Australian Good Birding Guide:
Northern Territory

Ted and Alex Wnorowski

ISBN N°: 978-0-6489564-5-7

Published in June 2024
in the paperback format

by Ted and Alex Wnorowski
Gladstone
Queensland
Australia
Mob. 0432 422 862
Email: awnorowski100@gmail.com
Website: www.australian-good-birding-guide.com

Subjects: Birdwatching – Australia
Birdwatching – Travel guidebooks

Front cover:	Rainbow Pitta, Howard Springs
Back cover:	
Horizontally, top:	Gouldian Finches
Vertically:	Black-bellied Crimson Finch, Long-tailed Finch, Gouldian Finch, Chestnut-breasted Mannikin
Horizontally, bottom:	Star Finch, Painted Finch
Spine:	Scaly-breasted Lorikeet

All photographs by Alex Wnorowski

Table of Contents

Introduction

Sunset over the Kakadu National Park

According to Geoscience Australia, Northern Territory covers over 1.3mln square kilometres (17.5% of surface area of Australia). Population of this Region is about 233,000 people, with 3 out of 5 (140,000) living in Darwin as per 2021 census.

Northern Territory Government has recently introduced fees, charged to out-of-State and international visitors, for camping in the national parks and reserves and for walking on several walking trails. NT residents are exempt. See the details here: https://nt.gov.au/parks/parks-pass to check if you'll need a pass for you stay.

Moreover, Uluru-Kata Tjuta National Park and Kakadu National Park are managed separately, and separate fees apply. The easiest way is to get a pass online:

- Kakadu: https://book.parksaustralia.gov.au/passes/kakadu/;
- Uluru: https://parksaustralia.gov.au/uluru/plan/passes-permits.html.

Northern Territory is divided into two distinctive climatic zones: the tropical Top End (from the coast to the level of Katherine), and the semi-arid Red Centre (all Outback south of the Top End).

The Top End is the scene of one of the most unique bird spectacles in the world – at the end of the dry season, when water becomes scarce, waterbirds congregate in incredible numbers. Thousands upon thousands of Magpie Geese, whistling-ducks, egrets, herons and cormorants can be seen on the remaining, shrinking wet areas. Such a bird mass is an unforgettable, rare sight, whether feeding or resting on the water or rising in the air together with an incredible noise of wing flapping, goose honking, ducks whistling.

Another spectacle takes place in the Red Centre in years when the drought eases and the endless red, dry plains get covered with the greenery. Populations of grass seed-eating birds such as Budgerigars, Cockatiels, Zebra Finches and Diamond Doves simply explode. Dense, iridescent blue-green clouds of Budgerigars descend for a drink on small waterholes. There may be a hundred thousand or more birds in a cloud. The trick is to be in the right place at the right time. A sight like that is on many a birder' bucket list.

Five endemic species can be found in Northern Territory. These are:

- Black-banded Fruit-Dove
- Chestnut-quilled Rock-Pigeon
- Hooded Parrot
- White-lined Honeyeater
- White-throated Grasswren.

The endemic Hooded Parrots, male on the right

Besides parrots and waterbirds, NT is famous for its mangrove specialists, escarpment specialists and finches. Australia has more birds that nearly exclusively live in and utilise the mangroves, than anywhere else in the world, and in the Northern Territory's mangroves you can find nearly all of them. These are:

- Chestnut Rail
- Great-billed Heron
- Striated Heron
- Broad-billed Flycatcher
- Mangrove Fantail
- Mangrove Gerygone
- Red-headed Honeyeater
- Collared Kingfisher
- Little Kingfisher
- Black Butcherbird
- Mangrove Yellow Whistler
- White-breasted Whistler
- Mangrove Robin
- Australian Yellow White-eye

Sandstone escarpment is one of the most spectacular landscapes of Northern Territory and it is home to several bird species that can be found only there:

- Black-banded Fruit-Dove
- Chestnut-quilled Rock-Pigeon
- White-quilled Rock-Pigeon
- White-lined Honeyeater
- White-throated Grasswren
- Sandstone Shrike-thrush
- Helmeted Friarbird, sandstone ssp. *ammitophila*
- Purple-backed Fairy-wren, lavender-flanked ssp. *dulcis*.

Another sought-after group are the colourful finches. Eleven species are found through the Northern Territory's savannah:

- Gouldian Finch
- Black-bellied Crimson Finch
- Double-barred Finch
- Long-tailed Finch
- Masked Finch
- Zebra Finch
- Star Finch
- Painted Finch
- Pictorella Mannikin
- Chestnut-breasted Mannikin
- Yellow-rumped Mannikin

In recent years, many changes have been introduced to bird nomenclature. Some species were split, other were lumped together, and some changed their common or Latin names. All taxonomy changes are recorded in the Birdlife's *Working List of Australian Birds*. In this book, we followed the latest revision of the *Working List*, v.4.3, dated October 2023. Otherwise, nomenclature used in this book follows the *Systematics and Taxonomy of Australian Birds* by Les Christidis and Walter E. Boles, CSIRO Publishing, 2008.

To help our readers navigate among the current changes, the main changes affecting birds of Northern Territory have been summarised below (species occurring in the Northern Territory are highlighted in **boldface**). Only time will tell how long these names will last; the review of the taxonomy system is ongoing.

Emerald Dove	Split into **Brown-capped Emerald-Dove** and Grey-capped Emerald-Dove
Banded Frut-Dove	Split into **Black-banded Frut-Dove** and Black-backed Fruit-Dove
Intermediate Egret	Split into **Plumed Egret** and Intermediate Egret
Gull-billed Tern	Spilt into **Australian Gull-billed Tern** and Common Gull-billed Tern (was: Asiatic ssp. of Gull-billed Tern)
Black-chinned Honeyeater	Split into **Golden-backed Honeyeater** and Black-chinned Honeyeater
Blue-faced Honeyeater	Split into **White-quilled Honeyeater** and Blue-faced Honeyeater
Crested Shrike-tit	Split into three species: **Eastern Shrike-tit**, Northern Shrike-tit and Western Shrike-tit.
Grey Whistler	Split into **Brown Whistler** and Grey-headed Whistler
Crimson Finch	Split into **Black-bellied Crimson Finch** and White-bellied Crimson Finch
Pied Imperial-Pigeon	This species was split into several new species. The species which was known as Pied Imperial-Pigeon in Australia is now called **Torresian Imperial-Pigeon**
Striated Grasswren	**Rufous Grasswren** was split from Striated Grasswren and incorporated Sandhill and Pilbara subspecies. Other changes were also made to the species.
Dollarbird	Name changed to **Oriental Dollarbird**.
Pied Cormorant	Name changed to **Great Pied Cormorant**
Crested Tern	Name changed to **Greater Crested Tern**
Eastern Curlew	Name changed to **Far Eastern Curlew**

The regions described in this book are: Darwin, Darwin Periphery, Litchfield NP & Surrounds, Arnhem Hwy Area, Kakadu NP, Katherine Region, Northwestern NT, Northeastern NT, Tennant Creek & Central Deserts, Alice Springs Area, McDonnell Ranges and Southern NT. The birds, like people, largely favour the coastal areas, which are described in the book in detail. However, many sought-after species can only be found in the arid landscape of the Outback.

Australian Good Birding Guide: Northern Territory

The Northern Territory climate has basically two seasons: the Wet (summer: Nov-Apr) and the Dry (winter: May-Oct). In the coastal regions, it is hot and humid in summer and hot and dry in winter. Arid, harsh climatic conditions prevail in the interior where in summer temperatures soar to 40°C and above during the day, dropping to perhaps 30°C at night, while in winter day temperatures are still high but at night the gauge easily drops to single digits and even frost. It does rain in the wet season in the Outback, except for the desert areas.

Travel must be planned carefully. Timing is crucial – it is not advisable to venture to the Top End in the wet season as widespread flooding occurs every year and roads may be flooded for weeks at a time, leaving you stranded. Even in the Darwin area, which generally has high bridges over the rivers, travelling in summer is not that pleasant, as you may get torrential rain nearly every day, and gloomy light conditions for your photos. On the other hand, the Red Centre is like a hot, dry oven in summer, while in winter the nights are freezing, making camping and caravanning quite unpleasant. In summary, the best time to travel to the Top End is May to October while for the Red Centre the best are the shoulder months (May or September). Remember, in the Outback, due to vast distances and sparse population, you must be self-sufficient for food, water and fuel (a long-range fuel tank is well advised).

The road safety reports on the NT public road network can be found here: https://roadreport.nt.gov.au/home. For the National Park alerts, park and road closures as well as the fire hazards, check the webpage https://nt.gov.au/parks and go to the individual Park' website. If you enter a closed road and consecutively get bogged up and require towing, you'll pay a hefty fine for that on top of your towing fees. If you lit a fire (even in a portable butane gas stove) when a total fire ban is imposed, you'll risk causing a bushfire and also face significant fines. The fire ban warnings may NOT be displayed in the National Parks, you do need to check the Park's website.

This Northern Territory Guide has been divided in our book into separate chapters. The approximate geographical locations of these areas are indicated on the Territory map below, with hyperlinks to the detailed birding information available in the ebook edition.

Northern Territory chapters

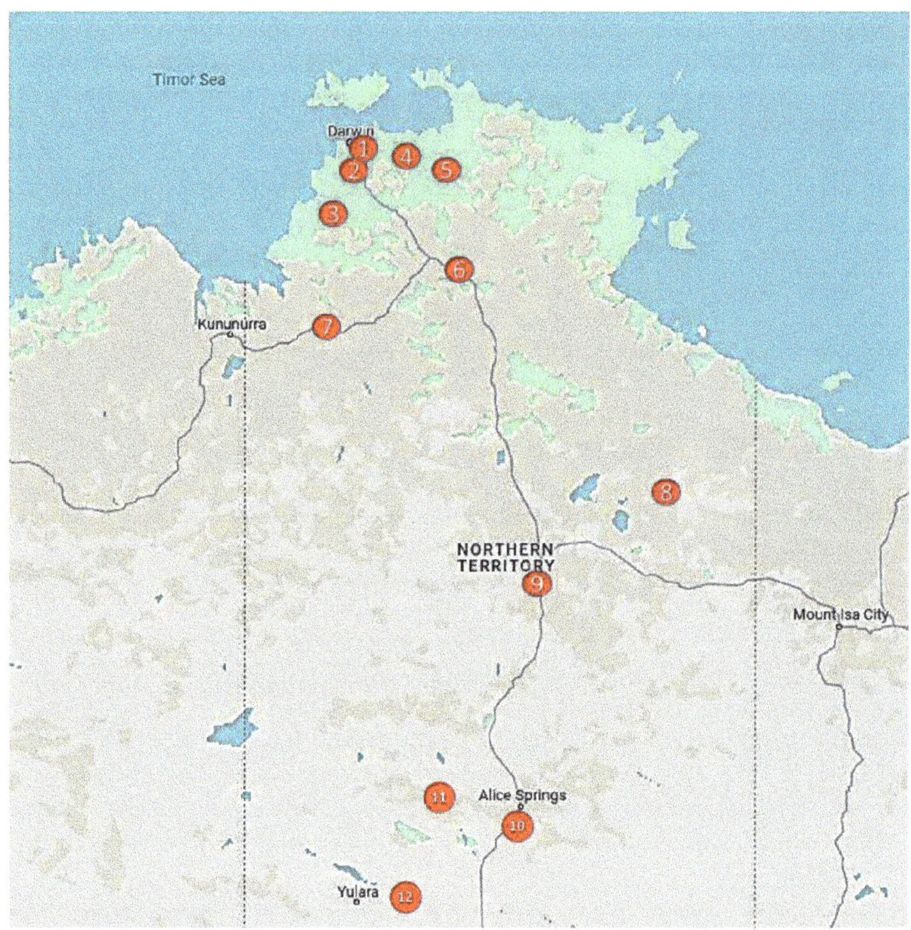

Darwin

Lee Point Beach
Lee Point
Casuarina Beach
Camerons Beach
Tiwi
Casuarina
Nightcliff
Darwin International Airport
Karama
Thorak - Deloraine-Knuckey...
Shoal Bay
East Point
Winnellie
Museum and Gallery of the Northern Territory
Berrimah
Holtze
Durack
Palmerston City

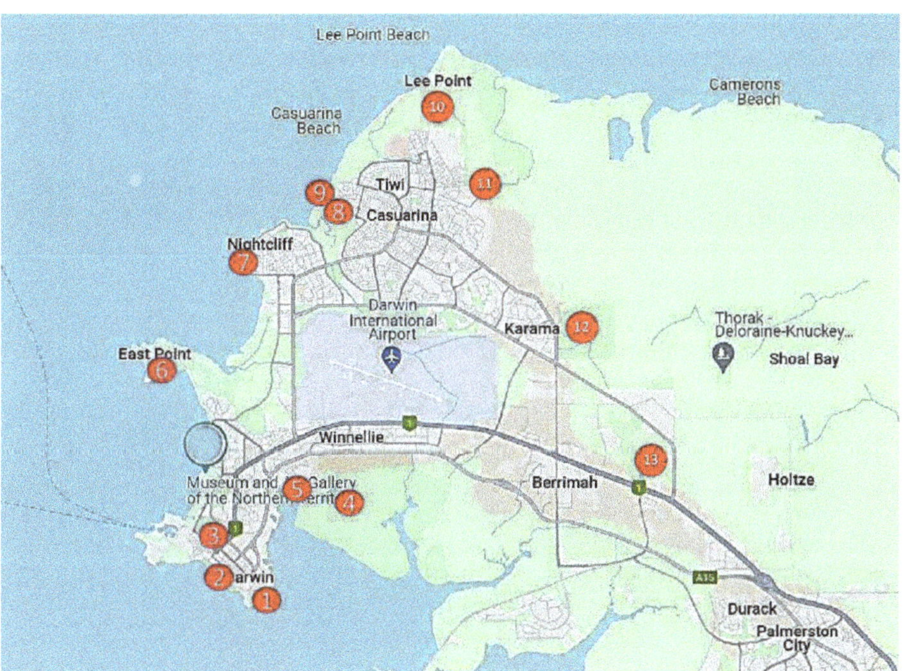

Darwin Harbour

Darwin Harbour, with its beauty and huge size, is a popular tourist destination. It is also a good place to look for seabirds. They are usually hanging around the Stokes Hill and Fishermans and Fort Hill Wharves. The most productive are visits to the Stokes Hill Wharf. Seabirds seen most often are Brown Boobies and Lesser Frigatebirds. Several vagrant gull species have visited the harbour. Black-headed Gulls were recorded several times; some stayed for many months, last one in 2018. Franklin's Gull was sighted at the Stokes Hill Wharf in April 2015 while Lesser Black-headed Gull in January 2017. There are also old records of a Black-tailed Gull that spent several months at the Fishermans Wharf. Many terns roost on the wharfs, including rarer species such as Brown Noddy, Bridled Tern, Roseate Tern and Common Tern. Peregrine Falcon, a migratory tundra falcon subspecies *calidus*, is sighted from time to time. Search the wharves for Eurasian Tree Sparrows – every few years they appear there, probably having smuggled themselves on a ship.

Eurasian Tree Sparrows

Fort Hill Parkland and Goyder Park, situated not far from the wharves to the northwest, are also worth your attention. You may come across Bush Stone-curlew, Green-backed Gerygone, White-breasted Woodswallow, Black-bellied Crimson Finch, Black Butcherbird, Green Oriole, Torresian Imperial-Pigeon and Brahminy Kite. Check the rocks along the shore for Common Sandpiper, Eastern Reef Egret, Ruddy Turnstone, Whimbrel, Black-naped Tern and Striated Heron.

Bicentennial Park

The park perches on the cliffs of Darwin Harbour along the Esplanade. It is one of the most popular green spaces in Darwin and is often visited by time-poor birders. The park stretches from the NT Parliament House to Doctor's Gully. You'll find here all necessary facilities such as park benches, picnic tables, toilets and walking tracks.

Orange-footed Scrubfowl

Over 170 bird species have been recorded in the Bicentennial Park. **Key species** are Orange-footed Scrubfowl, Rufous-banded Honeyeater, Brown Booby, Black Butcherbird, Mangrove Golden Whistler, Barking Owl, Tawny Frogmouth and Pacific Baza. Other birds of interest include Silver-backed Butcherbird, Little Bronze-cuckoo, Red-collared Lorikeet, Eastern Reef Egret, Common Sandpiper, Lesser Sand Plover, Greater Sand Plover, Bush Stone-curlew, Brown Whistler, Green Oriole, and Eastern Koel. Rarities include Masked Booby, Great-billed Heron, Black-eared Cuckoo, Fork-tailed Swift, Rufous Owl and Peregrine Falcon.

Bush Stone-curlews are abundant and breeding well in the park. A family of Barking Owls is resident here while Tawny Frogmouths are found regularly. Tame Orange-footed Scrubfowls are the main feature of the park, walking unhurriedly through the lawns. Various water features attract finches, in particular flocks of Chestnut-breasted Mannikins. Yellow-rumped Mannikins are observed from time to time among them.

Check the rocky shores for Common Sandpiper, Grey-tailed Tattler, Striated Heron and Eastern Reef Egret. Brown Boobies are often observed perched on the buoys and channel markers.

Other birds in the park include Helmeted Friarbird, Australasian Figbird, White-bellied Cuckoo-shrike, Varied Lorikeet, Forest Kingfisher, Rufous Whistler, White-gaped Honeyeater, Collared Sparrowhawk and Pacific Baza.

Darwin Botanic Gardens

George Brown Darwin Botanic Gardens offer a 42ha greenspace located just 2km from the Darwin CBD. Opening hours are 7am until 7pm. Besides the formal, historical parkland, other habitats here include mangroves, monsoon forest, rainforest and dry open woodland. Access to the Gardens is via Gardens Rd and Gilruth Av. The site facilities include a fantastic café, Visitor Centre and ample parking. Download the park map here: https://nt.gov.au/__data/assets/pdf_file/0006/194739/george-brown-darwin-botanic-gardens-map-v2.pdf.

A closeup of Rufous Owl

Over 160 bird species have been recorded in the Darwin Botanic Gardens. **Key species** are Rufous Owl, Barking Owl, Orange-footed Scrubfowl, Rose-crowned Fruit-Dove and Oriental Cuckoo (in summer). Other birds of interest include Torresian Imperial-Pigeon, Red-collared Lorikeet, Forest Kingfisher, Red-headed Honeyeater, Dusky Honeyeater, Helmeted Friarbird, Little Bronze-cuckoo, Black Butcherbird, Pacific Baza and Grey Goshawk. Rarities include Grey Wagtail, Pale-vented Bush-hen, Little Curlew, Little Kingfisher, Black-eared Cuckoo and Black-breasted Buzzard.

This Garden is the most reliable site for Rufous Owls in Darwin. In 2023, their favourite roost was in large trees at the start of Rainforest Walk. GPS coordinates there are 12°26'39"S and 130°50'19"E. Look also for them in Tiwi Wet Forest. Barking Owls also live in the Gardens and are easier to find. A family often roosts in trees surrounding Eva's Café and the playground. Also, check the trees around the water feature near the carpark. If spotlighting, you may also find Large-tailed Nightjar, Southern Boobook and plenty of Bush Stone-curlews.

Orange-footed Scrubfowls are here in large numbers and are tame, so it is easy to get photos. Pigeons are well-represented in the Gardens, in particular Torresian Imperial-Pigeon, Rose-crowned Fruit-Dove and Brown-capped Emerald-Dove. Among cuckoos, Little Bronze-cuckoo, Brush Cuckoo and Pheasant Coucal occur year-round. During the Wet, Channel-billed Cuckoo, Eastern Koel and Oriental Cuckoo appear. At the end of dry season, large flocks of Magpie Geese raid the lush lawns of the Gardens.

On the Rainforest Loop, search for Green-backed Gerygone, Brown Whistler, Forest Kingfisher, Green Oriole, Rufous-banded Honeyeater, Collared Sparrowhawk and Pacific Baza.

A part of the Botanic Gardens extends behind Gilruth Av into the dunes of Mindil Beach. To get there, take Larrakia Coastal Walk (1km one-way). The walk includes a boardwalk through the mangroves. The walk may produce Sacred Kingfisher, Collared Kingfisher, Mangrove Robin, Mangrove Gerygone, Large-billed Gerygone, Little Bronze-cuckoo and Australian Yellow White-eye.

Charles Darwin National Park

This small, 1,300ha National Park is an oasis of greenery squeezed in between densely built-up areas. It is located just 8km from the Darwin CBD. It protects the Port Darwin wetlands and the lush monsoon forest on the hillslopes.

Access is from Tiger Brennan Dr (A15) opposite Bowen St, well signposted. A sealed road leads to the top of the hill where you'll find a tranquil picnic area with picnic tables. barbecues and toilets. A viewing spot opens onto breathtaking views of Darwin and Timor Sea beyond. On your way up, you will pass several historical storage bunkers from WWII. The Park also has a network of walking and biking trails, the most important for birders are tracks along the mangroves. The Park is open daily from 8am to 7pm. For further information and the site map go to: https://nt.gov.au/__data/assets/pdf_file/0013/200065/charles-darwin-national-park.pdf.

A view on Darwin from the Charles Darwin National Park

Over 180 bird species have been recorded in the Charles Darwin National Park. **Key species** are Chestnut Rail, Mangrove Robin, Mangrove Golden Whistler, Silver-backed Butcherbird, Red-headed Honeyeater, Broad-billed Flycatcher and Common Cicadabird. Other birds of interest include Orange-footed Scrubfowl, Northern Rosella, Forest Kingfisher, Brown Whistler, Little Shrike-thrush, Green-backed Gerygone, Bar-breasted Honeyeater, Black Butcherbird, Arafura Fantail and Pacific Baza. Rarities include White-breasted Whistler, Little Kingfisher, Eastern Yellow Wagtail, Fork-tailed Swift and Square-tailed Kite.

We had good birding around the picnic area. The orange-flowering woollybutts were full of Helmeted Friarbirds, Silver-crowned Friarbirds, Little Friarbirds, Bar-breasted Honeyeaters, Brown Honeyeaters, White-gaped Honeyeaters, White-throated Honeyeaters, Rufous-banded Honeyeaters and White-quilled Honeyeaters.

Even Yellow-tinted Honeyeaters, rare in Darwin, were among them. A large flock of Red-collared Lorikeets was enjoying a bath under the working sprinklers. In the air, a small Collared Sparrowhawk was being chased by a Torresian Crow. A quick search of the surrounding bushland produced White-winged Triller, Varied Triller, Brown-capped Emerald-Dove, Eastern Koel and Australasian Figbird.

On the mangrove track, we heard Chestnut Rail calling and saw Shining Flycatcher, Lemon-bellied Flycatcher, Green-backed Gerygone and several Mangrove Robins.

Chestnut Rail Spots off Tiger Brennan Dr

Mangroves growing on the western side of Charles Darwin National Park, including the area on the west side of Sadgroves Creek, still support Chestnut Rails – this is in the centre of Durban! The spots of reported sightings are located along Stoddard Dr, Bayview Blvd and Tiger Brennan Dr, as described below.

Tiger Brennan Dr at 12°26’29’’S and 130°50’60’’E

This site is about 300m south of the intersection with Stoddard Dr. The site is marked by large concrete blocks, disposed off into the mangroves on the east side of the road. Stop by the roadside, wait patiently and listen to the Chestnut Rail calls – the birds may appear suddenly to fly over, perch or walk on the concrete blocks.

Collared Kingfisher hammering a hollow

This is also a good place to search for Mangrove Robin and Red-headed Honeyeater. Sulphur-crested Cockatoos and Little Corellas roost here in large numbers (up to 500 birds). Grey Goshawk is a regular in the area. Look also for Collared Kingfisher, Australian Yellow White-eye, Little Bronze-cuckoo, Mangrove Gerygone, Large-billed Gerygone and Shining Flycatcher.

Gonzales Road Boat Ramp

From Tiger Brennan Dr, turn east into Gonzales Rd and drive to a carpark by the boat ramp. The birds sometimes come out of the mangroves onto the mudflats at low tide. You may also spot Common Sandpiper, Whimbrel, Little Egret, Striated Heron on Australasian Darter on the mudflats. Collared Kingfisher, Australian Yellow White-eye and Shining Flycatcher are most common in the mangroves.

Stoddard Dr at 12°26'23''S and 130°51'08''E

A concrete path on the rockwall follows the mangroves along Stoddard Dr. From this footpath, inspect little outlets for the presence of Chestnut Rail. You also have a chance to get Mangrove Robin here. Other birds at this location include Brush Cuckoo, Brown Honeyeater and Torresian Imperial-Pigeon.

Bayview Boulevard at 12°26'27''S and 130°51'16''E

Find a passage from Bayview Blvd to the mangroves to the south, walk there and search for Chestnut Rails from the footpath. Look also for Mangrove Robin. In the late afternoon, you may witness hundreds of Torresian Imperial-Pigeons flying towards their night roost near the Dinah boat ramp.

East Point Reserve

The 200ha East Point Reserve is often the first place visited in Darwin by birders, as it is only 10min from the CBD. It offers a mosaic of habitats including monsoon forest, mangroves, beaches, parklands and grassy areas. This relatively small park can reward you with a large list of bird species sighted in a short time. The original monsoon forest of the East Point was sequestered by the Armed Forces during the Second World War, and today the area is full of historical military artefacts including the Military Museum.

The shoreline varies from rocky, through sandy to mangroves. The rocky shores are favoured by the roosting migratory waders. A superb mangrove boardwalk will take you to the shore. Sometimes, the tide is higher than the boardwalk, which gives you an eerie feeling of standing on the sea. Parklands and gardens surround the saline Lake Alexander in the southern part of the reserve. Another highlight of the reserve is a walking track through the monsoon forest.

To get there, take Gardens Rd, then continue in the northerly direction on Gilruth Av. The road later changes name to East Point Rd. When the road changes name again, to Alec Fong Lim Dr, you've reached the reserve so drive on, exploring various park attractions. You'll find here an extensive network of walking and cycling paths, many well-equipped picnic areas, several carparks, safe saltwater swimming in Lake Alexander and great views over Fannie Bay. Download the site map here: https://www.darwin.nt.gov.au/sites/default/files/publications/attachments/East_Point_Reserve_Lake_Alexander_Area_Map_FEB21_FINAL.pdf.

Over 220 bird species have been recorded in the East Point Reserve. **Key species** are Beach Stone-curlew, Chestnut Rail, Rainbow Pitta, Collared Kingfisher, Green-backed Gerygone, Rufous Owl and Grey Goshawk. Other birds of interest include waders, Rose-crowned Fruit-Dove, Red-headed Honeyeater, Orange-footed Scrubfowl, Mangrove Golden Whistler, Brown Whistler, Northern Fantail and Shining Flycatcher. Rarities include Little Ringed Plover, Painted Finch, House Swift, Flock Bronzewing, Black Noddy, Great Frigatebird and Peregrine Falcon.

Monsoon Forest Walk

Rufous-banded Honeyeater

A walking track through the monsoon forest commences at the carpark of the renowned Pee-Wee's at the Point restaurant. At the start of the walk, you'll see a gigantic communal mound of Orange-footed Scrubfowls; the birds themselves should not be too far away. Also, search the forest floor for Rainbow Pitta and Brown-capped Emerald-Dove. Cuckoos such as Little Bronze-cuckoo, Horsfield's Bronze-cuckoo, Brush Cuckoo and Eastern Koel, are common in the bush. Oriental Cuckoos appear in summer. In the forest's mid-storey, you may see Green-backed Gerygone, Large-billed Gerygone, Arafura Fantail, Northern Fantail, Lemon-bellied Flycatcher, Shining Flycatcher, Leaden Flycatcher, Brown Whistler, Olive-backed Oriole and Green Oriole. Honeyeaters are everywhere; look for White-gaped Honeyeater, Bar-breasted Honeyeater, Rufous-banded Honeyeater, White-quilled Honeyeater, Helmeted Friarbird and Silver-crowned Friarbird. Grey Goshawk is often observed in the bush. During the night, Large-tailed Nightjar or Rufous Owl may be calling.

Lake Alexander

This lake is the only saltwater body in Darwin which is safe for swimming. It is surrounded by parkland, where a flock of Magpie Geese regularly forages in the grass. Small numbers of waterbirds and waders should be present around the water, such as Common Greenshanks, Common Sandpipers, Marsh Sandpipers, Striated Herons, Little Egrets and Eastern Reef Egrets. Local Nankeen Night-Herons have a habit of hunting grasshoppers during the day, not minding the daylight or people milling about.

East Point Mangrove Boardwalk

Running through the mangroves, a 500m-long boardwalk is an aluminium structure, finishing in a pleasant landing with a seating arrangement. The high tide can sometimes submerge the boardwalk.

To get there, from Alec Fong Lim Dr turn into the boardwalk's carpark just north of Lake Alexander (signposted to the boardwalk). Find the entry to the walking track at the upper left corner of the carpark. The track runs through coastal scrub to the start of the boardwalk. The whole distance from the carpark to the boardwalk' landing is about 1km.

Mangroves at high tide at the end of the boardwalk

In the coastal scrub, look for Rose-crowned Fruit-Dove, Great Bowerbird, Common Cicadabird, Rufous Whistler, Brown Whistler, Paperbark Flycatcher, Lemon-bellied Flycatcher, Forest Kingfisher, Oriental Dollarbird, Green Oriole and Brown Goshawk. Many honeyeaters can be found here including Bar-breasted Honeyeater, White-throated Honeyeater, Rufous-banded Honeyeater and Banded Honeyeater.

The boardwalk is an ideal place to search for mangrove specialists. You may get here Collared Kingfisher, Mangrove Golden Whistler, Mangrove Robin, Australian Yellow White-eye, Black Butcherbird, Helmeted Friarbird, Red-headed Honeyeater, Shining Flycatcher and Broad-billed Flycatcher. Large-billed Gerygones are common along the boardwalk.

On the receding tide, you may observe a variety of waders coming to feed on the exposed mudflats. Some of them, such as Terek Sandpiper, Whimbrel and Grey-tailed Tattler, roost at high tide in large mangrove trees at the water-side margin of the mangrove forest. Other waders here include Common Sandpiper, Beach Stone-curlew, Lesser Sand Plover, Greater Sand Plover, Great Knot, Red Knot and Red-capped Plover.

White Rocks

This spot is located behind the Fannie Bay Equestrian Club. White Rocks can be reached via a 300m-long walk along the cliffs from Dudley Point Lookout. GPS coordinates are 12°24'39''S and 130°49'05''E. This is the place to watch seabirds, especially after gale winds and heavy rains that force the birds to move closer to the shore. Seen here were Lesser Frigatebird, Great Frigatebird, Bridled Tern and Brown Booby. Black Noddy was reported on the rocks in April 2020.

Far End Shores

The far end shores of East Point start behind the Fannie Bay Equestrian Club in the west and run behind the Military Museum grounds to extensive mangrove area in the east. Reefs, rocky platforms and rocky islands are dotted along the shoreline, providing roosting places to mixed flocks of waders. Common species include Pacific Golden Plover, Grey Plover, Lesser Sand Plover, Greater Sand Plover, Great Knot, Black-tailed Godwit, Bar-tailed Godwit, Whimbrel, Far Eastern Curlew, Ruddy Turnstone, Terek Sandpiper and Common Sandpiper. Several pairs of Beach Stone-curlews are using this area. Sooty Oystercatchers are sometimes found on the rocks. Other coastal species in the area include Little Tern, Australian Gull-billed Tern, Lesser Crested Tern, Caspian Tern, Eastern Reef Egret and Striated Heron.

Greater Sand Plovers

Check the horse paddocks behind the Military Museum. Mixed flocks of finches may be feeding there. Gouldian Finches were recorded among Double-barred Finches and Chestnut-breasted Mannikins. In the trees growing on the horse paddock, look also for Silver-backed Butcherbird, Oriental Cuckoo and Brush Cuckoo.

Take a walk through the Military Museum grounds. Bush Stone-curlews like to roost in the shade of scattered military equipment. You may also encounter Rose-crowned Fruit-Dove, Channel-billed Cuckoo, Rainbow Bee-eater, Green Oriole, Helmeted Friarbird, Little Friarbird, Green-backed Gerygone, Spangled Drongo, Brown Whistler, Lemon-bellied Flycatcher and, at night, Large-tailed Nightjar or Barking Owl.

Ludmilla Creek Mouth

To get there, from Alec Fong Lim Dr turn north into Colivas Dr and follow it to the end of the road. Extensive mangroves cover the mouth of the creek. When the mudflats get exposed at low tide, scan the mangroves between Ludmilla Creek and Colivas Dr for Chestnut Rail. Other birds in the area include Collared Kingfisher, Mangrove Robin, Shining Flycatcher, Broad-billed Flycatcher, Lemon-bellied Flycatcher, Northern Fantail and Black Butcherbird.

As the site is relatively secluded, waders choose to roost at high tide the saltpans along Colivas Dr. A large saltpan is located along Colivas Dr just south of the boatyards, at approximate GPS coordinates of 12°24’51’’S and 130°50’10’’E. It is surrounded by mangroves and vine thicket. It is used as a high tide roost, mostly by Whimbrels, Far Eastern Curlews, Common Greenshanks, Grey Plovers and occasionally by huge numbers of Great Knots. When water is present in the saltpans, look for Black-necked Stork, Black Bittern, Striated Heron, Little Egret and Buff-banded Rail. Small groups of waders roost also among the boats in the boatyards. While there, check the boatyards for finches; after the rain they come to drink water from the puddles.

Wader Sites on the Nightcliff Coast

Several high tide wader roosts and feeding grounds along the mangroves can be found along the coast in front of the densely populated Darwin suburbs of Coconut Grove and Nightcliff. The best sites are described below.

Off Aralia Street

The rock shelf at the end of Aralia St in the suburb of Nightcliff is a good high tide wader roost. Approximate GPS coordinates are 12°22'54''S and 130°50'29''E. You can leave your car in Sunset Park nearby.

Over 150 bird species have been recorded around the Aralia St wader spot. **Key species** are waders including Beach Stone-curlew. Other birds of interest include Collared Kingfisher, Shining Flycatcher, Lesser Frigatebird, Eastern Reef Egret, Lesser Crested Tern, Little Tern, Mangrove Gerygone and Broad-billed Flycatcher. Rarities include Barn Swallow, Rose-ringed Parakeet, Welcome Swallow, Fork-tailed Swift, White-throated Needletail, Elegant Imperial-Pigeon, Christmas Island Frigatebird (Jan-2014), Buff-banded Rail, Sooty Oystercatcher, Oriental Plover and Broad-billed Sandpiper.

In total, 34 species of waders have been recorded feeding and roosting in this area. Beach Stone-curlews and Sooty Oystercatchers are observed regularly. Common species here include Great Knot, Lesser Sand Plover, Greater Sand Plover, Pacific Golden Plover, Australian Pied Oystercatcher, Whimbrel, Far Eastern Curlew and Ruddy Turnstone. Among rarer species are Terek Sandpiper, Common Sandpiper, Sanderling, Grey Plover, Red Knot and Black-tailed Godwit.

A flock of Great Knots in breeding plumage plus a single Grey-tailed Tattler (front left)

This site is a good for Little Terns; they often roost with the waders. Rarer terns here include Brown Noddy, Common Tern and White-winged Black Tern. After stormy weather, influxes of Bridled Terns on the shore are observed. Brown Booby and Lesser Frigatebird are regularly observed from the shore, also mostly in bad weather.

In the surrounding mangroves, you have a chance to spot Mangrove Golden Whistler, Collared Kingfisher, Sacred Kingfisher, Shining Flycatcher and Broad-billed Flycatcher.

This site is good for birds of prey, especially White-bellied Sea-Eagle, Osprey and Australian Hobby. There are records of sightings of Peregrine Falcon, a migratory tundra subspecies *calidus*.

Off Orchard Road and Ostermann Street

This wader and mangrove specialist spot is located at the end of Orchard Rd and Ostermann St in the suburb of Coconut Grove. Approximate GPS coordinates for the mangroves in this area are 12°23’48’’S and 130°50’50’’E. Park your car at the end of Orchard Rd and find a path between the houses, leading to the mangroves. Similarly, park the car at the end of Ostermann St and walk towards the mangroves. Turn left and follow a narrow track along the beach; it will veer off into the mangroves, coming out right onto the harbour mudflats.

Over 160 bird species have been recorded at the Orchard Rd wader spot. **Key species** are Beach Stone-curlew, Chestnut Rail, White-breasted Whistler, Mangrove Golden Whistler, Mangrove Robin and Red-headed Honeyeater. Other birds of interest include waders, Azure Kingfisher, Black Butcherbird, Australian Yellow White-eye, Helmeted Friarbird, Little Bronze-cuckoo and Eastern Reef Egret. Rarities include Little Kingfisher and Mangrove Fantail.

This is a good spot to search for Chestnut Rail and other mangrove specialists. In particular, White-breasted Whistler and Mangrove Golden Whistler occur in good numbers. Three species of gerygones (Green-backed, Large-billed and Mangrove Gerygone) can be found here side-by-side. Grey Goshawk, a striking white-morphology bird, has been reported for years from this location.

Large flocks of waders are often feeding in front of mangroves, generally the same species composition as in Aralia St.

Charles Darwin University

The Casuarina campus of Charles Darwin University is located 12km of Darwin CBD, bordered by University Dr South, University Dr North, University Dr West and University Dr East. It is set on 60ha of urban parkland, adjacent from the south and west to the mangroves and riverine monsoon forest. A walking track to Casuarina Beach runs along University Dr South.

Over 140 bird species have been recorded at the campus of Charles Darwin University. **Key species** are Chestnut Rail, Rufous Owl, Green-backed Gerygone, Shining Flycatcher, Long-tailed Finch and Grey Goshawk. Other birds of interest include Common Sandpiper, Channel-billed Cuckoo, Black Butcherbird, Orange-footed Scrubfowl, Lemon-bellied Flycatcher, Northern Fantail, Brown Whistler, Red-headed Honeyeater and Osprey. Rarities include Grey Wagtail, Buff-banded Rail, Yellow-rumped Mannikin, Mangrove Fantail, Fork-tailed Swift and Black-breasted Buzzard.

Channel-billed Cuckoo

Rufous Owls can be heard calling from the campus. An active Osprey nest is located on a communication tower on the campus. Grey Goshawks breed on site (a well-known pair, one of white and the other of grey morphology). Look for their nest on a tree along the track. In the flowering paperbarks, look for Dusky Honeyeater, Bar-breasted Honeyeater, Red-headed Honeyeater, Rufous-banded Honeyeater and Little Friarbird. Expect also to come across Green-backed Gerygone, Large-billed Gerygone, Little Bronze-cuckoo, Helmeted Friarbird, Brown Whistler, Varied Triller and Arafura Fantail.

On the south side of the campus, a drainage outflow channel empties to Rapid Creek. Leave your car in the carpark off Lasharie Rd and walk up to a footbridge over the channel. A Common Sandpiper often spends summer in the outflow channel near the footbridge. Grey Wagtail was found in 2014 in the same place. Check the cricket grounds just south of the outflow channel carpark. Large-tailed Nightjars hunt there at dusk. Bush Stone-curlews are plentiful. During the day, flocks of Magpie Geese land on the oval to feed on the grass. Mixed flocks of finches should also be there, including Long-tailed Finch and Chestnut-breasted Mannikin.

The track running along the outflow channel will lead you over the footbridge to the north side of the channel. When you reach the mangroves at the end of the track, search the mudflats for Chestnut Rail. In the vegetation lining the creek, you may spot Azure Kingfisher, Collared Kingfisher or, occasionally, Little Kingfisher. The mangroves here are good for Mangrove Robin, Australian Yellow White-eye and Broad-billed Flycatcher.

Casuarina Coastal Reserve

This picturesque place protects 1,500ha of coastal habitats between the estuaries of Rapid Creek and Buffalo Creek. The reserve covers a narrow band of vegetation, stretching for 8km along the sandy beaches and dramatic cliffs of Darwin. The vegetation comprises mostly casuarina trees and coastal scrub. There are also areas of mangroves, paperbark forest and monsoon vine thickets. Access to the reserve is through Darwin's northern suburbs at Casuarina Dr, Trower Rd, Lee Point Rd and Buffalo Creek Rd. Well-equipped picnic areas can be found at Rapid Creek, Dripstone Cliffs, Lee Point and Buffalo Creek. Walking/biking trails run along the coast. There is also a bird hide in the Buffalo Creek area. Further information and a map can be found in the site's fact sheet, downloadable here: https://nt.gov.au/__data/assets/pdf_file/0011/200063/casuarina-coastal-reserve.pdf.

Waders at Lee Point, seen from the bird hide

The reserve protects important feeding and roosting wader habitats and is the best and most accessible place in the Northern Territory to look for Chestnut Rail.

Over 230 bird species have been recorded in the Casuarina Coastal Reserve. **Key species** are Chestnut Rail, Great-billed Heron, Gouldian Finch, Little Kingfisher, Mangrove Golden Whistler, Mangrove Fantail, Fork-tailed Swift and White-winged Black Tern. Other birds of interest include waders, seabirds, Oriental Cuckoo, Common Cicadabird, Arafura Fantail, Red-headed Honeyeater, Azure Kingfisher, Broad-billed Flycatcher, Brown Whistler, Australian Yellow White-eye, Large-tailed Nightjar and Grey Goshawk. Among the rarities are Franklin's Gull, Lesser Black-backed Gull, Black-headed Gull, Kentish Plover, Common Ringed Plover, Streaked Shearwater, Black Noddy, Matsudaira's Storm-Petrel, Painted Finch, Yellow-rumped Mannikin, Red-rumped Swallow, House Swift and Javan Pond Heron.

Buffalo Creek

Buffalo Creek is located in the eastern part of the reserve and is the most important place for birders. You'll find waders here as well as an easy access to Chestnut Rail.

To get there, from Lee Point Rd turn right into Buffalo Creek Rd and drive 2.5km to the Buffalo Creek mouth. A boat ramp and toilet are located at the end of the road. About 500m before the boat ramp, there is a sharp bend in the road to the right, with a spot by the roadside to park your car. GPS coordinates here are 12°20'09''S and 130°54'16''E. Walk across the monsoon forest to the beach. You'll find a bird hide at the beach-side fringe, strategically positioned in front of the high tide roost.

The beach and mudflats adjacent to the Buffalo Creek mouth support large numbers of waders. However, the star attraction of the area is Chestnut Rail. These elusive birds like to quietly emerge from the dense mangroves to the mud on the receding tide. The best way to spot one is to wait patiently at the boat ramp, scanning the muddy edges of the mangroves upstream of the mouth. We visited the place 2-3 times a day for a whole week and finally got good views of the bird foraging for about half an hour on the other side of the creek.

Chestnut Rail

While waiting for the rail, we enjoyed watching a couple of Azure Kingfishers and several Striated Herons, Eastern Reef Egrets and Brahminy Kites. There was also one Great Pied Cormorant. The creek mouth is also a good place to look for Little Kingfisher. To boost your chances to spot one (and also the Chestnut Rail), rent a dinghy and paddle upstream. You may even get Great-billed Heron. Just remember, crocodiles may be there, too.

An obscure track runs parallel to the creek immediately to the right of the boat ramp. It was trodden by and is used by anglers. The mangroves there are a good place to look for mangrove specialists including Mangrove Robin, Red-headed Honeyeater, Rufous-banded Honeyeater, Rose-crowned Fruit-Dove, Green-backed

Gerygone, Mangrove Fantail, Mangrove Golden Whistler, Broad-billed Flycatcher, Shining Flycatcher and Australian Yellow White-eye.

On the walk through the monsoon forest to the bird hide, look for Brown Whistler, Arafura Fantail, Northern Fantail, Brown-capped Emerald-Dove, Rose-crowned Fruit-Dove, Black Butcherbird, Little Bronze-cuckoo, Large-billed Gerygone, Rufous-banded Honeyeater and Pacific Baza. Along the track, you'll see several large breeding mounds of Orange-footed Scrubfowls.

Depending on the wind direction and the height of the tide, waders will be closer or further from the bird hide. 36 wader species have been recorded at this spot. The most numerous are Great Knots, forming flocks of up to 2,000 birds. Other common waders here include Greater Sand Plover, Lesser Sand Plover, Grey Plover, Pacific Golden Plover, Ruddy Turnstone, Common Greenshank, Bar-tailed Godwit, Black-tailed Godwit, Far Eastern Curlew and Sanderling. Several rare waders were sighted including Little Ringed Plover, Asian Dowitcher, Oriental Plover, Broad-billed Sandpiper, Little Stint, Red Knot and Common Redshank. Native waders are also present here including Beach Stone-curlew, Red-capped Plover, Sooty Oystercatcher and Australian Pied Oystercatcher.

Grey Plovers

Mixed flocks of terns roost together with the waders, mostly Greater Crested Terns but among them you may also find some Little Terns, Caspian Terns, Lesser Crested Terns, Common Terns, Australian Gull-billed Terns and Common Gull-billed Terns. Rare seabirds, such as Bridled Tern, Brown Noddy, Black Noddy and Pomarine Jaeger, may appear after the storms.

Four man-made ponds are located about 50m south of Buffalo Creek Rd, about 1km back from the boat ramp. A track leads to the ponds through a break in the fence. GPS coordinates here are 12°20'14''S and 130°54'04''E. Tall gamba grass surrounds the ponds. During our visit in 2022, we observed Gouldian Finches arriving at the water in large numbers. Other finches there included Black-bellied Crimson Finch, Chestnut-breasted Mannikin, Long-tailed Finch and Masked Finch. Check the pond margins for White-browed Crakes. Around the water, look for Comb-crested Jacana, Common Sandpiper, Pied Stilt, Nankeen Night-Heron, Buff-banded Rail and White-necked Heron. White-bellied Sea-Eagle regularly uses one of power poles near the ponds for roosting. In the gamba grasses, you may see Golden-headed Cisticola, Tawny Grassbird, Pheasant Coucal and Brown Quail. Oriental Cuckoos are reported from this site in summer. At night, Large-tailed Nightjar may hunt over the ponds.

Check the power lines along Buffalo Creek Rd. You may get White-bellied Cuckoo-shrike, White-breasted Woodswallow, Spangled Drongo, Brush Cuckoo, Little Bronze-cuckoo, Forest Kingfisher, Sacred Kingfisher or even Red-backed Kingfisher.

Lee Point

This is part of Casuarina Coastal Reserve is located at the end of Lee Point Rd. A large carpark is provided there next to a picnic area equipped with toilets, barbecues and shaded picnic tables. A 2km track runs along the coast to the mouth of Buffalo Creek, passing on its way the high tide wader roost with a bird hide, described in the previous section. A huge Orange-footed Scrubfowl breeding mound is located at the start of the walk. Oriental Cuckoo and Barn Swallow were recorded many times in summer at the Point. Bushland surrounding the picnic area may produce Torresian Imperial-Pigeon, Forest Kingfisher, Oriental Dollarbird, Varied Triller, Northern Fantail, Leaden Flycatcher, Paperbark Flycatcher and Pacific Baza.

Opposite the Point, a series of reefs emerge and submerge depending on the height of the tide. Check them out, as waders utilise them for feeding and roosting. Beach Stone-curlews are regularly seen there.

Moth Block

This area of woodland is situated just west of the Royal Darwin Hospital and can be reached from the hospital carpark at the corner of Hippocrates Rd and Paracelsus Rd. You need to find a walking track going west, cross Sandy Creek and continue to the beach, coming out onto the Free Beach carpark (a walk of about 1km one way). Along the creek, look for Little Kingfisher and Azure Kingfisher. You may also see Shining Flycatcher, Brown Whistler, Forest Kingfisher, Black Butcherbird, Helmeted Friarbird, Rose-crowned Fruit-Dove, Pacific Baza and Grey Goshawk. This is also a good place in summer for cuckoos including Channel-billed Cuckoo, Eastern Koel, Horsfield's Bronze-cuckoo, Little Bronze-cuckoo, Brush Cuckoo and Oriental Cuckoo. Look here for Rufous Owls; they are calling during the night and sometimes roost near the bike path on the hospital side of a little bridge. Other nocturnal birds in this patch of woodland include Large-tailed Nightjar (particularly active at the woodland boundary with mangroves), Australian Owlet-nightjar, Barking Owl and Nankeen Night-Heron.

Little Bronze-cuckoo

Daribah Road Section

To get there, take Daribah Rd from Trower Rd and follow it to the Daribah Rd carpark near the beach. Inspect the coastal strip from this carpark up to the Free Beach carpark further north. This beautiful, wide city beach is lined with casuarina trees and well-equipped with picnic facilities. When we visited in winter of 2022, leaking taps in the area were attracting finches, mostly Chestnut-breasted Mannikins and Black-bellied Crimson Finches. Among them were some Gouldian Finches. Even Yellow-rumped Mannikins and Painted Finches were recorded. Astonished numbers of Bush Stone-curlews live on the grounds; we saw a pair nearly under every bush or tree. This was also true for the open parkland areas in other parts of the Casuarina Coastal Reserve.

A short boardwalk runs through a patch of mangroves at the mouth of Sandy Creek. Keep an eye for Little Kingfisher; it is found there regularly. Other birds in the mangroves include Australian Yellow White-eye, Black Butcherbird, Varied Triller, Helmeted Friarbird, Brown Whistler and Rufous-banded Honeyeater. Waders are often seen in front of the mangroves, including Sanderling, Great Knot and Greater Sand Plover.

Dripstone Park

Access to the Dripstone picnic area is from Trower Rd. During our visit, Gouldian Finches were present, busy drinking water from the sprinklers and foraging on the lawns. They were mixed with other finches, mostly Double-barred Finches and Masked Finches. Other bird species in the park included Forest Kingfisher, White-bellied Cuckoo-shrike, Black-faced Cuckoo-shrike (plentiful), Varied Lorikeet, Little Corella, Straw-necked Ibis, Bar-shouldered Dove and Peaceful Dove. Tree Martins were flying high in the sky. Bush Stone-curlews were standing in the shade everywhere, nodding off in the heat of the afternoon.

Osprey was flying along the coast. A mixed flock of Lesser and Greater Sand Plovers with a couple of Terek Sandpipers was roosting at the foot of Dripstone Cliffs.

Rapid Creek Estuary

To get there, drive Trower Rd to the southern end of the Casuarina Coastal Reserve. A large carpark and a picnic area are located at the end of the road, near the mouth of Rapid Creek. A footbridge is provided on the Rapid Creek Barrage. A network of tracks connects the beach with the Charles Darwin University grounds to the northeast. These tracks run through eucalypt woodland and riverine monsoon forest. Mangroves grow around the creek mouth.

When we visited there, a large number of parrots and finches were feeding on the recently burnt grass in the large space between the in and out driveways. Substantial numbers of Gouldian Finches (ca. 30 birds) were in the finch flock. There were also Long-tailed Finches, Masked Finches and Black-bellied Crimson Finches. A separate flock of Little Corellas, Galahs and numerous Peaceful Doves was foraging nearby. House Sparrows and Rose-ringed Parakeets also reside on the grounds.

A pair of Beach Stone-curlews were standing at the mouth of the creek, they are resident there. A few Common Sandpipers and Far Eastern Curlews stood nearby.

Arafura Fantail

A flock of Grey-crowned Babblers was running on the lawn. During a walk towards the university, we came across Orange-footed Scrubfowl, Varied Triller, Lemon-bellied Flycatcher, Blue-winged Kookaburra, Brown Whistler, Dusky Honeyeater, Red-headed Honeyeater, Rufous Songlark and Arafura Fantail. This walk is also good for spotlighting. Rufous Owls can be heard from the woodland adjacent to the Rapid Creek bridge. Look also for Barking Owl and Large-tailed Nightjar. There will be plenty of Bush Stone-curlews. Tawny Frogmouths roost in the paperbarks along the walk. They can also be found on the south side of the footbridge, in the casuarina trees in the carpark.

Over the years, several vagrant species were recorded at the mouth of Rapid Creek. These include House Swift, Red-rumped Swallow and Javan Pond Heron.

Muirhead Bushland

The tall eucalypt forest in the estate of Breezes Muirhead covers 30ha at the corner of Lee Point Rd and Aldenham Dr and is bordered from the north by the Lee Point Caravan Park. This is a wildlife corridor linking the Casuarina Coastal Reserve with the Shoal Bay area. It is owned by the Defence Housing Australia and is being systematically bulldozed for suburban houses as it was rezoned for residential development in 2010. You'll still find here some bushland, grassland and a dam. This area is highly valued by the Darwinians who like to come and watch the wildlife here, in particular the finches that flock in large numbers to drink from the dam. Petitions have been lodged to have this piece of land protected as part of the Casuarina Coastal Reserve. We'll see...

The site shot to fame nationally and internationally in 2022 thanks to Gouldian Finches that suddenly appeared there in high numbers after decades of being very rare. We were lucky to stay at that time for two weeks in the Lee Point Caravan Park which is adjacent to the bushland and the dam. When we unhitched our caravan on a site assigned to us in the southeastern corner, we were surprised to see a large number of people with binoculars crowding just outside the fence, gawking in. Then we realised that around two sprinklers that were working continuously in the corner of the caravan park were hundreds of finches bathing and drinking, then roosting on the fence or surrounding bushes. And a lot of them were Gouldian Finches! We have never seen so many Gouldian Finches before! During our stay, we watched 30-150 Gouldian Finches daily, many of them green youngsters. They were mixed in flocks of Chestnut-breasted Mannikins, Double-barred Finches and Black-bellied Crimson Finches. We also observed Masked Finches and Long-tailed Finches but in much smaller numbers. Star Finches, Zebra Finches and Yellow-rumped Mannikins also appeared daily. Some birders even spotted a single Pictorella Mannikin one day.

Gouldian Finches at the Lee Point caravan park

Other birds utilising the dam and the sprinklers included Bar-breasted Honeyeaters, Rufous-banded Honeyeaters and many White-winged Trillers. During our stay, numbers of birdwatchers outside and inside the caravan park fence grew, as the news of the Gouldian Finch influx to the dam and the adjacent caravan park spread. Tour vans of birder operators started to arrive, several a day. The good folk of the caravan park kept running the sprinklers and the place turned into a birdwatching hotspot of the season.

To get there, drive Lee Point Rd north and stop at the southern boundary of the Lee Point Caravan Park. Leave your car on a wide road shoulder. A walking track along the boundary leads to the dam, there is also a network of obscure paths in the bush and tall grasses. A communication tower is located near your stop. A long-lasting, active Osprey nest sits on the tower.

Over 160 bird species have been recorded in the Muirhead Bushland. **Key species** are Gouldian Finch, Star Finch, Yellow-rumped Mannikin, Bar-breasted Honeyeater, Azure Kingfisher, Silver-backed Butcherbird, Osprey and Black-breasted Buzzard. Other birds of interest include other finches, Rufous-banded Honeyeater, Orange-footed Scrubfowl, Oriental Dollarbird, White-breasted Woodswallow, Rainbow Bee-eater, Forest Kingfisher, Lemon-bellied Flycatcher, Red-tailed Black-Cockatoo, Bush Stone-curlew and Barking Owl. Rarities include Black Bittern, Common Sandpiper, Pictorella Mannikin, Black-eared Cuckoo, Grey Fantail, Red-rumped Swallow and Black Falcon.

The dam outside the caravan park fence is the centre of activity, particularly before dusk when many birds come to roost in the bush and are getting the last sip of water before the night. When a large flock of Red-tailed Black-Cockatoos lands for a drink, it is a view to remember.

There are always some waterbirds on the dam, possibly Green Pygmy-geese, Glossy Ibises or Nankeen Night-Herons. Even Black Bittern is seen at the water edge from time to time. Azure Kingfishers are usually around the water.

A breeding population of Bar-breasted Honeyeaters lives in the bush. Look for their distinctive nests hanging from branches of paperbark trees. Other honeyeaters in the area include Brown Honeyeater, Banded Honeyeater, Rufous-banded Honeyeater, Dusky Honeyeater, White-throated Honeyeater, White-gaped Honeyeater and ever-present, noisy flocks of White-quilled Honeyeaters.

Grassy areas may produce (beside the finches) Tawny Grassbird, Brown Quail, Golden-headed Cisticola and Australasian Pipit. Apart from the Osprey, several other raptors nest around the site. We observed a Black-breasted Buzzard bringing nesting material to an old nest near the caravan park. Australian Hobby was attempting to take over the Osprey nest when they finished breeding. Tawny Frogmouths roost and nest in a tree along the boundary fence track. Also Whistling Kites and Brown Goshawks breed on site.

The Lee Point Village Resort & Caravan Park offers good birdwatching, especially at night. We enjoyed Bush Stone-curlew concerts each night, as 10 birds or so gathered at the 'stage' of a caravan turning area, flooded with the light from a streetlamp. Large-tailed Nightjars were hunting over the caravan storage yard. Barn Owls were roosting in the machinery yard on a roundabout near the reception. A pair of Barking Owls were duetting softly each night. We also noted Southern Boobook and Tawny Frogmouth on site.

As in many other caravan parks, trees inside the park are utilised as a night roost by many bird groups. We watched White-breasted Woodswallows forming long cuddles in the tree shading our caravan. Other trees were claimed by Varied Lorikeets, Red-collared Lorikeets, Rainbow Bee-eaters, Australasian Figbirds, Red-winged Parrots and several honeyeater species. Watching them all settle for the evening each day was an unforgettable spectacle, much better than TV.

White-breasted Woodswallows cuddling up for the night

While in the area, it is worth diverting for a while to the Muirhead Water Race site, a neglected wetland on the south side of Aldenham Rd. It is adjacent to the Buffalo Creek mangroves and Leanyer Sewage Ponds which frame it from the east and south, respectively. Several obscure tracks there can be used for birding. In 2022, an influx of Gouldian Finches and other finches was also noticed there. The area is also good for White-browed Crake, Buff-banded Rail, Nankeen Night-Heron and Pied Heron. Occasionally, Black Bittern is sighted. Look for Eastern Yellow Wagtails at the swamp edge in summer.

Brush Cuckoo, Little Bronze-cuckoo, Eastern Koel and Channel-billed Cuckoo are seen fairly often. We observed Green-backed Gerygone feeding a large Little Bronze-cuckoo chick. Oriental Cuckoos appear sporadically in summer.

Pacific Bazas and Brown Goshawks nest at this site. Grey Goshawks are regularly seen flying over the area.

Leanyer Sewage Ponds

This prime birdwatching site consists of eleven fenced stabilisation ponds and a large mangrove and wetland area outside the fence.

Access to the ponds used to be available to members of public upon completion of an online safety induction and signing of an online indemnity form on the NT Power and Water's website. This privilege was terminated. Only some birding tour operators may have special arrangements. Currently (as of mid-2024) the Power and Water still denies access to birdwatchers for "administrative" reasons. We hope this will change in the future; there is even a vague plan to build a permanent platform over the ponds.

Foot access to Leanyer WTP from the end of Hodgson Dr

In the meantime, a pipeline approach has been adopted by the birders who cannot be stopped going to this incredible site. To get there, drive to the end of Hodgson Dr in Leanyer and park your car before the boom gate (see photo). Continue on foot on a track through the open woodland to an obscure T-junction. Take the left fork; you'll see a pipeline after about 20m. Walk along the pipeline to the ponds' southern fence. The distance from the gate is about 1.5km. The path trodden by the birders along the fence is difficult, as the ground is uneven and slippery. Also, don't forget about the ever-present danger of crocodiles in the mangroves; we are indeed in the Far North. The best time to visit is Sep-Apr when migrant waders and possible rarities of all kinds appear.

The official access to the ponds, before the gate was locked, was from Fitzmaurice Dr, now useless. However, there is an outflow ditch running north parallel to the Sewage Ponds Rd's north-heading arm, starting just outside the gate in Fitzmaurice Rd. This ditch is worth checking; it may prove to be quite productive.

Over 240 bird species have been recorded around the Leanyer Sewage Ponds. **Key species** are Little Ringed Plover, Oriental Plover, Little Curlew, Eastern Yellow Wagtail, White-winged Black Tern, Little Kingfisher, Oriental Cuckoo, Barn Swallow and Great-billed Heron. Other birds of interest include waders, Pied Heron, Black Bittern, Wandering Whistling-Duck, Oriental Pratincole, Mangrove Gerygone, Broad-billed Flycatcher, Mangrove Robin, Australian Yellow White-eye, Azure Kingfisher, Brown Whistler, Tawny Grassbird and Rufous-banded Honeyeater. On the long list of rarities are Grey Wagtail, White Wagtail, Yellow Chat, Spotted Whistling-Duck, Freckled Duck, Garganey, Northern Pintail, Chestnut Teal, Australian Shelduck, Australasian Shoveler, Little Grebe, Black-headed Gull, Red-rumped Swallow, Yellow-rumped Mannikin, Star Finch and several waders as below.

An astonished number of 41 wader species has been reached for the ponds. The star attraction is Little Ringed Plover. This is the only place in Australia where 1-4 birds can be found regularly every summer. Common waders here include Sharp-tailed Sandpiper, Wood Sandpiper, Common Sandpiper, Marsh Sandpiper, Black-tailed Godwit, Whimbrel and Grey Plover. The number of vagrant species is still growing and includes Red-necked Phalarope (in 2020), Red Phalarope (in 2014), Broad-billed Sandpiper (in 2018), Pectoral Sandpiper, Little Stint (in 1986), Swinhoe's Snipe, Common Redshank and Ruff.

Ten species of terns are found at Leanyer Sewage Ponds. A flock of up to 300 White-winged Black Terns spends every summer here. Sometimes, they mix with common tern species as they prepare to migrate north.

The ponds are usually filled with waterbirds. Many stand in mixed groups on the causeways and bunds. Wandering Whistling-Ducks are typically most numerous, reaching 5,000 birds. Among them, look for Radjah Shelducks, Magpie Geese,

Plumed Whistling-Ducks and Australasian Grebes. Even Pink-eared Ducks and Hardheads may be present in good numbers. The endangered Freckled Ducks are sighted regularly. Vagrant waterbirds are listed in the site summary above.

A gang of male Hardheads

Eastern Yellow Wagtail and Barn Swallow are regular visitors in the Wet every year. Sightings of up to 30 Eastern Yellow Wagtails were reported; they feed at the pond edges, especially in the northwestern corner of the site. One or two Barn Swallows were observed flying over the ponds or perched on power lines.

Check the mangroves outside the pond fences. Nearly every mangrove specialist can be found there including Little Kingfisher, Broad-billed Flycatcher, Mangrove Robin and Mangrove Golden Whistler. Chestnut Rail may be calling from the mangroves. Occasionally, Great-billed Heron lands on the mudflats adjacent to the southern boundary of the ponds.

While you are in Leanyer, an outflow ditch in Fitzmaurice Dr is worth checking. During the Wet, Eastern Yellow Wagtail is often found here, as well as several waders such as Common Sandpiper, Wood Sandpiper, Marsh Sandpiper and Common Greenshank. Look also for Buff-banded Rail, Little Egret, Plumed Egret and White-necked Heron. Even Black-necked Stork can land in the ditch. The surrounding grassy areas may produce some finches. Black-bellied Crimson Finch, Double-barred Finch, Masked Finch and Chestnut-breasted Mannikin are quite common, while Gouldian Finch and Yellow-rumped Mannikin are sighted irregularly.

Marsh Sandpipers; in breeding plumage on the right

Such a large congregation of birds in the area attracts raptors; 19 species are on the site birdlist. Some, such as Whistling Kite, Black Kite, Brahminy Kite and White-bellied Sea-Eagle are always present, other, including Swamp Harrier, Grey Goshawk, Australian Hobby, Peregrine Falcon, Black Falcon and Black-breasted Buzzard, are much rarer.

We visited the ponds in June 2022 and adopted the pipeline approach from Hodgson Dr. At the start of the hike, a flock of finches was feeding in a recently burnt-out area, mostly Chestnut-breasted Mannikins and Black-bellied Crimson Finches. Among them were also some Gouldian Finches, Masked Finches and Long-tailed Finches. Red-tailed Black-Cockatoos were also foraging in the area subjected to backburning.

The flowering coral trees along the track were plastered with honeyeaters including Rufous-banded Honeyeater, Brown Honeyeater, Banded Honeyeater, White-gaped Honeyeater, Helmeted Friarbird and Little Friarbird. In the tall grasses along the pipeline, we came across Golden-headed Cisticola, Tawny Grassbird, Red-backed Fairy-wren and Australasian Pipit. Pale-vented Bush-hens were reported from the grassy areas near the pipeline but we did not sight them.

In swampy areas near the pipeline and on the mudflats nearby, we found Buff-banded Rail, Marsh Sandpiper, Common Greenshank, Red-kneed Dotterel, Little Egret and juvenile Nankeen Night-Heron. In the mangroves, we spotted Black

Butcherbird, Shining Flycatcher, Lemon-bellied Flycatcher, Common Cicadabird, Mangrove Gerygone, Green-backed Gerygone and Australian Yellow White-eye.

Looking through the wire fence, we could see masses of common ducks, herons, egrets and waders as described above. A flock of Royal Spoonbills was standing near the fence.

Holmes Jungle Nature Park

This 250ha park is located in Holmes, 20km from Darwin CBD on the fringe of the city's northern suburbs. It protects a small, isolated pocket of monsoon forest from the relentless urban encroachment. It also contains a substantial area of wetland, grassland and woodland. Palm Creek meanders through the area.

To get there, turn north off Vanderlin Dr into Shoal Bay Access Rd, then quickly into Holmes Jungle Rd (second right). The park is open between 8am and 6pm. There are two picnic areas: Hilltop the main one, and is equipped with toilets, shaded tables and excellent views of the park, while the Jungle Picnic Area near the Palm Creek offers just picnic tables. Walking trails run through the park. Further information with a site map can be found here: https://nt.gov.au/__data/assets/pdf_file/0009/200070/holmes-jungle-nature-park.pdf.

Over 210 bird species have been recorded in the Holmes Jungle Nature Park. **Key species** are Red-chested Button-quail, Red-backed Button-quail, King Quail, Zitting Cisticola, Red-headed Honeyeater, Rainbow Pitta and Eastern Yellow Wagtail. Other birds of interest include White-browed Crake, Black Bittern, Pied Heron, Forest Kingfisher, Rufous-banded Honeyeater, Green-backed Gerygone, Rose-crowned Fruit-Dove, Silver-backed Butcherbird, Black Butcherbird and Grey Goshawk. Rarities include Yellow Chat, Little Kingfisher, Swinhoe's Snipe, Little Ringed Plover, Asian Dowitcher, Pale-vented Bush-hen, Gouldian Finch, Yellow-rumped Mannikin, Eastern Grass Owl, Black-breasted Buzzard and Swamp Harrier.

Look for grassland birds at this site. A good area is past the turnoff to the Hilltop picnic site along Holmes Jungle Rd on your left, up to the fence. Brown Quails are the most common but you'll have a chance to see King Quail or one of the button-quails. Both Zitting and Golden-headed Cisticolas are found here so pay attention to the identification details. The grassland may also yield Brown Songlark, Tawny Grassbird, Horsfield's Bushlark and Australasian Pipit.

In October-November, the park gets flooded after heavy rains, and the wetland area increases in size. Masses of Magpie Geese, Wandering Whistling-Ducks and Plumed Whistling-Ducks land in the park. As the water starts receding, waders appear on the swampy edges including Sharp-tailed Sandpiper, Marsh Sandpiper, Wood Sandpiper, Pied Stilt, Swinhoe's Snipe, Red-kneed Dotterel, Oriental Pratincole, Far Eastern Curlew and many more. Rarities such as Little Ringed Plover or Ruff are sighted from time to time. The wetland is filled with egrets, herons and ibises, with Pied Heron particularly numerous. White-browed Crake, Buff-banded Rail or even Easter Yellow Wagtail may be skirting the swamp margins.

Rose-crowned Fruit-Dove

The rainforest path meanders along the creek and monsoon forest. There, look for Rainbow Pitta, Torresian Imperial-Pigeon, Rose-crowned Fruit-Dove, Brown-capped Emerald-Dove, Varied Lorikeet, Orange-footed Scrubfowl, Green-backed Gerygone, Arafura Fantail, Brown Whistler, Green Oriole, Common Cicadabird and Broad-billed Flycatcher. Scanning of the vegetation along the creek may produce Black Bittern, Nankeen Night-Heron and Azure Kingfisher.

The Hilltop picnic area may also prove productive, particularly for honeyeaters. You may get Rufous-banded Honeyeater, Bar-breasted Honeyeater, White-gaped Honeyeater, Red-headed Honeyeater, Banded Honeyeater, White-quilled Honeyeater, Yellow-throated Miner and Helmeted Friarbird there. Red-backed Fairy-wrens are abundant in the grass around the picnic area. Look also for Spangled Drongo, Rose-crowned Fruit-Dove, Australasian Figbird, Olive-backed Oriole, Green Oriole, Pheasant Coucal, Red-tailed Black-Cockatoo and Red-collared Lorikeet.

At night, Barking Owl, Rufous Owl, Bush Stone-curlew and Large-tailed Nightjar may be calling. Eastern Grass Owl used to be sporadically recorded in the grassy areas.

Knuckey Lagoons

Knuckey Lagoons from the picnic site at Fiddlers Lane

Knuckey Lagoons Conservation Reserve is an important wetland located 12km southeast of Darwin CBD. The four natural depressions in the reserve fill with water persisting throughout the Dry, although very little water is left by the end of the dry season. In the Wet, a single 50ha water body is formed, largely covered with waterlilies.

Three different routes lead to three different parts of the wetland, see descriptions in the relevant subsections below. A fact sheet with a map is downloadable here: https://nt.gov.au/__data/assets/pdf_file/0011/200072/knuckey-lagoons-conservation-reserve.pdf.

Over 200 bird species have been recorded in the Knuckey Lagoons Conservation Reserve. **Key species** are Eastern Yellow Wagtail, King Quail, Glossy Ibis, Swinhoe's Snipe, Little Curlew, Silver-backed Butcherbird and Zitting Cisticola. Other birds of interest include waders, White-browed Crake, Magpie Goose, Green Pygmy-goose, Pied Heron, Little Pied Cormorant, Brolga, Channel-billed Cuckoo, Horsfield's Bushlark, Rufous-banded Honeyeater, Common Cicadabird, Black-bellied Crimson Finch and Spotted Harrier. Rarities include Garganey, Northern Pintail, Freckled Duck, Yellow Chat, Black Falcon and Square-tailed Kite.

Magpie Goose

Waterbirds favour Knuckey Lagoons in the Dry, the numbers may be so huge that little water is visible from under the bird body mass. The numbers of Magpie Geese may reach over 5,000 birds by the of September and in October. Also abundant are Radjah Shelducks, Green Pygmy-geese, Wandering Whistling-Ducks and Plumed Whistling-Ducks. You can expect a variety of herons and egrets scattered in the shallow swamp, mainly Pied Herons, Plumed Egrets and Great Egrets. The site's wader list has 30 species. In particular, Marsh Sandpiper, Wood Sandpiper and Common Sandpiper are regularly here in summer. Among rare species are Little Ringed Plover, Oriental Plover, Long-toed Stint, Pectoral Sandpiper and Ruff.

In the surrounding bushland, look for Orange-footed Scrubfowl, Shining Flycatcher, Lemon-bellied Flycatcher, Rufous Songlark, Bar-breasted Honeyeater, Red-winged Parrot, Oriental Dollarbird, Large-billed Gerygone, Pheasant Coucal, Horsfield's Bronze-cuckoo and Oriental Cuckoo. On the list of 17 species of raptors are Swamp Harrier, Black-breasted Buzzard, Australian Hobby and White-bellied Sea-Eagle.

Snipe Swamp

To get to the Snipe Swamp, from Stuart Hwy (1) turn into Lagoon Rd and after 2km turn right into Randall Rd, a 200m unsealed track leading to the edge of the lagoon. Sometimes this track may be so boggy that it will be prudent to leave the car in Randall Rd. There are no facilities.

Grassland bordering Randall Rd often yields Swinhoe's Snipes in summer. Up to 30 birds have been reported. Look also for King Quail, Brown Quail, Red-backed Button-quail, Tawny Grassbird, Golden-headed Cisticola, Zitting Cisticola, Chestnut-breasted Mannikin and Long-tailed Finch.

Brolgas like to congregate at the edge of the swamp. Little Curlews have been recorded in huge flocks in summer. If you are lucky, Yellow Chats may be foraging on the drying mud.

Fiddlers Lane

To get to the Fiddlers Lane's part of Knuckey Lagoons, from Stuart Hwy (1) turn into McMillians Rd and after 2.2km turn left into Fiddlers La, a 200m unsealed track leading to the edge of the lagoon along a mango grove. A small picnic site is provided at the end of this track, otherwise there are no facilities.

This was our favourite part of the wetland, allowing an unobstructed view from a shady, grassy spot, where you can sit quietly at the picnic table under a tree and watch the birds passing close to you across the muddy edges of the lagoon. These could be White-browed Crakes, Comb-crested Jacanas or Eastern Yellow Wagtails. Brolgas and Black-necked Storks would wade stately through the swamp. If you visit in summer, Magpie Geese may sneak behind your back to the mango orchard to gorge on the fallen ripe mangoes.

Most of the rarities were recorded in this part of Knuckey Lagoons. Garganeys, Northern Pintails and Freckled Ducks like to spend time here. Several vagrant waders such as Ruff, Pectoral Sandpiper, Asian Dowitcher and Oriental Plover have also been sighted.

South End of Knuckey Lagoons

To get to the south end of the Knuckey Lagoons, from Stuart Hwy (1) turn into Thorak Rd, park your car and walk to the edge of the lagoon. There are no facilities.

The bird composition here will be similar to that of the other two parts of the site. Depending on the water reach, the birds may be closer or further away. It is worth noting that Silver-backed Butcherbirds are resident in the bushes by the water edge.

Darwin Periphery

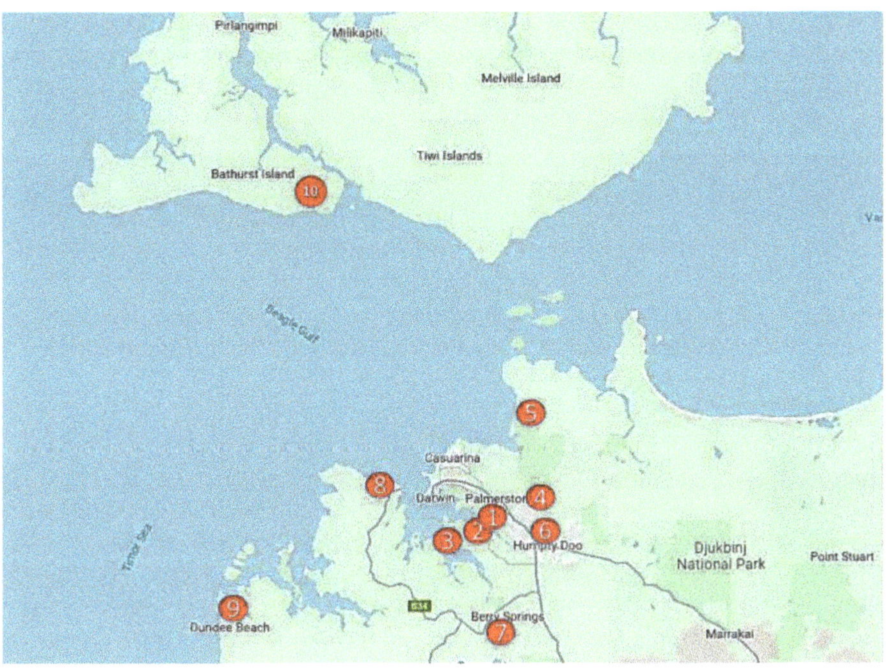

1 Palmerston WTP
2 Palmerston Pale-vented Bush-hen Sites
3 Channel Island
4 Howard Springs Nature Park
5 Tree Point Conservation Area
6 McMinns Lagoon Reserve
7 Berry Springs Nature Park
8 Wagait Beach
9 Dundee Beach
10 Tiwi Islands

Palmerston WTP

Palmerston Sewage Ponds are located 30km south of Darwin, in the suburbs of Archer and Marlow Lagoon in Palmerston City. This is still one of favourite birding location of many NT birders. The site used to be easily accessible from Catalina Rd. Now the access is more difficult, as NT Power and Water has barricaded a large end section of Catalina Rd before the ponds. Today it is still possible to walk around the ponds' perimeter, but the walk is longer and, to get there, requires walking through uneven ground and high grass.

To get there, drive down Catalina Rd, then turn right into Bridle Rd just past the railway tracks. You'll see a turf farm on the left; stop there at a small clearing about 50m from the turnoff. Walk down on the outside of the turf farm's fence and the bush to the ponds (less than 1km). Turn right and walk along the ponds fence until you get to an opening in the mangroves where you can look for the mangrove specialists. Watch for the crocks!

Over 210 bird species have been recorded around the Palmerston Sewage Ponds. **Key species** are Mangrove Fantail, Mangrove Robin, White-winged Black Tern, White-breasted Whistler, Mangrove Golden Whistler and Common Gull-billed Tern. Other birds of interest include waders, waterbirds, Whiskered Tern, Brown Whistler, Broad-billed Flycatcher, Chestnut Rail, Red-headed Honeyeater, Australian Yellow White-eye, Collared Kingfisher, Red-backed Button-quail, Bar-breasted Honeyeater and Common Cicadabird. Rarities include Little Kingfisher, Great-billed Heron, Grey Wagtail, Eastern Yellow Wagtail, Gouldian Finch, Broad-billed Sandpiper, Little Stint, Long-toed Stint, Oriental Plover, Swinhoe's Snipe, Red-necked Phalarope and Common Redshank.

Before you get to the ponds, it is worthwhile to visit the Palmerston Golf Course, located along University Ave. There are two large lakes on site, surrounded by wetland vegetation. The rare Australian Little Bittern was recorded in the reedbeds a couple of times. Other birds on the ponds include Green Pygmy-geese, Radjah Shelducks, Pied Herons, Nankeen Night-Herons and Comb-crested Jacanas.

The walk down the turf farm can be productive for many grassland birds. A long list of potentials includes Black-bellied Crimson Finch, Long-tailed Finch, Gouldian Finch (rare), Chestnut-breasted Mannikin, Brown Quail, Tawny Grassbird, Red-backed Button-quail and Golden-headed Cisticola. Also, Zitting Cisticola is sometimes reported from this spot.

When you reach the ponds' fence, check the outflow channel. This is the favourite place of Eastern Yellow Wagtails in summer. Mangroves surrounding the sewage ponds may prove to be the easiest place in NT to find Mangrove Fantail and

Mangrove Robin. The latter can be abundant in this area. In the mangrove clearing at the corner of the fence, look for Mangrove Golden Whistler, Black Butcherbird, White-breasted Whistler, Australian Yellow White-eye, Broad-billed Flycatcher and Shining Flycatcher. Listen to Chestnut Rails, they may even surprise you quietly coming out in the open.

Mangrove Fantail

Terns are often hunting over the ponds, especially Whiskered Terns and White-winged Black Terns. The latter congregate here in good numbers before their migration to the Northern Hemisphere in September. Both Australian Gull-billed Tern and Common Gull-billed Tern can be found at this site.

A staggering number of 41 species of waders features on the Palmerston Sewage Ponds birdlist, and the number of vagrant species is still growing. Some of the series of ponds are cyclically pumped out for desludging. When drying out, they attract a wide variety of waders. These include Common Sandpiper, Wood Sandpiper, Terek Sandpiper, Curlew Sandpiper, Sharp-tailed Sandpiper, Little Curlew, Black-tailed Godwit and Australian Pratincole. See the list of rarities in the site summary above.

Common ducks, egrets and herons gather on the ponds in large numbers. Even Great-billed Heron is here from time to time, probably arriving from Channel Island.

Palmerston Pale-vented Bush-hen Sites

A couple of spots in the Palmerston area are worth checking for this elusive species.

Mitchell Creek

Mitchell Creek's site is located not far from the Palmerston Sewage Ponds, at the corner of Roystonea Av and Lambrick Av. Concentrate on the northeast quarter of the intersection, at approximate GPS coordinates of 12°29'58"S and 131°00'08"E. However, there is no parking around this intersection. To get there, turn north into Farrar Blvd from Lambrick Av, then left into Tarakan Ct at the roundabout. You can park your car there and walk west towards the creek. The birds were flushed from dense grass in the area near the creek.

Other birds here include Brown Quail, Pheasant Coucal, Long-tailed Finch, Black-bellied Crimson Finch, Golden-headed Cisticola, Brush Cuckoo and Rufous-banded Honeyeater.

Finn Road at Weddell

To get there, from Stuart Hwy (1) south of Palmerston City and past the turnoff to Arnhem Hwy, turn right into Jenkins Rd. Turn first left into Finn Rd. The birds were recorded in dense grass about 100m south of the turnoff, at approximate GPS coordinates of 12°36'53"S and 131°00'33"E.

Channel Island

The 120ha Channel Island lies off the coast of NT, not far from Palmerston City. Most of the island is preserved as Channel Island Conservation Reserve. The ruins of historic leprosarium and the reefs surrounding the island are both heritage-listed sites. The rest of the island is utilised by a power station and an aquaculture centre. The island is connected to the mainland by a road bridge. To get there, take Elrundie Av from Palmerston City (it will later change name to Channel Island Rd) and drive about 20km to the island. Turn first left into Gas Facility Access Rd. A carpark at the end of the road has a resident Great Bowerbird maintaining an impressive bower. GPS coordinates for the carpark are 12°33'26"S and 130°51'49"E.

For the birdwatchers, tha main attraction of the island are Great-billed Herons that are sometimes seen foraging on the mudflats under the bridge. Stop near the bridge to see also an Osprey nest on a pylon. Other birds on the mudflats may include Far Eastern Curlew, Whimbrel, Great Knot, Terek Sandpiper, Grey Plover and Beach Stone-curlew.

Check out the place just before the turnoff to the boat ramp near the entrance to the Aquaculture Centre. Walk around the gate past the sign 'Restricted entry' – this is a well-used track allowing to get to the monsoon forest and the mangroves. Here, the selection of species typical of these habitats includes Rainbow Pitta, Rose-crowned Fruit-Dove, Mangrove Golden Whistler, Red-headed Honeyeater, Lemon-bellied Flycatcher, Varied Triller, Azure Kingfisher, Common Cicadabird and Black Butcherbird. Raptors include Osprey, Brahminy Kite and Grey Goshawk.

Black Butcherbird

Elizabeth River Boat Ramp

When driving on Channel Island Rd, it is a good idea to stop in the carpark for the Elizabeth River boat ramp, 2km south of Palmerston City. GPS coordinates for the carpark are 12°23'17"S and 130°58'38"E. Chestnut Rails are regularly found here while Great-billed Heron is sighted from time to time.

On the mudflats at the boat ramp, look for Far Eastern Curlew, Whimbrel, Grey-tailed Tattler, Radjah Shelduck, Little Egret, Striated Heron and Black-necked Stork.

In the mangroves, especially when grey mangroves are flowering, you'll see an abundance of Red-headed Honeyeaters. Look also for Mangrove Robin, Collared Kingfisher, Mangrove Gerygone, Northern Fantail, Brush Cuckoo and Helmeted Friarbird.

Middle Arm

This is another spot with a good chance of sighting a Great-billed Heron. To get there, from Channel Island Rd turn east in Jenkins Rd, then south into Finn Rd and then first right into Middle Arm Rd. Drive to the boat ramp at the end of the road. GPS coordinates are 12°38'55"S and 130°57'53"E.

One or two Great-billed Herons visit the mudflats near the boat ramp with some regularity. Look for waders at the muddy margins at low tide, including Terek Sandpiper, Common Sandpiper, Whimbrel, Far Eastern Curlew, Grey-tailed Tattler, Lesser Sand Plover and Greater Sand Plover.

Far Eastern Curlew

Search the mangroves north of the boat ramp for Little Kingfisher, Azure Kingfisher, Collared Kingfisher, Sacred Kingfisher, Chestnut Rail, Red-headed Honeyeater, Large-billed Gerygone, Mangrove Gerygone, Green-backed Gerygone, Black Butcherbird, Arafura Fantail, Shining Flycatcher, Lemon-bellied Flycatcher and Broad-billed Flycatcher.

Howard Springs Nature Park

This small park (286ha) is located 35km southeast of Darwin CBD. It is a fantastic place for a walk in a shady rainforest at any time of the day. The reserve protects habitats such as monsoon forest, extensive swamps and the riverine vegetation.

To get there from Darwin, from Stuart Hwy (1) take Howard Springs Rd just past Palmerston City. After 5km, drive through the entrance to Howard Springs Nature Park and continue to one of the two carparks. Gates to the park are open from 7:30am until 7pm. Swimming is prohibited in the large pool, but there are several shallow rocky splash pools for the kids. Good picnic areas are provided around the pools, well-equipped with sheltered picnic tables, barbecues and toilets. There is also a playground for children. A 1.8km walking circuit runs along the creek. Alternatively, take a short track to see the springs that feed the main pool. A fact sheet with the site map is downloadable here: https://nt.gov.au/__data/assets/pdf_file/0010/200071/howard-springs-nature-park.pdf.

Over 180 bird species have been recorded in the Howard Springs Nature Park. **Key species** are Rainbow Pitta, Black Bittern, Little Kingfisher, Azure Kingfisher, Silver-backed Butcherbird and Pacific Baza. Other birds of interest include Brown-capped Emerald-Dove, Torresian Imperial-Pigeon, Bar-breasted Honeyeater, Rufous-banded Honeyeater, Common Cicadabird, Arafura Fantail, Brown Whistler and Little Shrike-thrush. Rarities include Oriental Cuckoo, Rufous Owl, Gouldian Finch, Welcome Swallow and Grey Fantail.

The 1.8km Howard Creek Walk is the best place to look for Rainbow Pitta, especially the section from halfway to the furthest point (footbridge) on both sides of the loop. Look for them on the ground; in Sep-Feb also listen to their calls from elevated perches. The call is a very loud, distinctive 'we-wik to wik'. Other birds on the walk include Green Oriole, Green-backed Gerygone, Rose-crowned Fruit-Dove (plenty), Brown-capped Emerald-Dove, Dusky Honeyeater, Bar-breasted Honeyeater, Shining Flycatcher, Brush Cuckoo, Spangled Drongo, Little Shrike-thrush, Brown Whistler, Arafura Fantail and Brown Goshawk.

Check the vegetation around the main pool for Black Bittern, Little Kingfisher, Azure Kingfisher and Nankeen Night-Heron. Occasionally, Green Pygmy-geese and Radjah Shelducks may be found on the water while White-necked Heron or Common Sandpiper on the banks.

A pair of Silver-backed Butcherbirds is resident in the Woorabinda Youth Campground. Other birds there include Orange-footed Scrubfowl, Pheasant Coucal, Eastern Koel, Oriental Dollarbird, Bush Stone-curlew, White-bellied Cuckoo-shrike, Weebill and Little Corella. A group of Helmeted Guineafowls roams the grounds.

Immature male Eastern Koel

Tree Point Conservation Area

This site is located 65km east of Darwin. The reserve protects a mangrove-lined estuary in the northern part of Shoal Bay. The area also includes a narrow coastal strip of the monsoon vine thicket along the pristine beach of the Tree Point Peninsula. This a significant feeding and roosting site for the waders.

To get there, from Stuart Hwy (1) take Howard Springs Rd just past Palmerston City. Drive for 5km, then before the entrance to Howard Springs Nature Park continue on Gunn Point Rd for 30km. Turn left into Murrumujuk Dr, signposted just as 'Beach access', then at the fork in the road with a board 'Road rules on the beach' turn left. Drive along the beach to a locked gate. The last seven kilometres are unsealed, with the last two kilometres corrugated. Because of that section of the trip, a high-clearance 4WD is recommended. The tracks turn impassable after the rain. Leave the car at the gate and walk along the track or along the beach to the estuary.

There are no facilities in the park and no camping is allowed. The closest is the Gunn Point Campground or the Howard Springs township. A fact sheet is downloadable here: https://nt.gov.au/__data/assets/pdf_file/0010/200080/tree-point-conservation-area.pdf.

Over 100 bird species have been recorded in the Tree Point Conservation Area. **Key species** are Rainbow Pitta and waders including Beach Stone-curlew. Other birds of interest include Eastern Reef Egret, Rose-crowned Fruit-Dove, Large-billed Gerygone, Mangrove Gerygone, Little Bronze-cuckoo, Mangrove Golden Whistler, Brown Whistler, Varied Triller, Brown Quail and Osprey.

Lesser Crested Ten (front) with a group of Greater Crested Terns

Greater Sand Plovers roost here in large numbers. Beach Stone-curlews are resident. Other waders in the area include Grey Plover, Lesser Sand Plover, Great Knot, Red Knot, Ruddy Turnstone, Bar-tailed Godwit, Black-tailed Godwit, Terek Sandpiper, Sharp-tailed Sandpiper and Whimbrel. Little Terns and Lesser Crested Terns are often found here.

In the monsoon forest, look for Green Oriole, Red-headed Honeyeater, Rufous-banded Honeyeater, Varied Triller, Spangled Drongo, Rose-crowned Fruit-Dove and Black Butcherbird.

Check the grassy areas for Australasian Pipit, Golden-headed Cisticola and Horsfield's Bushlark. Raptors in the reserve include Australian Hobby, White-bellied Sea-Eagle, Osprey and Brahminy Kite.

McMinns Lagoon Reserve

This delightful, 50ha private reserve is located at 5 Dreamtime Dr in the rural suburb of McMinns Lagoon, 35km southeast of Darwin. The lagoon is covered by waterlilies and the site is breathtaking when they are flowering. Water is fringed with the paperbarks and grassland. The reserve is fenced to protect its environmental value.

McMinns Lagoon, seen from the lookout

There are several ways to reach the site, but the signposted route is via Girraween Rd from Stuart Hwy (1), turning south into McMinns Dr, then left into Orion Wy and finally right into Dreamtime Dr which will get you to a carpark at the end of the road. Go through the gate; walking to the right will get to a small lookout projecting into the lagoon, with a couple of picnic tables. If you turn left past the gate, you'll walk through bushland to the east of the lagoon. The track runs all around the lagoon but at high water parts of it are flooded. Foot access to this path is also from Lily Ln and Sayers Rd.

Over 190 bird species have been recorded in the McMinns Lagoon Reserve. **Key species** are King Quail, Swinhoe's Snipe, Eastern Yellow Wagtail, Oriental Cuckoo and Silver-backed Butcherbird. Other birds of interest include waders, waterbirds, Azure Kingfisher, Forest Kingfisher, Common Cicadabird, Little Bronze-cuckoo, Rufous-banded Honeyeater, Bar-breasted Honeyeater, Black Bittern, Pacific Baza, Osprey and Grey Goshawk. Rarities include Ruff, Garganey, Black Swan, Great-billed Heron and Rufous Owl.

We spent some time searching the scrub near the carpark, where a bird party was feeding on insects and small caterpillars. In that party we got Little Bronze-cuckoo, Horsfield's Bronze-cuckoo, Brush Cuckoo, Northern Fantail, Rufous Whistler, Little Friarbird, Varied Triller, White-winged Triller and a beautiful female Common Cicadabird.

Female Common Cicadabird

When we got the lookout, we sat at a picnic table, relaxing and watching the water. In the lagoon among the waterlilies were hundreds of Magie Geese with their bums up and heads in the water. Their deep honks were reverberating throughout the reserve. Among them were Green Pygmy-geese, Radjah Shelducks, Wandering Whistling-Ducks and Plumed Whistling-Ducks. About 200 Pied Herons were scattered along the water edges. Other waterbirds included White-necked Herons, Great Egrets, Plumed Egrets, Little Egrets, Black-necked Storks, Glossy Ibises and a pair of Brolgas. A flock of Royal Spoonbills was busy feeding close to the shore. Comb-crested Jacanas were walking on the lily pads. Swamp Harrier and several Black Kites, Whiskered Terns and Australian Gull-billed Terns were flying over the water. Australasian Darters were sunning their wings on the shore. Forest Kingfisher and Azure Kingfisher were perched near the water.

Twenty-two wader species have been recorded around the lagoon. It is a regular site for Swinhoe's Snipe in summer. Look also for Pied Stilt, Red-kneed Dotterel, Australian Pratincole, Wood Sandpiper, Marsh Sandpiper, Common Sandpiper and Little Curlew.

Other birds reported from this lagoon include Buff-banded Rail, Northern Rosella, Green Oriole, Lemon-bellied Flycatcher, Great Bowerbird, Dusky Honeyeater, Torresian Imperial-Pigeon and Barking Owl.

Berry Springs Nature Park

Berry Springs Nature Park is a picturesque, popular park, located about 50km south of Darwin. Cool off and relax here in one of the clear-water, shady thermal pools. In front of the hot springs are extensive shaded picnic areas equipped with picnic tables and barbecues. A loop walk will take you to the monsoon rainforest and woodland; expect good birding there. Other facilities include kiosk, toilets and a spacious carpark. To get there, from Stuart Hwy (1) turn into Cox Peninsula Rd (B34) and drive about 10km to a well signposted turnoff to the right to the Nature Park. Then there is a short drive to the carpark. Opening hours are 8am-6:30pm. A fact sheet with a map can be downloaded here: https://nt.gov.au/__data/assets/pdf_file/0009/200061/berry-springs-nature-park-fact-sheet.pdf.

Adjacent to the hot springs is the Territory Wildlife Park, tucked in the monsoon rainforest. It has a good collection of Northern Territory birds in a series of walk-in aviaries. Wild bird population is very similar to that of the neighbouring hot springs.

Brown-capped Emerald-Dove

Over 150 bird species have been recorded in the Berry Springs Nature Park. **Key species** are Rainbow Pitta, Brown-capped Emerald-Dove, Brown Whistler, Arafura Fantail, Shining Flycatcher and Silver-backed Butcherbird. Other birds of interest include Brown-capped Emerald-Dove, Rose-crowned Fruit-Dove, Little Shrike-thrush, Common Cicadabird, Red-headed Honeyeater, Azure Kingfisher, Green-backed Gerygone, White-bellied Cuckoo-shrike, Black-bellied Crimson Finch, Large-tailed Nightjar and Pacific Baza. Rarities include Partridge Pigeon, Oriental Cuckoo, Grey Fantail, Rufous Owl, Black Falcon and Square-tailed Kite.

Rainbow Bee-eaters were swooping over the pools where we were enjoying a pleasant soak, and Shining Flycatchers were picking insects from the pandanus leaves that line the pools. Azure Kingfishers were hunting from the banks and Black Falcon was flying overhead. Bliss...

When we moved to the picnic area, we were treated to an exquisite concert by the ensemble of about 15 Spangled Drongos. One bird was clearly the soloist, had a different call and led the singing. The rest created the background music. The performance lasted about 15 minutes, with some of the backup singers leaving or joining the band.

We searched the rainforest around the hot pools for Rainbow Pitta, with no success. However, we ticked off Brown-capped Emerald-Dove, Orange-footed Scrubfowl, Brown Whistler, Rufous Whistler, Torresian Imperial-Pigeon, Eastern Koel, Lemon-bellied Flycatcher, Northern Fantail, Arafura Fantail, White-breasted Woodswallow, Little Bronze-cuckoo and Brown Goshawk.

Wagait Beach

The little, sleepy coastal town of Wagait Beach is located just 8km west of Darwin, as the crow flies, but on the opposite side of Darwin Harbour. You can get there on a 15min passenger ferry from Cullen Bay in Darwin to the Mandorah Jetty. Taking a bicycle onboard is advisable. Otherwise, it is a 150km drive from Darwin via Stuart Hwy (1) and then Cox Peninsula Rd (B34) past Berry Springs. In Wagait Beach, you'll find a supermarket, public toilets near the sports area, and some coffee- and food-serving places (if open). We didn't see a fuel station.

You'll be rewarded here with 10km of secluded beaches cobbled with colourful soft rocks. As the houses have crept onto the beach, public access to the water is preserved only between some of the properties; look for signs denoting designated walkways. Still, you may get an evil eye from a property owner.

Rocks on the sand at Wagait Beach

Over 100 bird species have been recorded in Wagait Beach. **Key species** are Beach Stone-curlew, Little Tern and Silver-backed Butcherbird. Other birds of interest include waders, Tawny Frogmouth, Great Bowerbird, Grey-crowned Babbler, Brolga, Bar-breasted Honeyeater, Broad-billed Flycatcher, Northern Fantail, Red-winged Parrot and Pacific Baza. Rarities include Black-eared Cuckoo, Eastern Yellow Wagtail and Great-billed Heron.

We walked through this town in the morning, and it was a birdwatcher's treat. Flocks of parrots were frolicking in the street and in the backyards. Particularly delightful were Red-winged Parrots, common there. Plenty of Great Bowerbirds were flying between the properties. Honeyeaters were teeming in the flowering eucalypt trees; we noted White-quilled Honeyeater, Dusky Honeyeater, White-throated Honeyeater, Yellow-throated Miner and Silver-crowned Friarbird. There was a pair of very loud Silver-backed Butcherbirds near Erickson Cre. Other birds in town included Rainbow Bee-eater, Red-tailed Black-Cockatoo, Bush Stone-curlew, Varied Triller and Striated Pardalote. At night, you may hear howls of dingoes prowling the streets.

We found four pairs of Beach Stone-curlews within the short 2km distance of the beach in front of the houses. There was also one small saltwater crocodile, sunbathing in front of an empty holiday house, looking innocently like a plastic toy. The beach also yielded Australian Pied Oystercatcher, Ruddy Turnstone, Terek Sandpiper and a small flock of Little Terns.

Beach Stone-curlew

About 2km west of town, there is a shallow swamp at the mouth of Wagait Creek, surrounded by the mangroves. You can walk there along the beach at low tide from the end of Erickson Cre. If there is water in the swamp, Brolgas like to congregate there; flocks up to 50 have been recorded. Look also for Black-necked Stork, Radjah Shelduck, Common Greenshank, Pied Heron, White-necked Heron, Plumed Egret and Straw-necked Ibis. In the mangroves, you may come across Broad-billed Flycatcher, Little Bronze-cuckoo and Australian Yellow White-eye. On the walk to the swamp, keep an eye on the scrub; you may get Bar-breasted Honeyeater, Pallid Cuckoo, White-breasted Woodswallow, Lemon-bellied Flycatcher and Pacific Baza.

Another place worth checking is the Mandorah Jetty, located at the eastern end of Charles Point Rd. It is a good spot for waders. Beach Stone-curlews are nearly always on the beach. Terek Sandpipers and Greater Sand Plovers often roost together at high tide. Look for Little Terns nearby. Other birds along the beach include Red-capped Plover, Common Sandpiper, Ruddy Turnstone, Whimbrel, Far Eastern Curlew and Eastern Reef Egret.

Dundee Beach

Dundee Beach is a small coastal town and a very popular fishing spot. It is located 120km southwest of Darwin on the shores of Fog Bay. It has pristine beaches and is surrounded by the monsoon vine thicket and patches of mangroves. To get there, from Darwin take Stuart Hwy (1) and then turn into Cox Peninsula Rd (B34). After passing Litchfield Park Rd turn left into Fog Bay Rd. Towards the end, the road name changes to Namarada Dr; it will take you to the boat ramp with a large carpark and a caravan park right behind it. The last stretch of the road is named Dundee Pl.

Dundee Beach is another wader site. Observe them best foraging on the receding tide on the mudflats in front of the boat ramp. Unmarked public access paths to the beach from Marege Dr are also worth checking.

Over 140 bird species have been recorded in Dundee Beach. **Key species** are Beach Stone-curlew, Little Tern, Mangrove Fantail, Bar-breasted Honeyeater, Rainbow Pitta, Brown-capped Emerald-Dove, Fork-tailed Swift, Lesser Frigatebird and Grey Goshawk. Other birds of interest include waders, Orange-footed Scrubfowl, Common Cicadabird, Silver-backed Butcherbird, Rufous-banded Honeyeater, Red-headed Honeyeater, Rose-crowned Fruit-Dove, Brown Quail, Black-bellied Crimson Finch, Great Pied Cormorant and Osprey. Rarities include Bridled Tern, Common Gull-billed Tern, Brown Noddy, Little Curlew and Star Finch.

Australian Gull-billed Terns, breeding and non-breeding plumage

Twenty-three wader species have been recorded here. Beach Stone-curlews are resident. Regularly reported are Terek Sandpiper, Common Sandpiper, Greater Sand Plover, Lesser Sand Plover, Grey Plover, Whimbrel, Ruddy Turnstone, Grey-tailed Tattler and Australian Pied Oystercatcher. Terns are also occurring in a good variety including White-winged Black Tern, Common Tern, Australian Gull-billed Tern, Common Gull-billed Tern, Lesser Crested Tern, Bridled Tern and Caspian Tern.

In the monsoon thicket, look for Rainbow Pitta, Common Cicadabird, Northern Fantail, Black Butcherbird, Brown Whistler, Rufous-banded Honeyeater, Large-billed Gerygone, Green-backed Gerygone and Forest Kingfisher.

There is a reasonable chance to find Mangrove Fantail in the mangroves here. Walk north for about 1km from the end of Namarada Dr on a track at the edge of mangroves. For example, the birds have been seen around the GPS position of 12°42'28"S and 130°21'18"E. Look also for Mangrove Gerygone, Black Butcherbird, Shining Flycatcher, Red-headed Honeyeater and Australian Yellow White-eye.

Nocturnal birds in the area include Barking Owl, Southern Boobook, Large-tailed Nightjar and Bush Stone-curlew.

Tiwi Islands

Tiwi Islands sit in the Arafura Sea 80km north of Darwin. Melville Island and Bathurst Island are populated, while several smaller islands are uninhabited. Tiwi Islands form the second largest, after Tasmania, land mass off the Australian coast. Vegetation here includes open eucalypt forest, paperbark forest, monsoon rainforest, mangroves, freshwater swamps, grassland as well as coastal dunes and saltmarshes. The tall open forest (tropical savannah) dominated by stringybarks, woollybutts and bloodwoods covers nearly 80% of the islands. Due to the island's lengthy isolation from the mainland, a high level of endemics among plants and animals is found on the subspecies level.

A visitor permit is required to visit Tiwi Islands and the surrounding waters, except for day visitors and organised tours. For permits go to Tiwi Land Council's website at https://www.tiwilandcouncil.com/index.cfm?fuseaction=page&p=219&l=1&id=68. Regular flight service from Darwin is available on Fly Tiwi, see http://www.flytiwi.com.au/. The flight takes 30min. A Sealink ferry to Wurrumiyanga on Bathurst Island and Paru on Melville Island takes 2.5hrs and sails on Thu, Fri and Sun. There are also weekly barges calling at various settlements on both islands. Wurrumiyanga offers accommodation, car rental, fuel, shops and restaurants. A map of the islands, showing transport options, can be downloaded here: https://www.tiwilandcouncil.com/documents/Uploads/Maps/14_Tiwi-Islands_Tourism-Transport-Map.pdf.

Over 190 bird species have been recorded on Tiwi Islands. **Key species** are Red Goshawk, Spotted Whistling-Duck, Beach Stone-curlew, Chestnut Rail, Partridge Pigeon, Roseate Tern, Chestnut-backed Button-quail, Mangrove Robin and Masked Owl. Other birds of interest include waders, terns, Mangrove Golden Whistler, Oriental Cuckoo, Rose-crowned Fruit-Dove, Rainbow Pitta, Black Butcherbird, Red-headed Honeyeater, Green-backed Gerygone, Azure Kingfisher, Little Shrike-thrush and Brown Whistler. Among the rarities are Little Kingfisher, Swinhoe's Snipe, Oriental Plover, Mangrove Fantail, Eastern Yellow Wagtail, Galah and Hardhead.

Little Shrike-thrush

Birding can be rewarding on the islands. The star attraction is the endangered Red Goshawk, probably the rarest bird of prey in Australia. The total Australian population size is estimated at 700 pairs (or less) including about 100 pairs on Tiwi Islands. Melville Island is the easiest place to find this species, we advise contacting the Land Rangers to help you. The birds favour the tall eucalypt forest, particularly in the riparian habitats along coastal watercourses. There is about 18,000ha of tall forest on Tiwi Islands, and this species is thriving there.

Another good bird is Chestnut Rail. They are relatively tame here and can be found on the mudflats south of Wurrumiyanga, Maxwell Creek boat ramp or Paru Barge Landing.

In grassy areas, search for Australian Bustard, Red-backed Button-quail, Chestnut-backed Button-quail, Chestnut-breasted Mannikin and Black-bellied Crimson Finch. At night, you may hear Masked Owl calling. This will be an endangered Tiwi Island subspecies *melvillensis*. Other nocturnal birds include Large-tailed Nightjar, Barking Owl, Tawny Frogmouth, Southern Boobook and plenty of Bush Stone-curlews.

Both the largest Tiwi Islands and many small islets scattered around, are utilised by the seabirds for breeding. In particular, Seagull Island 4km north of Melville Island is home to the world-largest colony of Greater Crested Terns – 60,000 pairs. Among them breed Silver Gulls and small numbers of Roseate Terns and Black-naped Terns. In September, large flocks of Common Terns and Little Terns roost here before their migration to the Northern Hemisphere. In the waters around Tiwi Islands, you have a chance to spot seabirds such as Lesser and Great Frigatebird, Brown Booby, Bridled Tern, Sooty Tern, Wilson's Storm-Petrel, Streaked Shearwater and Tropical Shearwater (very rare).

Bathurst Island

White-bellied Sea-Eagle

Wurrumiyanga is the largest settlement (pop. 2,000) on Bathurst Island. An inter-island ferry connects the township with Paru on Melville Island. Birding on Bathurst Island is generally conducted around Wurrumiyanga. Take a walk to the jetty, visit sewage ponds, scan the airstrip or hike a bit further to Wanyanga Beach opposite

Buchanan Island. Look for Little Kingfishers in the mangroves near the ferry where you may also spot Little Tern, Common Tern, Lesser Crested Tern and Greater Crested Tern (usually roosting on the ferry). Roseate Tern is occassionally recorded. The mangroves may also yield Mangrove Gerygone, Little Bronze-cuckoo and Australian Yellow White-eye. Offshore, look for Brown Boobies on buoys and navigation markers.

On the beach up to the jetty, look for waders such as Beach Stone-curlew, Common Sandpiper, Terek Sandpiper, Far Eastern Curlew, Whimbrel and Black-tailed Godwit. Red-headed Honeyeaters are very common in the patches of mangroves. Several raptors are usually patrolling the area, including White-bellied Sea-Eagle, Brahminy Kite and Australian Hobby.

Partridge Pigeons have been sighted near the Wurrumiyanga Airport, e.g. at GPS coordinates of 11°46'34''S and 130°34'16''E. The airport may also produce Northern Rosella, Australian Pratincole, Pheasant Coucal, Brown Quail, Golden-headed Cisticola and Brown Goshawk.

In patches of forest through the township, look for Northern Fantail, White-bellied Cuckoo-shrike, Green Oriole, Little Shrike-thrush, Brown Whistler, Shining Flycatcher, Rufous-banded Honeyeater and Pacific Baza.

It is worth checking out the sewage ponds. To get there, drive along Malawu St past the supermarket in the northerly direction until the end of the road (the road name will change to Sewage Ponds). GPS coordinates are 11°45'19''S and 130°37'36''E. In the three ponds surrounded by the forest, Spotted Whistling-Ducks are found from time to time. A selection of waders around the ponds includes Marsh Sandpiper, Common Sandpiper, Common Greenshank, Sharp-tailed Sandpiper, Little Curlew and Grey-tailed Tattler. Waterbirds include Radjah Shelduck, Wandering Whistling-Duck, White-winged Black Tern and Australian Gull-billed Tern. In the surrounding bush, look for Collared Kingfisher, Forest Kingfisher, Red-headed Honeyeater, White-winged Triller, Large-billed Gerygone, Arafura Fantail and Grey Goshawk. Saltwater crocodiles are often sighted in the sewage ponds, so beware.

A good wader site is Medina Inlet, near Wanyanga Beach 5km south of town. Beach Stone-curlew is nearly always there, while in summer Terek Sandpiper, Bar-tailed Godwit and Far Eastern Curlew are also guaranteed. A small flock of Little Terns usually roosts on the beach, they breed on the Buchanan Island nearby.

Melville Island

Melville Island is more important to birders than Bathurst Island, thanks to a good chance of spotting a Red Goshawk. Some places worth visiting are listed below.

Baru Barge Landing

This site is located at the end of Barge Landing Rd, on the side of the channel opposite to Wurrumiyanga, at GPS coordinates of 11°44’44’’S and 130°38’27’’E. Here, Chestnut Rails pop often onto the mudflats from the mangroves. Search also for Red-headed Honeyeater, Australian Yellow White-eye, Lemon-bellied Flycatcher, Green Oriole and Red-winged Parrot.

Maxwell Creek Area

Visit the Maxwell Creek Sewage Ponds off Pirlangimpi Rd, at GPS coordinates of 11°32’53’’S and 130°33’59’’E. The closest landmark is the Memorial Airfield. For years now, a small flock of Spotted Whistling-Ducks have been observed on the three ponds among the Plumed and Wandering Whistling-Ducks. Partridge Pigeons regularly come to drink here. Scan the pond edges in search of Common Sandpiper, Marsh Sandpiper, Wood Sandpiper, Common Greenshank and Brolga. In the surrounding bushland, look for Rufous-banded Honeyeater, Yellow-tinted Honeyeater, Helmeted Friarbird, Northern Fantail and Great Bowerbird.

Check out the Maxwell Creek boat ramp, located at GPS coordinates of 11°31’55’’S and 130°35’37’’E. To get there, from Pirlangimpi Rd turn into a track near the Memorial Airfield and drive along the edge of a tree plantation for about 3km to get to the boat ramp. It is a good spot for Chestnut Rails. Other birds in the area include Black Butcherbird, Red-headed Honeyeater, Dusky Honeyeater, Large-billed Gerygone, Mangrove Gerygone, Brown Whistler, Little Shrike-thrush and Shining Flycatcher.

While driving along the track to the boat ramp, check out the Maxwell Creek Forest Camp, located at the plantation edge at GPS coordinates of 11°32’53’’S and 130°34’41’’E. A well-known Red-Goshawk nest is located not far from Maxwell Creek (Land Ranger’s help will be indispensable). The main prey of this particular pair are Blue-winged Kookaburras, and the skulls of the consumed birds are strewn under the nest. At the camp and adjacent plantation, look for Partridge Pigeon, Rainbow Pitta, Pheasant Coucal, Varied Triller and Bar-shouldered Dove (plentiful here). A walk in the plantation may produce Brush Cuckoo, Forest Kingfisher, Green-backed

Gerygone, Rose-crowned Fruit-Dove, Brown-capped Emerald-Dove, Orange-footed Scrubfowl, Torresian Imperial-Pigeon, Dusky Honeyeater, Brahminy Kite and Black-breasted Buzzard.

Dusky Honeyeater

Milikapiti Area

There are several active nests of Red Goshawks around Milikapiti. Their exact locations are known to the Land Rangers.

Again, the local sewage ponds in Milikapiti are of interest. The ponds are located at GPS coordinates of 11°25'47"S and 130°40'49"E. To get there, drive on Milikapiti Internal, section along the coast, in the southerly direction. Take the first track left into the bush and continue south to the three ponds. This is a well-known place for Spotted Whistling-Ducks. Other waterbirds on the ponds include Wandering Whistling-Ducks, Radjah Shelducks, Grey Teals and an occasional Hardhead. Tawny Frogmouths are often roosting near the ponds. Eastern Yellow Wagtail was recorded on the Milikapiti Sewage Ponds several times.

A barge landing is located at the end of Milikapiti Internal north of the settlement, also worth visiting. GPS coordinates are 11°24'49"S and 130°40'03"E. Spotlighting may be successful here, as Masked Owls have been reported from this site. Other nocturnal birds include Australian Owlet-nightjar, Southern Boobook, Tawny Frogmouth and plentiful Bush

Stone-curlews. Nankeen Night-Herons roost near the water. Bushland birds here include Brown-capped Emerald-Dove, Rose-crowned Fruit-Dove, Olive-backed Oriole, Green-backed Gerygone, Bar-breasted Honeyeater, Dusky Honeyeater and Spangled Drongo.

Mangrove species and waders can be found along the Track. To get there, drive on Milikapiti Internal, section along the coast, in the southerly direction. Pass the first track left into the bush, leading south to the three ponds, and take the next track to the left. Drive to the creek mouth at GPS coordinates of 11°26'33"S and 130°41'03"E. Look for Great Knot, Lesser Sand Plover, Greater Sand Plover, Far Eastern Curlew, Terek Sandpiper, Common Sandpiper and Whimbrel. Among the mangroves, you may spot Mangrove Robin, Mangrove Golden Whistler, Australian Yellow White-eye, Broad-billed Flycatcher, Red-headed Honeyeater, Rufous-banded Honeyeater, Brown Whistler and Azure Kingfisher. Listen intently, Chestnut Rails can be heard there.

Terek Sandpipers roosting in the mangroves

Another productive spot is the Milikapiti Farm, located along Milikapiti Access opposite Australia Post, 500m from the airport. Search the vine thicket along the track at GPS coordinates of 11°25'15"S and 130°39'38"E for Green-backed Gerygone, Black Butcherbird, Oriental Cuckoo, Rose-crowned Fruit-Dove, Brown Whistler, Common Cicadabird, Northern Rosella, Varied Lorikeet and Southern Boobook.

Litchfield NP & Surrounds

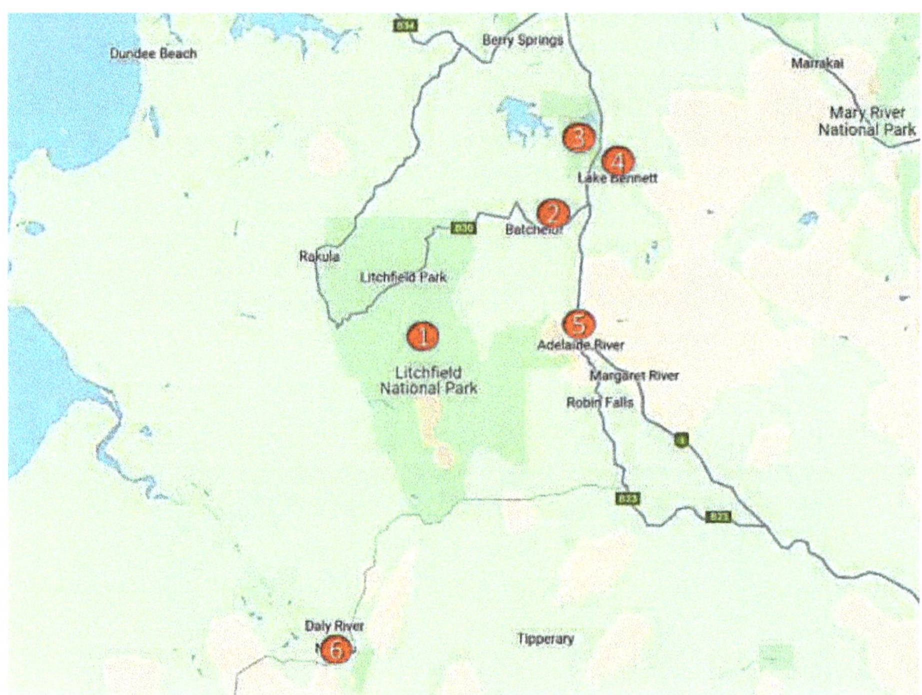

1 Litchfield National Park
2 Batchelor
3 Manton Dam Recreational Area
4 Lake Bennett
5 Adelaide River
6 Daly River

Litchfield National Park

This very popular 150,000ha National Park is located near the township of Batchelor, 120km southwest of Darwin. The Park features numerous stunning waterfalls cascading into crystal-clear pools, iconic magnetic termite mounds and sandstone pillars of Lost City. Vegetation in the Park consist mostly of grassy woodland dominated by woollybutts, stringybarks and banksia. In the gorges and near the campgrounds, there are areas of dense monsoon thicket. Dense stands of pandanus and other riparian vegetation grow along the watercourses.

There are two main routes to the Park, both starting from Stuart Hwy (1).

- via Berry Springs: from N1 turn west into Cox Peninsula Rd (B34), then past Berry Springs turn south into Litchfield Park Rd (B30).
- via Batchelor: from N1 turn west into Batchelor Rd (B30). The road will change name to Rum Jungle Rd and then to Litchfield Park Rd, retaining its number. B30 runs through the entire National Park.

Roads to most of the Park's attractions are sealed which explains the popularity of the place. However, in the south part of the Park, a 4WD paradise has been created, with a network of vehicular rough tracks.

The Park offers fantastic facilities including a Visitor Centre with a café at Wangi Falls, several well-equipped picnic areas and camping grounds and a network of walking tracks suitable for various fitness levels. See also the Park fact sheet here: https://nt.gov.au/__data/assets/pdf_file/0012/200073/litchfield-national-park.pdf.

Over 180 bird species have been recorded in Litchfield National Park. **Key species** are Red Goshawk, Azure Kingfisher, Rainbow Pitta, Silver-backed Butcherbird, Silver-crowned Friarbird, Banded Honeyeater, Little Woodswallow and Pacific Baza. Other birds of interest include Orange-footed Scrubfowl, Little Shrike-thrush, Rose-crowned Fruit-Dove, Lemon-bellied Flycatcher, Shining Flycatcher, Great Bowerbird, Grey Fantail, Black-tailed Treecreeper, Black-bellied Crimson Finch and Mistletoebird. Rarities include Oriental Honey-buzzard, Square-tailed Kite, Black Falcon, Peregrine Falcon, Little Kingfisher, Gouldian Finch, Partridge Pigeon, Hooded Robin, Hooded Parrot, Eastern Yellow Wagtail and Emu.

The Park is good for raptors; 21 species have been recorded. The star attraction is Red Goshawk, with a few breeding pairs still hanging on here. The places to look for them are Greenant Creek (Tjaetaba Falls), Tjaynera Falls and Surprise Creek Falls. The rare vagrant, Oriental Honey-buzzard, appeared here in August 2020. Other birds of prey, besides the ones listed in the site summary, include Black-breasted Buzzard, Little Eagle, Grey Goshawk, Australian Hobby, Wedge-tailed Eagle and White-bellied Sea-Eagle.

Magnetic Termite Mounds

The tiny magnetic termites construct the unbelievable, thin structures that can last a hundred years. A mound is up to 2m tall, and its thin edge is always directed north-south. Hundreds of such structures stand densely on a flat ground at this site. They can be admired from a viewing platform and a boardwalk. The site is the first significant stop past the park entrance from Batchelor. It is located at GPS coordinates of 13°06'09''S and 130°50'42''E.

Magnetic termite mounds

During our visit, a single Partridge Pigeon was sitting at the edge of access road. A small flock of Sulphur-crested Cockatoos was foraging among the mounds. Silver-backed Butcherbird and Pied Butcherbird were singing, each perched on top of a mound. Nankeen Kestrel was hovering over this grassy area. In the sparse trees near the carpark were White-gaped Honeyeaters, White-quilled Honeyeaters, White-throated Honeyeaters and White-bellied Cuckoo-shrike. Eastern Koel was calling.

This site is often visited for spotlighting. You may encounter Large-tailed Nightjar, Spotted Nightjar, Barn Owl, Barking Owl and Tawny Frogmouth. Bush Stone-curlews are plentiful and favour this area to practice their group singing.

Emus live in the Park, although are rare and difficult to spot. However, from time to time have been sighted wandering between the mounds.

In the Wet (summer), the area can get waterlogged. Glossy Ibis, Australian White Ibis and even Brolga arrive at such times to forage between the mounds.

Buley Rockhole

This is a popular tourist spot with natural swimming holes and waterfalls. Site GPS coordinates are 13°06'48''S and 130°47'12''E. To get there, from Litchfield Park Rd (B30) turn north into Buley Florence Rd, then left into Buley Rockhole Rd, and drive to the carpark. Picnic tables and toilets are provided on top of a track descending to the swimming hole.

We met plenty of cheeky Great Bowerbirds in the carpark area. There were also Red-winged Parrots, Red-tailed Black-Cockatoos, White-bellied Cuckoo-shrikes and White-quilled Honeyeaters there. In the bush along the walk, we came across Spangled Drongo, Green Oriole, Oriental Dollarbird, Dusky Honeyeater and Varied Lorikeet. Silver-backed Butcherbird was calling angrily.

Chestnut-backed Button-quail, Partridge Pigeon, Northern Rosella, Tawny Frogmouth and Australian Hobby have also been reported from this site.

Florence Falls

This charming swimming hole is located at the end of Buley Florence Rd past the Buley Rockhole. It has two campgrounds; the bigger one is for 4WD campers only as a steep section has to be conquered to get there. A 1km walking trail runs through the monsoon forest. A 3km walk along Florence Creek connects this site with Buley Rockhole.

A large flock of Rainbow Bee-eaters regularly roosts in the trees of the 4WD campground. A pair of Silver-backed Butcherbirds is resident there. Look also for Little Woodswallow, Great Bowerbird, Mistletoebird, Silver-crowned Friarbird and Pacific Baza. At night, you may hear Southern Boobook, Australian Owlet-nightjar and Bush Stone-curlew.

The monsoon forest walk may yield Green-backed Gerygone, Brown-capped Emerald-Dove, Rufous-banded Honeyeater, White-throated Honeyeater, Bar-breasted Honeyeater, Little Shrike-thrush, Shining Flycatcher, Northern Fantail, Northern Rosella and Rose-crowned Fruit-Dove.

Partridge Pigeons are occasionally found along access road. There are also rare records of Red Goshawk from this area.

Tabletop Swamp

Tabletop Swamp

This site is located at GPS coordinates of 13°10'39''S and 130°44'48''E, a 200m drive off the main thoroughfare (Litchfield Park Rd, B30). You'll find there a carpark, a few picnic tables and a walking path along the beautiful, seasonal billabong. It is surrounded by paperbark forest with bulrushes and waterlilies in the water. It serves as a refuge for waterbirds in the dry season. Large flocks of Magpie Geese arrive then to feed there. Australasian Grebes regularly come to breed on the billabong. You may also get Glossy Ibis, White-necked Heron, Nankeen Night-Heron, Green Pygmy-goose and Comb-crested Jacana. Azure Kingfishers are resident. Straw-necked Ibises come in large flocks (60-100 birds) every evening to roost in the paperbarks.

Bar-breasted Honeyeaters nest in the area. You may also come across Dusky Honeyeater, White-quilled Honeyeater, White-gaped Honeyeater and Silver-crowned Friarbird. The rare Common Cicadabirds are found here regularly. In the surrounding woodland, look also for Jacky Winter, Green Oriole, Lemon-bellied Flycatcher, Leaden Flycatcher, Paperbark Flycatcher and Pacific Baza.

Tolmer Falls

Tolmer is one of the most spectacular waterfalls in the Park, and can be admired from a viewing platform at the top of the gorge which can be reached via a short walk from the carpark. You may choose to return by a longer, 1.6km Tolmer Loop Walk. GPS coordinates for the lookout are 13°12'19''S and 130°45'50''E.

We found plenty of Silver-crowned Friarbirds in the carpark. The surrounds yielded Red-winged Parrot, Northern Rosella and Silver-backed Butcherbird. The loop walk gave us Channel-billed Cuckoo, White-winged Triller, Little Woodswallow, Tree Martin, Brown Falcon and Wedge-tailed Eagle.

Red Goshawk was recorded in May 2023, flying over the site.

Greenant Creek (Tjaetaba Falls)

Green Oriole

A 2.7km return walk leads to the top of Tjaetaba Falls. It follows Greenant Creek upstream, climbing steeply to the falls' lookout. Swimming is not allowed at the base of the falls.

Red Goshawks breed along the creekline so this is the site that offers a chance, although still slim, to sight them in the Park. Other raptors include Black-breasted Buzzard, Pacific Baza, Black Falcon, Brown Goshawk and Australian Hobby. The sighting of Oriental Honey-buzzard in 2020 was from this site.

When we arrived there, Common Cicadabird was calling from the carpark area and displaying. Rose-crowned Fruit-Dove was consuming a Carpentaria palm fruit. Along the creek, we found Forest Kingfisher, Torresian Imperial-Pigeon, Helmeted Friarbird, Dusky Honeyeater, Little Shrike-thrush, Little Woodswallow, Varied Triller and Green Oriole.

Birds reported from the walk by others include Partridge Pigeon, Brown Quail, Rainbow Pitta and Red-backed Fairy-wren.

Tjaynera Falls

This site is reached via Litchfield Daly Railroad Rd (on the Park map called Reynolds 4WD Tk), a 4WD track running south from Litchfield Park Rd (B30) to Daly River Rd. The track passes several deep river crossing so a 4WD vehicle is a must.

To get to the Tjaynera Falls (Sandy Creek) campsite, drive south for approximately 7km, then make east and continue for 2km on Tjaynera Falls Tk to the campsite. GPS coordinates are 13°14'58"S and 130°44'42"E. A 1.8km walking track leads from the campsite to the falls where you will find a large, crystal-clear plunge pool and no people.

This is the best place to look for Red Goshawk in the Park. A well-known nest used to be located near the carpark but it collapsed in 2021 and the birds moved elsewhere in the area. Look for Gouldian Finches; these were observed foraging along the access track. At the waterfall, check the surrounding riparian vegetation for the presence of Black Bittern and Azure Kingfisher. On your way to the waterfall, you may come across Rose-crowned Fruit-Dove, Brown-capped Emerald-Dove, Oriental Dollarbird, Banded Honeyeater, Bar-breasted Honeyeater, Little Shrike-thrush, Silver-backed Butcherbird, Lemon-bellied Flycatcher, Shining Flycatcher, Pacific Baza and Brown Goshawk.

Surprise Creek Falls

To get there, drive along Litchfield Daly Railroad Rd (on the Park map called Reynolds 4WD Tk) for 28km from the turnoff from Litchfield Park Rd, then turn east into a 500m track leading to the Surprise Creek Falls carpark. Take a short walk through the monsoon forest to a large swimming hole. Look for Black Bittern around the edges of the pool and the creek. Black-tailed Treecreepers are regularly found in the savannah woodland. When grevilleas are in bloom, you should get

Dusky Honeyeater, Banded Honeyeater, White-throated Honeyeater and Rufous-throated Honeyeater. Along the walk, you may also encounter Black-bellied Crimson Finch, Little Woodswallow, Olive-backed Oriole, Little Shrike-thrush, Rose-crowned Fruit-Dove and Bush Stone-curlew.

Wangi Falls

This is the main tourist destination in the Park. It is reached via Wangi Falls Rd off Litchfield Park Rd (B30). You will find a Visitor Centre and extensive picnic and camping grounds at the end of the road. A large plunge pool has formed at the base of the waterfall. During the Wet, the pool may be closed for swimming. A 1.6km return walk starts at the pool with a viewing platform, runs through the monsoon forest and then climbs to the top of the escarpment.

Dramatic Wangi Falls

During our visit, the place was crowded due to school holidays. In spite of that, or perhaps because of that, the area around the café was teeming with birds eyeing a possible suitable morsel. We saw Great Bowerbirds, White-quilled Honeyeaters, Red-collared Lorikeets, Sulphur-crested Cockatoos, Red-winged Parrot and Little Friarbirds. Much shyer, but still approaching, were Orange-footed Scrubfowls and Bush Stone-curlews. Black Kites had a field day, skilfully extracting barbecued sausages from the hands of innocent small children.

On the walk to the waterfalls, we encountered Little Shrike-thrush, Varied Triller, Rufous Whistler, Spangled Drongo, Rainbow Bee-eater, Shining Flycatcher, Dusky Honeyeater, White-bellied Cuckoo-shrike and Mistletoebird. Azure Kingfishers were perching on the branches.

Other birds reported from this location include Little Woodswallow, Northern Rosella, Brown-capped Emerald-Dove, Common Cicadabird, Rainbow Pitta, Brush Cuckoo, Grey-crowned Babbler and Black-breasted Buzzard. Square-tailed Kites and Little Eagles were observed here a few times.

Cascades

To get there, from Litchfield Park Rd (B30) turn into Cascades Rd and drive to a large carpark. Toilets and picnic tables are provided there, as is a viewing platform over the swamp.

This site is considered to be quieter and more tranquil than other swimming holes in Litchfield National Park. The creek trickles over a wide, 200m-long old lava flow, forming several shallow waterholes. Separate walking tracks lead to the Lower Cascades (2.6km return) and Upper Cascades (3.4km return). The walks are long, steep and partly in full sun, but worth it when you get to the water.

The place was very loud when we checked out this site, as the woollybutts were flowering and were plastered with noisy Silver-crowned Friarbirds and White-quilled Honeyeaters. At the edge of this rowdy group were also White-throated Honeyeaters, Rufous-throated Honeyeaters, Rufous-banded Honeyeaters, Bar-breasted Honeyeaters, Brown Honeyeaters, Banded Honeyeaters and Varied Lorikeets.

The swamp was dry and overgrown with grasses. In the grass, we found Brown Quails, Red-backed Fairy-wrens, Golden-headed Cisticolas and Double-barred Finches. Brown Falcon was hunting over the area.

Other bird species that can be found at this site included Azure Kingfisher, Olive-backed Oriole, Rainbow Pitta, Grey-crowned Babbler, Shining Flycatcher, Oriental Dollarbird, Brush Cuckoo and Spotted Nightjar.

Batchelor

This small town is best known as the gateway to the magnificent Litchfield National Park. It is situated just off Stuart Hwy, about 100km south of Darwin. It used to be a uranium mining town, but since the mining was discontinued it is just a stopover for tourist travelling to the National Park. If you stay here, check some birding spots.

Batchelor WTP

From Batchelor Rd (B30) turn south onto Coach Rd, then, passing the airfield on the left, turn first right into Sargent Rd. The ponds are visible from the road, GPS coordinates are 13°03'19''S and 131°01'04''E. This site has become know when a rare vagrant, White Wagtail, appeared there in June 2022.

Over 110 bird species have been recorded around the Batchelor WTP. **Key species** are Radjah Shelduck, Black Bittern, Silver-backed Butcherbird, Northern Rosella and Black-breasted Buzzard. Other birds of interest include Wandering Whistling-Duck, Plumed Whistling-Duck, Pied Heron, Black-fronted Dotterel, Wood Sandpiper, Common Sandpiper, Channel-billed Cuckoo, Black-faced Woodswallow, Masked Woodswallow, Oriental Dollarbird and Yellow-throated Miner. Rarities include White Wagtail and Partridge Pigeon.

Wood Sandpiper with a couple of Black-fronted Dotterels on a levee

Radjah Shelducks breed on the ponds. Wandering Whistling-Ducks and Plumed Whistling-Ducks congregate here. Waders, such as Common Greenshank, Common Sandpiper, Wood Sandpiper, Sharp-tailed Sandpiper and Marsh Sandpiper, arrive during the Wet. Occasionally, Black Bitterns and White-necked Heron can be found around the ponds.

In the surrounding bushland, look for White-breasted Woodswallow, Varied Triller, Channel-billed Cuckoo, Forest Kingfisher and Oriental Dollarbird. Raptors are represented by Australian Hobby and Black-breasted Buzzard.

Rum Jungle Lake

To get there, turn south from Litchfield Park Rd into Poett Rd and drive to the carpark. Approximate GPS coordinates at the lake are 13°02'05''S and 130°59'53''E.

Over 110 bird species have been recorded around the Rum Jungle Lake. **Key species** are Black Bittern, Azure Kingfisher, Broad-billed Flycatcher and Silver-backed Butcherbird. Other birds of interest include Orange-footed Scrubfowl, Green-backed Gerygone, Little Woodswallow, Great Bowerbird, Diamond Dove, Torresian Imperial-Pigeon, Bar-breasted Honeyeater, Lemon-bellied Flycatcher, Chestnut-breasted Mannikin and Brown Goshawk. Rarities include Common Sandpiper, Gouldian Finch and Black Falcon.

Black Bitterns were observed in vegetation at the inlet near the toilet block. Finches, mostly Chestnut-breasted Mannikins, come for a drink in large numbers. Occasionally, Gouldian Finches are with them. A Great Bowerbird's bower is located in the vicinity of the carpark.

Waterbirds here include White-necked Heron, Nankeen Night-Heron, Common Sandpiper, Radjah Shelduck and Brolga. Other birds at the site include Forest Kingfisher, Azure Kingfisher, Paperbark Flycatcher, Rufous-banded Honeyeater, White-throated Honeyeater, White-winged Triller and Barking Owl.

Coomalie Creek Crossing

The site is located on Stuart Hwy (1) 1.5km south of the turnoff to Batchelor. A car can be safely parked at the western shoulder of the highway. From there, you can find a vantage point to scan the creek.

Look for Black Bittern and Azure Kingfisher. Other birds in the riparian vegetation include Little Bronze-cuckoo, Shining Flycatcher, Arafura Fantail, Large-billed Gerygone, Rose-crowned Fruit-Dove, Brown Whistler, Banded Honeyeater and Pheasant Coucal.

Manton Dam Recreation Area

Manton Dam was the first reliable drinking water supply for Darwin. The site is located along Stuart Hwy about 70km south of Darwin. Today, it is a popular recreation area, utilized for fishing and boating. Crocodiles are regularly removed but swimming is still not recommended. The dam is surrounded by the savannah woodland and monsoon forest.

To get there, from Stuart Hwy (1) turn west into Manton Dam Recreation Reserve Rd and drive 4km to the boat ramp and picnic area with good facilities. Opening hours are from sunrise to sunset. Park pass is required for the out-of-state visitors. A site fact sheet with a map can be downloaded here: https://nt.gov.au/__data/assets/pdf_file/0013/200074/manton-dam-recreation-area.pdf.

Over 120 bird species have been recorded in the Manton Dam Recreation Area. **Key species** are Green Pygmy-goose, Black-tailed Treecreeper, Brown-capped Emerald-Dove, Shining Flycatcher, Broad billed Flycatcher, Arafura Fantail, Yellow-tinted Honeyeater and Black-breasted Buzzard. Other birds of interest include Black-necked Stork, Comb-crested Jacana, Nankeen Night-Heron, Common Cicadabird, Azure Kingfisher, Little Shrike-thrush, Silver-crowned Friarbird, Tree Martin, Wedge-tailed Eagle and Osprey. Rarities include Square-tailed Kite.

Male Green Pygmy-Goose

Birding is good around the picnic area and the boat ramp. Common Cicadabirds are resident and often very vocal. Other birds in that area include Northern Rosella, Great Bowerbird, Lemon-bellied Flycatcher, Brush Cuckoo, Green-backed Gerygone and Sacred Kingfisher. In the forest, search for Rainbow Pitta, Little Shrike-thrush, Shining Flycatcher and Arafura Fantail. Birds on the water include Green Pygmy-goose, Nankeen Night-Heron, Wandering Whistling-Duck and Great Egret.

A good selection of honeyeaters can be found in the reserve including Banded Honeyeater, Rufous-throated Honeyeater, Rufous-banded Honeyeater, Dusky Honeyeater, Silver-crowned Friarbird and plenty of White-quilled Honeyeaters. At night, Bush Stone-curlew, Australian Owlet-nightjar and Barking Owl may be calling.

Lake Bennett

This man-made freshwater lake is located 80km south of Darwin, set up in 450ha of tropical wilderness. It offers several types of accommodation on its shores. De Lago Resort allows public access for swimming, canoeing and birding around the lake.

To get there, from Stuart Hwy (1) turn east into Chinner Rd 10km south of the turnoff to Manton Dam. Chinner Rd wraps around the whole dam.

Over 120 bird species have been recorded at Lake Bennett. **Key species** are Buff-sided Robin, Azure Kingfisher, Northern Rosella, Silver-backed Butcherbird and Spotted Harrier. Other birds of interest include Grey-crowned Babbler, Sacred Kingfisher, Arafura Fantail, Rainbow Pitta, Orange-footed Scrubfowl, Red-tailed Black-Cockatoo, Diamond Dove, Black-bellied Crimson Finch and White-bellied Sea-Eagle. Rarities include Great Crested Grebe and Square-tailed Kite.

The sought-after species of this site is Buff-sided Robin. Look for them at the creek along Heathers Lagoon Rd, about 50-70m past the end of the bitumen. Another spot is bushland near the dam wall. Also, inspect any other place with the right conditions. For Black Bittern, search the dense vegetation at the creek mouths. The best place for Rainbow Pitta is bushland at the creek crossing in Chinner Rd just north of De Lago Resort. In the same location, look also for Arafura Fantail, Bar-breasted Honeyeater, Forest Kingfisher and Azure Kingfisher.

Birds common on the resorts' grounds include Grey-crowned Babbler, Oreen Oriole, Red-winged Parrot, Double-barred Finch, White-bellied Cuckoo-shrike and Silver-backed Butcherbird.

Check the surrounding paddocks, especially along Heathers Lagoon Rd, for Horsfield's Bushlark, Australasian Pipit, Double-barred Finch and Spotted Harrier.

Adelaide River

The township of Adelaide River is located on the banks of Adelaide River, 115km south of Darwin along Stuart Hwy. It is a small service centre, noted for its Adelaide River Wartime Civilian Cemetery, the only wartime cemetery on the Australian soil. The town is an important rest stop for travellers on Stuart Hwy, offering fuel, accommodation and basic supplies. The iconic Adelaide River Inn is the place where some of the Crocodile Dundee scenes were filmed. One of the memorable stars of the movie, Charlie the buffalo, was stuffed after he peacefully ended his life, and now he stands in the bar of the Adelaide River Inn.

Several small birding spots are worth visiting in the area, as described below. Barking Owls may be duetting during the night. Sometimes, Emus are seen wandering down the main drag.

Adelaide River WTP

To get there, from Stuart Hwy (1) north of the township turn east into Silverton Rd (it will change name to Sewer Ponds Rd). Drive 1km to the ponds. GPS coordinates at the ponds are 13°13’52”S and 131°06’23”E.

Radjah Shelduck

The three ponds are surrounded by paddocks, woodland and dense forest. Check the paddocks for the presence of Magpie Geese, Glossy Ibises, Straw-necked Ibises and Brolgas. Woodland may produce Red-winged Parrot, Varied Lorikeet, Cockatiel, Silver-crowned Friarbird, Dusky Honeyeater, Yellow-tinted Honeyeater, Northern Fantail, Rufous Whistler, Spangled Drongo, Masked Woodswallow and Black-faced Woodswallow.

Common waterbirds congregate on the ponds. You may get Radjah Shelducks with their cute ducklings. Search the water edge for the waders, such as Red-kneed Dotterel, Black-fronted Dotterel, Common Sandpiper, Marsh Sandpiper, Wood Sandpiper and Oriental Pratincole. Finches coming to drink include Masked Finch, Long-tailed Finch and Black-bellied Crimson Finch.

Riverside Park

This is the parkland with scattered tall trees and adjacent monsoon thicket along the Adelaide River. It proved to us to be very productive. The park is lining the Memorial Tce from the main road to the cemetery.

Varied Lorikeet

During our visit, the orange-flowering woollybutts were teeming with honeyeaters. We got Bar-breasted Honeyeater, Rufous-throated Honeyeater, Rufous-banded Honeyeater, White-throated Honeyeater, Banded Honeyeater and the rare Yellow-tinted Honeyeater. The very noisy mixed flocks of Varied Lorikeets and Red-collared Lorikeets were flying from tree to tree. Lemon-bellied Flycatchers were perched on lower branches across the park. Small flocks of finches were feeding in grassy areas. We saw Masked Finches and Long-tailed Finches among Double-barred Finches. Sitting side-by-side on the power lines were Sacred Kingfisher, Forest Kingfisher and Red-backed Kingfisher as well as several doves and White-breasted Woodswallows.

Near the river, in dense clumps of bamboo, we spotted Arafura Fantail, Northern Fantail and Shining Flycatcher. Grey Goshawk was perching in a tree, patiently enduring harassment from the honeyeaters.

A flock of Grey-crowned Babblers was foraging among the leaf litter, annoying a pair of Bush Stone-curlews that were napping under a tree in the heat of the day.

Adelaide River Wartime Civilian Cemetery

The cemetery is located at the end of Memorial Tce, adjacent to the Riverside Park. We saw a pair of Tawny Frogmouths roosting in a pink-flowering bauhinia tree near the gate. Bush Stone-curlews were roosting in their typical cemetery location – between the tombstones. Red-tailed Black-Cockatoos were feeding in a large flock on the ground. A family of Grey-crowned Babblers was moving swiftly through the lawns. A mixed flock of finches comprised Masked Finches, Long-tailed Finches, Black-bellied Crimson Finches and Double-barred Finches. Dusky Honeyeaters, feeding on the snakeweed flowers, were aggressively attacked by Brown Honeyeaters. A large flock of Masked Woodswallows was circling overhead.

We were excited to spot a Rainbow Pitta in the parkland just opposite the cemetery, hopping on the ground, turning leaf litter in search of food. A flock of Magpie Geese landed on the paddocks bordering the cemetery, to join Cattle Egrets and Straw-necked Ibises there. The surrounding bushland yielded Brush Cuckoo, Sacred Kingfisher, Rainbow Bee-eater, Rufous Whistler, Brown Whistler, White-winged Triller, Lemon-bellied Flycatcher, Willy Wagtail and Great Bowerbird.

Old Stuart Highway Bridge

The old Adelaide River bridge is just next to the current bridge. You can leave the car on a remnant of an old service road and walk down to the river. GPS coordinates are 13°14’25’’S and 131°06’28’’E.

Old Stuart Hwy bridge over the Adelaide River

This is the place to look for Black Bittern, Azure Kingfisher and Nankeen Night-Heron; they all favour roosting and hunting under the bridges. Other birds in the area include Shining Flycatcher, Oriental Dollarbird, Green-backed Gerygone, Brush Cuckoo, Little Bronze-cuckoo, Arafura Fantail, Brown Goshawk and Pacific Baza. Flocks of Black-bellied Crimson Finches come to drink in the puddles in the riverbed. An occasional waterbird here may be Black-necked Stork, Radjah Shelduck, Pied Heron or Great Egret.

Mt Bundy Station

Mt Bundy is a small working cattle station that also provides tourist accommodation. You should be warned: to enhance the 'real experience' of a farm stay, the guests may be asked to participate in the station chores. On the bright side, there is a bar on site.

The property is located 4km east of the Adelaide River township. To get there, from Stuart Hwy (1) south of town make left into Haynes Rd and drive to the property, sprawled along the banks of Adelaide River.

Over 120 bird species have been recorded at the Mt Bundy Station. **Key species** are Buff-sided Robin, Bar-breasted Honeyeater, Rainbow Pitta, Azure Kingfisher, Arafura Fantail and Varied Lorikeet. Other birds of interest include White-necked Heron, Red-tailed Black-Cockatoo, Olive-backed Oriole, Grey-crowned Babbler, Red-kneed Dotterel, Masked Finch, Black-bellied Crimson Finch, Tawny Grassbird and Brown Goshawk. Rarities include Black Bittern, Yellow-billed Spoonbill and Black Falcon.

Great Bowerbirds and Grey-crowned Babblers can be seen around the campground. White-breasted Woodswallows come to roost overnight, forming large cuddles on the tree branches, sometimes 400 birds. Feral Helmeted Guineafowls and Indian Peafowls will be walking across the grounds.

In the flowering trees in the vicinity of the homestead, look for White-gaped Honeyeater, Rufous-banded Honeyeater, Dusky Honeyeater and White-quilled Honeyeater.

Birds drink from leaking sprinklers or taps around the property; use it in your birding. In particular, finches are partial to the dripping water. Look for Black-bellied Crimson Finches, Chestnut-breasted Mannikins and Masked Finches.

There are several small farm dams on the station. A variety of waterbirds can be seen there including Pink-eared Duck, Hardhead, Radjah Shelduck, Pied Stilt, Black-fronted Dotterel, Glossy Ibis, Great Egret and Australasian Grebe.

Daly River

Daly River flows 350km from the confluence of Flora River and Katherine River to the Timor Sea. There is also another Daly River - a small, remote NT town sitting on the banks of Daly River, 220km southwest of Darwin. It is one of those quirky Outback towns that Northern Territory seems to specialise in. It is nothing more than a few caravan parks, a general store and the compulsory pub. The number of residents is small until the time of a national or state barramundi angling competition when the town bursts at seems with the visitors. In the Wet, the place is flooded *at nauseam* and every 10-15 years the water comes so high that everybody needs to be evacuated. This is the stereotypical north Australia, as imagined by the southern Australians: oppressively hot and humid, and full of crocodiles, snakes, spiders, wild pigs and buffalos - and they are right. Vegetation here is lush and green, mostly mangroves, rainforest, giant bamboo and pandanus.

The area has become accessible to birdwatchers and anglers when the road was sealed. Access is from Stuart Hwy (1) where you can take Dorat Rd (23) at either end, then turn west into Daly River Rd (28) and drive 110km to Daly River.

Good birdwatching usually happens around the caravan parks and fishing lodges scattered along the river. You may also consider heading to Douglas Daly where Douglas and Daly Rivers meet, to experience hot springs and amazing rock formations. Access to this area is from Dorat Rd separate to that of Daly River, see details below.

Over 130 bird species have been recorded in the Daly River area. **Key species** are Great-billed Heron, Black Bittern, Mangrove Golden Whistler, Rainbow Pitta, Oriental Cuckoo and Fork-tailed Swift. Other birds of interest include Glossy Ibis, Rose-crowned Fruit-Dove, Azure Kingfisher, Arafura Fantail, Little Shrike-thrush, Shining Flycatcher, Rufous-banded Honeyeater, Orange-footed Scrubfowl, Large-tailed Nightjar, Grey Goshawk and Pacific Baza. Rarities include Masked Owl, Eastern Grass Owl and Little Eagle.

Lee and Jenny's Bushcamp

This site is located on Daly River off Wooliana Rd, near the Sinclairs Daly River Fishing Retreat. GPS coordinates are 13°39'50''S and 130°39'29''E. This is a very good place to search for Mangrove Golden Whistler. Also, Great-billed Herons have been recorded many times along the river. Red-tailed Black-Cockatoos and Little Corellas arrive in the evening to roost on the property. Black-bellied Crimson Finches nest in the veranda eaves. At the end of summer, large flocks of Fork-tailed Swifts are observed feeding over the area, riding an edge of the impending storm.

Rainbow Pittas are resident on the property. Other birds found here include Star Finch, Orange-footed Scrubfowl, Brown Whistler, Little Shrike-thrush, Forest Kingfisher, Azure Kingfisher, Shining Flycatcher, Arafura Fantail, Rufous-banded Honeyeater and Torresian Imperial-Pigeon. The nocturnal birds can be very vocal, in particular Large-tailed Nightjar, Barking Owl and Bush Stone-curlew.

Search for Red-chested Button-quails along the access road to the property.

Sinclairs Daly River Fishing Retreat

Turn off Wooliana Rd at GPS coordinates of 13°42'10''S and 130°40'15''E. This spot is good for nocturnal birds; even Masked Owl was reported from here. Large-tailed Nightjars hunt insects over the property nearly every evening. Bush Stone-curlews, Barking Owls and Southern Boobooks are very vocal.

Bush birds around this site include Rose-crowned Fruit-Dove, Varied Lorikeet, Green Oriole, Rainbow Pitta, Mangrove Golden Whistler, Forest Kingfisher and Great Bowerbird.

Check the riverbanks for Black Bittern, Great-billed Heron, Nankeen Night-Heron, Pied Heron, Royal Spoonbill, Radjah Shelduck and Glossy Ibis. A monotonous clatter of Australasian Darters can be heard all day. Whistling Kites nest along the river. You may also spot Pacific Baza, Australian Hobby or White-bellied Sea-Eagle.

Male Australasian Darter drying its wings in the sun

Douglas Daly Holiday Park

Douglas Daly Holiday Park sits on the banks of Douglas River 40km from Stuart Hwy (1) via Borat Rd and Oolloo Rd. The Douglas Daly area is famous for its hot springs, fabulous fishing, picturesque gorges and abundance of wildlife. At the back of Douglas Daly Holiday Park, you can visit river sites such as the Arches Waterhole, twin pools, thermal pool and natural spa.

Buff-sided Robin, Azure Kingfisher and Black Bittern are often found on the property. Occasionally, Little Kingfisher can be sighted. White-breasted Woodswallows roost here in cuddles in their hundreds. Great Bowerbirds are common and tame. Rainbow Pittas are tame, too. Other birds in the area include Paperbark Flycatcher, Shining Flycatcher, Lemon-bellied Flycatcher, Arafura Fantail, Green Oriole, Bar-breasted Honeyeater, Dusky Honeyeater, Green-backed Gerygone, Long-tailed Finch, Black-bellied Crimson Finch and Gouldian Finch. Even Emu was recorded at times.

Butterfly Gorge Nature Park

To get there, from Oolloo Rd north of Douglas Daly Holiday Park turn east into Hot Springs Rd, signposted to Hot Springs. The road is decent to the Tjuwalyin (Douglas) Hot Springs which used to be a major tourist attraction but were sadly closed over a monetary dispute and no resolution seems to be on the horizon. Anyway, from the hot springs, take Butterfly Gorge Rd and drive 17km on a terrible 4WD track to the Butterfly Gorge, situated at the base of a low sandstone plateau. It boasts sheer rocky cliffs edged with dense riverine vegetation. Carpark is provided at the end of the road, from where you can take a walk through the gorge with several pools formed in the dry season. Gouldian Finches come to drink there. Black Bittern and Azure Kingfisher are regularly found near the water. Little Woodswallow will be flying along the cliffs.

Great-billed Heron was recorded several times by the pools. In summer, Oriental Cuckoos may occasionally appear. Other birds found in the area include White-throated Gerygone, Arafura Fantail, Shining Flycatcher, Bar-breasted Honeyeater, Dusky Honeyeater, Little Shrike-thrush, Rose-crowned Fruit-Dove, Masked Finch, Northern Rosella, Large-tailed Nightjar and Australian Owlet-nightjar.

Arnhem Highway Area

1 Fogg Dam Conservation Area
2 Arnhem Highway
3 Djukbinj National Park
4 Leaning Tree Lagoon Nature Park
5 Marrakai Road
6 Mary River National Park
7 Bamurru Plains

Fogg Dam Conservation Area

This 1,600ha reserve is one of Darwin's most productive and famous birding spots. Thousands of waterbirds congregate here, different species in different seasons of the year. The site is located approximately 90km southeast of Darwin, a short drive from the turnoff off Arnhem Hwy (36). Easy access is available year-round, with all roads sealed and usually not flooded.

The dam was built in mid-1950' to provide irrigation water to a new business idea for this area – rice farming. The project ultimately failed but the birds gained. The dam provides a dry season refuge for wildlife and the abandoned rice fields feed thousands of geese and other waterbirds. The area has been declared a nature reserve and convenient facilities for birdwatchers and other tourists were built. This shallow wetland is always beautiful but turns simply stunning when lotus lilies and waterlilies are blooming. The surrounding monsoon forest and paperbark forest are also part of the reserve.

Fogg Dam

To get there, turn from Stuart Hwy (1) into Arnhem Hwy (36). Drive east for 25km, then turn left into Anzac Pde. Drive 6km and turn left into Fogg Dam Rd. Drive to the carpark before the dam wall to explore the forest area. Facilities here include the toilets (the only one on site), picnic tables and spacious carparking areas on both sides of the road. Two walks start from there. From the carpark, you can drive (but not walk) on the dam wall up to the Pandanus Lookout on the other side of the water. You'll find there a carpark, picnic site and a fantastic viewing platform. The road over the dam wall is a single lane and a lot of tourist buses go over it, so drive carefully and plan to pull over into narrow bays along the shoulder; the oncoming traffic is visible most of the way. The best time to visit is between December and July. Accommodation can be found in the roadhouses along Arnhem Hwy. Further info and a site map can be downloaded here: https://nt.gov.au/__data/assets/pdf_file/0016/200068/fogg-dam-conservation-reserve-fact-sheet-and-map.pdf.

Over 260 bird species have been recorded in the Fogg Dam Conservation Reserve. **Key species** are Little Kingfisher, Magpie Goose, Black-necked Stork, White-browed Crake, Black Bittern, Pale-vented Bush-hen, Comb-crested Jacana, Rainbow Pitta, Oriental Cuckoo, Grey Goshawk and Pacific Baza. Other birds of interest include waterbirds, waders, Buff-banded Rail, Azure Kingfisher, Forest Kingfisher, Little Pied Cormorant, Little Bronze-cuckoo, White-bellied Cuckoo-shrike, Arafura Fantail, Bar-breasted Honeyeater, Orange-footed Scrubfowl and Shining Flycatcher. Rarities include Oriental Reed-Warbler, Eastern Yellow Wagtail, Little Ringed Plover, Baillon's Crake, Spotless Crake, Australian Little Bittern, Great-billed Heron, Swinhoe's Snipe, Gouldian Finch, Pictorella Mannikin, Yellow Chat, Common Pheasant, King Quail, Red Goshawk and Black Falcon.

Anzac Parade

Barn Owl

The 6km stretch of the road between Arnhem Hwy to the turnoff to Fogg Dam Rd is one of the best sites in NT for spotlighting. In particular, Barn Owls are abundant here. There are reports of up to 30 birds counted in one visit. Eastern Grass Owls are recorded here from time to time, while Barking Owls and Bush Stone-curlews are common. Other nocturnal birds in the area include Large-tailed Nightjar, Spotted Nightjar, Southern Boobook, Tawny Frogmouth and Nankeen Night-Heron. In 2005, several Letter-winged Kites were recorded along Anzac Pde.

During the day, check the powerlines for the presence of Brown Falcon, Forest Kingfisher, Sacred Kingfisher, Red-backed Kingfisher, Pallid Cuckoo and Tree Martin. The grassland may produce Horsfield's Bushlark, Australian Bustard, Golden-headed Cisticola, Australian Pratincole, Tawny Grassbird and Straw-necked Ibis.

The area is very good for raptors. Whistling Kites and Black Kites are often observed in large numbers (200 birds). Occasionally, you may also see Black-breasted Buzzard, Black-shouldered Kite, Spotted Harrier or even Little Eagle.

Monsoon Forest Walk

The 3.6km return Monsoon Forest Walk starts from the first carpark near the toilet block. It runs through several habitats, first through the monsoon forest, then paperbark forest, then traces the edge of a floodplain.

In the big trees around the toilets, you may spot Brown Whistler, Little Shrike-thrush, Lemon-bellied Flycatcher, Northern Fantail and Orange-footed Scrubfowl. In the dense monsoon forest along the first 200m from the trailhead, search for Rainbow Pitta, Brown-capped Emerald-Dove and Rose-crowned Fruit-Dove. Further down, in the paperbark forest, look for Dusky Honeyeater, Rufous-banded Honeyeater, Little Bronze-cuckoo, Arafura Fantail, Shining Flycatcher, Paperbark Flycatcher, Green Oriole, Green-backed Gerygone, Varied Triller and Common Cicadabird.

The edge of the floodplain is the best place to look for Little Kingfisher and Azure Kingfisher. The former is often using the path railings as hunting perches. Puddles of water in the floodplain attract waterbirds such as White-browed Crakes, Black-necked Storks, Pied Stilts and Purple Swamphens. Grassy areas at the end of the walk may produce Australian Bustard, Horsfield's Bushlark, Purple-backed Fairy-wren, Black-bellied Crimson Finch and Masked Finch.

Raptors along the walk include Brown Goshawk, Grey Goshawk, Collared Sparrowhawk and Pacific Baza. Swamp Harrier may be flying over the floodplains.

Woodland to Waterlilies Walk

The 2.2km return Woodland to Waterlilies Walk runs through the monsoon forest and paperbark forest that fringe the floodplains. A boardwalk leads to the dam. The walk starts from the carpark on the left side of the road (coming in).

The grassy fringes of the floodplains may yield Tawny Grassbird, Zitting Cisticola, Golden-headed Cisticola, Horsfield's Bushlark, Brown Songlark, Black-bellied Crimson Finch and Long-tailed Finch. Gouldian Finches are recorded sporadically. On the floodplains, you may get Little Kingfisher and Azure Kingfisher. White-browed Crakes are quite common in the area. Bar-breasted Honeyeaters breed along the walk; look for their distinctive nests, hanging from branches over the water.

At the end of the walk, look for Baillon's Crakes; these were sighted here several times, last in April 2023. Waterbirds favouring this corner of the dam include Comb-crested Jacana, Australasian Darter, Glossy Ibis, Nankeen Night-Heron, Green Pygmy-goose and Red-kneed Dotterel.

Bush bird selection along the walk is similar to that of the Monsoon Forest Walk, as described in the previous section.

Dam Wall

The 1km-long, one-lane sealed road on top of the causeway offers excellent and convenient viewing across the dam covered with lotus and lilies to the left, and wild ricefield floodplains to the right. Two shaded viewing platforms have been erected along the dam road, with a car bay next to each.

Check the entry to the causeway; it is a favourite spot of Black Bittern. Also Nankeen Night-Herons regularly roost there. Reeds and cumbungi near the start of the causeway are the place where the vagrant Oriental Reed-Warbler was observed in summer over several years.

We visited Fogg Dam several times, and every time we watched huge masses of waterbirds congregating on the floodplains. White egrets, mostly Great Egrets, were scattered over the area up to the horizon. Foraging closer to the dam wall in dense, mixed groups were Magpie Geese, Plumed Whistling-Ducks, Wandering Whistling-Ducks, Radjah Shelducks, Pied Herons, Glossy Ibises and Australian White Ibises.

White-browed Crake

Underneath a viewing platform in the middle of the dam wall we got Buff-banded Rail and a couple of White-browed Crakes. In the lotus fields were plenty of very active White-bellied Cuckoo-shrikes and Black-faced Cuckoo-shrikes. Several Shining Flycatchers and Restless Flycatchers were hunting insects. A beautiful Forest Kingfisher was perched on nearly every lotus seedhead.

A few miserably-looking bushes are scattered along the mid-section of the wall. These were extensively used by bush birds, especially when they arrived for a drink. These included Black-bellied Crimson Finches, White-breasted Woodswallows, White-winged Trillers and Rainbow Bee-eaters. There was also Horsfield's Bronze-cuckoo and Pheasant Coucal. Tawny Grassbird was trilling loudly from a bush top. Australian Gull-billed Terns and Whiskered Terns were flying over the wetland.

When water levels raise above the dam wall, an unbelievable spectacle happens, as nearly every fish-eating bird from the area arrives to sit on the flooded dam wall, picking up fish clearly visible when passing over the flooded road. Particularly impressive are herons and egrets; you can encounter ten species side-by-side. At such times, Nankeen Night-Herons fish readily during the day.

Pandanus Lookout

This double-story viewing platform is located at the far end of the dam wall. It allows excellent views over the northern section of the wetland. A carpark for this facility is large enough for big tourist buses to turn. Therefore, the place is always full of people, especially at sunrise and sunset.

When we got there, the lagoon in front of the platform was packed with the waterbirds. They seemingly did not mind the presence of a large saltwater crocodile sunning itself among them. It was apparently not hungry as there was a leftover of a feral pig's carcass nearby, to which it did not pay any attention. On the other hand, Pied Herons were feasting on the carcass with delight.

Nankeen Night-Herons were roosting in a tree at a small bridge over a culvert past the dam wall. The carpark yielded Rainbow Bee-eater, Broad-billed Flycatcher, Green Oriole, Leaden Flycatcher, Red-winged Parrot, White-throated Honeyeater and Spangled Drongo.

Nankeen Night-Heron

Arnhem Highway

The 100km section of Arnhem Hwy (36) between Stuart Hwy (1) and the border of Kakadu National Park can be very productive. You'll find here numerous wetlands, although many of them are ephemeral. It is also worth stopping at the roadside to check out dense, long grasses at the verge of the tropical savannah woodland. Look there for finches, in particular Gouldian Finch. Keep your eyes peeled for raptors; these are abundant in the area. You can stay in one of several good roadhouses on the way. They offer shady, spacious camping grounds, where birding is also good.

Over 150 bird species have been recorded along Arnhem Hwy. **Key species** are Gouldian Finch, Masked Finch, Long-tailed Finch, Partridge Pigeon, Silver-backed Butcherbird and Mangrove Golden Whistler. Other birds of interest include raptors, waterbirds, Northern Rosella, Black-tailed Treecreeper, Varied Lorikeet, Red-backed Button-quail, Red-chested Button-quail, Australian Bustard, Red-backed Kingfisher and Barking Owl. Among the rarities are Great-billed Heron, Hooded Parrot and Black Falcon.

Beatrice Hill Rest Area

Rest area is located 3.5km west of the Adelaide River Bridge and 1km west from the prominently signposted turnoff to the Window on the Wetlands. The rest stop's GPS coordinates are 12°38'25''S and 131°18'28''E. On the opposite, north side of the road, you'll see Beatrice Lagoon, which during the Wet spills over 120ha.

While resting at a picnic table, we watched Black-necked Storks, Magpie Geese, Nankeen Night-Herons, Great Egrets, Plumed Egrets, Little Egrets, Glossy Ibises, Radjah Shelducks, Pied Herons, Wandering Whistling-Ducks and Plumed Whistling-Ducks. A Red-browed Crake popped out of the vegetation. A pair of Black-breasted Buzzards were soaring overhead. In the bushes of the rest area were Green-backed Gerygone and Arafura Fantail.

In summer, Little Curlews stop at this lagoon. There is a record of a sighting of four thousand birds that landed in the short grass.

Adelaide River Bridge

Adelaide River crosses Arnhem Hwy 30km southeast of the turnoff from Stuart Hwy. As many as four 'jumping crocodiles' tourist ventures operate in close proximity on the river, with the original enterprise just next to the bridge. Search for Mangrove Golden Whistler in the riverbank vegetation, in particular in clumps of bamboo at the Jumping Crocodile Cruises. Check also the trees on the northern side of the bridge, on the west bank of the river – you can drive there along a short track.

Along the river, look also for Broad-billed Flycatcher, Arafura Fantail, Mangrove Gerygone, Red-headed Honeyeater, Brown Whistler, Shining Flycatcher and Australian Yellow White-eye. Oriental Cuckoos are sighted in summer.

When we checked out the Jumping Crocodile Cruises, Grey Goshawk was roosting in the tree by the carpark. Brahminy Kite and Wedge-tailed Eagle were flying overhead. Red-tailed Black-Cockatoos and Little Corellas were hanging out near the café tables. A flock of Torresian Imperial-Pigeons flew across the river.

A man-eater size crocodile emerging next to your boat

Adelaide River Jumping Crocodile Experience

To get there, turn from Stuart Hwy (1) into Arnhem Hwy (36). Drive east for 25km, then turn left into Anzac Pde. Drive past the turnoff to Fogg Dam and continue to the end of Anzac Pde. After the road turns south, pass the turnoff to the left to the Humpty Doo Barramundi Farm, then turn left into a dirt track leading to the river cruises operation called Jumping Crocodile Experience.

About 500m before the boat ramp is a small billabong to the left. There, we experienced one of the weirdest, most wonderful sighting of our life. The billabong was filled to the brim with Pied Herons, there were at least 8,000 birds, some even of rufous morphology. Among them, were small numbers of Great Egrets, Plumed Egrets, Royal Spoonbills, Masked Lapwings, Whiskered Terns and Australian Gull-billed Terns. We realised later that a large area of barramundi production (100 saline ponds) is located just to the north and the bird gathering was possibly related to a mass raid planned on the fish farm.

A mass gathering of Pied Herons

Adelaide River, along with Mary River, have the highest saltwater crocodile density in NT. The salties are fed several times a day during the tourist boat cruises. As we arrived at the boat ramp, a hundred-strong flocks of Whistling Kites and Black Kites were roosting around the cruise office. During the trip, the kites that could still eat something, accompanied our boat to snatch chicken morsels from the crocodiles.

Waterbirds along the river included Magpie Geese, Brolgas, Pied Herons, Striated Herons and Glossy Ibises. Azure Kingfishers and Sacred Kingfishers were hunting from overhanging branches. Riverine vegetation produced Rainbow Bee-eater (plenty), Rufous-banded Honeyeater, Red-headed Honeyeater, Broad-billed Flycatcher, Paperbark Flycatcher, Collared Kingfisher, Channel-billed Cuckoo and a single female Mangrove Golden Whistler.

Corroboree Park Tavern

This roadhouse, featuring a fantastic pub, is located on Arnhem Hwy (36) halfway between Darwin and Kakadu National Park, with the Adelaide River to the west and Mary River to the east. Stop here for a meal and cold beer or, even better, stay for a few days to explore Fogg Dam and Mary River National Park. Corroboree Billabong cruises are booked there, with an option of a pickup from the roadhouse.

We thoroughly enjoyed our stay in the Tavern's caravan park, it was a very good base for our explorations. The resident Silver-backed Butcherbirds were calling every day from the tree shading our van site. Tame Great Bowerbirds were everywhere. We located a bower near the second gate, on the west side of the roadhouse. Pheasant Coucals were walking on the green lawn from one epiphyte-covered tree trunk to the next, as we watched them while sipping a cold one in the pub's garden.

Red-backed Kingfishers were perching on the power lines in front of the roadhouse. Other birds on the wires included Forest Kingfisher, Sacred Kingfisher, Blue-winged Kookaburra, Peaceful Dove and Brown Falcon.

Nocturnal birds were fantastic in the campground. Barking Owls and plentiful Bush Stone-curlews were very vocal. Spotlighting produced a Large-tailed Nightjar perched on a clothesline by the laundry block. We also heard Tawny Frogmouth, Australian Owlet-nightjar and Southern Boobook.

Other birds in the caravan park included Channel-billed Cuckoo, Red-winged Parrot, Green Oriole, Varied Triller, Lemon-bellied Flycatcher, White-quilled Honeyeater, Dusky Honeyeater and Brown Goshawk.

Mary River Excavation Pits

The site is located on the western side of Arnhem Hwy (36) about 10km northwest of the Mary River crossing and 850m southeast of the Mary River NP information bay. GPS coordinates are 12°52'04"S and 131°35'48"E. A small pull-off provides foot access to a gravel extraction area surrounded by woodland.

Two small ephemeral waterholes form in the gravel pit. This is a Gouldian Finch site, they come here to drink, especially in the morning, about 2hrs after dawn. Other finches that accompany them may include Black-bellied Crimson Finches, Masked Finches and Double-barred Finches. Waterbirds are recorded in the Wet, including Black Bittern, Nankeen Night-Heron, White-necked Heron and Buff-banded Rail.

Silver-backed Butcherbirds are often found here. The woodland may also yield Weebill, Paperbark Flycatcher, Rose-crowned Fruit-Dove, Varied Lorikeet, Red-backed Kingfisher and White-winged Triller.

Check the spot near the information board, at GPS coordinates of 12°51'39"S and 131°35'42"E. Gouldian Finches feed in this area now and then. Look also for Masked Finch, Red-backed Kingfisher, Black-tailed Treecreeper and Wedge-tailed Eagle.

Mary River Crossing

This site is located 79km from the turnoff from Stuart Hwy (1). A boat ramp is situated on the western side of the river. Great-billed Herons are occasionally sighted there. Black Bitterns are resident in the riverine vegetation. The best way to look for them is by boat – these can be organised by the Mary River Wilderness Retreat nearby. Other birds you may spot along the river include Grey Goshawk, Azure Kingfisher, Buff-sided Robin, Arafura Fantail, Oriental Dollarbird, Buff-breasted Honeyeater and Northern Fantail. Mangrove Golden Whistler is seen occasionally. White-bellied Sea-Eagles are nesting by the river.

Mary River Wilderness Retreat

After a recent change in ownership, Mary River Wilderness Retreat has changed its name to Breeze Holiday Park. It is located on the banks of Mary River, on 150ha of bushland adjacent to the Mary River National Park. A wide range of accommodation is offered, from bungalows to safari tents, caravan sites and camping sites. The property has 3km of river frontage where you can choose a place to camp. There is also a restaurant and two swimming pools. Boats are available for hire.

Over 170 bird species have been recorded on the grounds of Mary River Wilderness Retreat (Breeze Holiday Park). **Key species** are Great-billed Heron, Black Bittern, Azure Kingfisher, Rainbow Pitta, Black-tailed Treecreeper, Buff-sided Robin, Arafura Fantail and Pacific Baza. Other birds of interest include Silver-backed Butcherbird, Varied Lorikeet, Banded Honeyeater, Dusky Honeyeater, Green Oriole, Torresian Imperial-Pigeon, Green-backed Gerygone, Little Woodswallow, Masked Woodswallow and White-bellied Sea-Eagle. Rarities include Black-eared Cuckoo, Rufous Owl, Grey Falcon and Red Goshawk.

Bamboo Walk runs on the grounds parallel to Mary River, passing several small billabongs on its way. This setup is excellent for birding. Great-billed Herons visit these billabongs from time to time. The birds were observed booming and displaying on a tree. Also on this trail, look for Arafura Fantail, White-bellied Cuckoo-shrike, Green-backed Gerygone, Brown Goshawk and Shining Flycatcher.

Huge flocks of Little Corellas come to roost overnight in trees near the river. During our visit, Australian Figbirds were everywhere. There were plenty of honeyeaters, mostly Dusky Honeyeaters. We also got Bar-breasted Honeyeater, White-gaped Honeyeater, White-throated Honeyeater and Silver-crowned Friarbird. Sitting on a big bough, a Pacific Baza was consuming a large stick insect. We also came across Purple-backed Fairy-wren, Rufous Whistler, Brush Cuckoo, Masked Woodswallow, Black-faced Woodswallow and Australian Hobby.

Australian Figbird, northern yellow ssp.

Rainbow Pittas are often found on the resort grounds, coming out onto the lawn near the edge of the forest. Red Goshawk was sighted in the camping area in 2018. Grey Falcon flew over the site in 2019.

Bark Hut Inn

This roadhouse is located on Arnhem Why (36) at the western edge of Kakadu National Park. It is a good place to refuel and refresh while exploring Mary River or Kakadu National Parks. The pub is full of memorabilia to keep your mind busy during a meal.

Remember to cast an eye into an outdoor enclosure where they keep a buffalo, emus and a large crocodile. The enclosure is visited by many wild birds eager to participate in the feed. We spotted four Partridge Pigeons calmly invading the enclosure of the croc. Finches were feeding in the buffalo trough, later coming to drink from the crocodile pool. The mixed flock comprised Gouldian Finches, Double-barred Finches and Chestnut-breasted Mannikins.

Partridge Pigeons in the crocodile enclosure at Bark Hut Inn

In the trees around the property, we spotted White-bellied Cuckoo-shrike, Rainbow Bee-eater, Red-tailed Black-Cockatoo, Red-winged Parrot, Banded Honeyeater and White-quilled Honeyeater.

Djukbinj National Park

The 55,440ha Djukbinj National Park is located about 80km southeast of Darwin along Arnhem Hwy (36). The Park largely covers the Adelaide River catchment. Water is in abundance here year-round therefore this area is important for feeding, roosting and breeding of many bird species. The Park protects major breeding grounds of Magpie Geese, Brolgas, egrets and herons. In the past, the area was Marrakai Station, where water buffalos were roaming in large herds. The current National Park is jointly managed with the local Aboriginal people. Because of that, it is still their traditional hunting grounds. There are no facilities except for carparks and lookouts, and no camping is allowed. A 25km scenic drive runs by a network of billabongs, from Scott Creek to the Twin Billabong. The Park is visited only in the dry season and even then a 4WD vehicle is needed.

To get there, from Arnhem Hwy take Arnhem Hwy-Woolner Rd (on the Park map it is called Djukbinj Rd). GPS coordinates at the turnoff are 12°42'35''S and 131°25'37''E. See also the Park's fact sheet with a map, downloadable here: https://nt.gov.au/__data/assets/pdf_file/0014/200066/djukbinj-national-park.pdf.

Over 120 bird species have been recorded in the Djukbinj National Park. **Key species** are Partridge Pigeon, Black Bittern, Azure Kingfisher, Black-tailed Treecreeper and Spotted Nightjar. Other birds of interest include waterbirds, Forest Kingfisher, Bar-breasted Honeyeater, Oriental Dollarbird, Pallid Cuckoo, Brush Cuckoo, Brown Whistler, Black-necked Stork and Brolga.

Look for Partridge Pigeons at the start of the drive, up to 200m from the highway.

A good birding spot is along the Scott Creek crossing, about 6km north of the turnoff from Arnhem Hwy. The best time to visit is the early dry season, when water is still flowing in the creek. The file snakes are migrating upstream and there is an abundance of small fish. Every possible fish-eating bird species is represented at this shallow crossing at that time to gorge on an easy meal. You should see Nankeen Night-Herons, Pied Herons, Little Egrets, Plumed Egrets, Great Egrets, White-necked Herons, Royal Spoonbills, Black-necked Storks, Little Black Cormorants and all ibises. Azure Kingfishers hunt small fish from the branches. Raptors, some eyeing fish, some other birds, position themselves on the trees nearby. Look for White-bellied Sea-Eagles, Whistling Kites, Black Kites, Australian Hobbies and Peregrine Falcons.

There will be waders in the drying billabongs including Common Sandpiper, Marsh Sandpiper, Sharp-tailed Sandpiper, Pied Stilt and Red-kneed Dotterel. Many nectar-feeders would be in the flowering trees such as Rufous-banded Honeyeater, Bar-breasted Honeyeater, Dusky Honeyeater, Red-headed Honeyeater, Yellow-throated

Miner, Helmeted Friarbird, Little Friarbird, Red-collared Lorikeet and Varied Lorikeet. Bushland along the track may also yield Green Oriole, Forest Kingfisher, Orange-footed Scrubfowl, Leaden Flycatcher, Broad-billed Flycatcher, Little Shrike-thrush, Weebill, Brown-capped Emerald-Dove, Large-billed Gerygone, Long-tailed Finch and Channel-billed Cuckoo.

Leaning Tree Lagoon Nature Park

Leaning Tree Lagoon is located off Arnhem Hwy (36) at Marrakai, about 80km southeast of Darwin. To get there, 11km west of Corroboree Park Tavern turn south into a 300m track leading to the lagoon, well signposted from the main road. On the other side of Arnhem Hwy is Djukbinj National Park.

Leaning Tree Lagoon

This is a quiet enclave, nearly completely covered with beautiful white waterlilies. The park is popular with locals who come here for a picnic and to watch waterbirds congregating on the water. The lagoon doubles in size and connects with other waterways of the Adelaide River floodplain during the Wet. Be crockwise, salties may be present in the lagoon year-round.

Camping is permitted but there are no facilities. A walking track runs along the lagoon; it may not be passable at places. The park gets closed after heavy rains.

Over 150 bird species have been recorded in the Leaning Tree Lagoon Nature Park. **Key species** are Green Pygmy-goose, Oriental Cuckoo (summer), Black-necked Stork and Glossy Ibis. Other birds of interest include Comb-crested Jacana, Magpie Goose, Whiskered Tern, Pied Stilt, Azure Kingfisher, Rainbow Pitta, Forest Kingfisher, Black-tailed Treecreeper, Oriental Dollarbird, Red-winged Parrot, Swamp Harrier and Black-breasted Buzzard. Rarities include Black Swan, Australian Wood Duck, Great Crested Grebe, Little Curlew, Red-necked Avocet and White-winged Black Tern.

Many Pygmy-geese breed in the park. Then, large post-breeding flocks form here. Magpie Geese also favour this place, especially in the late Dry. In early summer (Oct-Nov), waders appear such as Sharp-tailed Sandpiper, Wood Sandpiper, Common Sandpiper, Common Greenshank and Australian Pratincole.

Woodland at the site may produce Banded Honeyeater, Red-tailed Black-Cockatoo, Black-tailed Treecreeper, White-bellied Cuckoo-shrike, Rainbow Pitta, Varied Triller, Forest Kingfisher, Sacred Kingfisher, Varied Lorikeet and White-throated Gerygone. Check the grassland for Brown Quail, Golden-headed Cisticola, Masked Finch, Long-tailed Finch and Black-bellied Crimson Finch.

Marrakai Road

Turnoff to Marrakai Rd, often referred to as Marrakai Track, is from Arnhem Hwy (36) about 3km northwest from the Corroboree Park Tavern. This unsealed road is a known Gouldian Finch site, and many bird tour operators include this stop in their trip itinerary. A 30km section of the road, starting from the Purple Mango Café 5km from the highway, up to the Adelaide River crossing, is the place to look for finches. Along the road, there are various farm-utilised habitats such as grassy woodland, grassland, monsoon forest, paperbark forest and wetlands. The latter become expansive after heavy rains.

Over 150 bird species have been recorded along Marrakai Road. **Key species** are Gouldian Finch, Partridge Pigeon, Buff-sided Robin, Black Bittern, Banded Honeyeater, Little Woodswallow, Arafura Fantail, Red-backed Button-quail and Black-breasted Buzzard. Other birds of interest include Brown Quail, Australian Bustard, Red-backed Kingfisher, Northern Rosella, Black-tailed Treecreeper, Rufous-banded Honeyeater, Rufous Songlark, Jacky Winter, Masked Finch, Weebill, Silver-backed Butcherbird and Spotted Nightjar. Rarities include Little Curlew, Common Cicadabird and Zitting Cisticola.

Partridge Pigeons are usually found near the Purple Mango Café. The best spot for Buff-sided Robin is vegetation at the Margaret River crossing, about 30km from Arnhem Hwy. For Gouldian Finches, look in the right habitat anywhere along the road but particularly in the freshly burnt areas.

We stopped at the first creek crossing, about 5km from the highway, at GPS coordinates of 12°46′45′′S and 131°27′02′′E. We found there a couple of Gouldian Finches among Double-barred Finches, Masked Finches and Long-tailed Finches. In the surrounding bushland, we got Northern Rosella, Red-tailed Black-Cockatoo, Black-tailed Treecreeper, Rufous Songlark, White-winged Triller, Varied Lorikeet, Weebill and Collared Sparrowhawk.

Huge numbers of Diamond and Peaceful Doves could be seen along the road. Flowering paperbarks attracted Rufous-banded Honeyeaters, Rufous-throated Honeyeaters, Banded Honeyeaters, Dusky Honeyeaters, Singing Honeyeaters and Little Friarbirds. Little Woodswallows were flying overhead in surprisingly large numbers (about 30 birds). Marrakai Rd was also good for raptors; we observed Spotted Harrier, Swamp Harrier, Brown Falcon, Wedge-tailed Eagle and Black-breasted Buzzard.

We found Buff-sided Robins quite easily at the Margaret River crossing. Vegetation there also produced Shining Flycatcher, Lemon-bellied Flycatcher, Arafura Fantail, Northern Fantail, Varied Triller, Pheasant Coucal, Black-bellied Crimson Finch and Brush Cuckoo. Black Bittern flushed from the paperbark swamp. A pair of Brolgas was walking through the short grass. Fairy Martins were flying over the crossing.

Black-bellied Crimson Finch

If you go there spotlighting, you may encounter Red-backed Button-quails or Chestnut-backed Button-quails on the roadside. Look also for Spotted Nightjar, Southern Boobook and Bush Stone-curlew.

Adelaide River crossing is a good birding spot. GPS coordinates are 12°55'35''S and 131°15'59''E. On the northern side of the road, you'll find a carparking space and a trailhead to a billabong. Red Goshawk was recorded here a couple of times. Search also for Azure Kingfisher and Nankeen Night-Heron. On the water, you may get Green Pygmy-goose, Radjah Shelduck or Glossy Ibis. Riparian vegetation may yield Shining Flycatcher, Little Shrike-thrush, Green-backed Gerygone, Bar-breasted Honeyeater, Banded Honeyeater, Northern Fantail and Little Bronze-cuckoo.

Another potential place to stop is 1km west of the Adelaide River crossing. A small billabong, surrounded by grassland, is located on the southern side of the road. GPS coordinates are 12°55'38''S and 131°15'34''E. In winter, masses of birds come here to drink. In particular, Peaceful Doves, Bar-shouldered Doves and finches favour this location. Gouldian Finches are occasionally spotted among Black-bellied Crimson Finches. In the surrounding grassland, look for Australian Bustard, Tawny Grassbird and Golden-headed Cisticola. Zitting Cisticolas can also be found in the area.

Spotted Harriers may be patrolling the grassland. Other raptors here include Black-breasted Buzzard, Brown Goshawk, Wedge-tailed Eagle and Little Eagle. Other birds at this location include Tree Martin, Paperbark Flycatcher, Azure Kingfisher, Black-necked Stork, Little Woodswallow, White-browed Woodswallow and Red-backed Kingfisher.

Mary River National Park

This sprawling 121,500ha National Park is located 11km east of Darwin. It stretches along Mary River from the coast to Arnhem Hwy, then continues south for further 50km. The Park comprises several sections, often separate from each other, with the two largest sections sited north and south of the highway like a bow tie.

The Park protects part of the Mary River catchment with its floodplains, billabongs, lagoons, canals, tropical woodland, paperbark forest and monsoon forest. Its wetlands are home to a vast variety of waterbirds, the biggest barramundi to catch and the largest saltwater crocodiles to watch for. Over 200 bird species are on the Park's birdlist.

In the Dry (May-Sep) most of the Park becomes accessible, however many roads are unsealed so a 4WD is a must. Different access routes lead to different attractions of the Park, but all routes start from Arnhem Hwy (36). One of the best ways of exploring the area is to take a wildlife-watching boat cruise on the Mary River or Corroboree Billabong. Camping is allowed at Shady Camp and at Couzens Lookout. There are several picnic areas including Mary River Crossing and Mistake Billabong. At some billabongs, there are boat ramps and viewing platforms. There are two 4WD tracks (Hardies Tk and Wildman Tk) and several walking trails. Accommodation is available along Arnhem Hwy and Point Stuart Rd. A fact sheet with a map can be downloaded here: https://nt.gov.au/__data/assets/pdf_file/0014/200075/mary-river-national-park.pdf.

Corroboree Billabong

This gorgeous water body is located approximately 100km southeast of Darwin. In our opinion, this is one of the most picturesque spots in the whole NT. The billabong consists of a series of long, periodically interconnected wetlands which get cut off from Mary River in the Dry. The water edges are lined with rows of stunning lotus lilies and waterlilies.

Corroboree Billabong wetlands

To explore the wetland, hire a charter boat or embark on a tourist cruise. The best are the sunrise cruises. Book through the Corroboree Park Tavern or online at https://www.wetlandcruises.com.au/.

To get to the Corroboree Billabong boat ramp, turn north from Arnhem Hwy (36) 1km east of the Corroboree Park Tavern into Marrakai Access, then turn right into Corroboree Access which will get you to the cruise boat. The total length of the road is 20km, with the last 2km unsealed.

Over 170 bird species have been recorded around the Corroboree Billabong. **Key species** are Little Kingfisher, Azure Kingfisher, Black-necked Stork, Radjah Shelduck, Arafura Fantail, Bar-breasted Honeyeater, Oriental Cuckoo, Large-tailed Nightjar and White-bellied Sea-Eagle. Other birds of interest include Magpie Goose, Green Pygmy-goose, Pied Heron, Plumed Egret, Glossy Ibis, Australasian Darter, Whiskered Tern, Green-backed Gerygone, Black-bellied Crimson Finch, Red-headed Honeyeater, Whistling Kite, Swamp Harrier and Black-breasted Buzzard. Rarities include Swinhoe's Snipe, Red-necked Avocet, Black Falcon and Red Goshawk.

We took the sunrise boat trip which pays more attention to the birdlife. While driving to the boat ramp still in the dark, we came across several nocturnal birds including Bush Stone-curlew, Large-tailed Nightjar, Barking Owl and a Barn Owl which was sitting on the fence by the cruise office. About 20 Nankeen Night-Herons were perched on the trees, boats and on the ground. Black-bellied Crimson Finches were building a nest under the roof of the office area.

During the trip, we saw plenty of Great Egrets, Plumed Egrets, Pied Herons, Australasian Darters, Radjah Shelducks, Wandering Whistling-Ducks and Magpie Geese. The latter had just arrived for the season. Black Bittern flew over our heads, flushed from the bushes. We passed a long-established Black-necked Stork nest, with two chicks inside.

The tour operator pointed out to us a double nest of White-bellied Sea-Eagle and said that the female had rejected the larger nest, so her partner had to construct the second, smaller nest a bit higher, and that nest was now used by the pair. Several Whistling Kite nests were active along the shores of the billabong. One of them was taken over by Australian Hobby. Other raptors during the trip were Brown Goshawk, Pacific Baza and Black Falcon.

We enjoyed watching Azure Kingfishers which spaced themselves out at regular intervals along the shore. The rarer Little Kingfisher also made an appearance. Bar-shouldered Doves sat in the bushes everywhere, sunning themselves in the morning sun. A Bar-breasted Honeyeater's nest was hanging over the water.

Other birds during the cruise included Green Oriole, Olive-backed Oriole, Collared Kingfisher, Forest Kingfisher, Red-headed Honeyeater, Rufous-banded Honeyeater, Australian Yellow White-eye, White-throated Gerygone, Tawny Grassbird, Glossy Ibis, Yellow-billed Spoonbill, Green Pygmy-goose and Shining Flycatcher.

The trip was also satisfying for its beautiful sunrise and the picturesque watery landscapes of lotus and waterlilies. Crocodiles were everywhere which added a pinch of excitement to the otherwise serene surroundings.

Hardies Lagoon

Hardies Lagoon is located 10km north of Arnhem Hwy (36) via Hardies Lagoon Rd (unsealed). The turnoff is 4.5km east of the Corroboree Park Tavern, at GPS coordinates of 12°47'19''S and 131°32'30''E. A camping site is located by the lagoon at the end of Hardies Lagoon Rd. You'll also find here a boat ramp and a track running through the forest along the water. Be careful, when we arrived, a monster croc was resting on the boat ramp, just under the warning sign about the crocodiles.

Paperbark Flycatcher

On the walk, we observed Brown Goshawk gorging on a Pacific Baza (as we later confirmed by the plucked primaries). Arafura Fantail was hopping on the track in front of us. Rainbow Bee-eaters were hunting over the water. Other birds we saw in the area included Northern Fantail, Paperbark Flycatcher, Lemon-bellied Flycatcher, Shining Flycatcher, Broad-billed Flycatcher, Brush Cuckoo, Little Bronze-cuckoo, Dusky Honeyeater, Rufous-banded Honeyeater, Weebill and Whistling Kite. There were plenty of agile wallabies on the grounds.

Nocturnal birds at this site include Australian Owlet-nightjar, Barking Owl and Bush Stone-curlew.

Bird Billabong

This aptly named billabong is popular with the birders. To get there, turn north from Arnhem Hwy (36) into Hardies 4WD Tk at GPS coordinates of 12°54'07"S and 131°37'36"E. This track runs past Bird Billabong about 4km from the turnoff. Further information about Hardies Tk can be found in the fact sheet downloadable here: https://nt.gov.au/__data/assets/pdf_file/0015/200076/mary-river-national-park-hardies-4wd-track-information-sheet.pdf.

From the carpark, take a stroll to the billabong. There is a viewing platform over the water. However, the return walk is nearly 5km.

Over 180 bird species have been recorded around the Bird Billabong. **Key species** are Gouldian Finch, Radjah Shelduck, Green Pygmy-goose, Magpie Goose, Pink-eared Duck, Silver-backed Butcherbird, Swamp Harrier and White-bellied Sea-Eagle. Other birds of interest include waders, Glossy Ibis, White-necked Heron, Australian Gull-billed Tern, Australasian Darter, Australian Reed-Warbler, Cockatiel, Pallid Cuckoo, White-winged Triller, Bar-breasted Honeyeater and Forest Kingfisher. Rarities include Dusky Moorhen, Buff-sided Robin, Great-billed Heron, Flock Bronzewing, Red Goshawk, Black Falcon and Little Eagle.

Gouldian Finches are found here regularly. Look for them in the grass around the carpark and along the walking track. We found them feeding in the freshly burnt area near the carpark. Foraging with them were Long-tailed Finches, Masked Finches and Double-barred Finches as well as several Red-tailed Black-Cockatoos.

Bird Billabong is an important breeding ground for Radjah Shelducks so they can often be seen here with ducklings in tow.

In winter and spring (dry season), the billabong is filled with thousands of waterbirds, in particular Magpie Geese, Plumed Whistling-Ducks and Wandering Whistling-Ducks. You will also get here Glossy Ibis, Pied Heron, White-necked Heron, Royal Spoonbill and Yellow-billed Spoonbill. As the billabong is drying out, the emerging muddy edges attract the waders, including Black-fronted Dotterel, Red-kneed Dotterel, Marsh Sandpiper, Wood Sandpiper, Sharp-tailed Sandpiper, Common Greenshank and Black-tailed Godwit. Masses of Magpie Larks are often seen feeding among the waders. White-winged Black Terns and Whiskered Terns may be flying over the billabong.

Savannah woodland along the billabong supports good numbers of Black-tailed Treecreepers. In the flowering trees, look for Varied Lorikeet, Banded Honeyeater, Rufous-throated Honeyeater and Silver-backed Butcherbird.

The impressive number of 21 raptor species has been recorded around the billabong. Common species are Brown Goshawk, Swamp Harrier, Spotted Harrier, Whistling Kite and Black Kite. You may also come across Grey Goshawk, Square-tailed Kite, Black-breasted Buzzard or Osprey.

Mary River Billabong

Mary River Billabong is located on Hardies 4WD Tk approximately 5km north of Arnhem Hwy (36) and 1.5km from the turnoff to Bird Billabong. The turnoff to Hardies Tk from the highway is located at GPS coordinates of 12°54'07"S and 131°37'36"E. Further information about Hardies Tk can be found in the fact sheet downloadable here: https://nt.gov.au/__data/assets/pdf_file/0015/200076/mary-river-national-park-hardies-4wd-track-information-sheet.pdf.

We watched Nankeen Night-Heron and White-necked Heron there, standing at the water edge, not fussed about a large saltwater crocodile basking in the sun nearby. Azure Kingfisher was perched on an overhanging branch. Osprey and Brahminy Kite were patrolling the area.

On the walk around the billabong, we encountered Arafura Fantail (plenty), Red-headed Honeyeater, Australian Yellow White-eye, Northern Fantail, Varied Triller, Weebill, Green-backed Gerygone and Pacific Baza. A flock of Black-bellied Crimson Finches arrived for a drink of water. In the bushes near the carpark, we got Red-winged Parrot, Red-tailed Black-Cockatoo, Great Bowerbird and Lemon-bellied Flycatcher.

Rockhole Boat Ramp

This is a popular access point to Mary River. One of Mary River cruise options (Mary River Wetland Cruises) starts from here. These cruises are reported to be very productive. To get there, make left from Point Stuart Rd and head west on Rockhole Rd to the boat ramp. You'll find picnic tables and toilets there.

Over 130 bird species have been recorded on the Mary River Wetland Cruises. **Key species** are Black Bittern, Buff-banded Rail, Black-necked Stork, Red-kneed Dotterel, Azure Kingfisher, Arafura Fantail, Banded Honeyeater, Black-breasted Buzzard and White-bellied Sea-Eagle. Other birds of interest include Green Pygmy-goose, Wandering Whistling-Duck, Comb-crested Jacana, Plumed Egret, Rufous-banded Honeyeater, Red-winged Parrot, Pacific Baza and Swamp Harrier. Rarities include Little Kingfisher, Great-billed Heron and Buff-sided Robin.

A large nest of White-bellied Sea-Eagles is located not far from the boat ramp. You will see many more White-bellied Sea-Eagles on this trip, they are abundant there. Herons should be plentiful along the way, including Nankeen Night-Heron, Pied Heron, White-necked Heron, Striated Heron, Plumed Egret and Little Egret. Even Great-billed Heron is seen from time to time. Black Bittern may be hiding in the clumps of pandanus.

Vegetation along the river may yield Golden-headed Cisticola, Arafura Fantail, Leaden Flycatcher, Broad-billed Flycatcher, Forest Kingfisher, Sacred Kingfisher, Oriental Dollarbird, Barking Owl, Collared Sparrowhawk and Pacific Baza.

Mistake Billabong

This small billabong is located on the western side of Point Stuart Rd, 3km south of Opium Creek Tk. A short, 500m track runs to the billabong through the forest. GPS coordinates at the track entry are 12°37′52″S and 131°46′35″E.

Comb-crested Jacana daddy with two small chicks

White-browed Crakes are regularly found along the water edges. Black-necked Stork is also seen frequently. Waterbirds on the billabong include Green Pygmy-goose, Comb-crested Jacana, Glossy Ibis, Whiskered Tern and plenty of Magpie geese. The site is good for raptors including Black-breasted Buzzard, White-bellied Sea-Eagle, Pacific Baza, Swamp Harrier, Collared Sparrowhawk and Australian Hobby. In the woods, look for Black-tailed Treecreeper, Green-backed Gerygone, White-breasted Woodswallow, Masked Woodswallow, Forest Kingfisher and Little Shrike-thrush.

Point Stuart Wilderness Lodge

The Lodge is located on Point Stuart Rd, approximately 170km east of Darwin. To get there, from Arnhem Hwy (36) take Point Stuart Rd and drive north for 35km. The last 7km are unsealed. The Lodge is situated in a good place to explore the wilderness of Mary River National Park. It offers a variety of accommodation as well as birding tours and 4WD wildlife safaris.

Black-breasted Buzzards are regularly seen around the Lodge. On the extensive lodge grounds, you have a chance to find Red-backed Kingfisher, Rainbow Pitta, Common Cicadabird, Australian Bustard, Tree Martin, Green-backed Gerygone, Brown Whistler, Orange-footed Scrubfowl, Oriental Dollarbird and Blue-winged Kookaburra. A pair of Tawny Frogmouths is often roosting near the house. At night, you may get Large-tailed Nightjar, Barking Owl and Bush Stone-curlew.

Adult female Blue-winged Kookaburra

A small, shallow dam is situated at the back of the property. It can be productive for waterbirds such as Black Bittern, Nankeen Night-Heron, Pied Heron, Yellow-billed Spoonbill, Glossy Ibis, Black-fronted Dotterel, Pink-eared Duck and Radjah Shelduck.

From the back right-hand corner of the Lodge's campground, you enter the Jimmy Creek Monsoon Forest Walk. The path is about 2km long and has sections of boardwalk. This area is often teeming with birds. Orange-footed Scrubfowls have built an enormous communal nest mound here. Rainbow Pitta is regularly seen on the forest floor. Fruit-eating birds should not disappoint; you may spot Torresian

Imperial-Pigeon, Rose-crowned Fruit-Dove, Brown-capped Emerald-Dove, Channel-billed Cuckoo, Eastern Koel, Green Oriole and Olive-backed Oriole. Other birds here include Brown Whistler, Arafura Fantail, White-bellied Cuckoo-shrike, Varied Triller, Rufous-banded Honeyeater, Dusky Honeyeater and Shining Flycatcher.

Shady Camp

To get there, from Arnhem Hwy (36) take Point Stuart Rd. Pass the turnoff to the Point Stuart Wilderness Lodge on your way. Turn left into Harold Knowles Rd, then left into Shady Camp Rd and drive to the river. The distance from the Arnhem Hwy turnoff is 54km with the first 30km sealed.

This is a popular fishing spot with a boat ramp, picnic area, campground, toilets and a shaded crocodile viewing platform. A barrage divides the river to prevent saltwater entering the freshwater wetland. It has created the habitat for the waders which allows to observe them on the mudflats during the low tide.

Over 130 bird species have been recorded around the Shady Camp. **Key species** are Great-billed Heron, Mangrove Golden Whistler, Mangrove Robin and Black Falcon. Other birds of interest include waders, Pied Heron, Azure Kingfisher, Glossy Ibis, Torresian Imperial-Pigeon, Broad-billed Flycatcher, Shining Flycatcher, Banded Honeyeater, Rufous-banded Honeyeater and Black Butcherbird. Rarities include Little Kingfisher, Zitting Cisticola, Yellow-billed Spoonbill and Fork-tailed Swift.

Black-tailed Godwit

Great-billed Herons appear with surprising regularity on the mudflats at low tide. Chestnut Rails have also been recorded coming out of the mangroves. Eighteen species of waders are on the site's birdlist including Whimbrel, Far Eastern Curlew, Common Sandpiper, Marsh Sandpiper, Black-tailed Godwit, Great Knot, Australian Pratincole and Pied Stilt. Common Sandpipers are often roosting with Pacific Golden Plovers and Common Greenshanks on rocks on the saltwater side of the barrage.

Look for Little Kingfisher, it may be perched just right beside the viewing platform. The platform may also come useful when locating Black Bittern and Black-necked Stork, both usually found on the freshwater side of the barrage.

Check the mangroves for Mangrove Golden Whistler, Mangrove Robin, Shining Flycatcher, Azure Kingfisher, Collared Kingfisher and Mangrove Gerygone.

Nocturnal birds in the area include Barn Owl, Barking Owl, Large-tailed Nightjar and Bush Stone-curlew.

Bamurru Plains

This is not a typical birding site. It is an Outback luxury camp, inspired by the luxury camps of southern Africa. It is sometimes called the Australian Okavango. It offers the lodge, safari tents, bungalows, airboats, river cruises and daily safari drives. The 30,000ha property sits on the coastal floodplains of Mary River at the edge of the Kakadu National Park. Wildlife is plentiful here, with large crocodiles, water buffaloes, wallabies and huge numbers of waterbirds. It is still a working water buffalo station, so you can get a real 'Crocodile Dundee' experience here. You can walk around the property only with a guide (for safety reasons).

The site is located 3hr drive from Darwin. To get there, from Stuart Hwy (1) turn into Arnhem Hwy (36) and drive for about 100km. At 77km, stop at the Bark Hut Inn which is the furthest point where you can contact the Lodge about your imminent arrival. The number to call is 08 8978 8977. If your phone does not work there (only Telstra phones have coverage), ask the Inn staff to make the call for you. This is essential, as the Lodge personnel has to open the property gate for you and transfer the guests to the Lodge vehicles for the last leg of the drive. Bark Hut Inn has also the last fuel, so do not neglect to top up for the return journey. From the Inn, continue for 23km, then turn left into Point Stuart Rd. Next, turn left into Harold Knowles Rd, signposted to Shady Camp. Ignore the two turnoffs to Shady Camp. Continue straight over a cattle grid, passing the turnoff to Melaleuca. Pass over another cattle grid and then further on go through a gate (this may be closed, please leave this gate as you find it). Finally, you will go over another cattle grid and arrive at a gate labelled 'Swim Creek Station'. This is the boundary of Bamurru

Plains. You are required to wait for a guide to meet you there at the agreed time. The guide will escort your vehicle to the property where it will remain safely parked. You'll then be moved into a 4WD vehicle to be driven to the safari lodge, with a 30 min drive time.

You can also get to the lodge on a light plane or by organised transfer from Darwin. Further details of this type of transport can be found on the Lodge website at https://www.bamurruplains.com/. The Lodge is open from 1 March to 31 October.

Your satisfaction with the waterbirds will depend on the level of water on the floodplains. Even Great-billed Heron is possible here. The memories of masses of geese, ducks, storks, ibises, herons, terns and Little Corellas you'll take from Bamurru are truly one of the kind. Bush birds are also plentiful however you cannot get to them without a guide so your good relationship with a safari vehicle driver will be directly proportional to the length of your birdlist.

A pair of Black-necked Storks, female (yellow eye) in the foreground

Kakadu National Park

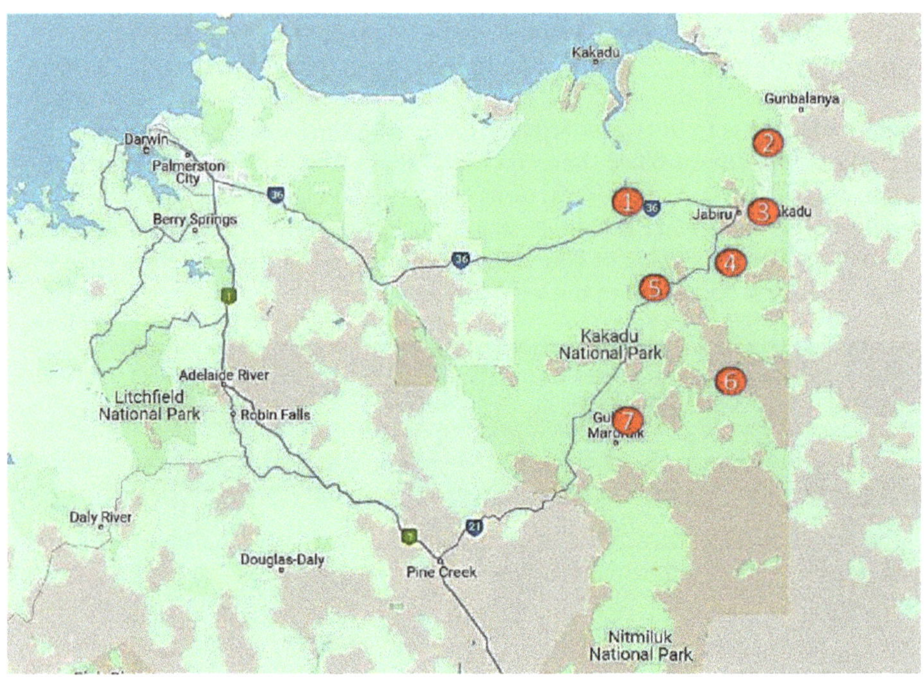

Kakadu National Park is located in the three Alligator Rivers region. It is the second largest national park in Australia (after the Munga-Thirri - Simpson Desert NP in South Australia, created in 2021). It covers over 2 million hectares and is roughly the size of Wales or 2/3 of Belgium. It stretches 200km from north to south and 100km from east to west. This World Heritage area is renowned for its sandstone plateaus, spectacular gorges, escarpments, wetlands and waterfalls. The Park is also home to the oldest and finest collections of Aboriginal rock art.

Tropical savannah woodland covers nearly 80% of the Park. There are also large areas of monsoon forest. The enormous wetland areas with a network of billabongs, rivers and swamps are used by millions of waterbirds and migratory birds as well as astounding numbers of crocodiles and other wildlife. The importance of these wetlands is reflected in their Ramsar and World Heritage status. Some of the savannah habitats in the Park have been identified by Birdlife International as IBA (Important Bird Areas) because they support endangered populations of Gouldian Finches, Red Goshawks, Partridge Pigeons and Chestnut-backed Button-quails.

Tropical savannah is dotted with termite mounds

Arnhem Hwy (36) in the north and Kakadu Hwy (21) in the south offer sealed access to the Park. Jabiru is the only town in the Park, and you can get all your daily necessities there. You need a car to explore the Park and be mindful of long distances between destinations. Most of the waterfalls and sandstone escarpment areas can only be reached by a 4WD vehicle.

Tourist infrastructure in the Park is good including numerous camping sites, a wide range of accommodation from lodges to caravan parks, three visitor centres, a network of walking tracks, picnic sites, boardwalks and more. Car rental is available in Jabiru, Katherine and Darwin. Daily coach service from Darwin to Kakadu NP stops in Jabiru, Cooinda, Bowali Visitor Centre and Nourlangie Rock. More than 200 commercial tour operators run day trips and longer safaris to the Park; some of them specialise in birding tours. The range of activities offered in Cooinda and Jabiru include helicopter or fixed-wing plane scenic flights, boat cruises and canoe hire. Further information and maps of individual Park areas are available in many local guides, e.g. the one downloadable here: http://vazivite.free.fr/australie/topend/kakadu_guide.pdf.

The astounding number of over 290 bird species features on the Kakadu National Park's birdlist, more than a third of all birds recorded in Australia. The particularly sought-after species include White-throated Grasswren, Red Goshawk, Gouldian Finch and Partridge Pigeon. A list of sites where these species have been recorded in the Park is provided below with further details in the relevant site descriptions.

Having said that, the best way to secure a sighting of White-throated Grasswren or Red Goshawk is to book a birding trip with a specialist tour operator. Several Red Goshawks' old and current nests are scattered throughout the Park. White-throated Grasswren is an elusive NT endemic that can practically be found only in this park, and only in the old spinifex habitat. Due to the very aggressive backburn regime implemented in NT according to the Aboriginal tradition (we were told by a Ranger that up to 80% of land is burnt every year!), the areas of old spinifex are scarce, and the bird is very rare.

Red Goshawk:

- Harriet Creek Rest Stop
- Big Nellie Creek
- Bukbukluk Lookout
- Moline Rockhole
- Mary River Ranger Station
- Gerowie Creek Crossing
- Information stop on Arnhem Hwy.

White-throated Grasswren:

- Jim Jim Falls (the best chance)
- Barrk Malan Walk at the top of Jim Jim Falls
- Yurmikmik Walks
- Koolpin Gorge
- Gunlom Falls (historical sightings)
- Gunlom Escarpment (historical sightings).

Partridge Pigeon:

- Mardugal
- Djarradjin Campground (Muirella Park)
- Maguk
- Jabiru Airport
- Aurora Kakadu Lodge and Caravan Park, Jabiru

- Ubirr
- Gubara
- Anbangbang Billabong.

Gouldian Finch:
- Harriet Creek Rest Area
- Gerowie Creek Crossing
- Maguk
- Yurmikmik Walks
- Koolpin Gorge
- Mamukala Wetlands
- Buba Walk
- Bardedjilidji
- Ubirr
- During our visit in winter 2022 this species was present in the freshly burnt areas across the whole Park, feeding in mixed flocks with other finches.

South Alligator River

Wetlands of Kakadu

This section of the Park extends along Arnhem Hwy (36) and includes several birding sites such as Mamukala Wetlands, South Alligator Boat Ramp and Gungarre Walk.

Key species are Buff-sided Robin, waterbirds and waders including Oriental Pratincole and Little Curlew. Other birds of interest include White-winged Black Tern, Bar-breasted Honeyeater, Broad-billed Flycatcher, Lemon-bellied Flycatcher, Paperbark Flycatcher, Arafura Fantail, Long-tailed Finch, Masked Finch and Black-breasted Buzzard. Among the rarities are Freckled Duck, Red Goshawk, Great-billed Heron, White Wagtail, Eastern Yellow Wagtail, Pale-vented Bush-hen, Dusky Moorhen and Hooded Robin.

Information Stop on Arnhem Hwy

This site is located on Arnhem Hwy (36) 1.5km west of the turnoff to Two Mile Hole at the GPS position of 12°48'04''S and 132°07'42''E.

A pair of Red Goshawks nest in the area, so you'll have a chance to sight them here. Several other sizeable nests can be found in trees around the information stop, used by Torresian Crows, Pied Butcherbirds and Australian Hobbies.

In the surrounding bushland, look for Black-tailed Treecreeper, Rufous Whistler, Northern Rosella, Weebill, Grey-crowned Babbler and Silver-crowned Friarbird. Chestnut-backed Button-quails were recorded at the edge of the access road.

Two Mile Hole Camping Area

Two Mile Hole is a secluded billabong and a fishing spot popular among the locals. It is however rarely visited by tourists. To get there, drive for about 20km from the western entrance of the National Park, then turn north (well signposted) into a 4WD track and drive 12km to the camping area. GPS coordinates there are 12°41'32''S and 132°09'03''E. There are no facilities or a boat ramp. You'll be driving through savannah woodland, traversing two deep creek crossings. A 4WD vehicle is a must.

Gouldian Finches are found along the access track. Look also for Masked Finches, Red-tailed Black-Cockatoos, Varied Lorikeets, Paperbark Flycatchers, White-winged Trillers and Australian Owlet-nightjars.

On the billabong, you can observe Black-necked Stork, White-necked Heron, Nankeen Night-Heron, Glossy Ibis, Red-kneed Dotterel and Azure Kingfisher. Tree Martins nest in a tree near the water. There are also numerous saltwater crocodiles.

You'll be camping with dingoes, agile wallabies, feral donkeys and a few thousands of Little Corellas.

Gungarre Walk

This 3.6km circuit track starts at the large banyan tree near the Aurora Kakadu Resort on the south side of Arnhem Hwy (36). The path runs through the monsoon forest before reaching woodland and grassland, and then continues to the billabong with a floating walkway leading to a viewing platform.

The monsoon forest may produce Rainbow Pitta, Orange-footed Scrubfowl, Common Cicadabird, Arafura Fantail, Little Shrike-thrush and Brown Whistler. In woodland, look for Varied Lorikeet, Rufous-banded Honeyeater, Dusky Honeyeater, Brush Cuckoo, Collared Sparrowhawk and Brown Goshawk. Masked Finch, Long-tailed Finch and Brown Quail may be found in the grassland.

As you reach the billabong, you will be faced with masses of waterbirds. Search also for White-browed Crake, Black Bittern, White-necked Heron, Glossy Ibis and Whiskered Tern. Swamp Harriers often fly over the area. The billabong can also be reached via a shorter walk starting behind the Aurora resort.

When we were passing Aurora Resort, the property was shut down and deserted however sprinklers were operating along the access road to the resort. The water attracted over 500 Little Corellas which were displaying their comical antics on the sprinklers and on the lawn. We stopped for a while and watched these endearing birds at play. We also spotted two Barking Owls roosting on a tree nearby.

Little Corellas frolicking under the sprinklers

South Alligator Boat Ramp

This site is located 8km west of Mamukala Wetlands and 2km east of Gungarre Walk. GPS coordinates are 12°39'39''S and 132°30'15''E. A large picnic area is provided at the boat ramp. Adjacent to the picnic site and the carparks is extensive grassland.

This is a fantastic birding site, and we enjoyed our stop there thoroughly. White-breasted Woodswallows were cuddling in a tree overhanging our picnic table. There were hundreds of Peaceful Doves and Rainbow Bee-eaters around. Torresian Crows were nesting at the picnic site. Other birds there included Lemon-bellied Flycatcher, Paperbark Flycatcher, Spangled Drongo, Arafura Fantail, Olive-backed Oriole and Green Oriole.

In the grassland, we observed Zitting Cisticola, Golden-headed Cisticola, Red-backed Fairy-wren, Double-barred Finch, Black-bellied Crimson Finch, Horsfield's Bronze-cuckoo and Tawny Grassbird. Spotter Harrier and Black-shouldered Kite were hunting over the grass.

Brahminy Kite

Mangroves along the river produced Collared Kingfisher, Azure Kingfisher, Australian Yellow White-eye, Red-headed Honeyeater, Shining Flycatcher, Broad-billed Flycatcher and Brahminy Kite. On the mudflats were two Common Sandpipers and a single Nankeen Night-Heron. We also flushed Black Bittern from a tree near the boat ramp. In summer, check the pillars under the bridge – their shelves are used by the waders such Common Sandpipers, Grey-tailed Tattlers and Lesser Sand Plovers for roosting at high tide.

Spotlighting can be rewarding here, especially around the carpark. There is an abundance of Barn Owls, often seen hunting over the grassland and adjacent floodplains. Other nocturnal birds include Barking Owl, Southern Boobook, Tawny Frogmouth and Bush Stone-curlew.

A culvert is located 500m west of the bridge. A wetland stretches on both sides of the road. GPS coordinates there are 12°39'52"S and 132°29'25"E. During our visit in June 2022, we observed a large flock of Magpie Geese and a variety of waders, mostly Pied Stilts but also Black-fronted Dotterels, Red-kneed Dotterels, Marsh Sandpipers, Australian Pratincoles and Common Greenshanks. A flock of 50 Glossy Ibises was feeding at the edge of the mudflats among Pied Herons. There were also a couple of Brolgas, Black-necked Storks and skulking Buff-banded Rails. In the scrubby vegetation nearby, we spotted Green-backed Gerygone, Broad-billed Flycatcher, Black-bellied Crimson Finch and Tawny Grassbird. Pheasant Coucal was hooting from a tree. At the end of summer, this site is often used by White-winged Black Terns that are getting ready to fly north for the winter. Swinhoe's Snipe and Oriental Plover are recorded here from time to time.

Mamukala Wetlands

This is an iconic, very popular tourist site, located on Arnhem Hwy (36) 7km east of the South Alligator River bridge. The turnoff to a short, sealed driveway to a spacious carpark is very well signposted.

At the end of a short walk, you'll find a large bird hide and a viewing platform overlooking a great expanse of flowering lotus lilies. The bird hide is most productive at high water levels, so in the Wet. However, we were there in the Dry and only saw plenty of Comb-crested Jacanas, Purple Swamphens and Green Pygmy-geese. Numerous Forest Kingfishers, Paperbark Flycatchers, White-bellied Cuckoo-shrikes and Black-faced Cuckoo-shrikes were perching on the lotus flower stems sticking out of the water. Australasian Darter was perched on the platform railings. A White-browed Crake was foraging under the bird hide floor. Australian Reed-Warblers, Tawny Grassbirds and Golden-headed Cisticolas were calling from the reeds and rushes at the edge of the swamp.

In the freshly-burnt area near the carpark, we observed a mixed flock of Peaceful Doves, Diamond Doves, Long-tailed Finches and several juvenile Gouldian Finches. A Silver-backed Butcherbird was calling. A short walk to the hide was very productive, with plenty of Lemon-bellied Flycatchers accompanying us on the way. There were also Rufous-banded Honeyeaters, White-winged Trillers, Rufous Whistlers, Brush Cuckoos and Red-winged Parrots. A couple of Partridge Pigeons walked along the access road while several raptors, including a pair of Black-breasted Buzzards, were flying overheard.

Lemon-bellied Flycatcher

Take a 3km circular walk along the edge of the billabong to really see the waterbirds. This is a great birding spot, particularly in the late Dry (Aug-Oct) when thousands of Wandering Whistling-Ducks, Plumed Whistling-Ducks, Radjah Shelducks, Magpie Geese, Great Egrets, Plumed Egrets, Pied Herons, Glossy Ibises, Whiskered Terns and Australian Gull-billed Terns descend on the area. They congregate mostly in the shallows of the southern section of the wetland which can only be reached on foot via an Aboriginal hunting track (often waterlogged and impassable, so not recommended here). Smaller numbers can be observed from the circular walk, so look for suitable vantage points.

Waders appear in large numbers at Mamukala at the end of the Dry, usually late September and October. Pied Stilts form large breeding colonies on the 'islands' emerging from the disappearing water. Red-kneed Dotterels also breed in good numbers here. Migratory waders recorded regularly in the area include Marsh Sandpiper, Sharp-tailed Sandpiper, Wood Sandpiper, Common Sandpiper, Common Greenshank and Black-tailed Godwit. At the end of November, Little Curlews, Oriental Plovers and flocks of Oriental Pratincoles appear in the southern part of the wetland, to feed in the short grasses.

Search the muddy edges of the wetland for Eastern Yellow Wagtail, a regular summer visitor. In April 2023, a single White Wagtail was sighted there.

In taller grasses and tussock grass, look for Long-tailed Finch, Masked Finch, Black-bellied Crimson Finch and Double-barred Finch. Red-chested Button-quail is occasionally found in dense grass along the circular walk.

Nocturnal birds at Mamukala include Bush Stone-curlew, Barking Owl, Spotted Nightjar and Large-tailed Nightjar.

Ubirr and Surrounds

This section of the National Park is located on the Park's eastern border about 45km northeast of Jabiru along East Alligator River. The landscape here includes sandstone islets and stacks, and stunning rock formations with natural rock shelters adorned with ancient Aboriginal rock paintings. This area is reached via a sealed road. To get there, just before the turnoff to Jabiru turn north into Arnhem Hwy-Oenpelli Rd and drive to the river.

Key species are Chestnut quilled Rock-Pigeon, Black-banded Fruit-Dove, Sandstone Shrike-thrush, Gouldian Finch and Peregrine Falcon. Other birds of interest include Partridge Pigeon, Helmeted Friarbird, Little Woodswallow, White-breasted Woodswallow, Rainbow Pitta, Grey-crowned Babbler, Brush Cuckoo, Large-billed Gerygone, Long-tailed Finch, Pacific Baza and Black-breasted Buzzard. Rarities include Great-billed Heron, Little Kingfisher, White-lined Honeyeater and Common Cicadabird.

Merl Camping Ground

This spacious, shaded camp is an ideal base for the exploration of the Ubirr area, famous for its picturesque sunrises and sunsets. To get there, from Arnhem Hwy-Oenpelli Rd turn north into the campground as signposted, about 1km before the turnoff to Ubirr Art Site. Approximate GPS coordinates for this site are 12°25'36''S and 132°57'17''E. Facilities include hot showers, toilets, barbecues and picnic tables. A short walk to Cahill's Crossing starts here.

The campground is a good place for Partridge Pigeon (we spotted five of them). Other birds we found there included Forest Kingfisher, Green Oriole, Orange-footed Scrubfowl, Spangled Drongo, Silver-crowned Friarbird, Rufous-banded Honeyeater, Red-winged Parrot, Green-backed Gerygone and Pacific Baza.

Forest Kingfisher

Chestnut-backed Button-quail have been recorded along the walking trail to the Cahill's Crossing.

Try spotlighting in the campground. Bush Stone-curlews are common. Barn Owls, Barking Owls and Tawny Frogmouths often roost in the camp. The rare Masked Owls have also been reported.

Bardedjilidji Sandstone Walk

The walk starts at the upstream East Alligator River's carpark, the first one on the Bardedjilidji Rd. This 2.5km circular path wanders through many habitats including sandstone formations, grassland, pandanus thicket, monsoon forest, tropical woodland and the wetlands along East Alligator River. When you walk close to the river, watch for the crocodiles and wild pigs.

Along the first 1km, search for Chestnut-quilled Rock-Pigeons and Sandstone Shrike-thrushes roosting on the sandstone cliffs. Peregrine Falcons are sometimes seen flying along the cliffs. Check the recently burnt area for finches. Gouldian Finches are often found here in mixed flocks with Long-tailed Finches and Masked Finches.

In the monsoon forest, Black-banded Fruit-Doves may be quietly feeding in rock fig trees.

Other birds on the walk include Channel-billed Cuckoo, Oriental Dollarbird, Leaden Flycatcher, Shining Flycatcher, Dusky Honeyeater, Little Woodswallow and Rose-crowned Fruit-Dove.

Spotted Nightjars are common in the Dry, often flushed while roosting on the ground.

Cahills Crossing

Cahills Crossing at low tide

The notorious crossing on the East Alligator River has a mysterious draw on anglers, making them fish from the causeway. They do that under a watchful eye of saltwater crocodiles on both sides of the crossing. To our knowledge, in the last 20 years there were two fatalities and many near-misses. An elevated viewing platform on the western side of the river allows to observe natural behaviour of both species in the wild.

Arnhem Land's visitors and residents can traverse the river in 4WD vehicles. Some, however, attempt to do the same in 2WD cars, even at high tide. Therefore, several car wrecks are scattered near the causeway. Anyway, to get to the other side, you'll need a permit as it is Aboriginal land.

The best time to be on the platform is at the spring tide between August and October, when you can observe numerous crocodiles that line up to lay in wait for the mullet migrating upstream, as fish going over the causeway swim straight into their mouths. At the same time, fish-eating birds congregate on the riverbanks for an easy hunt. These include Nankeen Night-Herons, Pied Herons, Striated Herons, Great Egrets, Little Egrets, Black-necked Storks and cormorants.

Also on the western side of the river, a walking trail runs north through the monsoon forest. Look there for Rainbow Pitta, Arafura Fantail, Brown-capped Emerald-Dove, Shining Flycatcher, Rose-crowned Fruit-Dove, White-quilled Honeyeater and Rufous Whistler. Occasionally, Great-billed Heron lands near the Cahills Crossing. Other rare birds here include Black Bittern and Buff-banded Rail.

Manngarre Rainforest Walk

This 1.5km circular walk runs mostly through the monsoon forest, with glimpses of East Alligator River. At the northern end of the path is a raised observation platform built around a large banyan fig tree and above a large boulder. Access is from the carpark opposite the Border Store (signposted).

It is a good place to look for Rainbow Pitta. Other birds you may see on the walk include Mangrove Golden Whistler, Arafura Fantail, Orange-footed Scrubfowl, Azure Kingfisher, Green Oriole, Shining Flycatcher, Dusky Honeyeater, White-throated Honeyeater and Bar-breasted Honeyeater.

Australian Hobbies are often found roosting in dead trees near the Border Store. Other raptors in the area include Pacific Baza, Grey Goshawk, Brown Goshawk and Black-breasted Buzzard.

Ubirr

To get there, from Arnhem Hwy-Oenpelli Rd 40km from Jabiru, turn north into Ubirr Rd and drive to a carpark near the Rock Art Site, passing the Border Store on your way. The whole area is well signposted.

Take a 1km circular walk that skirts the base of the sandstone outliers. On your way, you will pass several exceptional Aboriginal Art rock galleries. A short but steep, 500m return climb from the base leads to Nadab Lookout. It offers an outstanding panoramic view of the floodplain below. It featured in the movie Crocodile Dundee. The Ubirr site facilities include toilets and sheltered benches.

Ubirr landscape

Ubirr is a good place to look for the escarpment specialists such as Sandstone Shrike-thrush and Chestnut-quilled Rock-Pigeon. Black-banded Fruit-Doves and White-lined Honeyeaters are also present but are much rarer.

As we arrived, Partridge Pigeon welcomed us in the carpark. On the walk, we got Red-backed Kingfisher, Sacred Kingfisher, Rainbow Bee-eater (plentiful there), Paperbark Flycatcher, White-gaped Honeyeater, Helmeted Friarbird and White-bellied Cuckoo-shrike. Sandstone Shrike-thrush was calling loudly from the rock. Little Woodswallows were flying along the rockface. A flock of finches including Gouldian Finches was feeding on the track leading to the carpark.

From the lookout, you may see waterbirds on the floodplains such as Magpie Geese, Great Egrets, Plumed Egrets and Black-necked Storks. Raptors in attendance may include Black-breasted Buzzard, Brown Goshawk, Brown Falcon, Wedge-tailed Eagle and Peregrine Falcon.

Jabiru Area

Jabiru is a small former mining town, situated in the heart of Kakadu National Park. It provides all services you are likely to need during your travel and is a perfect base to explore the Park. In the town and its surrounds there are several places worth visiting. Keep checking the sky for the raptors and at night go for spotlighting. Nearly all nocturnal birds can be found here.

Key species are Partridge Pigeon, Oriental Cuckoo, Red-backed Button-quail, Bar-breasted Honeyeater, Black-tailed Treecreeper and Black-breasted Buzzard. Other birds of interest include Brown Quail, Common Sandpiper, Azure Kingfisher, Hardhead, Channel-billed Cuckoo, Red-tailed Black-Cockatoo, Northern Rosella, Little Corella, Paperbark Flycatcher and Bush Stone-curlew. Among the rarities are Red Goshawk, Great-billed Heron, Great Crested Grebe, Swinhoe's Snipe, Australian Wood Duck, Little Kingfisher, Gouldian Finch, Welcome Swallow and Zitting Cisticola.

Jabiru Airport

The airport is located on Arnhem Hwy-Oenpelli Rd, 5km west of the junction of Arnhem Hwy (36) and Kakadu Hwy (21). Flights over the escarpment go from there.

Brown Falcon

The place is known for Partridge Pigeons; they are resident in the grass outside the terminal building. We saw three birds near the airport fence. Other birds in the area include Straw-necked Ibis, Rainbow Bee-eater, White-quilled Honeyeater, Little Corella, Australian Hobby, Brown Goshawk and Brown Falcon.

Jabiru WTP

To get there, take Whites Rd from Arnhem Hwy (36) near the turnoff to Jabiru Dr. After 300m turn right into Elsherana Rd and drive to the ponds (opposite the rubbish tip). GPS coordinates for this site are 12°39'34"S and 132°51'11"E.

Partridge Pigeons are often seen around the ponds and at the rubbish tip's fences. In early summer, large numbers of Green Pygmy-geese congregate on the ponds. Other warbirds seen in large numbers are Hardhead, Pink-eared Duck and Australasian Grebe. Look also for Hoary-headed Grebe, Glossy Ibis and White-necked Heron. Waders here include Oriental Plover, Common Sandpiper, Black-fronted Dotterel and Red-kneed Dotterel.

Other birds in the area include Brown Quail, Paperbark Flycatcher, White-winged Triller and Red-backed Kingfisher. Raptors are usually plentiful, especially Black Kites and Whistling Kites, often roosting in good numbers near the ponds.

Jabiru Lake

This man-made, now neglected reservoir stretches along Civic Dr, with multiple access points to the water. A 2.5km loop trail runs around the lake. Look here for Green Pygmy-goose, Hardhead, Radjah Shelduck, Glossy Ibis and Nankeen Night-Heron. The lake is not crock-free so be careful near the water.

Partridge Pigeons are often found around the lake, particularly in the parkland area. When the lake is drying up, White-browed Crakes and waders appear on the muddy shores. Look for Common Sandpiper, Sharp-tailed Sandpiper, Black-fronted Dotterel and Australian Pratincole. Swinhoe's Snipes were recorded a few times.

In the wetland vegetation around the open water, you should get Australian Reed-Warbler, Tawny Grassbird and Golden-headed Cisticola. A large flock of Little Corellas is always present on the lawns of the picnic areas. In March-April, good numbers of Channel-billed Cuckoos feed in trees around the lake. In summer, Oriental Cuckoos are regularly recorded.

Among many rarities showing up in the area are Red Goshawk, Great-billed Heron, Gouldian Finch, Black Bittern, Great Crested Grebe and Dusky Moorhen.

Aurora Kakadu Lodge and Caravan Park

This large facility is called in short Kakadu Lodge. It is located in Jabiru Dr opposite the Anbinik Kakadu Resort. It offers lodge accommodation, safari tents, cabins and a spacious caravan park with a swimming pool and a restaurant. Sprinklers are working daily on site, so birds come in droves for a drink and a bath. We spent a week there in winter 2022 when controlled burn was conducted outside the property fences. A lot of birds kept to the caravan park where vegetation was untouched, while others liked foraging in the burnt areas. Birding was excellent.

The star attraction was Partridge Pigeon. We counted up to 18 birds feeding just outside the fence, on the ground still smouldering at places. Each evening, a 1,000-strong flock of Little Corellas was descending onto the caravan park, perhaps just to seek refuge from the fires. To the contrary, Red-tailed Black-Cockatoos and Red-winged Parrots were following the fire lines everywhere in the Park, to forage on the roasted insects and seeds.

Partridge Pigeons feeding in the fresh prescribed burn area

The most visible in the caravan park were Grey-crowned Babblers and Great Bowerbirds that were ignoring the crowds of travellers and their mobile homes. The sprinklers were repeatedly visited by Long-tailed Finches, Masked Finches, Black-bellied Crimson Finches, White-quilled Honeyeaters, White-gaped Honeyeaters, White-throated Honeyeaters, Rufous-throated Honeyeaters, Green Orioles, Northern Rosellas and Grey shrike-thrushes. Other birds on the grounds included

Orange-footed Scrubfowl, Varied Triller, Paperbark Flycatcher, White-throated Gerygone, Brown Goshawk and Mistletoebird. At night, Barking Owls were duetting, alternating with the cries of Bush Stone-curlews.

Bowali Visitor Centre

The Centre is situated on Kakadu Hwy (21) about 2.5km south of its intersection with Arnhem Hwy (36). This large facility offers information on the local Aboriginal history and on the Park's geology, wildlife and flora.

Look for Partridge Pigeons on the grounds; we saw one behind the building. Tawny Frogmouths and Barking Owls were roosting in the trees. A pair of Bush Stone-curlews were napping near the logs supporting the path to the Centre. Plenty of Orange-footed Scrubfowls and Grey-crowned Babblers were working the grounds. We also found Olive-backed Oriole, Brown-capped Emerald-Dove, White-gaped Honeyeater, Dusky Honeyeater, Brush Cuckoo and Northen Fantail.

A 1km walk connects Bowali Centre with the southern end of Jabiru Dr in town. Red-backed Button-quails have been many times recorded along this track. Look also for Weebill, Channel-billed Cuckoo, Horsfield's Bronze-cuckoo, Eastern Koel, Green Oriole, Sacred Kingfisher and Australian Owlet-nightjar.

Malabanjbanjdju Campground

This spacious, well-shaded campground is for those who wish to experience that remote Outback camp feeling while still staying close to the action (Jabiru, Yellow Waters). It is located on Kakadu Hwy (21) about 13km south of Jabiru. Site facilities include fire rings, toilets and picnic tables.

Our visit in winter of 2022 was very productive, particularly among the freshly burnt grasses and bushes. At the entrance to the site, hundreds of Peaceful Doves, Diamond Doves and Bar-shouldered Doves were feeding among the ashes. Together with them were three Partridge Pigeons. Further down along the access track, we encountered a mixed flock of Masked, Long-tailed and Double-barred Finches with a few Gouldian Finches and White-winged Trillers among them. Little Woodswallows and Rainbow Bee-eaters were landing on the ground, picking up roasted morsels. A flock of Red-tailed Black-Cockatoos had two Hooded Parrots with them. Black Kites and Whistling Kites were catching prey at the verge of smouldering residual fires.

We stopped by a delightful, serene billabong at the end of the road, with wallabies grazing on the shores, some carrying a Wille Wagtail on their backs. Cattle Egrets were alongside them, treating them like cattle. A large crock on the bank was smiling wide with his mouth open. Just in front of us, a pair of Wandering Whistling-

Ducks was busy feeding and watching over their enormous family of 17 half-grown ducklings. The parents were constantly watchful front and back. When one of the parents dipped its head in the water to feed, the other was always on alert.

A large family of Wandering Whistling-Ducks on the billabong

The billabong also yielded Black-necked Stork, successfully extracting one slimy fish after another from the mud, Nankeen Night-Herons, White-necked Herons, Great Egrets, Plumed Egrets, Green Pygmy-geese and plenty of Comb-crested Jacanas with chicks. A large, screeching flock of Litte Corellas suddenly descended on the billabong, disturbing the peace.

In the bush by the billabong, we found Paperbark Flycatcher, Lemon-bellied Flycatcher, Shining Flycatcher, Pheasant Coucal, Azure Kingfisher, Bar-breasted Honeyeater and Green-backed Gerygone.

Other birds reported from this site include Black-tailed Treecreeper, Oriental Dollarbird and Black-breasted Buzzard.

Burdulba Billabong

The campsite situated at the Burdulba Billabong is located just 1km south of the southern entrance to the Malabanjbanjdju Campground described above. GPS coordinates for the turnoff are 12°46’32’’S and 132°45’22’’E. The camp area is about 1.5km from the highway.

Red Goshawk is sporadically reported from this site. Black Bitterns and Nankeen Night-Herons are regularly flushed from the vegetation surrounding the billabong.

In the surrounding woodland, you may get Forest Kingfisher, Red-backed Kingfisher, Sacred Kingfisher, Little Shrike-thrush, Brown Whistler, Little Woodswallow, Bar-breasted Honeyeater, Rufous-banded Honeyeater and Shining Flycatcher. Nocturnal birds in the campground include Spotted Nightjar, Australian Owlet-nightjar, Tawny Frogmouth and Bush Stone-curlew.

Nourlangie Area

An extensive sandstone escarpment with pockets of monsoon forest and one of most spectacular Aboriginal rock art galleries await you here. To get there, turn south off Kakadu Hwy (21) 19km southwest of the Bowali Visitor Centre (well signposted). Follow the sealed Nourlangie Rd to different birding spots.

Key species are White-lined Honeyeater, Black-banded Fruit-Dove, Chestnut-quilled Rock-Pigeon, Sandstone Shrike-thrush and Peregrine Falcon. Other birds of interest include Partridge Pigeon, Black-tailed Treecreeper, Brown-capped Emerald-Dove, Helmeted Friarbird, Little Woodswallow, Lemon-bellied Flycatcher, Channel-billed Cuckoo and Silver-backed Butcherbird. Among the rarities are Hooded Parrot, Gouldian Finch, Black-eared Cuckoo, Emu, Little Ringed Plover, Pectoral Sandpiper, Yellow-tinted Honeyeater, Fork-tailed Swift, Masked Owl and Rufous Owl.

Gubarra Walk

This 6km return walk runs through the wetlands (Gubarra Pools), open woodland and monsoon forest to the escarpment. The rocky Gubarra Pools provide refuge for fish when the floodplains dry out.

To get there, drive on Nourlangie Rd for 6km, then turn left into an unsealed, poorly maintained track at GPS coordinates of 12°49’34’’S and 132°47’56’’E. Drive 8.5km, passing an airstrip, then driving along its northern edge, then continuing until you’ll get to the carparks on the left at 12°50’31’’S and 132°51’31’’E. Your walk starts here.

Partridge Pigeons can be found on the vehicular access track. Look also for Black-tailed Treecreepers in the woodland along the road. You may also come across Brown Quail, Red-backed Button-quail, Bush Stone-curlew and Black-faced Woodswallow. In the carpark area, Hooded Plovers are recorded from time to time.

Gubarra Walk, leading to the escarpment, is good for Chestnut-quilled Rock-Pigeon, Helmeted Friarbird, Northern Rosella, Red-backed Kingfisher, Lemon-bellied Flycatcher and Weebill. In the monsoon forest close to the escarpment, look for Black-banded Fruit-Dove in the rock figs in the gorge. Also, White-lined Honeyeaters may be feeding near the escarpment. Other birds in the monsoon forest include Rainbow Pitta, Little Shrike-thrush, Shining Flycatcher, Green-backed Gerygone, Common Cicadabird and Buff-sided Robin. Check the escarpment cliffs for Sandstone Shrike-thrush, Little Woodswallow and Peregrine Falcon.

In the area around Gubarra Pools look for Black Bittern and Nankeen Night-Heron. Black-bellied Crimson Finches and Long-tailed Finches come here for a drink.

Nawurlandja Lookout

To get there, drive 10.5km on Nourlangie Rd and then turn into a short access road signposted to the Nawurlandja Lookout. A 600m return walk leads from the carpark to the lookout. Sandstone Shrike-thrushes are perhaps easier to find there than at their main site of Nourlangie Rock. This is also arguably the best place to watch the sun risings and setting over the Nourlangie Rock.

Look also for Black-banded Fruit-Doves, mostly in winter when rock fig trees are fruiting. Small flocks fly over here from the Nourlangie Rock. Rocky areas are also a great spot for Chestnut-quilled Rock-Pigeon. Chestnut-backed Button-quails and Red-backed Button-quails are sighted at times along the access road. Black-tailed Treecreeper, Rainbow Bee-eater, Orange-footed Scrubfowl, Brush Cuckoo, Lemon-bellied Flycatcher, Helmeted Friarbird, Silver-backed Butcherbird, Grey Goshawk and Brown Falcon can be found along the access road and at the rock base.

Anbangbang Billabong

Less than 1km from the Nourlangie Rock carpark, turn into Anbangbang Billabong Tk (sealed) and drive 1.5km to an expansive picnic site along the billabong equipped with picnic tables. There are plenty parking spaces here and a 2.5km circular walk around the billabong. The walk offers spectacular views of Nourlangie Rock and the escarpment, featured in the Crocodile Dundee movie.

There is an abundance of waterbirds and other wildlife. Wallabies and wallaroos graze at the water edge in the morning and at dusk. Occasionally, Emu dads with chicks walk across the plain. A large camp of little red flying-foxes is established nearby. Salties can be lurking in the shallow water.

In the early Wet, various waders are using the exposed muds including Sharp-tailed Sandpiper, Marsh Sandpiper, Wood Sandpiper, Common Sandpiper, Pied Stilt,

Black-fronted Dotterel and Red-kneed Dotterel. Several rarities have been recorded here including Little Ringed Plover, Little Curlew and Pectoral Sandpiper.

Waterbird numbers can reach giant proportions here, mostly Magpie Geese, Green Pygmy-geese, Wandering Whistling-Ducks and Plumed Whistling-Ducks. Herons, egrets, spoonbills and ibises are dotted around the shallow billabong. A Black-necked Stork or two are nearly always there, adding to the beauty and serenity of the landscape.

In the surrounding woodland, you may find Shining Flycatcher, Azure Kingfisher, Paperbark Flycatcher, Lemon-bellied Flycatcher, Bar-breasted Honeyeater, Rufous-banded Honeyeater, Northern Rosella and Brown Goshawk. Along the access road, look for Partridge Pigeon, Pheasant Coucal and Brown Quail.

Nourlangie Rock

Gunwarddehwarde Lookout at Nourlangie Rock

Nourlangie Rock is one of the best places in the Park to search for three of the NT endemic birds: White-lined Honeyeater, Black-banded Fruit-Dove and Chestnut-quilled Rock-Pigeon. To get there, from Kakadu Hwy (21) take Nourlangie Rd and drive 13km on a good sealed road to the carpark. From there, a 1.5km circular walk leads through the monsoon forest and woodland to rock art galleries.

While driving along Nourlangie Rd, be on the lookout for Partridge Pigeons; they often roost at the edge of the road. Scan the sky for raptors, searching for Black-breasted Buzzard, Black Falcon and Brown Goshawk. Bushland along the road may yield Varied Lorikeet, Forest Kingfisher, Dusky Honeyeater, Silver-crowned Friarbird, Grey-crowned Babbler and Rufous Whistler.

Silver-crowned Friarbird in a flowering tree

Along the circuit walk, look for the escarpment endemics. This site gets very busy with tourists, so for the best result come early, before the buses start to arrive.

White-lined Honeyeaters are found at the base of Nourlangie Rock, near the painting galleries. We saw one, hanging from a flowering tree between the rocks and calling.

For Black-banded Fruit-Doves, check the fruiting rock figs and native nutmeg trees. We observed a couple of birds gorging on the fruit of a completely leafless fig tree, allowing unobstructed views. That was in the gully near the Gunwarddehwarde Lookout. Look for them also behind the main rock shelter at the lower gallery.

In the monsoon forest, you may come across Rainbow Pitta, Eastern Koel, Brown-capped Emerald-Dove, Channel-billed Cuckoo, Great Bowerbird, Northern Fantail, Helmeted Friarbird and Shining Flycatcher.

When we walked in the dry woodland, we encountered hundreds of very noisy Silver-crowned Friarbirds feeding in brightly-coloured flowering trees. We also ticked off Olive-backed Oriole, Varied Triller, Rainbow Bee-eater, Brown Honeyeater and White-gaped Honeyeater.

A short climb to the Gunwarddehwarde Lookout rewarded us with the calls of Sandstone Shrike-thrushes, singing loudly from the rock ledges. Chestnut-quilled Rock-Pigeon flew onto a cliff ledge. Red-tailed Black-Cockatoos landed in a woollybutt tree where Varied Lorikeets and Red-collared Lorikeets were already feeding on its blossom. The endemic black wallaroos were moving among the rocks.

Bubba Wetlands

To get there, from Kakadu Hwy (21) 26km south of the Bowali Visitor Centre turn south into a sealed road to Muirella Park (now called Djarradjin Campground). Drive 6km to the carpark. A 4km circular Bubba Walk runs around the wetlands through the paperbark forest, open woodland and freshwater mangroves. GPS coordinates at the trailhead are 12°51’11”S and 132°45’01”E.

The wetlands are known for the largest congregations of Green Pygmy-geese in the Park. Other noteworthy waterbirds here include Azure Kingfisher, Glossy Ibis, Brolga, Royal Spoonbill, Nankeen Night-Heron and Great-billed Heron (rare). This is also a regular site for Black Bittern.

Glossy Ibises

Bubba Walk may produce Paperbark Flycatcher, Shining Flycatcher, White-winged Triller, Arafura Fantail, Northern Fantail, Rufous-throated Honeyeater, Little Woodswallow, Little Friarbird and Silver-backed Butcherbird.

In the spacious campground, look for Partridge Pigeons. Little Woodswallows are regularly observed flying overhead. Emu was seen several times. Other birds here include Varied Lorikeet, Sacred Kingfisher, Forest Kingfisher, Great Bowerbird, Brown Whistler, Little Shrike-thrush and Lemon-bellied Flycatcher.

The selection of nocturnal birds in the Muirella Campground includes the rare Rufous Owls which are recorded from time to time. Masked Owl was reported in 2021. More common night birds include Spotted Nightjar, Large-tailed Nightjar, Barking Owl (very vocal), Australian Owlet-nightjar and Bush Stone-curlew.

Raptors in the area include White-bellied Sea-Eagle, Grey Goshawk and Black-breasted Buzzard.

Mirrai Lookout

To get there, 30km south of the Bowali Visitor Centre turn south from Kakadu Hwy (21) and drive 200m on a sealed road to the carpark. A 1.8km return walk leads to a viewing platform. The climb to the lookout is very steep but the views of the plateau and escarpment are worth it.

In the bushland near the carpark, search for Black-tailed Treecreeper as well as Rufous Whistler, Red-winged Parrot, Australian Owlet-nightjar and Grey Shrike-thrush. On the walk to the summit, you'll have a good chance to spot White-lined Honeyeater or Black-banded Fruit-Dove. Other birds on the walk include Northern Fantail, Weebill, Little Shrike-thrush, Leaden Flycatcher, Shining Flycatcher and Varied Lorikeet.

Yellow Waters Section

This section includes Yellow Waters, Cooinda Lodge, Mardugal, Gungurul and Barramundi Billabong.

Yellow Waters is a series of billabongs surrounded by floodplains and extensive woodland. It is situated in the centre of the National Park at the confluence of Jim Jim Creek and South Alligator River. A Yellow Waters boat cruise is a must when visiting the Kakadu. It will give you an unmissable opportunity to photograph masses of waterbirds and saltwater crocodiles in the beautiful setting of lush wetland vegetation with fields of flowering waterlilies and lotus lilies. Best for the birders are the morning cruises.

Key species are Great-billed Heron, Little Kingfisher, Azure Kingfisher, Black Bittern, Gouldian Finch and Red Goshawk. Other birds of interest include waterbirds, Partridge Pigeon, Buff-sided Robin, Bar-breasted Honeyeater, Banded Honeyeater, Channel-billed Cuckoo, Rainbow Pitta, Silver-backed Butcherbird, Barking Owl, White-bellied Sea-Eagle and Black-breasted Buzzard. Rarities include Sarus Crane, Australian Painted-Snipe, Pale-vented Bush-hen, Dusky Moorhen, Hooded Parrot, Rufous Owl, Masked Owl, Square-tailed Kite and Black Falcon.

Yellow Waters

The turnoff to Cooinda Rd that leads to Yellow Waters and Cooinda Lodge is off Kakadu Hwy (21) 50km south of Jabiru and 160km north of Pine Creek. To get to Yellow Waters, drive along Cooinda Rd, pass the turnoff to the Warradjan Aboriginal Centre, then turn right into Yellow Waters Rd and drive to the large carparks at the jetty. All cruises start here. A 500m boardwalk meanders past the jetty, skirting the billabong. A walking trail runs from here to the Cooinda campground.

Yellow Waters: tour boat view

Most of the tourist interest on the cruises focuses on the crocodiles but birders will find these cruises also worthwhile due to the massive numbers of waterbirds on the billabongs. During our latest trip to the Kakadu (June 2022), we took the first cruise out in the morning. Barking Owls were still calling in the forest. Little Kingfisher was perching on the railings of the jetty. We spotted a pair of Azure Kingfishers on the moored boats. The faithful Van Gough, an old crocodile that years ago lost one ear, was lurking in the water, silently watching the boarding tourists. We were wondering whether he was posing for photos or drooling.

We spotted nearly all Australian heron and egret species on the cruise. Plumed Egrets and Pied Herons were everywhere and in large numbers. Black Bittern was flushed from vegetation by the boat movement while Great-billed Heron flew low across one of the forks of the billabong, allowing just a fleeting glimpse of it. Huge flocks of Plumed Whistling-Ducks were piled up on the muds of the mangroves, mixed with smaller numbers of Wandering Whistling-Ducks, Radjah Shelducks, Pink-eared Ducks, Glossy Ibises, Royal Spoonbills, Australasian Darters, Little Black Cormorants and Little Pied Cormorants. There was also a single Great Cormorant. Flocks of Green Pygmy-geese were foraging among the waterlilies, and Comb-crested Jacanas were walking on the lily pads with their chicks. Black-necked Storks waded in the shallows, picking up eels from the flooded grass. Three Brolgas were dancing in the morning sun.

Water buffalos were wallowing in the mud, accompanied by a large, noisy flock of Masked Lapwings. At the water edge were numerous Pied Stilts and a few Marsh Sandpipers, Wood Sandpipers, Common Sandpipers and Black-fronted Dotterels. Rainbow Bee-eaters were hawking insects while a Channel-billed Cuckoo was being chased by an angry mob of White-quilled Honeyeaters. In the vegetation lining the water channels, we spotted Paperbark Flycatcher, Shining Flycatcher (very common here), Bar-breasted Honeyeater, Brown Honeyeater and Horsfield's Bronze-cuckoo.

Several raptors were spotted during the cruise. The most impressive were White-bellied Sea-Eagles but we also got Whistling Kite, Black Kite, Brown Goshawk and Australian Hobby. A pair of Barking Owls were roosting in a large paperbark tree. Our tour guide pointed them out to us and said it was their favourite spot.

Female Pheasant Coucal at the Yellow Waters boardwalk

After the cruise, we took another stroll along the boardwalk and got White-browed Crake and Buff-banded Rail just at the start. Pheasant Coucal was sitting on the railing at the other end of the boardwalk and reluctantly moved to a bush when we approached. A juvenile Nankeen Night-Heron was struggling in the water, flapping its wings, in danger of being picked up by a crocodile resting nearby. It must not have been hungry though, so the bird managed to crawl out onto the dry land. We checked the next day – the young heron was still in the area, alive.

Several consecutive visits to the boardwalk yielded Horsfield's Bronze-cuckoo, Shining Flycatcher, Australian Reed-Warbler, Tawny Grassbird, Golden-headed Cisticola and Brown Quail.

In the forest surrounding the carpark, we found Rainbow Pitta, Lemon-bellied Flycatcher, Leaden Flycatcher, Bush Stone-curlew, Barking Owl, Pacific Baza and Grey Goshawk.

Cooinda Lodge

This village-style property, also called Gagudju Lodge, is situated near Yellow Waters. It offers a wide variety of accommodation including a spacious campground with two large swimming pools, and has a fuel station, store, bar and restaurant. The property is surrounded by the dense monsoon forest. To get there, drive for

4.5km along Cooinda Rd, passing the turnoffs to the Warradjan Aboriginal Centre and to Yellow Waters, to arrive at the Cooinda Lodge.

We camped nearly for a week in Cooinda, enjoying the abundance of birds in the area. Very loud Green Orioles live in trees around the campsite. We also saw Varied Trillers, White-winged Trillers, Olive-backed Orioles and numerous White-bellied Cuckoo-shrikes. A variety of nectar-feeders including Dusky Honeyeater, White-throated Honeyeater, Bar-breasted Honeyeater, Varied Lorikeet, Red-collared Lorikeet, Silver-crowned Friarbird and Yellow-throated Miner hanged around the flowering gum trees.

The camp edges are lined with very dense vegetation where plague-proportion mosquito numbers were breeding. If you could withstand their onslaught, you could find there Arafura Fantail, Northern Fantail, Shining Flycatcher, Paperbark Flycatcher, Lemon-bellied Flycatcher, Little Bronze-cuckoo and Weebill.

In the open-air restaurant, the cheeky White-quilled Honeyeaters, Red-collared Lorikeets and Great Bowerbirds were inspecting any vacated tables. In fact, even the presence of guests did not deter them to claim what they regarded their catch.

White-quilled Honeyeater

You can have good birding while soaking in the warm swimming pool. We were observing an active nest of Torresian Crow in a communication tower. A pair of Australian Hobbies were ferociously attacking the crows, attempting to dislodge the crows from the nest. By the time we left, they still hadn't succeeded. Other raptors, circling in the sky over the swimming pool, included Black Kite, Whistling Kite,

White-bellied Sea-Eagle, Black-breasted Buzzard and Collared Sparrowhawk (chased by White-quilled Honeyeaters).

Cooinda was excellent for nocturnal birds. Bush Stone-curlews and Barking Owls were calling every night. One evening, we flushed a Large-tailed Nightjar at the access road. More species were reported by other birders including the rare Masked Owl and Rufous Owl.

Adjacent to the Cooinda grounds is Home Billabong. You can find there a good selection of waterbirds including rarer species such as Buff-banded Rail, Red-kneed Dotterel, Yellow-billed Spoonbill and White-browed Crake. Azure Kingfishers are nearly always there. Bar-breasted Honeyeaters nest in trees near the water.

Warradjan Aboriginal Cultural Centre

The Centre is located in Cooinda Rd 3.5km from Kakadu Hwy (21) and 1km from the Cooinda Lodge. This is one of several Aboriginal centres in the National Park, featuring a range authentic handmade arts and crafts.

It may be worthwhile to stop here for a moment to look for Partridge Pigeons, often hanging out around the Centre. We also spotted a family of Bush Stone-curlews roosting at the Centre's doorstep. Other birds in the area include Arafura Fantail, Olive-backed Oriole, Great Bowerbird, Little Bronze-cuckoo, Varied Triller and Orange-footed Scrubfowl.

Mardugal

Mardugal, also called Mardukal, is located just south of Kakadu Hwy (21) 2km south of the turnoff to Yellow Waters. You'll find here two large camping grounds (No.1 and No.2) and a billabong. There are two walking tracks: the 2km Gun-gardun Walk is excellent for forest birds while a shorter Mardugal Billabong Walk with a boardwalk and a viewing platform is good for waterbirds. The abundant facilities include hot showers, toilets, barbecues and picnic tables.

On the billabong walk, there is a chance to spot Little Kingfisher. Azure Kingfishers are common. On the billabong, you are likely to see Green Pygmy-geese, Comb-crested Jacanas, Wandering Whistling-Ducks, Plumed Whistling-Ducks, Radjah Shelducks and Nankeen Night-Herons. Black-necked Storks and Glossy Ibises are the regulars here. Cattle Egrets may accompany the wallaroos that come to the water. You may also be lucky to sight Great-billed Heron or Black Bittern.

Cattle Egrets are often seen near the wallaroos

In the bush on the billabong walk, expect to see Green Oriole, Pheasant Coucal, Little Bronze-cuckoo, Broad-billed Flycatcher, Shining Flycatcher, Leaden Flycatcher, Paperbark Flycatcher, Bar-breasted Honeyeater and Rufous-throated Honeyeater.

The Gun-gardun walks starts at the caravan section of the Mardugal Camp 2 area. You'll walk mostly through the open woodland. The walk can be productive for Black-tailed Treecreeper - to find them, search the stringybark woodland. Keep an eye for Partridge Pigeons wandering on the forest floor. There is also a good chance to find Buff-sided Robin on this walk. Among common birds are Green Oriole, Rufous Whistler, Little Shrike-thrush, Northern Fantail, Arafura Fantail as well as Paperbark Flycatcher, Lemon-bellied Flycatcher, Shining Flycatcher, Leaden Flycatcher and Broad-billed Flycatcher. Other birds in the area include Common Cicadabird, Little Woodswallow, Dusky Honeyeater, Banded Honeyeater, Brush Cuckoo, Varied Triller and Sacred Kingfisher.

Mardugal is a good area for the nocturnal birds. Rufous Owls have been recorded here from time to time while Barking Owls, Bush Stone-curlews and Australian Owlet-nightjars are common.

Jim Jim Billabong

Please note that Jim Jim Billabong is located near Yellow Waters, not near the Jim Jim Falls. This stunning campground is used mostly as a fishing spot. To get there, 6km south of Cooinda turn off Kakadu Hwy (21) into Jim Jim Billabong Rd and drive about 5km on a dirt track. This road is often terrible; a 4WD is advisable. GPS coordinates at the turnoff are 12°57'34''S and 132°32'01''E.

Black-tailed Treecreepers are quite easy to find here. Search also for Grey-crowned Babbler, Little Woodswallow, Orange-footed Scrubfowl, Diamond Dove, Great Bowerbird, Spangled Drongo and Red-tailed Black-Cockatoo. A good selection of honeyeaters can be enjoyed, including Bar-breasted Honeyeater, Banded Honeyeater, White-quilled Honeyeater, Rufous-throated Honeyeater, Rufous-banded Honeyeater and Dusky Honeyeater.

Around the billabong, look for Little Kingfisher and Azure Kingfisher. A small flock of Hooded Parrots was spotted in the campsite in September 2022. Emus are visiting the camping grounds from time to time. Raptors in the area include Black-breasted Buzzard, White-bellied Sea-Eagle, Swamp Harrier, Black Kite and Whistling Kite.

Jim Jim Falls Area

The main feature of this section of the National Park are Jim Jim Falls and Twin Falls. Additionally, you'll find here beautiful gorges, plunge rock pools, cliff faces of the escarpment and a vast area of a plateau looking over the undulating plains below. Vegetation is mostly open woodland with pockets of monsoon forest in the gorges. The plateau is sparsely vegetated with small trees and shrubs and has the spinifex groundcover, dense at places.

To get there, 40km south of Bowali Information Centre turn south off Kakadu Hwy (21) into Jim Jim Falls Rd. Drive 60km to the Jim Jim Falls carpark or continue further on for 10km to the Twin Falls. Take note that Jim Jim Falls Rd is a difficult, 4WD only track, rough, corrugated, with section of deep sand, and basically a bone-shattering experience, requiring serious 4WD driving skills. Also, to get to the Twin Falls you'll need to traverse a deep water crossing. The whole route is open only in the dry season and even then it may be kept closed by the Park management. Commercial 4WD tours are an option, if the road is open, if you wish to visit this area.

The magnificent landscape of the Kakadu escarpment

Key species are White-throated Grasswren, Chestnut-quilled Rock-Pigeon, Sandstone Shrike-thrush, White-lined Honeyeater, Black-banded Fruit-Dove, Red-chested Button-quail, Red-backed Button-quail and Peregrine Falcon. Other birds of interest include Helmeted Friarbird, Purple-backed Fairy-wren (lavender-flanked ssp.), Partridge Pigeon, Little Woodswallow, Masked Woodswallow, Banded Honeyeater and Spotted Nightjar. Among the rarities are Grey Wagtail, Golden-backed Honeyeater, Yellow-tinted Honeyeater and Little Eagle.

The endemic White-throated Grasswren, is the star attraction of the falls area. This rare and elusive species can still be found here but you'll need to put in a lot of time and effort. The birds are usually found on the plateau just behind the Jim Jim Falls.

The quintessential White-throated Grasswren habitat consists of 50% of cover of rocks, 20% of old, unburnt spinifex, and 30% of low, sparse shrubs. The unburnt old spinifex is the most important component because if burnt too often, the birds would disappear from the site for a long time. For example, the Gunlom Falls area, where the birds used to be fairly common, was burnt so frequently, following the Aboriginal tradition, that the birds are gone from there. The two Jim Jim Falls sites are now the only places accessible to tourists. The stronghold of the species in the National Park remains the Arnhem Land plateau where there is no infrastructure to approach them.

Garnamarr Campground

The Garnamarr Campground is located 50km from the highway and 10km from the Jim Jim Falls carpark. Facilities include showers, toilets, fire rings, barbecues and picnic tables. Drinking water is available.

Partridge Pigeons are found here regularly. Bush Stone-curlews nest in the camp area. You may also come across Little Woodswallow, Great Bowerbird, Northern Rosella, White-lined Honeyeater and White-bellied Cuckoo-shrike.

Jim Jim Falls

A carpark is provided 1km from Jim Jim Falls. Two walks start from the carpark. The longer Barrkmalan Walk, 8km return, 6-8hrs to complete, is a challenging trail, climbing steeply to the escarpment and crossing the plateau to the top of the Jim Jim Falls. On the way up, you go through several patches of monsoon forest and open woodland. Up on the plateau, the trail runs over a large area of sandstone pavement with area of sparse old spinifex and shrubs. This is the place to look for the White-throated Grasswren. Many birders climb this track before dawn to make a good start in the early morning for their search.

The shorter, 1km return Jim Jim Plunge Pool Walk, branches off the longer track not far from the carpark. It runs through the monsoon forest, following the northern side of Jim Jim Creek beneath the escarpment, to end at the plunge pool at the base of a 200m one-drop waterfall, surrounded by 150m high cliffs. In the dry season, the waterfall stops flowing.

Along the short walk, search for White-lined Honeyeater, Black-banded Fruit-Dove, Rainbow Bee-eater, Little Shrike-thrush, Common Cicadabird, Spangled Drongo and Pacific Baza. Near the pool, you can occasionally encounter Nankeen Night-Heron, White-faced Heron, Black Bittern or Australasian Darter. In 2015, Grey Wagtail was recorded at the water edge. Finches come to drink from the pool, with Double-barred Finches, Black-bellied Crimson Finches and Masked Finches likely to visit.

If braving the long walk to the plateau, look in the woodland for Rainbow Bee-eater, Red-tailed Black-Cockatoo, Leaden Flycatcher, Masked Woodswallow and White-winged Triller. Grevilleas are often flowering profusely in the woodland and are magnet to Silver-crowned Friarbirds, Helmeted Friarbirds, White-lined Honeyeaters, Banded Honeyeaters, Grey-fronted Honeyeaters and Varied Lorikeets. In the pockets of monsoon forest, search for Black-banded Fruit-Dove, Rainbow Pitta, Orange-footed Scrubfowl and Northern Rosella. Climbing the escarpment, keep your eyes peeled for Chestnut-quilled Rock-Pigeon, Sandstone Shrike-thrush, Little Woodswallow and White-lined Honeyeater. Check the sky for raptors such as

Peregrine Falcon, Black-breasted Buzzard, Little Eagle, Wedge-tailed Eagle and Australian Hobby. When you reach the plateau, scan the right habitat for White-throated Grasswren. However, you'll have a better chance to find Purple-backed Fairy-wren (lavender-flanked), Weebill and finches there.

Southern Section

This section of Kakadu covers the area on the southern border, reaching up to the Nitmiluk National Park. It features the most beautiful gorges in the Park, numerous waterfalls with the plunge pools at the base of the escarpment, and the spinifex-cladded plateaus. Vegetation here includes open woodland, monsoon forest and spinifex grassland. Facilities in this section are basic or non-existent. A network of neglected rough tracks requires the use of 4WD vehicles and can be accessed only in the Dry. Gunlom Falls are the main attraction of the area.

Key species are White-throated Grasswren (very rare), White-lined Honeyeater, Black-banded Fruit-Dove, Chestnut-quilled Rock-Pigeon, Sandstone Shrike-thrush and Black-breasted Buzzard. Other birds of interest include Banded Honeyeater, Helmeted Friarbird, Purple-backed Fairy-wren (lavender-flanked ssp.), Silver-backed Butcherbird, Little Woodswallow, Red-winged Parrot, Northern Rosella, Varied Sittella, Partridge Pigeon and Black-tailed Treecreeper. Rarities include Red Goshawk, Hooded Parrot, Gouldian Finch, Rufous Owl, Grey Falcon, Black Falcon, Square-tailed Kite and Oriental Honey-buzzard.

Male Red-winged Parrot

Maguk Campground

To get there, drive 92km southwest from the Bowali Visitor Centre, then turn east into a 4WD track signposted to the Barramundi Billabong. GPS coordinates at the turnoff are 13°15'19''S and 132°22'05''E. Drive for 12km, then turn right towards the camping area and drive for another 1km. Along this route, you'll see towering in a grassy woodland, often 5m tall, termite mounds. Be on the lookout for Partridge Pigeon, Black-tailed Treecreeper, Red-winged Parrot, Banded Honeyeater, Little Woodswallow, White-breasted Woodswallow, Red-tailed Black-Cockatoo and Long-tailed Finch in this habitat.

At the campsite, you may see Red-collared Lorikeets, Silver-crowned Friarbirds, Dusky Honeyeaters, Shining Flycatchers, Bush Stone-curlews, Northern Rosellas, Weebills and White-bellied Cuckoo-shrikes.

A 2km return walk runs from the carpark. It crosses the Barramundi Creek and continues through the monsoon forest and paperbarks to a rocky gorge with a picturesque, small waterfall with a plunge pool, home to freshwater crocodiles. In the monsoon forest look for Rainbow Pitta, Brown-capped Emerald-Dove, Torresian Imperial-Pigeon, Orange-footed Scrubfowl, Varied Triller and Shining Flycatcher.

In the gorge, you may come across White-lined Honeyeater, Black-banded Fruit-Dove, Sandstone Shrike-thrush, Helmeted Friarbird, Little Woodswallow and Black-breasted Buzzard. Search for Black Bittern, Nankeen Night-Heron, Azure Kingfisher and Oriental Dollarbird near the plunge pool.

Gungurul Campground

It is one of the Kakadu quietest camping areas and it boasts an abundance of wildlife. The site is located 58km south of Cooinda, with the turnoff to the west from Kakadu Hwy (21) at 13°17'10''S and 132°20'38''E. It lies about 4.5km south from the turnoff to Maguk. Drive about 1km to reach a small billabong with a camping site among the paperbark trees. The rare Red Goshawk is one of the birds you may be lucky to spot while exploring the area. Look for Buff-sided Robin in the vegetation near the billabong. A pair of Grey Goshawks nest in trees near the campsite, one bird of white, the other of grey morphology. Barking Owls and Australian Owlet-nightjars may be calling during the night.

The area near the carpark was recently burnt when we visited in June 2022. Mixed flocks of finches and doves were feeding on the ground, comprising Gouldian Finches, Long-tailed Finches, Masked Finches, Diamond Doves and Peaceful Doves. Fresh foliage was sprouting on the blackened twigs, being infested by small caterpillars. Mixed groups of insectivores were feeding on them including White-winged Trillers, Varied Trillers, Weebills, Large-billed Gerygones, Grey Shrike-thrushes, Rufous Whistlers and Leaden Flycatchers.

Male Varied Triller

Masked Woodswallows and Little Woodswallows were flying about. On the walk near the billabong, we ticked off Great Egret, White-necked Heron, White-bellied Sea-Eagle, Azure Kingfisher, Arafura Fantail and Bar-breasted Honeyeater.

Gunlom Falls

This spectacular 80m high waterfall was commemorated in the famous Crocodile Dundee movie, promoting the beauty of Australia to the world. At the base of the waterfall is the Gunlom plunge pool. To get there, from Kakadu Hwy (21) take an unsealed Gimbat Rd 2km north of the Information Bay – Mary River Ranger Station. Drive for 26km to a T-junction, where you'll turn left to travel 11km to the Gunlom Camping and Day-use Area at the end of the road. Facilities there include showers, toilets and picnic tables. However, the site has been closed since 2019 by the Aboriginal Authority claiming its sacred status. Check the current situation before embarking on a visit.

Gunlom offers several areas worth exploring such as the campground, a walk to the plateau past the plunge pool and a walk to the Murrill Billabong.

Gunlom Lookout Walk

The 2km return walking trail to the top of the falls starts at the day-use area. The path winds through the pandanus and paperbarks to the plunge pools, then climbs steeply onto the escarpment to reach the lookout on the plateau. The Gunlom Falls site used to be the most accessible and most reliable site for White-throated Grasswren. Due to excessive backburn, the old unburnt spinifex has disappeared, and the birds vanished with it. The last record is from 2009.

The monsoon forest at the base of a plunge pool can be very productive for honeyeaters. Look for Banded Honeyeater, White-gaped Honeyeater, Dusky Honeyeater, White-throated Honeyeater, Bar-breasted Honeyeater, Brown Honeyeater and Silver-crowned Friarbird. Also, Buff-sided Robin may be found in this area. Other birds include Oriental Dollarbird, Spangled Drongo, Shining Flycatcher, Azure Kingfisher, Common Cicadabird, Rainbow Pitta, Rose-crowned Fruit-Dove, Varied Triller and Rufous Whistler.

When walking along the creek, search for Black Bittern and Nankeen Night-Heron. In the thicket near the escarpment, White-lined Honeyeaters are often found.

As you climb the escarpments, look for raptors circling on the thermals. These include Wedge-tailed Eagle, Little Eagle, Black-breasted Buzzard, Brown Goshawk and Australian Hobby. Occasionally, rarer species appear such as Black Falcon, Peregrine Falcon or Square-tailed Kite. In 2004 Oriental Honey-buzzard, and in 2011 Grey Falcon, were observed here.

While searching for White-throated Grasswren on the plateau, you may encounter other sandstone specialists such as Sandstone Shrike-thrush, Chestnut-quilled Rock-Pigeon, Helmeted Friarbird and Purple-backed Fairy-wren (lavender-flanked).

Gunlom Camping Area

At the Gunlom campground, you may come across Bush Stone-curlew, Orange-footed Scrubfowl, Pheasant Coucal, Brush Cuckoo and Little Friarbird. On the traffic island of the day-use area, Rainbow Bee-eaters regularly nest on the ground. Red Goshawks were recorded a few times in the trees at the camping area. You may also find Little Woodswallow, Varied Lorikeet, Northern Rosella and Blue-winged Kookaburra (nesting in the camp).

Spotlighting should reveal the regular nocturnal species such as Barking Owl, Tawny Frogmouth and Australian Owlet-nightjar. Also, Spotted Nightjar is recorded in the dry season while Rufous Owls have been seen or heard occasionally. During spotlighting, Chestnut-backed Button-quails and Red-backed Button-quails were sighted near the campground.

Murrill Billabong Walk

Behind the campground, you'll find the trailhead to Murrill Billabong, a little muddy waterhole lined with reeds and stands of tall bamboo. This 2.5km return track runs past the billabong along the banks of South Alligator River and the plains covered with open woodland.

At the billabong, expect to find Azure Kingfisher, Blue-winged Kookaburra, Plumed Whistling-Duck, Radjah Shelduck, Great Egret, Plumed Egret, Nankeen Night-Heron, Black-necked Stork and the ever-present saltwater crocodiles. A couple of water buffaloes may be wallowing in the water. Search the clumps of bamboo for Northern Fantail and Arafura Fantail. Buff-sided Robin may be nearby.

Plumed Egret in breeding plumage

The woodland part of the walk may produce Partridge Pigeon, Great Bowerbird, Northern Rosella, Masked Finch, Black-bellied Crimson Finch, Long-tailed Finch, Striated Pardalote, Masked Woodswallow, Green Oriole, Silver-backed Butcherbird and Brown Goshawk.

Kambolgie Campground

To get there, from Kakadu Hwy (21) take an unsealed Gimbat Rd 2km north of the Information Bay – Mary River Ranger Station. Drive for 13km. The campground's approximate GPS coordinates are 13°30'08''S and 132°23'39''E. You will find here basic facilities with toilets, picnic tables and fire rings.

Partridge Pigeons are common in the area and often walk across the campground to get to a nearby creek. The campground is also visited by Red-winged Parrots, Red-tailed Black-Cockatoos, Northern Fantails, White-gaped Honeyeaters, Rainbow Pittas, Bush Stone-curlews and White-quilled Honeyeaters. Barking Owls are calling at night. Occasionally, Red Goshawk is observed in the area.

Check the creek for Black Bittern. Vegetation along the creek may produce Arafura Fantail, Azure Kingfisher, Shining Flycatcher, Lemon-bellied Flycatcher and Black-bellied Crimson Finch.

Yurmikmik Walks

This site is a series of interconnected walking tracks that offer a chance (although slim) of finding White-throated Grasswren. The tracks are accessible in the Wet, so provide a rare wet season experience, with the waterfalls cascading at full force. To get there, from Kakadu Hwy (21) take an unsealed Gimbat Rd 2km north of the Information Bay – Mary River Ranger Station. Drive for 21km to the Yurmikmik carpark on the right side of the road. Cross the Plum Tree Creek on a swaying footbridge and follow one of the tracks described below.

- Boulder Creek Walk – 2km return;
- Yurmikmik Lookout Walk – 5km return;
- Motor Car Falls Walk – 8km return;
- Kurrundie Creek Walk – 11km return.

All walks start and finish in the carpark. The first two walks are shorter, and are marked with paint on the posts and rocks; the longer trails are unmarked. A map of the walking area can be downloaded here: https://parksaustralia.gov.au/kakadu/pub/yurmikmik.pdf.

Boulder Creek Walk

At the start of the walk, check the banks of Plum Tree Creek where Rainbow Bee-eaters and Striated Pardalotes breed in the burrows. The path runs through the open woodland to Boulder Creek where fan palms and rock figs grow among the boulders. These attract many Black-banded Fruit-Doves and other fruit-eaters such as Great Bowerbird, Australasian Figbird and Rose-crowned Fruit-Dove. Search also for White-lined Honeyeater, Helmeted Friarbird, Pheasant Coucal and Northern Fantail. Along the creek, you may spot Azure Kingfisher and Nankeen Night-Heron.

In the woodland, search for Jacky Winter, Black-faced Woodswallow, Leaden Flycatcher, Banded Honeyeater and Weebill.

Yurmikmik Lookout Walk

This is one of the favourite Kakadu NP tracks. It runs to the lookout through a shady monsoon forest, stony ridges and a plateau. Several spinifex-clad areas can be seen on the higher section of the walk where you can try your luck to locate White-throated Grasswren. Flocks of Gouldian Finches have been reported from this walk as they come to drink from small waterholes. Other birds in the area include Chestnut-quilled Rock-Pigeon, Diamond Dove, Purple-backed Fairy-wren, Little Woodswallow and Brown Goshawk.

Kurrundie Creek Walk

This is a difficult, long trail and walkers usually bush-camp overnight along the way. Peregrine Falcons have for years been nesting on the cliff ledge near the Kurrundie Creek Falls.

Motor Car Falls Walk

This walk is an old, disused vehicular track running through the open woodland, low ridges and the plateau. Be on the lookout for finches, in particular for Gouldian Finch. Also, Hooded Parrots were found here a few times. In patches of monsoon forest, search for Rainbow Pitta and Black-banded Fruit-Dove. Other birds along the walk include Partridge Pigeon, Shining Flycatcher, Paperbark Flycatcher, Sandstone Shrike-thrush, Black-tailed Treecreeper, White-lined Honeyeater and Red-tailed Black-Cockatoo.

Male Red-tailed Black-Cockatoo

Yurmikmik at 13°30'43"S and 132°26'11"E

To get there, drive 1km further on from the Yurmikmik carpark. The site is located on the eastern side of the Plum Tree Creek, at the second creek crossing. The search area is about 1km wide, where old spinifex grows between the dark conglomerate rocks. White-throated Grasswrens were recorded here as recently as September 2021.

Other birds in this area include Little Woodswallow, Purple-backed Fairy-wren, Sandstone Shrike-thrush and Chestnut-quilled Rock-Pigeon. Near the creek crossing, look for Gouldian Finch, Paperbark Flycatcher, Brush Cuckoo, Partridge Pigeon, Bush Stone-curlew and Black-breasted Buzzard.

Koolpin Gorge

Koolpin Gorge, also known as Jarrangbarnmi Gorge, is one of the most stunning gorges in the National Park, featuring cliffs, waterfalls, plunge pools, rapids and huge fallen boulders. To get there, from Kakadu Hwy (21) take an unsealed Gimbat Rd 2km north of the Information Bay – Mary River Ranger Station. Drive for 26km to the T-junction, then turn right to continue on Gimbat Rd (the left turn will get you to Gunlom Falls, described earlier). Continue for 10km to a ford crossing on the South Alligator River. After the water crossing, drive further 8km on a tough 4WD track to the Jarrangbarnmi Camping Ground. A 3km return walk allows to enter the gorge from the campground. You'll need to negotiate several rapids, large boulders, rock pools and small waterfalls. The trail has no markers.

Permits for camping and bushwalking, including the day-use area, have to be obtained well in advance (like a year earlier, as numbers of visitors are restricted) from here: https://www.dcceew.gov.au/sites/default/files/env/resources/cbcfe81f-6fb0-4e3a-9d7b-27a05a5b7eca/files/kakadu-jarrangbarnmi-access-permit-2016_1.pdf. You'll also need to collect the site gate key at the Mary River Ranger Station. Contact kakadu.permits@dcceew.gov.au with questions and seeking further guidance.

This is the place where you can still search for the White-throated Grasswrens. The search area on the sandstone plateau near the gorge is located 1km north of the campground at the approximate GPS coordinates of 13°29'42"S and 132°34'56"E. Other birds there include Chestnut-quilled Rock-Pigeon, Sandstone Shrike-thrush, Black-banded Fruit-Dove, Helmeted Friarbird, White-lined Honeyeater and Banded Honeyeater. Along the walk, look for Gouldian Finches that landed for a drink.

Birds around the campground include Northern Rosella, White-breasted Woodswallow, Masked Woodswallow, Little Woodswallow, Leaden Flycatcher, Forest Kingfisher, Dusky Honeyeater, Silver-crowned Friarbird, Brush Cuckoo, Common Bronzewing and Weebill.

Red Goshawk Sites

The southern area of Kakadu National Park features several spots along Kakadu Hwy (21), including places outside the Park boundary, where Red Goshawks are nesting. The exact nest locations are usually known by the tour operators. You may still try to locate the birds yourself. Listed below are the most likely areas where Red Goshawks may be spotted.

Gerowie Creek Crossing

This site is located 8km north of the Bukbukluk Lookout and 74km south of the turnoff to Cooinda, at GPS coordinates of 13°26'06"S and 132°16'25"E. A Red Goshawk nest is located near the creek crossing. Black-breasted Buzzard is also nesting in this area.

It is also a good place to search for Buff-sided Robin and Black Bittern in the riparian vegetation near the bridge. Finches come to drink at the creek. Look for Gouldian Finch, Chestnut-breasted Mannikin and Black-bellied Crimson Finch. We also saw a herd of wild horses drinking from the creek.

Other birds at this spot include Bar-breasted Honeyeater, Arafura Fantail, Oriental Dollarbird, Shining Flycatcher, White-throated Gerygone, Nankeen Night-Heron and Collared Sparrowhawk.

Bukbukluk Lookout

This a lovely picnic spot for lunch, located 82km south of the turnoff to Cooinda, and just a short distance from Kakadu Hwy. GPS coordinates for the turnoff are 13°29'24"S and 132°15'00"E. A short, 500m walk leads to the lookout. The most important reason for a stop here is of course Red Goshawk. The birds nest in the area and have been observed in a display flight over the lookout. Other raptors often seen soaring over the lookout include Black-breasted Buzzard, Brown Goshawk and Whistling Kite.

Silver-backed Butcherbirds can be found near the picnic area. Other birds here include Northern Rosella, Pied Butcherbird, Silver-crowned Friarbird, Channel-billed Cuckoo and Red-winged Parrot.

Just 1.8km north of the turnoff to the Bukbukluk Lookout is Bukbukluk Creek crossing, a spot worth stopping along the highway. Black Bitterns are often observed in the riparian vegetation or feeding in the creek bed. Look also for Shining Flycatcher, Lemon-bellied Flycatcher, Little Shrike-thrush, Northern Rosella, Little Bronze-cuckoo, Brush cuckoo and Arafura Fantail.

Mary River Ranger Station

This site is located 10km northeast of the Mary River Roadhouse on the northern side of the highway. The Station offers information and interpretative displays. There are toilets in the information centre and some picnic tables to sit outside. Red Goshawks nest on the Station grounds. As we arrived, a pair of Silver-backed Butcherbirds welcomed us to the National Park with loud, melodic vocalizations. We also got Northern Rosella, Common Bronzewing, Varied Triller, Silver-crowned Friarbird (plentiful), Yellow-throated Miner and White-quilled Honeyeater.

Silver-backed Butcherbird

Other birds reported from this location include Chestnut-backed Button-quail, Partridge Pigeon, Buff-sided Robin, Brown Quail, Tawny Frogmouth and Southern Boobook.

Fern Wall Creek Crossing

This site is located 3km north of the Park's southern border at GPS coordinates of 13°35'12"S and 132°14'13"E. Red Goshawks were reported here in flight a few times. Other birds in the area include Partridge Pigeon, Silver-backed Butcherbird, White-breasted Woodswallow, White-throated Honeyeater, Dusky Honeyeater and Wedge-tailed Eagle.

Big Nellie Creek

Big Nellie Creek crossing on the Kakadu Hwy (21) is located 34km northeast of Pine Creek. GPS coordinates are 13°40'18"S and 132°00'33"E. Stop along the highway near the creek.

Red Goshawk was recorded in this area several times. Black Bittern and Nankeen Night-Heron may be found along the creek. Hooded Parrots visit occasionally. Other birds include Varied Sittella, Yellow-tinted Honeyeater, Brown Honeyeater, Silver-crowned Friarbird, Red-backed Kingfisher, Little Woodswallow, Rufous Songlark, White-winged Triller and Northern Rosella.

Harriett Creek Rest Stop

This Red Goshawk stop is a free campground located outside Kakadu NP just 200m off Kakadu Hwy (21), 30km from Pine Creek. GPS coordinates are 13°40'43"S and 131°59'05"E. You'll find here plenty of shady trees and a creek nearby. Nesting Red Goshawks were recorded at this site. Also, Black-breasted Buzzards may be circling overhead.

Birds in the campsite include Red-tailed Black-Cockatoo, Northern Rosella, Yellow-throated Miner, Silver-backed Butcherbird, Partridge Pigeon, Red-backed Fairy-wren, Rainbow Bee-eater, Little Woodswallow and Green Oriole. Also a good spot to look for Hooded Parrots outside Pine Creek.

Rainbow Bee-eaters – female at the bottom, with two juveniles

Katherine Region

This chapter covers birding sites along Stuart Hwy from Pine Creek to Renner Springs north of Threeways Roadhouse.

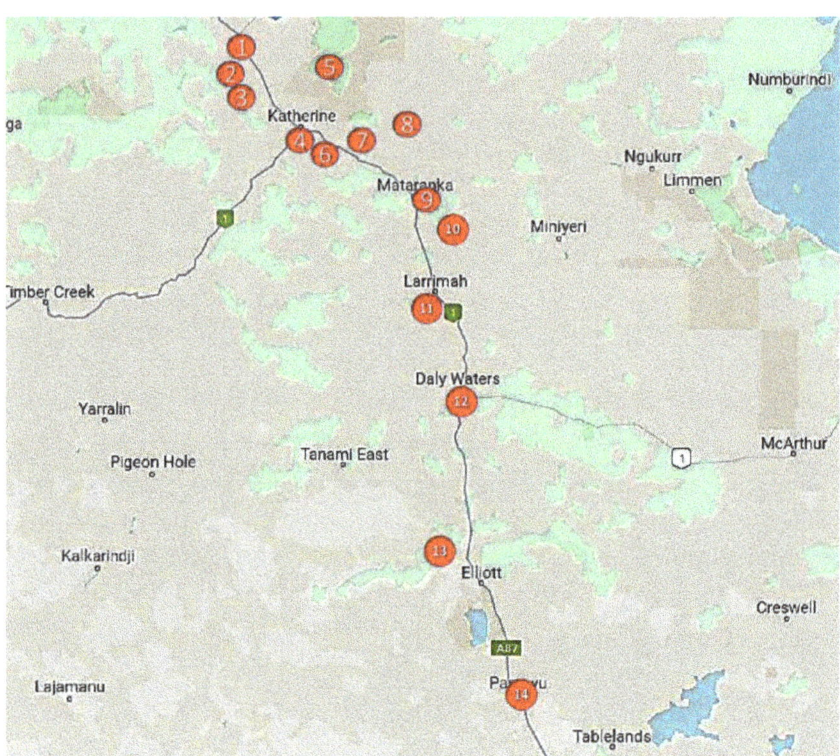

1 [Pine Creek]
2 [Umbrawarra Gorge Nature Park]
3 [Fergusson River Crossing]
4 [Katherine]
5 [Nitmiluk National Park]
6 [Cutta Cutta Caves Nature Park]
7 [Leach Lagoon]
8 [Central Arnhem Road]
9 [Elsey National Park and Mataranka]
10 [Warloch Ponds]
11 [Alexander Forrest Memorial Rest Area]
12 [Daly Waters Hi-Way Inn]
13 [Newcastle Waters]
14 [Renner Springs Desert Inn]

Pine Creek

This small, former gold mining town is located 220km southeast of Darwin and 90km northwest of Katherine at the crossroads of Darwin and Kakadu National Park routes. A lot of gold was taken out around Pine Creek between 1870 and 1995, when all mining activities had ceased. Today it is a quaint tropical village, where birdwatchers rejoice thanks to the guaranteed presence of Hooded Parrots. This is the best place in the whole NT to see this endemic species. The town offers a range accommodation including caravan parks, RV camping grounds, cabins and hotel rooms. These is fuel, general store and several attractions, mostly linked to the bygone mining era. The town is surrounded by savannah woodland and eucalypt tall forest dominated by Darwin woollybutt and Darwin stringybark. There are also smaller areas of monsoon rainforest and tussock grassland.

Over 190 bird species have been recorded around Pine Creek. **Key species** are Hooded Parrot and Gouldian Finch. Other birds of interest include Northern Rosella, Azure Kingfisher, Red-backed Button-quail, Chestnut-backed Button-quail, Silver-backed Butcherbird, Long-tailed Finch, Masked Finch, Red-collared Lorikeet, White-quilled Honeyeater, Green Oriole and Great Bowerbird. Among the rarities are Grey Falcon, Red Goshawk, Oriental Plover, Partridge Pigeon, Eastern Yellow Wagtail, Yellow-rumped Mannikin, Star Finch and Fork-tailed Swift.

Lazy Lizard Caravan Park

Male Hooded Parrot

This caravan park is located in the centre of Pine Creek, at 299 Millar Tce, off Main Tce (the road taking you to and from Stuart Hwy). We spent a week in this lovely place in June 2022. It proved to be the best spot in town to enjoy Hooded Parrots. Every day, we observed flocks of 30-100 birds. Many of them were juvenile which indicates a good population growth. They usually appeared at the fuel station in front of the caravan park in the morning, as soon as the sprinklers were switched on. Before and after their bath, they were frolicking on the roof of the caravan park's restaurant and the nearby Railway Resort. During the day, they were frequenting Meyse's Café near the Pine Creek Hotel and any other place where sprinklers were working, including the grounds inside our caravan park. At noon, they could be spotted snoozing in trees of the Water Gardens.

Each evening, our Lazy Lizard Caravan Park was witnessing a spectacle of thousands of Red-collared Lorikeets returning to roost in trees in and around the caravan park. At the same time, a large cloud of flying-foxes was leaving the same trees, moving in the opposite direction to feed overnight in the surrounding woods.

Several tame and very cheeky Great Bowerbirds live in the campsite. An active bower is located between the old railway tracks near the caravan park entrance.

A Great Bowerbird's bower constructed on an old railway line

Nectar feeders were extensively using the flowering trees and bushes. We noted White-gaped Honeyeater, Dusky Honeyeater, Rufous-throated Honeyeater, Little Friarbird and Silver-crowned Friarbird. Grey-crowned Babblers built several massive nests in the van park; some of which were taken over by White-quilled

Honeyeaters. Pheasant Coucals were calling every morning, and finches such as Long-tailed Finch, Masked Finch and Double-barred Finch were coming for a drink. At night, we could hear Southern Boobook, Barking Owl, Tawny Frogmouth and Bush Stone-curlew.

Other birds in the Lazy Lizard Caravan Park included Green Oriole, Olive-backed Oriole, White-breasted Woodswallow (a big flock coming to roost), Sacred Kingfisher, Rainbow Bee-eater, Silver-backed Butcherbird and Brown Goshawk.

In the Wet, an occasional flock of Fork-tailed Swifts is reported flying over the town.

Pine Creek Water Gardens

The gardens are located in the centre of township, between the Main Tce and Railway Tce, just south of Lazy Lizard Caravan Park. The gardens were created when the railway tracks were pulled out, leaving a line of unsightly trenches. These were converted to a series of ponds and parkland was planted around them. The result is quite enchanting. Hooded Parrots are regularly found here, roosting in trees in the hot afternoon.

Pine Creek Water Gardens

Among birds visiting the ponds for a drink are Red-winged Parrots, Apostlebirds, Dusky Honeyeaters, Paperbark Flycatchers and a variety of finches. You may be lucky to find Azure Kingfisher, Sacred Kingfisher, Pallid Cuckoo, Eastern Koel, Bar-breasted Honeyeater and even Star Finch.

Railway Museum and Miners Park

These two adjacent sites are located along the Main Tce just north of Lazy Lizard Caravan Park. A creek meanders on the border of Miners Park, with several permanent waterholes filled with water even in the Dry. This is the place to search for finches, particularly near the water. Gouldian Finches are found here regularly. Look also for Black-bellied Crimson Finch, Masked Finch and Chestnut-breasted Mannikin. Occasionally, Star Finch is seen. Hooded Parrots sometimes visit this area.

Pine Creek WTP

To get to the ponds, from Stuart Hwy (1) about 500m north of the southern turnoff to Main Tce, turn into Sewer Ponds Pine Creek Rd (not signposted) and drive approximately 1km in the easterly direction. The ponds are on the left side of the road, just before the cemetery. Approximate GPS coordinates are 13°48’47’’S and 131°50’49’’E. The site is fenced so you’ll need to walk around to find suitable vantage points.

Pine Creek WTP is very popular with the birders; over 180 species are on its birdlist, including a number of rarities such as Star Finch, Wood Sandpiper, Swinhoe’s Snipe, Little Curlew, Oriental Plover, Yellow-rumped Mannikin, Black Falcon and Little Eagle. Eastern Yellow Wagtails and Common Sandpipers can be spotted foraging on the ponds in summer. In total, 18 wader species have been recorded. Commonly found are Black-fronted Dotterel, Red-kneed Dotterel, Pied Stilt, Oriental Pratincole, Sharp-tailed Sandpiper and Red-capped Plover.

Waterbirds can be seen on the ponds, sometimes in good numbers. These include Radjah Shelduck, Plumed Whistling-Duck, Hardhead, Pink-eared Duck, Green Pygmy-goose, Australasian Grebe, Glossy Ibis, White-necked Heron, Pied Heron and Black-necked Stork.

Gouldian Finches regularly visit the ponds in winter. Other finches at this site include Chestnut-breasted Mannikin, Black-bellied Crimson Finch, Long-tailed Finch, Masked Finch and Double-barred Finch.

In the surrounding grassy areas, you may come across Brown Quail, Red-backed Button-quail, Chestnut-backed Button-quail, Golden-headed Cisticola, Horsfield's Bushlark and sometimes even King Quail, Partridge Pigeon or Zitting Cisticola.

Small flocks of Hooded Parrots occasionally come to the water while other parrots, such as Red-tailed Black-Cockatoo, Red-winged Parrot, Varied Lorikeet and Red-collared Lorikeet, are common.

Birds gathering on the ponds attract raptors such as Black-breasted Buzzard, Australian Hobby, Collared Sparrowhawk, Spotted Harrier and Peregrine Falcon.

Pine Creek Cemetery

This site is located at the end of Sewer Ponds Pine Creek Rd, just north of the sewage ponds. Approximate GPS coordinates are 13°48'36''S and 131°50'48''E. A large carpark is provided in front of the cemetery, with giant termite mounds scattered throughout. It is surrounded by savannah woodland and grassland.

During our visit, finches were feeding in a mixed flock on the cut grass. These were mostly Double-barred and Long-tailed Finches, with a couple of juvenile Gouldian Finches and several Masked Finches.

A large flock of Red-tailed Black-Cockatoos enjoyed foraging in the freshly burnt area. Together with them were three Hooded Parrots. While walking in the grass along the cemetery fence, we flushed a few Brown Quails and a couple of Chestnut-backed Button-quails. A family of Bush Stone-curlews was snoozing between the headstones. Jacky Winter was perched on the cemetery fence.

In the woods, we got Black-tailed Treecreeper, Varied Sittella, Rainbow Bee-eater, Rufous Songlark and Brush Cuckoo. Australian Hobby was roosting on a dead tree.

Pussy Cat Flats RV Campground

This is a racecourse site where you can park your caravan for as little as $10 per night. The site is located along Kakadu Hwy (21); about 1km from the turnoff from Stuart Hwy (1). GPS coordinates are 13°48'29''S and 131°50'18''E.

Hooded Parrots regularly roost in the campground, we saw two flying overhead. Other birds there include Cockatiel, Red-winged Parrot, Red-tailed Black-Cockatoo, Northern Rosella, Pied Butcherbird, Little Friarbird, White-breasted Woodswallow (plentiful), Grey-crowned Babbler, Great Bowerbird, Masked Finch and Red-backed Kingfisher.

Copperfield Dam

Copperfield Dam near Pine Creek

This water body is accessed from Stuart Hwy (1) about 4km south of Pine Creek via Umbrawarra Rd, also referred to as Umbrawarra Gorge Rd. Drive west for 1.8km and at the GPS position of 13°51'08''S and 131°49'22''E turn north into Copperfield Dam Tk (not signposted) and drive 1km to a picnic area by the dam. There are two shaded picnic tables, carpark and toilets (these are quite in a distance). The site looked neglected when we visited.

Over 140 bird species have been recorded at the Copperfield Dam. **Key species** are Black-tailed Treecreeper, Hooded Parrot, Partridge Pigeon, Chestnut-backed button-quail, Gouldian Finch and Northern Rosella. Other birds of interest include Green Pygmy-goose, Azure Kingfisher, Shining Flycatcher, Banded Honeyeater, Varied Lorikeet, Silver-backed Butcherbird, Oriental Dollarbird, Australian Owlet-nightjar and Brown Goshawk. Among the rarities are Glossy Ibis, Wood Sandpiper, Little Curlew, Black Bittern, Purple Swamphen and Little Eagle.

During our visit, there were just a few birds on the lake including Radjah Shelduck, Great Egret, Comb-crested Jacana and Azure Kingfisher. The woods produced Black-faced Woodswallow, White-bellied Cuckoo-shrike, Rufous Whistler, Paperbark Flycatcher and Silver-backed Butcherbird. Three Chestnut-backed Button-quails flushed from the grass.

Jollys Dam

Just 50m after turning to Umbrawarra Rd from Stuart Hwy (1), turn north into Jollys Dam Rd (not signposted). The access to the water is from the side tracks at the northern and southern ends of the lake, leading to a tall dam embankment. A visit there can be productive for waterbirds and bush birds. Our findings at the south section included Black Bittern (flushed from a paperbark tree), Radjah Shelduck, Little Egret, Plumed Egret, Glossy Ibis, Black-fronted Dotterel, Red-kneed Dotterel, Azure Kingfisher and Brown Goshawk. Tawny Grassbirds were calling while Black-bellied Crimson Finches and Double-barred Finches were drinking at the water edge. We also got Paperbark Flycatcher, Leaden Flycatcher, Shining Flycatcher and plenty of Rainbow Bee-eaters.

Female Shining Flycatcher

Umbrawarra Gorge Nature Park

This 970ha park is the NT's hidden gem. It features a strikingly beautiful gorge with red cliffs and overhanging sandstone outcrops. To get there, from Stuart Hwy (1) about 4km south of Pine Creek turn west into Umbrawarra Rd, also called Umbrawarra Gorge Rd. Drive 22km to the camping site. The road is bad, corrugated, with many steep dips and creek crossings, so access is for 4WDs only. The campsite is small; book online while planning your visit. Best visited in mid-dry season.

A carpark is provided near the entrance. The site is equipped with toilets, picnic tables and wood-fired barbecues. From the camp, an easy 1km walk leads to the gorge. At the end of the walk is a waterhole with a small beach. However, in-depth exploration of the gorge requires a lot of rock jumping and water wading. Further information can be found in the Umbrawarra Gorge Fact Sheet at https://nt.gov.au/__data/assets/pdf_file/0011/200081/umbrawarra-gorge-nature-park.pdf.

Over 110 bird species have been recorded in the Umbrawarra Gorge Nature Park. **Key species** are Partridge Pigeon, Silver-backed Butcherbird, Little Woodswallow and Bar-breasted Honeyeater. Other birds of interest include Azure Kingfisher, Banded Honeyeater Paperbark Flycatcher, Varied Lorikeet, Northern Rosella, Red-tailed Black-Cockatoo, Nankeen Night-Heron, Spangled Drongo, Striated Pardalote, Tawny Frogmouth and Brown Goshawk. Among the rarities are Gouldian Finch, Hooded Parrot, Grey Falcon, Square-tailed Kite and Little Eagle.

The star attraction of the park is Partridge Pigeon. Flocks up to 30 birds are sometimes counted. Several records of Grey Falcon exist for the park, with the last one dated June 2022. Flowering trees attract plenty of honeyeaters including Bar-breasted Honeyeater, Banded Honeyeater, Dusky Honeyeater, Brown Honeyeater, Helmeted Friarbird, Little Friarbird and Silver-crowned Friarbird.

The campground may yield Silver-backed Butcherbird, Oriental Dollarbird, Yellow-throated Miner, Silver-crowned Friarbird, Mistletoebird and Northern Rosella. Tawny Frogmouths and Brown Goshawks regularly nest in the camp. During the night, look and listen to Southern Boobook, Barking Owl and Bush Stone-curlew.

The gorge and its access track may produce Nankeen Night-Heron, Little Woodswallow, Masked Finch, Long-tailed Finch, Golden-backed Honeyeater, Northern Fantail and Red-collared Lorikeet.

Check the creek crossing on Umbrawarra Rd near the campground. If water is present, Azure Kingfisher may be there. Another productive creek crossing is located 6km before the camp at the GPS position of 13°53'16''S and 131°47'372''E. We got Partridge Pigeon walking across the road there. A constant stream of finches, including four Gouldian Finches, was landing at a waterhole in the creek bed. The orange-flowered woollybutts were attracting Varied Lorikeets, Banded Honeyeaters, Bar-breasted Honeyeaters and all three species of friarbirds. We flushed Chestnut-backed Button-quails while wandering through the grass. Other birds there included Little Woodswallow, White-browed Woodswallow, Red-backed Kingfisher, Paperbark Flycatcher and Weebill.

Fergusson River Crossing

Fergusson River passes under the road bridge along Stuart Hwy about 33km south of Pine Creek and 57km north of Katherine. There is also a railway bridge over the riverbed nearby. Site approximate GPS coordinates are 14°04'10''S and 131°58'44''E. During the Dry, the rives turns into a series of disconnected pools which, together with their grassy verges, may potentially yield Gouldian Finches and Hooded Parrots. However, Stuart Hwy doesn't have a safe and convenient parking near the bridge. You may wish to park up to 500m south or north of the bridge and find your way to the riverbed on foot. There are remnants of an old road near the bridge that may be useful for the hike, but access is generally difficult.

Over 100 bird species have been recorded at the Fergusson River Crossing. **Key species** are Gouldian Finch and Hooded Parrot. Other birds of interest include Black Bittern, Black-tailed Treecreeper, Northern Rosella, Silver-backed Butcherbird, Varied Sittella, Varied Lorikeet, Cockatiel, Banded Honeyeater, Red-browed Pardalote, Little Woodswallow, Long-tailed Finch and Australian Owlet-nightjar. Among the rarities are Painted Finch, Star Finch and Little Eagle.

Fergusson River East of Stuart Highway

Walk along the dry riverbed in the easterly direction from the bridge for about 200m where the waterholes usually form in the dry season. Check the large trees overhanging the waterholes for roosting Nankeen Night-Herons or Black Bittern.

Gouldian Finches and Hooded Parrots visit these waterholes for a drink, sometimes in good numbers. You may also spot Masked Finch, Long-tailed Finch, Black-bellied Crimson Finch, Northern Rosella, Peaceful Dove and Paperbark Flycatcher. In the surrounding bushes look for Rufous-throated Honeyeater, Banded Honeyeater, Yellow-tinted Honeyeater, White-gaped Honeyeater and Varied Lorikeet.

Rufous-throated Honeyeater

Fergusson River West of Stuart Highway

Walk along the dry riverbed in the westerly direction from the bridge for about 200m until you get to a pool with a small stony beach. In the morning, finches and other birds come to drink here in good numbers. Patient stalking for 1-2hrs will give you a good chance of sighting some Gouldian Finches and Hooded Parrots. Azure Kingfishers are regularly observed fishing here and Black-necked Storks sometimes visit the site. Otherwise, the bird selection around the waterhole is similar to that on the east side of the bridge.

Along the riverbed, look also for Silver-backed Butcherbird, Shining Flycatcher, Oriental Dollarbird, Cockatiel, Hooded Robin and Brown Goshawk.

Stuart Highway 1.5km South of Fergusson River

This site is a roadside stop next to an ephemeral wetland. GPS coordinates are 14°04’59’’S and 131°59’18’’E. When water is present in the wetland, Hooded Parrots visit to get a drink. If there are any freshly burnt areas, check whether finches are present, foraging on seeds released by the fire. Gouldian Finches, Masked Finches, Long-tailed Finches and Chestnut-breasted Mannikins have been recorded here. In the surrounding woodland, you may encounter Jacky Winter, Golden-backed Honeyeater and Northern Rosella.

Stuart Highway 3km South of Fergusson River

This is a wayside stop on the eastern side of the highway at GPS coordinates of 14°05'45''S and 131°59'22''E. Railway tracks and a creek bed are located nearby. This patch of savannah is very productive for finches including Gouldian Finches which are observed here regularly. Hooded Parrots also frequent the area. Other birds at this site include Australian Bustard, Black-tailed Treecreeper, Yellow-tinted Honeyeater, Banded Honeyeater, Varied Sittella, Northern Shrike-tit, White-throated Gerygone and Hooded Robin (rare).

Katherine

Katherine, a small NT town, is located on the banks of Katherine River at the crossroads of Stuart Hwy and Victoria Hwy, 320km south of Darwin. The town is surrounded by the plains covered with savannah woodland. There are several hills scattered within the plains. Nitmiluk National Park, situated east of town, boasts a spectacular, world-famous Katherine Gorge, now called Nitmiluk Gorge. Katherine offers many good birding spots in town and around it. There are also hot springs which create warm-water pools in the Katherine River, great to soak away the sweat and grime of a birdwatching morning.

Katherine WTP

This very popular birding site is located about 5km south of town. Take Novis Quarry Rd from Victoria Hwy (1). At the T-junction turn right; the ponds will be on your left in 400m. Approximate GPS coordinates for the ponds are 14°30'13''S and 132°14'06''E. Inspect the perimeter of the ponds and the adjacent woodland.

Over 200 bird species have been recorded at the Katherine Wastewater Treatment Plant. **Key species** are waders, Barn Swallow (Wet), Eastern Yellow Wagtail (Wet), Red-chested Button-quail, White-winged Black Tern (Wet) and Black-breasted Buzzard. Other birds of interest include Radjah Shelduck, Magpie Goose, Australian Bustard, Silver-crowned Friarbird, Red-backed Kingfisher, Paperbark Flycatcher, Oriental Dollarbird and Horsfield's Bushlark. Rarities include Common Tern, Freckled Duck, Baillon's Crake, Glossy Ibis, Flock Bronzewing, Star Finch, Gouldian Finch, Yellow Chat, Citrine Wagtail and Black Falcon.

The site is known for its waders; 27 species have been recorded and you can expect something new every time you visit. Common migratory waders include Wood Sandpiper, Common Sandpiper, Sharp-tailed Sandpiper, Marsh Sandpiper, Common

Greenshank, Pacific Golden Plover and Oriental Pratincole. Small flocks of Oriental Plovers are recorded regularly. Rarer migratory waders include Black-tailed Godwit, Curlew Sandpiper, Broad-billed Sandpiper, Little Curlew, Ruff, Long-toed Stint and Swinhoe's Snipe. Among common native waders found here are Australian Pratincole, Red-kneed Dotterel, Pied Stilt and Bush Stone-curlew.

Long-tailed Stint (front) is called a 'mini version' of Sharp-tailed Sandpiper (back)

A good selection of waterbirds includes Green Pygmy-goose, Hardhead, Hoary-headed Grebe, Yellow-billed Spoonbill, White-necked Heron, Nankeen Night-Heron, Pied Heron, Caspian Tern, Australian Gull-billed Tern as well as masses of Plumed Whistling-Ducks. Regular visitors include Brolga and Black-necked Stork.

Flock Bronzewings, Chestnut-breasted Mannikins, Gouldian Finches, Northern Rosellas and a selection of honeyeaters arrive each day for a drink. Eastern Yellow Wagtails are regularly found around the ponds in summer.

In the surrounding woodland and near Katherine River look for Varied Lorikeet, Red-collared Lorikeet, Green Oriole, Northern Fantail, Shining Flycatcher, Arafura Fantail, White-gaped Honeyeater and Banded Honeyeater. Brown Songlarks and Horsfield's Bushlarks are regularly displaying over the paddocks. At night, Spotted Nightjars may be hunting over the paddocks. Look for Red-chested Button-quails at the edge of long grass near the railway tracks north of the ponds.

When paperbarks are flowering, large flocks of Little Friarbirds descend on the area. Look also for Yellow-tinted Honeyeater, Rufous-throated Honeyeater and White-quilled Honeyeater.

A resident pair of White-bellied Sea-Eagles nests on the banks of Katherine River behind the ponds. Other raptors here include Wedge-tailed Eagle, Australian Hobby, Swamp Harrier and plenty of Black Kites. Among nocturnal birds are Tawny Frogmouth, Barking Owl and Australian Owlet-nightjar. There are records of Rufous Owl which occasionally visits camps of flying-foxes along the river.

Manbulloo Homestead Caravan Park

This caravan park is located on Katherine River just south of the WTP. To get there, from Victoria Hwy (1) take Murnburlu Rd and drive west to the river. This site is known for an occasional presence of Great-billed Heron, but you'd need to rent a canoe and paddle downstream in search of this elusive bird.

Over 110 bird species have been recorded at the Manbulloo Homestead Caravan Park and surrounding property. **Key species** are Hooded Parrot, Northern Rosella, Australian Bustard, Horsfield's Bushlark, Star Finch and Black-breasted Buzzard. Other birds of interest include Great Bowerbird, Red-tailed Black-Cockatoo, Red-browed Pardalote, Torresian Imperial-Pigeon, Pheasant Coucal, Spotted Harrier and Bush Stone-curlew. Rarities include Great-billed Heron, Little Eagle, Ground Cuckoo-shrike and Eastern Grass Owl.

Hooded Parrots come to drink from the livestock water troughs along the access road. Star Finches and Masked Finches can occasionally be spotted. Look for Australian Bustards on the paddocks, groups of 15-20 birds have been observed. Other birds here include Golden-headed Cisticola, Brown Songlark, Tawny Grassbird and Brown Quail. Check the power lines for Pallid Cuckoos, Red-backed Kingfishers and Black-faced Woodswallows. Eastern Grass Owls were observed several times at dusk, flying slowly along the access road. More common are Barn Owls, often seen perched on the fences at night.

Around the campsite, there are plenty of Great Bowerbirds, White-gaped Honeyeaters, White-quilled Honeyeaters, White-bellied Cuckoo-shrikes and very tame Bush Stone-curlews. Look for Oriental Dollarbirds, Northern Fantails, Tree Martins, Leaden Flycatchers, Shining Flycatchers, Paperbark Flycatchers, White-bellied Sea-Eagles and Nankeen Night-Herons along the river. Well, perhaps even a Great-billed Heron will happen!

White-gaped Honeyeater

Chinaman and Chainman Creek Crossings

These two confusingly named creeks that cross the Victoria Hwy (1) may prove to be lucky for you. The Chinaman Creek crossing is located on Victoria Hwy 16km southwest of Katherine at the GPS position of 14°34'29"S and 132°10'38"E. Chainman Creek crossing is 4km further down the road at 14°36'06"S and 132°08'52"E. The waterholes at both crossings and any burnt out areas for up to 10km west of Chinaman Creek may produce Gouldian Finches and Hooded Parrots.

Over 140 bird species have been recorded in the area of Chinaman and Chainman Creek Crossings. **Key species** are Hooded Parrot, Gouldian Finch, Chestnut-crowned Button-quail, Red-chested Button-quail, Pale-vented Bush-hen, Northern Rosella and Black-breasted Buzzard. Other birds of interest include Masked Finch, Long-tailed Finch, Red-tailed Black-Cockatoo, Masked Woodswallow, Rufous Songlark, Olive-backed Oriole, Grey-fronted Honeyeater, Brolga, Tawny Frogmouth and Spotted Harrier. Rarities include Black Bittern, Northern Shrike-tit, Yellow-rumped Mannikin, Golden-backed Honeyeater, Ground Cuckoo-shrike and Zitting Cisticola.

Chinaman Creek crossing

Waterhole at the Chinaman Creek crossing

In the Dry, the creek turns into a series of small waterholes and the best birding is to walk in the northerly direction along the creek bed for about 50m up to a fence. Birds come to drink here in the early morning and late afternoon. Also, on the southern side of the road you may wish to explore several short firebreaks ending at the boundary fence.

In June 2022, we observed various finches, including two juvenile Gouldian Finches, drinking from the waterhole at the crossing. Long-tailed Finches, Double-barred Finches and Masked Finches appeared in good numbers. A pair of Hooded Parrots also made and appearance, landing in a bush before approaching the water. In the woodland nearby, we got Masked Woodswallows in large numbers and also Little Friarbird, Silver-crowned Friarbird, Red-winged Parrot, Olive-backed Oriole, White-winged Triller and Varied Sitella. A flock of Red-tailed Black-Cockatoos and a couple of Hooded Parrots and Diamond Doves landed on a burnt-out patch near the fence. We walked a firebreak south of the highway and observed Pale-vented Bush-hen emerging from the groundcover. Later, Chestnut-backed Button-quail flushed from the dense grass.

Chainman Creek Crossing

Look for quails and button-quails along the road. There are several short firebreaks from the highway to the fences on both sides of the road and longer tracks along the fences for you to explore. We found three Chestnut-backed Button-quails at the edge of dense grass near the crossing. Stony bare ground in the woodland and the newly burnt areas can yield finches, doves and parrots. We observed a group of Gouldian Finches, Long-tailed Finches and a couple of Hooded Parrots in this habitat. A large flock of Cockatiels foraged on the ground. White-winged Trillers were walking with them. Pacific Baza had a nest near the creek.

Woodland also produced Black-tailed Treecreeper, Horsfield's Bronze-cuckoo, Olive-backed Oriole, Golden-backed Honeyeater, Banded Honeyeater, Yellow-tinted Honeyeater, Varied Lorikeet, Jacky Winter and Apostlebird. Azure Kingfisher was perching on an overhanging branch.

Raptors along the highway included Spotted Harrier, Brown Falcon, Wedge-tailed Eagle and Black-breasted Buzzard.

Katherine Showgrounds

Access to the site is from Victoria Hwy (1). To get there, opposite Rundle Park take a track called Murphy St, leading to the Showgrounds. Of interest to a birdwatcher is the drainage line encircling the site perimeter. If water is present, look for finches which come here for a drink. You may come across Black-bellied Crimson Finch, Double-barred Finch, Long-tailed Finch, Masked Finch and Chestnut-breasted Mannikin. Look also for Tawny Grassbird, Brown Songlark, Rufous Songlark, Brown Quail and Australian Bustard. Apostlebirds are often seen foraging on the showgrounds. When the showgrounds are flooded in the Wet, waterbirds appear including Magpie Geese, Plumed Whistling-Ducks and Radjah Shelducks. Occasionally Wood Sandpipers and Marsh Sandpipers may pay a visit. In summer 2024, a pair of Red-rumped Swallows was reported.

The rare Yellow-rumped Mannikins can be occasionally found along the drainage channel and in a small wetland at the north end of the Country Club adjacent to the Showgrounds. Access is from Railway Tce behind the BP station on Stuart Hwy. In the Wet, the Country Club wetland may also produce Wood Sandpiper, Buff-banded Rail, Golden-headed Cisticola, Glossy Ibis and a selection of common waterfowl.

Flat Rock

Flat Rock is a popular fishing camp on Edith River, located at the GPS of 14°17'23''S and 131°52'24''E. The distance from Katherine is 54km. To get there, drive north on Stuart Hwy (1) from Katherine, then turn left into Edith Farms Rd. In Edith, turn into Beasley Rd and follow it to the camp at the end of the road. Birdwatching is conducted along a rough track along the river.

Over 100 bird species have been recorded at Flat Rock. **Key species** are Rainbow Pitta, Azure Kingfisher, Nankeen Night-Heron, Shining Flycatcher, Buff-sided Robin, Green-backed Gerygone, Northern Rosella and Pacific Baza. Other birds of interest include Radjah Shelduck, Common Sandpiper, Oriental Dollarbird, Varied Lorikeet, White-throated Gerygone, Northern Fantail and Barking Owl. Among the rarities are Great-billed Heron, Black-eared Cuckoo and Rufous Owl.

Azure Kingfishers regularly fish along the creek. Rainbow Pitta is quite often recorded at the edge of the forest. Vegetation surrounding the creek may yield Rainbow Bee-eater, Rufous Whistler, Spangled Drongo, Australian Yellow White-eye, Silver-backed Butcherbird, Bar-breasted Honeyeater, Dusky Honeyeater, Lemon-bellied Flycatcher, Arafura Fantail and Weebill.

Waterbird selection along the creek includes Nankeen Night-Heron, Great Egret, Brolga and Black-necked Stork.

This site is good for the nocturnal birds; besides those mentioned above you may hear or see Southern Boobook, Tawny Frogmouth and Australian Owlet-nightjar.

Donkey Camp Weir

Donkey Camp is located northeast of Katherine. Turn north from Stuart Hwy (1) into Gilles St at the Katherine Hotel and follow the road (it will change name to Gorge Rd at the Katherine Hospital) for about 9km up to the sign announcing the 'Pandanus Farm'. Turn north at the GPS position of 14°25'04''S and 132°19'45''E and drive 500m through a private property on a track lined with large trees. You will reach a carpark near the pump station (a small building at the far end). Go over the gate and follow a wide track down to the river. Turn left to the weir.

Katherine River at Donkey Camp

This is one of the most accessible sites along Katherine River to search for Great-billed Heron. Check the rocks on the other side of the river near the weir. We got a fleeting glance of one bird that on our arrival lifted from the weir wall to promptly vanish behind the tall trees. The birds that stayed put on the wall were a single Common Sandpiper and a flock of Radjah Shelducks. Azure Kingfisher was fishing along the riverbanks. We got good views of a Black Bittern flying into the pandanus thicket. A group of Nankeen Night-Herons was roosting in a large gum tree.

Birds in the surrounding dense vegetation included Shining Flycatcher, Leaden Flycatcher, Green Oriole, Northern Fantail, Arafura Fantail and plenty of Black-bellied Crimson Finches. In the flowering paperbarks, we got Banded Honeyeater, Dusky Honeyeater, White-gaped Honeyeater, Brown Honeyeater, Rufous-banded Honeyeater and Silver-crowned Friarbird. Red-collared Lorikeets and Varied Lorikeets were plentiful. We also noted Oriental Dollarbird, Pheasant Coucal, Lemon-bellied Flycatcher, White-bellied Cuckoo-shrike and Pacific Baza. In mango trees nearby, Great Bowerbirds were gorging on ripening mangoes, while Straw-necked Ibises foraged underneath.

Nitmiluk National Park

This large, 292,000ha property, formerly known as Katherine Gorge National Park, is located about 320km south of Darwin. The land is owned by the Aboriginal people and the Park is managed jointly by them and Parks and Wildlife Commission of NT. The Park sits northeast of Katherine and is accessed via sealed roads. The Park is divided in two sections: southern part with Nitmiluk Gorge and northern part featuring Edith Falls (a.k.a. Leliyn).

The main attraction of the Park is the deep, picturesque Nitmiluk Gorge, carved out in the sandstone country by Katherine River. Tropical savannah grows on the sandstone cliffs above the gorge, while lush rainforest thrives in the gullies and in giant cracks in the gorge walls. The Park has rich Aboriginal history, with rock art scattered through the area.

Over 180 bird species have been recorded in the Nitmiluk National Park. **Key species** are Chestnut-quilled Rock-Pigeon, Sandstone Shrike-thrush, Great-billed Heron, Gouldian Finch, Hooded Parrot and Peregrine Falcon. Other birds of interest include Azure Kingfisher, Varied Lorikeet, Northern Rosella, Black Bittern, Silver-backed Butcherbird, Common Cicadabird, Apostlebird, Northern Shrike-tit, Red-chested Button-quail, Masked Finch and Barking Owl. Rarities include Partridge Pigeon, Little Kingfisher, White-lined Honeyeater, Fork-tailed Swift, Grey Wagtail, Square-tailed Kite, Black Falcon, Grey Falcon and Little Eagle.

Nitmiluk Gorge

To get to Nitmiluk Gorge, turn north from Stuart Hwy (1) in Katherine into Gilles St at the Katherine Hotel and follow the road for 30km (it will change name to Gorge Rd out of town) to a large Visitor Centre and a carpark at the end of the road. The Visitor Centre offers a café, curio shop, information desk, bbq, toilets, etc. A large caravan park and lodge-type accommodation are located next to the Visitor Centre. A network of walking trails criss-crosses the Park.

A jetty and a boat ramp facility, with its own spacious carpark, is located on Katherine River north of the Visitor Centre. A variety of boat tours in the gorge system depart from the jetty. The boats are operated by the Park-owned Nitmiluk Tours. Book a tour at https://www.nitmiluktours.com.au/gorge-experiences/#touring. Tickets are also available from virtually all accommodation venues in Katherine. Advanced bookings are essential. Further information can be found in the Nitmiluk Fact Sheet with a map, downloadable at https://nt.gov.au/__data/assets/pdf_file/0007/200104/nitmiluk-national-park-fact-sheet-and-map.pdf.

Gorge Boat Cruises

The high cliffs of Nitmiluk Gorge, home of Chestnut-quilled Rock-Pigeons

A gorge boat cruise is not exactly a birding trip but you cannot miss it. It is a magic experience, especially in the morning. The majestic gorge is confined between the coloured, towering walls of artistic shapes, with fissures, stacks and strange rock formations, some plunged in a deep shadow, other glistening in the light of the rising sun.

Eight gorges are lined up in the gorge system. The extent of a gorge boat trip depends on the season and level of water in the gorges. Typically, up to 4 gorges can be visited in the dry season, with the last two in a second boat which is reached by the tourist after a short hike among the boulders.

Before boarding, check the trees near the jetty. A resident pair of White-bellied Sea-Eagles and a few Australasian Darters often roost there. Cast an eye on the railings of other moored boats; Azure Kingfishers regularly use them as launching pads in their fish hunting. There are occasional records of Little Kingfishers using the same spots. Even Great-billed Heron is sometimes seen on the rocks on the other side of the river, if you take the first boat. Later, boat traffic becomes so heavy that all birds move away. Also check the rocks for Common Sandpiper and Nankeen Night Heron.

During the trip, keep your eyes peeled for the two sought-after species of the area: Chestnut-quilled Rock-Pigeon and Sandstone Shrike-thrush. The latter are easier to spot on the rock shelves, being more vocal in the early morning and particularly loud in the section between the first and second gorge. The Rock-Pigeons are seen occasionally less than 1km from the jetty. Indeed, we sighted them near the Baruwei Lookout.

Fairy Martins collecting mud for their nests

Large flocks of Fairy Martins fly over the water. In several place, you will see their bottle-shaped nests under the rock shelves, with the rock stained with their droppings. Little Woodswallows are resident and flying along the cliffs. Patches of vegetation growing on the cliff walls may produce Shining Flycatcher, White-gaped Honeyeater, Brown Honeyeater, White-quilled Honeyeater, Paperbark Flycatcher, Forest Kingfisher and Blue-winged Kookaburra; the latter often very vocal, with calls resonating through the gorge. There is a good chance to see many raptors along the way such as Peregrine Falcon, Osprey, Black Kite, Whistling Kite and Australian Hobby. Peregrine Falcons nest in the second gorge and the boats often stop there for a closer look.

Nitmiluk Gorge Tourist Facilities

The areas around the Visitor Centre, camping grounds and the parkland around the jetty carpark are often bursting with birds. It is worth spending some time there.

Near the Visitor Centre, you can encounter Silver-backed Butcherbird, Grey-crowned Babbled, Apostlebird, Rainbow Bee-eater, Green Oriole, Oriental Dollarbird, Rufous Whistler, White-breasted Woodswallow, White-quilled Honeyeater, Little Friarbird, Channel-billed Cuckoo and Black-bellied Crimson Finch.

On the grounds near the jetty, look for Forest Kingfisher, Sacred Kingfisher, Silver-crowned Friarbird, Northern Fantail, Red-collared Lorikeet, Torresian Imperial-Pigeon, Bar-breasted Honeyeater, Weebill and Pacific Baza. Occasionally, Little Eagle is reported. Broad-billed Flycatchers can be found in the paperbarks around the jetty's carpark.

Spotlighting around the Visitor Centre, campground and parkland may produce Tawny Frogmouth, Bush Stone-curlew, Barking Owl and Southern Boobook

Baruwei Loop

This 4.8km return walk climbs up a steep section of the escarpment to the Baruwei Lookout, then follows the clifftop, finally descending back to the Visitor Centre. In summer (Sep-Feb), it is extremely hot and rugged on top of the escarpment so prepare well and choose the distance that suits your fitness level.

Along the walk, be on the lookout for Gouldian Finches and the escarpment specialists: Chestnut-quilled Rock-Pigeon, Sandstone Shrike-thrush and White-lined Honeyeater. Other birds include Little Woodswallow, Masked Woodswallow, Red-winged Parrot, Leaden Flycatcher, Diamond Dove, Varied Triller and Rufous-banded Honeyeater.

Sixteen raptor species have been recorded in the area. These include Peregrine Falcon, Wedge-tailed Eagle, Grey Goshawk, Osprey, White-bellied Sea-Eagle and Black-breasted Buzzard. A rare raptor, Oriental Honey-buzzard, was recorded in April 2021.

Edith Falls Section

To get to Edith Falls, drive north from Katherine on Stuart Hwy for 42km, then turn east into Edith Falls Rd (sealed). If arriving from Pine Creek, follow Stuart Hwy south for 48km to the turnoff to Edith Falls Rd. Drive 19km to the falls. You'll find a large carpark with a kiosk at the end of the road. The site's picnic area and campground are equipped with toilets, showers, benches, shelters and barbecues. The falls' plunge pool is just a couple of hundred metres away. You can swim there; the cold water is very refreshing in the heat of the day. A walking trail runs to the top of the falls. Further information can be found in the Edith Falls Fact Sheet with a map, downloadable at https://nt.gov.au/__data/assets/pdf_file/0008/413837/leliyn-edith-falls-fact-sheet-and-map.pdf.

Edith Falls Road

On your way to Edith Falls, it is worth stopping several times along Edith Falls Rd in search of Gouldian Finches and Hooded Parrots.

The first and best stop is at the Edith River crossing, located at the junction of Stuart Hwy and Edith Falls Rd, just north of the turnoff from the highway. Several obscure paths lead to the riverbed where waterholes form in the Dry, attracting finches searching for water. Get there early, 7am-8:30am, find a good seat and wait patiently for the birds to arrive, sometimes in their hundreds.

In May 2022, we observed a couple of Gouldian Finches that visited this site together with Long-tailed, Masked and Black-bellied Crimson Finches. Other birds coming for a drink included Red-winged Parrots, Cockatiels, Northern Rosellas, Diamond Doves, Paperbark Flycatchers, Bar-breasted Honeyeaters, Brown Honeyeaters, Dusky Honeyeaters and White-winged Trillers. Azure Kingfisher was perched on a branch overhanging the water. In the surrounding woodland, we spotted Northern Fantail, Little Woodswallow, Silver-backed Butcherbird and Brush Cuckoo. Collared Sparrowhawk perched hiding in a bush.

About 200m-300m from the junction, you'll find a waterhole outside of the riverbed, with a small carpark provided. GPS coordinates are 14°11'03''S and 132°02'18''E. Look for finches there; Hooded Parrots were also recorded. Waterbirds are often encountered, including Radjah Shelduck, Black Bittern, Little Egret, White-necked Heron, Brolga, Australasian Grebe and Black-fronted Dotterel. Keep your eyes peeled for Partridge Pigeons; they may also come to the waterhole for a drink. Woodland here may produce Black-tailed Treecreeper, Varied Sittella, Jacky Winter and Oriental Dollarbird. While walking through grassy areas, you have a chance to flush Red-backed Button-quails or Chestnut-backed Button-quails. Some rarer raptors, such as Little Eagle, Square-tailed Kite and Black-breasted Buzzard, have been reported from this spot.

Approximately 5km east of the junction with the highway, at GPS coordinates of 14°11’26”S and 132°04’32”E, there is a small creek crossing and an ephemeral wetland by the road. Hooded Parrots and Gouldian Finches are regularly found there. Other birds in this area include Black Bittern, Nankeen Night-Heron, Banded Honeyeater, Little Woodswallow and Black-breasted Buzzard.

Another spot, and a good one, is located 5.6km east of the turnoff from the highway. Pull over from Edith Falls Rd into a large circular turn in at GPS coordinates of 14°11’14”S and 132°04’57”E. Isolated waterholes form in the creek, where Hooded Parrots and Gouldian Finches are often found in the late Dry. Look also for Black Bittern. Check the tall trees in the area; they are the favourite roosting place of Hooded Parrots. Other birds reported from this location include Northern Rosella, Jacky Winter, Shining Flycatcher, Red-browed Pardalote, Forest Kingfisher, Varied Lorikeet, Bush Stone-curlew, Paperbark Flycatcher, White-gaped Honeyeater, Spotted Nightjar and Australian Owlet-nightjar. The 16 raptor species recorded in the area include Spotted Harrier, Australian Hobby, Black-breasted Buzzard and such rarities like Red Goshawk and Grey Falcon.

The next stop is about 10km further down the road, at the GPS coordinates of 14°10’25”S and 132°07’19”E, where a bridge spans the Edith River. Hooded Parrots and Gouldian Finches are found regularly in the area, particularly in the late Dry. Some finch species are abundant, including Black-bellied Crimson Finch, Masked Finch and Long-tailed Finch. Look for Black Bittern and Azure Kingfisher along the river edges lined with dense pandanus. Fifteen honeyeater species are recorded at this site including Yellow-tinted Honeyeater, Bar-breasted Honeyeater, Banded Honeyeater, White-quilled Honeyeater, Dusky Honeyeater, Helmeted Friarbird and Silver-crowned Friarbird. You may also come across Leaden Flycatcher, Lemon-bellied Flycatcher, Shining Flycatcher, Rufous Whistler, Little Shrike-thrush, Chestnut-backed Button-quail and Australian Bustard.

Edith Falls Area

Edith Falls lower pool

The lower pool is excellent not only for a refreshing dip in the cool water but also for birding. Black Bitterns and Azure Kingfishers are resident and regularly found perched in the pandanus around the pool. Other birds in this spot include Shining Flycatcher, Dusky Honeyeater, White-gaped Honeyeater, Paperbark Flycatcher, Nankeen Night-Heron and Australasian Grebe. A rare vagrant, Grey Wagtail, spent a few months around the pool in summer 2019.

The campground features tame Great Bowerbirds and Bush Stone-curlews. Look also for Oriental Dollarbird, Red-tailed Black-Cockatoo, Eastern Koel, Pheasant Coucal, Varied Lorikeet, Common Cicadabird, Brown Goshawk and a variety of honeyeaters.

A 2.6km Leliyn Circuit runs from the Visitor Centre to the top of the falls. You have a chance to spot Gouldian Finches and Hooded Parrots on this walk. You may also come across Black-tailed Treecreeper, Northern Shrike-tit, Little Woodswallow, White-throated Gerygone, Purple-backed Fairy-wren, Little Bronze-cuckoo and Olive-backed Oriole. Raptors will not disappoint; look for Black-breasted Buzzard, Wedge-tailed Eagle, Pacific Baza and Square-tailed Kite. Grey Falcon was recorded here a few times.

Cutta Cutta Caves Nature Park

This small, 1,500ha property is located 30km south of Katherine. The main attraction of the park are its spectacular caves. The land is covered with tropical savannah with small patches of rainforest thicket. Interestingly, the rainforest trees, such as banyan, are able to grow in this dry landscape because their roots find moisture in the humid air of the caves below. The fruits produced profusely by the rainforest feed a variety of birds including bowerbirds and figbirds.

To get there, drive south on Stuart Hwy (1) from Katherine, then turn west to the park as signposted. Drive 1km on a sealed road to the Visitor Centre where you'll find ample parking. Facilities include a kiosk and picnic grounds with shelters and toilets. A 1km circular Karst Walk leads to the caves. Another short walking track runs through the savannah woodland. In the dry season, the park is open daily from 8:30am to 4:30pm. The site is closed from December till March. Further information is provided in the Cutta Cutta Caves NP Fact Sheet, downloadable here: https://nt.gov.au/__data/assets/pdf_file/0017/200096/cutta-cutta-caves-nature-park-fact-sheet-and-map.pdf.

About 50 bird species are on the Cutta Cutta Caves birdlist. **Key species** are Red-chested Button-quail, Red-backed Button-quail, Long-tailed Finch and Northern Rosella. Other birds of interest include Red-tailed Black-Cockatoo, Red-winged Parrot, White-throated Honeyeater, White-gaped Honeyeater, Silver-crowned Friarbird, Varied Lorikeet and Tawny Frogmouth. Rarities include Red-browed Pardalote, Golden-backed Honeyeater and Little Eagle.

Our visit happened to be on a very hot afternoon. Sprinklers were working at full force on the lawns around the Visitor Centre. Masses of birds were making use of this shower, bathing and drinking. This included Double-barred Finches, Long-tailed Finches, Masked Finches, Zebra Finches, Great Bowerbirds, Grey-crowned Babblers, Silver-crowned Friarbirds, Diamond Doves, Olive-back Orioles and very vocal White-gaped and White-throated Honeyeaters.

In a tree near the Visitor Centre, we spotted a roosting pair of Tawny Frogmouths. Savannah Woodland Walk produced Banded Honeyeater, Yellow-tinted Honeyeater, Rufous-throated Honeyeater, White-winged Triller and Northern Fantail. A group of Red-chested Button-quails flushed from the grass. Red-backed Button-quails and Brown Quails were also recorded at this site.

Northern Fantail

As we were leaving, a large flock of Red-tailed Black-Cockatoos landed near the entrance gate in the area still smouldering from a recent controlled burn.

Leach Lagoon

This large, shallow lagoon is located on the eastern side of Stuart Hwy (1) 40km southeast of Katherine and 4km north of the turnoff to Central Arnhem Rd. A large rest area with toilets is located by the roadside opposite the lagoon. GPS coordinates are 14°37'56''S and 132°37'27''E. During the Dry, very little water remains in the lagoon.

Over 140 bird species have been found on and around Leach Lagoon. **Key species** are waders, Brolga, Black-necked Stork, Glossy Ibis, Red-chested Button-quail, Northern Rosella and Common Cicadabird. Other birds of interest include Apostlebird, White-throated Gerygone, Oriental Dollarbird, Green Pygmy-goose, Tawny Grassbird, Jacky Winter, Great Bowerbird, Silver-crowned Friarbird and White-bellied Sea-Eagle. Rarities include Freckled Duck, Black-tailed Treecreeper, Dusky Moorhen, Little Grassbird, Oriental Plover and Swinhoe's Snipe.

Bird composition changes with the changing water levels. In the Dry, particularly at its end in Oct-Nov, most visible are Black-necked Storks (up to 20 birds) and Brolgas, scattered around the area. You will also see waders, gathering here on the exposed mud. 15 species have been recorded, including Common Greenshank, Marsh Sandpiper, Wood Sandpiper, Red-kneed Dotterel, Pied Stilt, Australian Pratincole and Oriental Pratincole. In the wet season, waterbirds dominate, including Magpie Goose, Radjah Shelduck, White-necked Heron, Royal Spoonbill, Yellow-billed Spoonbill, Plumed Whistling-Duck and Wandering Whistling-Duck.

In the surrounding grassland, look for Australian Bustard, Red-chested Button-quail, Brown Quail, Brown Songlark, Rufous Songlark and Tawny Grassbird. Woodland birds in the area include Little Bronze-cuckoo, Pallid Cuckoo, Long-tailed Finch, Grey-crowned Babbler and Olive-backed Oriole.

Central Arnhem Road

The turnoff from Stuart Hwy (1) to Central Arnhem Rd (24) is located about 45km south of Katherine. The first section of the road is sealed up to about 40km mark. Coincidentally, the sealed segment is the best site in the whole NT for the much-coveted species, Northern Shrike-tit. Several spots that could be helpful in search for this difficult species are listed below.

In total, over 110 bird species have been recorded along Central Arnhem Rd. **Key species** are Northern Shrike-tit, Gouldian Finch, Hooded Parrot and Red-backed Button-quail. Other birds of interest include Red-browed Pardalote, Australian Bustard, Banded Honeyeater, Golden-backed Honeyeater, Apostlebird, Pallid Cuckoo, Little Woodswallow, Black-tailed Treecreeper, Jacky Winter, Varied Sittella, White-throated Gerygone. Long-tailed Finch and Australian Owlet-nightjar. Rarities include Grey Falcon, Black Falcon, Little Eagle and Hooded Robin.

Central Arnhem Rd at 14°38'12''S and 132°41'09''E

This spot is located 3km east of Stuart Hwy, at the Roper Creek crossing. Apart from Northern Shrike-tit, look here for Little Woodswallow, Red-backed Kingfisher, Jacky Winter, Rufous Songlark, Yellow-tinted Honeyeater, Banded Honeyeater and Golden-backed Honeyeater. Finches coming to drink, include Gouldian Finch, Masked Finch, Double-barred Finch and Long-tailed Finch. Chestnut-backed Button-quails can be found in grassy areas.

Central Arnhem Rd at 14°37'54''S and 132°41'18''E

This place is about 4km east of Stuart Hwy. Apart from Northern Shrike-tit, look for Gouldian Finches here. You may also get Black-tailed Treecreeper, Apostlebird, Cockatiel, Red-tailed Black-Cockatoo and Wedge-tailed Eagle.

Black-tailed Treecreeper

Central Arnhem Rd at 14°36'40"S and 132°42'16"E

This is one of the best spots for the Northern Shrike-tit. It is located about 6km from Stuart Hwy. Gouldian Finches and Hooded Parrots were observed in good numbers, particularly most recently, in 2022-23. In autumn, Masked Woodswallows appear in large numbers, but you can also see White-browed Woodswallows, Black-faced Woodswallows and Little Woodswallows.

Search for Hooded Robins, rare in the North. They are resident in the area.

Honeyeaters here include Yellow-tinted Honeyeater, Rufous-throated Honeyeater, Golden-backed Honeyeater, Banded Honeyeater, Bar-breasted Honeyeater, Silver-crowned Friarbird and Helmeted Friarbird.

Red-chested Button-quails, Red-backed Button-quails or Brown Quails can be flushed from the grassy areas.

Central Arnhem Rd at 14°36'09"S and 132°42'42"E

This spot is located 6.5-7km east of Stuart Hwy. Northern Shrike-tits have been reported nesting there. Other birds in the area include Pallid Cuckoo, Brush Cuckoo, Chestnut-backed Button-quail, Gouldian Finch, Grey-fronted Honeyeater, Hooded Parrot and Black-breasted Buzzard.

Central Arnhem Rd at 14°35'12"S and 132°43'31"E

This site is located 12km northeast of Stuart Hwy. Apart from Northern Shrike-tits, this is also a good spot for Gouldian Finches, Hooded Parrots and Silver-backed Butcherbirds. Other birds in the area include Black-tailed Treecreeper, Varied Sittella, Little Woodswallow, Red-backed Kingfisher, Golden-backed Honeyeater, Long-tailed Finch, Rufous Songlark, Varied Lorikeet and Apostlebird. Be on the lookout for some rare raptors like Square-tailed Kite, Black-breasted Buzzard and Black Falcon.

Central Arnhem Rd at 14°31'44"S and 132°47'14"E

Now you are about 15km from Stuart Hwy at the Maranboy Creek crossing. A Police Station is located nearby. Northern Shrike-tits are hard to find here but there is waterhole in the creek where these birds may come to drink. Cockatiels may arrive in large flocks. Hooded Parrots and Gouldian Finches are reported from time to time. Look also for Black-necked Stork, Nankeen Night-Heron, Azure Kingfisher, Black Bittern, Great Egret and Plumed Egret. Even Grey Falcon was seen several times.

Cockatiels at a waterhole

Bush birds in the surrounding woodland include Grey-crowned Babbler, Banded Honeyeater, Yellow-tinted Honeyeater, Sacred Kingfisher, Red-backed Kingfisher, Olive-backed Oriole, Apostlebird and Rufous Whistler.

Central Arnhem Rd at 14°33'36"S and 133°03'57"E

This site is located approximately 50km from Stuart Hwy. If you reach the Beswick Creek settlement, you have to go back 1km. If you are game to drive that far, you may get some finches at a waterhole; most common are Chestnut-breasted Mannikin, Double-barred Finch, Long-tailed Finch and Masked Finch. However, you may also encounter Star Finch, Gouldian Finch or Pictorella Mannikin.

Elsey National Park and Mataranka

This 13,800ha Park is located near Stuart Hwy (1) 100km south of Katherine and 420km south of Darwin. The legendary township of Mataranka is located on Stuart Hwy, partially within the National Park. The main attraction of the Park are the fantastic, crystal clear thermal springs that stay at about 34-36°C year around. Several historic sites in the Park include a replica of the Mataranka Homestead, home of Jeannie Gunn, the author of the iconic Australian novel *We of the Never Never*. The famous movie of the same title was also filmed there.

The main vegetation in the National Park is tropical woodland, with long stretches of paperbark woodland, pandanus and stands of mature palms along the Roper River and its tributaries.

Elsey National Park consists of two sections: Bitter Springs in the north and Mataranka Homestead in the south. Each section has its own fabulous thermal pools that are magnet for tourists. Three sealed roads lead to various parts of the Park. The roads may become impassable during the Wet.

The Bitter Springs section is reached via Martin Rd. Turn east off Stuart Hwy at the north end of the Mataranka village. Mataranka Homestead is located at the end of Homestead Rd. To get there, turn east off Stuart Hwy 1.5km south of the Mataranka village. To visit the southeastern section of the Park along Roper River, turn from Homestead Rd into John Hauser Dr 1.5km from the turnoff from Stuart Hwy. Many Park facilities are located along this road including the Jalmurark Campground, 4 Mile Picnic Area and several hiking trails to the river. Toilets are available only in Jalmurark. At some river access points there are boat ramps.

Mataranka Homestead offers good facilities including a restaurant, a large caravan park, toilets and a short track to the Mataranka Thermal Pool. Bitter Springs have a more natural, bush setting, there is no resort around them. You'll find here a large carpark, toilets and a circular walk along Little Roper River around the thermal pools. Which pools are better? It's a personal preference, we loved both locations. Take a couple of foam noodles with you, bobbing up and down in the warm water is a singularly pleasant experience.

Further information on Elsey National Park and the site map can be downloaded here: https://nt.gov.au/__data/assets/pdf_file/0018/200097/elsey-national-park-fact-sheet-and-map.pdf.

Over 180 bird species have been recorded in the Elsey National Park. **Key species** are Red Goshawk, Rufous Owl, Black Bittern and Northern Shrike-tit. Other birds of interest include Azure Kingfisher, Paperbark Flycatcher, Shining Flycatcher, Banded Honeyeater, Northern Fantail, White-throated Gerygone and Apostlebird. Rarities include Grey Falcon, Square-tailed Kite, Great-billed Heron, Flock Bronzewing, Rock Dove, Buff-sided Robin and Hooded Robin.

A unique road sign on Stuart Hwy catches your eye in the Mataranka village, called, perhaps a bit overinflated, Mataranka Central: 'Attention: Brolgas crossing the road'. And indeed, when we stopped there one day, a family of three Brolgas were stately walking between the people and parked cars at the busy Sunday market in the park beside the main road, peeping into the stalls. No kidding! A noisy hotel pub with gambling was just across the road on the other side; we were wondering if the Brolgas were heading there afterwards. Next year, we stopped in the same park for a picnic lunch, and three Brolgas came up to our table.

A family of Brolgas checking out our rig at a picnic site in Mataranka Central

Bitter Springs Section

The bird that attracts birders to this site is Red Goshawk. It can be found all along Martin Rd, from Territory Manor Caravan Park to Bitter Springs. Its preference is a tall riverine forest and watercourses, in particular the northern side of Little Roper River. Over the years, there were several well-known Red Goshawk nests along Martin Rd, some even in a caravan park, but mostly on private properties. To protect the breeding birds (from the birders) the locations are now kept secret.

Territory Manor Caravan Park

This site is located in Martin Rd in the Mataranka village. A pair of Red Goshawks were nesting in the van park for years but now their nest is occupied by Black Kites. Whistling Kite, Pacific Baza and Brown Goshawk are also nesting on the grounds. We also observed Black-breasted Buzzard and Australian Hobby flying overhead.

A large flock of feral Indian Peafowl roams the van park, some resident here, other arriving every evening from elsewhere to roost in big trees scattered through the site. There are lots of other tame, inquisitive birds on the grounds. These include Apostlebirds, White-quilled Honeyeaters, Varied Lorikeets, Red-collared Lorikeets, Great Bowerbirds, Grey-crowned Babblers, Blue-winged Kookaburras and Green Orioles.

Azure Kingfishers and Sacred Kingfishers are resident on a small dam behind the restaurant, which is maintained for the barramundi. In this location, look also for Forest Kingfisher, Nankeen Night-Heron, Shining Flycatcher, Paperbark Flycatcher, Oriental Dollarbird, Banded Honeyeater, White-bellied Cuckoo-shrike, Long-tailed Finch and Channel-billed Cuckoo.

Bitter Springs Cabins and Camping

This charming caravan park is adjacent to the National Park, at a walking distance to thermal pools. A morning walk in the woodland around the site and along the Little Roper River may produce Azure Kingfisher, Nankeen Night-Heron, Radjah Shelduck, Pheasant Coucal, Lemon-bellied Flycatcher, Shining Flycatcher, Olive-backed Oriole, Arafura Fantail, Rufous-throated Honeyeater, Bar-breasted Honeyeater and Silver-crowned Friarbird.

Red Goshawk regularly nests around the Bitter Springs Cabins not far from the turnoff to the site from Martin Rd.

At night, you may hear Southern Boobook, Australian Owlet-nightjar, Bush Stone-curlew and occasionally Rufous Owl.

Bitter Springs Circular Walk

A magnificent palm forest at Bitter Springs thermal pools

This 1.5km walk runs along the Little Roper River from the carpark to the thermal pools, coming back on the other side of the river. You may get here Azure Kingfisher, Common Cicadabird, Green-backed Gerygone, White-throated Gerygone, Shining Flycatcher, Paperbark Flycatcher, Northern Fantail, Black-bellied Crimson Finch, Rufous-banded Honeyeater, Bar-breasted Honeyeater and Buff-sided Robin. Nankeen Night-Herons often roost just beside the pools.

Be on the lookout for Red Goshawk; there are several records from trees in the carpark. You may have a slightly better chance to spot a Square-tailed Kite (last record from the Bitter Springs area is from June 2022). Other raptors include Grey Goshawk, Brown Goshawk, Pacific Baza, Wedge-tailed Eagle and Australian Hobby.

Rarer birds recorded in the Bitter Springs section include Great-billed Heron (usually seen flying over the area), Black-necked Stork and Dusky Moorhen. Rufous Owl is sometimes observed in the thermal pools' carpark.

John Hauser Drive

In the southeastern section of the National Park, best birding is along Roper River that runs parallel to John Hauser Dr. There are several access points to the river along this road.

Botanic Walk

This 5.5km circular walking trail to the river starts and ends at a small carpark at GPS coordinates of 14°56'20"S and 133°08'26"E.

Square-tailed Kites and Black-breasted Buzzards were recorded several times along the walk. Other raptors in the area include White-bellied Sea-Eagle, Pacific Baza and Brown Falcon. Along the walk, look for Arafura Fantail, Shining Flycatcher, Paperbark Flycatcher, Rufous Whistler, White-gaped Honeyeater, Dusky Honeyeater, Grey-fronted Honeyeater, Golden-backed Honeyeater and Banded Honeyeater. Hooded Robins have also been recorded.

Look for Black Bittern, Nankeen Night-Heron and Azure Kingfisher along the riverbanks.

Wabalarr Rest Area

Roper River at Wabalarr, note the massive croc trap

This riverside picnic spot is located just 100m from John Hauser Dr. GPS coordinates for the off-road carpark are 14°56'52''S and 133°12'33''E. We flushed Black Bittern and Nankeen Night-Heron from the trees lining the river. The spot was still showing the signs of a recent flood and was in disrepair. However, we found a place to sit and enjoy watching the birds flying over the river from one side to the other. Among them were Torresian Imperial-Pigeons, Channel-billed Cuckoos, Pheasant Coucals, Oriental Dollarbirds, White-quilled Honeyeaters, Pacific Baza and plenty of Red-collared Lorikeets. Little Bronze-cuckoo was calling from the bushes.

Red-collared Lorikeets seeking water at the dripping taps

In the dry woodland growing on the tall banks, we found Rufous Whistler, Forest Kingfisher, Banded Honeyeater, Brown Honeyeater, Red-winged Parrot and Collared Sparrowhawk. Spotted Nightjar was also reported from this location.

Jalmurark Campground

This is a large, complex site with a criss-cross of walking tracks and river access points. The birdlife here is abundant. The most visible during our visit were Great Bowerbirds. We located an active bower at the camping Site #11 at the GPS coordinates of 14°57'10''S and 133°13'17''E. The bower was tastefully decorated on both sided with white snail shells, and was sprinkled with green foliage. As we watched it, nine birds were attending to the bower.

A large flock of Apostlebirds was advancing through the campground. In the flowering paperbark trees around the site, were got White-gaped Honeyeater, Yellow-tinted Honeyeater, White-throated Honeyeater and Varied Lorikeet. Two Tawny Frogmouths were roosting in a tree near the amenities block. Behind this building we found a double bower of Great Bowerbirds, one bigger, one smaller. Perhaps the owner decided to expand or maybe the bird from a smaller bower was helping himself to the construction materials from the main residence.

At the river, we noted Azure Kingfisher, Nankeen Night-Heron, Common Sandpiper, Australasian Darter, Radjah Shelduck, Shining Flycatcher, Pheasant Coucal, Dusky Moorhen and White-bellied Sea-Eagle. Other birds we got at this site included Bar-shouldered Dove, Cockatiel, Tree Martin, Green Oriole, Leaden Flycatcher and Australian Figbird.

Nocturnal birds reported from Jalmurark include Barking Owl, Bush Stone-curlew, Southern Boobook and Spotted Nightjar.

Mataranka Homestead

The most common birds on the grounds of Mataranka Homestead were Great Bowerbird, Apostlebird and White-quilled Honeyeater. A huge group of feral Indian Peafowl was landing in the trees each evening for a night roost. At night, Rufous Owl was calling in the caravan park. Other birds were similar to those in other parts of Elsey National Park.

Warloch Ponds

This site is located on both sides of Stuart Hwy (1) approximately 20km south of Mataranka, 8km north of the south end of Elsey Cemetery Rd. GPS coordinates are 15°06’13’’S and 133°04’40’’E.

Black Bitterns are regularly found there. Other waterbirds include Brolga, Glossy Ibis, Green Pygmy-goose, Magpie Goose, Radjah Shelduck, Royal Spoonbill, Black-necked Stork and Plumed Egret. Finches come to drink here, including Pictorella Mannikin, Star Finch, Masked Finch and Long-tailed Finch. Look also for Northern Shrike-tit, Australian Bustard, Banded Honeyeater, Masked Woodswallow, Little Woodswallow, Peregrine Falcon and Black-breasted Buzzard.

Warloch Rest Area

This site is located on the eastern side of the highway 20km south of Warloch Ponds and 41km north of Larrimah, at GPS coordinates of 15°14'11"S and 133°06'53"E.

Look here for the rare Northern Shrike-tits. They occur in the savannah trees mostly west of the rest stop. Investigate the 250m-long strip on the other side of the road.

Finches come to drink here from the puddles formed by a leaking tank by the toilet block. You should get Long-tailed Finch, Masked Finch, Double-barred Finch and, if lucky, also Gouldian Finch.

In the surrounding savannah look for Black-tailed Treecreeper, Pallid Cuckoo, Horsfield's Bronze-cuckoo, Masked Woodswallow, Varied Sittella, Apostlebird, Golden-backed Honeyeater, Yellow-tinted Honeyeater, Singing Honeyeater and Helmeted Friarbird. Grassland may produce Brown Quail, Red-backed Button-quail and Red-backed Fairy-wren.

Golden-backed Honeyeater

Alexander Forrest Memorial Rest Area

This site is located on Stuart Hwy (1) 38km south of Larrimah and 220km south of Katherine, at the GPS coordinates of 15°51'37''S and 133°24'17''E. This excellent free RV camp has two large water tanks, painted purple. Water has been dripping for years from the tanks' piping and somebody had a presence of mind to put collecting trays and perching branches under the drip of the tank that is closer to the toilets. This has become the favourite drinking place for finches and other local birdlife. Inevitably, this site has become a regular stop for birders to watch Gouldian Finches along Stuart Hwy.

We stopped there twice, in autumn and in winter 2022. Gouldian Finches were there on both occasions, arriving several times a day to drink, 4-20 birds at a time. They were mostly green juveniles. While waiting for Gouldian Finches to come in hope of a good photo, we also observed Long-tailed Finches, Masked Finches, Double-barred Finches, Chestnut-breasted Mannikins, Yellow-tinted Honeyeaters, Brown Honeyeaters, Rufous-throated Honeyeaters, Little Friarbirds, Peaceful Doves, Diamond Doves, Common Bronzewings, Great Bowerbirds and a single Pictorella Mannikin.

Masked Woodswallows and a Little Friarbird

In the profusely flowering tall bloodwoods around the site, we observed masses of Masked Woodswallows and also honeyeaters such as Little Friarbird, Silver-crowned Friarbird, Bar-breasted Honeyeater, Grey-fronted Honeyeater, Banded Honeyeater and Golden-backed Honeyeater. At night, Bush Stone-curlews were breaking the night calm with their piercing calls. Tawny Frogmouth was catching insects near the site streetlamp. Southern Boobook and Australian Owlet-nightjar were calling.

Other birds at this spot included Golden-headed Cisticola, Red-backed Fairy-wren, Jacky Winter, Apostlebird, White-winged Triller, Little Woodswallow, Black-faced Woodswallow, Brown Quail and Cockatiel.

Daly Waters Hi-Way Inn

Daly Waters Hi-Way Inn is a popular roadhouse located at the corner of Stuart Hwy (1) and Carpentaria Hwy (1), about 600km south of Darwin. It offers good facilities for the weary travellers. The roadhouse is surrounded by savannah woodland and is known for a large flock of Red-tailed Black-Cockatoos that often come to roost in trees on the grounds. A temporary wetland is located behind the roadhouse, where many birds visit to drink. In particular, look for finches such as Masked, Long-tailed, Zebra and Double-barred Finch. Small numbers of Yellow-rumped Mannikins have also been recorded. Occasionally, wetland birds stay for a while, including Black-fronted Dotterel, Marsh Sandpiper, Nankeen Night-Heron and White-necked Heron.

Golden-backed Honeyeaters are resident on the grounds. Other birds in the area include White-throated Honeyeater, Grey-fronted Honeyeater, Red-winged Parrot, Budgerigar, Cockatiel, Apostlebird, White-fronted Chat and Paperbark Flycatcher. Large flocks of White-browed Woodswallows come to roost in the trees, cuddling up together in long lines.

Stuart Hwy at 16°15'27''S and 133°23'37''E.

This site is located on Stuart Hwy (1) about 6km north of Daly Waters Hi-Way Inn. You'll find here a patch of woodland that is worth a stop. Locate a track leading to the aerodrome – Northern Shrike-tits can be found there. Look also for Brown Quail, Varied Lorikeet, Little Woodswallow, Black-faced Woodswallow, Masked Finch and Budgerigar.

Newcastle Waters

Newcastle Waters is an interesting ghost town with a large, nearly permanent waterhole nearby. The site is located about 3km west of Stuart Hwy (A1) via Newcastle Waters Rd. GPS coordinates are 17°22'23"S and 133°24'39"E. The turnoff is situated 23km north of Elliott. You'll find here a number of well-preserved buildings such as Jones Store and Junction Hotel. Newcastle Waters is surrounded by a 1mln ha cattle station of the same name.

Over 150 bird species have been recorded in Newcastle Waters. **Key species** are waders and waterbirds including Brolga and Glossy Ibis, as well as Apostlebird, Australian Reed-Warbler, Black Falcon and Black-breasted Buzzard. Other birds of interest include Budgerigar, Cockatiel, Sacred Kingfisher, Red-backed Kingfisher, Great Pied Cormorant, Paperback Flycatcher, Banded Honeyeater, Yellow-tinted Honeyeater, Diamond Dove, Grey-crowned Babbler, White-winged Triller and Rufous Songlark. Rarities include Yellow Chat, Pictorella Mannikin, Freckled Duck, Australian Shelduck, Pied Heron, Great Cormorant, Australian Spotted Crake, Oriental Pratincole, Little Curlew, Wood Sandpiper, Golden-backed Honeyeater, Black Honeyeater and Little Eagle.

Masses of waterbirds congregate around the waterhole, with the biggest flocks formed by Magpie Geese and Plumed Whistling-Ducks. Brolgas gather in flocks of 10-15 birds. Other regulars on the water include Australian Gull-billed Terns, Royal Spoonbills, Plumed Egrets and Nankeen Night-Herons.

A typical selection of waders includes Sharp-tailed Sandpiper, Red-kneed Dotterel, Black-fronted Dotterel, Red-necked Avocet, Red-capped Plover and Australian Pratincole.

Australian Shelduck is a rarity in NT

When the waterhole is shrinking but water is still there, other water sources in the area may have already disappeared, and the traffic to Newcastle Waters increases. At such times, you may observe flocks of Budgerigars, Diamond Doves, Zebra Finches and a variety of honeyeaters.

The birds crowding around the waterhole attract raptors; 17 species have been recorded. A pair of resident Black Falcons are often observed. Look also for White-bellied Sea-Eagle, Peregrine Falcon, Black-breasted Buzzard, Australian Hobby, Wedge-tailed Eagle or Swamp Harrier.

Other birds near the waterhole include Masked Woodswallow, Black-faced Woodswallow, Pallid Cuckoo, Varied Lorikeet, Rainbow Bee-eater and Emu.

Renner Springs Desert Inn

This roadhouse is a welcomed stop on the endless Stuart Hwy. It is located 160km north of Tennant Creek and 820km south of Darwin. It offers a fuel station, restaurant, motel and a small, recently spruced up caravan park. There is also a swimming pool. Several large trees on the grounds are utilised by birds for roosting and nesting. Behind the caravan park is a wetland with a muddy spring and an old windmill. Another waterhole is on the adjacent property. These waterholes attract birds in the Dry, so Renner Springs is a good place for an overnight stop.

Over 160 bird species have been recorded in Renner Springs. **Key species** are Brolga, Australian Bustard, Grey-fronted Honeyeater, Spinifex Pigeon and Black-breasted Buzzard. Other birds of interest include Nankeen Night-Heron, Rainbow Bee-eater, Red-tailed Black-Cockatoo, Apostlebird, White-breasted Woodswallow, Oriental Dollarbird, Rufous Songlark, Western Gerygone and Black Kite. On the long list of rarities are Grey Falcon, Black Falcon, Little Eagle, Freckled Duck, Great Cormorant, Oriental Plover, Wood Sandpiper, Australian Painted-snipe, Pictorella Mannikin, House Sparrow and Welcome Swallow.

Black Kite chick on its nest on the old windmill at Renner Springs

We stayed a couple of nights at Renner Springs in winter 2022 and spent a lot of time observing a nearly fledged Black Kite chick that was making efforts to get ready to fly. The nest was constructed on the old windmill. The chick was fed with the roadkill, mostly cane toads, and scraps from the restaurant. After hours of wing flapping and walking along the horizontal bar, always ending with a cautious retreat to the nest, the bird finally made its first flight on the morning of our departure. We were proud as if that were the first steps of our own child. At the bottom of the kite's nest, several Zebra Finches made their own nests. That turned the structure into an apartment building.

Brown Goshawks had their nest with a chick in the tree standing in the middle of the caravan park (that tree may no longer be there after the renovations). Other raptors in the area included Wedge-tailed Eagle, Black-breasted Buzzard and Australian Hobby. Spotted Harriers were hunting over the farmland south of the roadhouse.

Five Brolgas were honking and prancing around the wetland. A resident domestic goose joined in the vocalisation and looked as if it yearned to fly away with them. Fairy Martins were repairing their bottle-shaped mud nests around the motel. Behind the restaurant, a noisy flock of about 200 Little Corellas chose a tree for roosting above a drying clothesline. Bugger. The whole day, a line of small bush birds was queueing for the waterhole, perching on bushes growing at the water edge. They were paying little attention to the tourists and their caravans. We observed Grey-fronted Honeyeater, Brown Honeyeater, Singing Honeyeater, Yellow-tinted Honeyeater, Zebra Finch, Double-barred Finch, White-winged Triller, Budgerigar and Cockatiel. A small flock of Spinifex Pigeons was landing at dusk at the dam of the neighbouring property.

Every evening, flock of small birds, mostly Rainbow Bee-eaters and various honeyeaters, were arriving from the surrounding farmland to roost overnight in a few tall trees near the fuel pumps. Bush Stone-curlews were serenading during the night. We also watched Barn Owl in the light coming from the restaurant.

In summer (the Wet), 18 species of waders have been recorded in Renner Springs including Common Sandpiper, Sharp-tailed Sandpiper, Common Greenshank, Marsh Sandpiper, Pied Stilt, Red-necked Avocet, Australian Pratincole, Oriental Pratincole, Black-fronted Dotterel and Red-kneed Dotterel. Many waterbirds have also been reported, such as Buff-banded Rail, Nankeen Night-Heron, White-necked Heron, Black-tailed Native-hen, Pink-eared Duck, Hardhead, Grey Teal, Glossy Ibis, Yellow-billed Spoonbill, Whiskered Tern and White-winged Black Tern.

The section of Stuart Hwy between Elliott and Renner Springs is very good for raptors, with 18 species recorded. Our findings included Spotted Harrier, Black-breasted Buzzard, Black Falcon, Brown Falcon, Nankeen Kestrel and plenty of Black Kites and Whistling Kites.

Northwestern NT

1 [Buntine Highway](#)
2 [Victoria Highway](#)
3 [Victoria River Roadhouse](#)
4 [Timber Creek](#)
5 [Judbarra Gregory National Park](#)
6 [Jasper Gorge](#)
7 [Keep River National Park](#)

Buntine Highway

Buntine Hwy (96) is a 580km regional road that runs north-southwest through the Northern Territory. It starts at Victoria Hwy (1) half-way between Katherine and Timber Creek, and leads via Top Springs and Kalkarindji to intersect with Duncan Rd in Western Australia. The 360km section from Victoria Hwy to Kalkarindji is a single-lane sealed road. The remaining part is unsealed and unfenced.

The road runs through various habitats, with savannah woodland being the predominant landscape. The only decent place to stay along the road is the Top Springs Roadhouse.

Over 130 bird species have been recorded along Buntine Hwy. **Key species** are Gouldian Finch, Pictorella Mannikin, Purple-crowned Fairy-wren, Northern Shrike-tit, Golden-backed Honeyeater and Black-breasted Buzzard. Other birds of interest include Red-backed Kingfisher, Paperbark Flycatcher, Apostlebird, Jacky Winter, Banded Honeyeater, Long-tailed Finch, Masked Finch, Red-browed Pardalote and Spotted Harrier. Rarities include Yellow-rumped Mannikin, Buff-sided Robin, Star Finch, Grey Falcon and Little Eagle.

Buntine Hwy at 15°18’11’’S and 131°34’18’’E

A pair of Long-tailed Finches

This spot is located not far from the turnoff from Victoria Hwy. A local ephemeral waterhole attracts finches in the dry season. Look for Gouldian Finch, Long-tailed Finch, Masked Finch, Double-barred Finch, Pictorella Mannikin and Yellow-rumped Mannikin. Keep an eye on the sky; Black-breasted Buzzards have been observed here several times.

Buntine Hwy at 15°19'07''S and 131°34'59''E

There is a creek crossing at this location, about 2km from the turnoff from Victoria Hwy. Inspect any waterholes in the creek bed as well as bushland up to 1km before and 1km past the crossing. Gouldian Finches are recorded here frequently among the more common species. You may also come across Yellow-rumped Mannikin and Star Finch. Northern Shrike-tits have been sighted in the bush near the creek. Hooded Robins are occasionally reported from this site.

Look also for Jacky Winter, Weebill, Varied Sittella, White-winged Triller, Grey-fronted Honeyeater, Banded Honeyeater, Yellow-tinted Honeyeater and Masked Woodswallow. In the grassland, you may find Brown Quail, Australian Bustard, Golden-headed Cisticola and Rufous Songlark. Spotted Harrier was recorded.

Buntine Hwy at 15°20'07''S and 131°35'07''E

This is Humbles Creek crossing, about 5km from the Victoria Hwy turnoff. A water tank near the road is often leaking, which attract the birds. This is another spot where a variety of finches can be found. It is particularly reliable for Gouldian Finches. Also, large numbers of Star Finches are reported to come for a drink here.

Check the roadside trees for Northern Shrike-tits and Golden-backed Honeyeaters.

When paperbarks are blooming, you may experience masses of pollen- and nectar-feeding birds including Masked Woodswallows, Varied Lorikeets, Yellow-tinted Honeyeaters, Banded Honeyeaters, Rufous-throated Honeyeaters, Silver-crowned Friarbirds and Little Friarbirds.

Other birds in the area include Budgerigar, Black-faced Woodswallow, Northern Fantail, Great Bowerbird, Oriental Dollarbird, Black-tailed Treecreeper and Horsfield's Bronze-cuckoo.

Buntine Hwy at 15°33'01"S and 131°38'38"E

This place is located 35km from the Victoria Hwy turnoff. There is a small dam here, not visible from the road. Look for a farm track to the right and walk about 100m to the dam. This is a good place for the waders; you may also encounter Australian Pelicans, Black-necked Storks, Hardheads, White-necked Herons, Plumed Whistling-Ducks, Purple-crowned Fairy-wrens, Apostlebirds and Spotted Harriers, or even catch a glimpse of a Grey Falcon.

Top Springs

Top Springs is located at the crossroads of Buntine Hwy (96) and Buchanan Hwy (80), 165km from the Victoria Hwy turnoff and 290km from Katherine. It has the population of 3, a roadhouse and a caravan park. The main magnet of this place is a remote Aussie pub filled with memorabilia. Stop here for a cold beer and the famous Outback hospitality. At the back of the pub is a waterhole which can be very productive for raptors and finches.

Over 120 bird species have been recorded around Top Springs. **Key species** are Grey Falcon, Black Falcon, Gouldian Finch, Pictorella Mannikin and Spinifex Pigeon. Other birds of interest include Black-breasted Buzzard, Spotted Harrier, Apostlebird, Bar-shouldered Dove, Black-tailed Treecreeper, Red-browed Pardalote, Purple-backed Fairy-wren, Chestnut-backed Button-quail, Long-tailed Finch and Masked Finch. Rarities include Common Myna, Flock Bronzewing, Buff-banded Rail and Little Eagle.

Top Springs offers you a good chance to spot a Grey Falcon flying over the roadhouse or harassing pigeons and parrots near the waterhole. Altogether, 16 raptor species have been recorded in the area. A hundred or more Black Kites hang around the roadhouse. Other birds of prey include Wedge-tailed Eagle, Australian Hobby, Brown Falcon and Black-shouldered Kite.

The most visible birds are the parrots, particularly when Budgerigars and Cockatiels arrive for a drink. Ten finch species are present in the area. Pictorella Mannikins are recorded in huge flocks. Look also for Star Finch, Black-bellied Crimson Finch, Long-tailed Finch, Masked Finch and Gouldian Finch. Honeyeaters are represented by 16 species including Golden-backed Honeyeater, White-plumed Honeyeater, Yellow-tinted Honeyeater, Grey-fronted Honeyeater, Banded Honeyeater, Spiny-cheeked Honeyeater and Yellow-throated Miner. During the Wet, large flocks of Oriental Pratincoles may appear.

Masked Finch with a juvenile Gouldian Finch sneaking in into the frame

Other birds in the area include Sacred Kingfisher, White-winged Triller, Rainbow Bee-eater, Australian Bustard, Horsfield's Bushlark, Purple-backed Fairy-wren, White-throated Gerygone and Tree Martin.

A single Common Myna was recorded near the roadhouse in July 2016.

Kalkarindji

The township of Kalkarindji is located 360km from the Victoria Hwy turnoff. The bitumen ends here. Victoria River flows through Kalkarindji and a large waterhole in the riverbed under the bridge retains water year-round. A robust, isolated population of Purple-crowned Fairy-wrens lives there, easy to watch from the bridge.

Finches come daily to drink from the waterhole. Most common are Long-tailed Finch, Black-bellied Crimson Finch and Zebra Finch. Yellow-rumped Mannikins are occasionally encountered. Large flocks of Straw-necked Ibises regularly roost in trees near the bridge. Wetland birds include Radjah Shelduck, White-necked Heron, Black-necked Stork, Brolga and Common Sandpiper.

In woodland along the river, look for Buff-sided Robin, Paperbark Flycatcher, Rufous Songlark, Red-backed Kingfisher, Azure Kingfisher, Jacky Winter, White-gaped Honeyeater, Rufous-throated Honeyeater, Varied Lorikeet and Brown Goshawk.

The township is ruled by Great Bowerbirds. Several bowers have been established. Australian Bustards can be spotted in grassland at the edges of town.

Victoria Highway

The length of Victoria Hwy (1) in NT is 470km, all sealed. The road runs northeast-southwest from Katherine to the WA border through the vast savannah plains fringed by escarpment country. There are several spots along the route with waterholes, creek crossings and rivers where you can stop in search of finches, button-quails and raptors. Some of the more promising spots are described below.

Mathison Rest Area

This spot is located at the GPS coordinates of 15°08’23”S and 131°41’02”E, about 25km northeast of the junction with Buntine Hwy (96). You’ll find toilets here and a water tank that is usually leaking, attracting birds. A flock of Apostlebirds lives around the rest area. Other birds include Masked Finch, Long-tailed Finch, Yellow-tinted Honeyeater, Budgerigar and Australian Owlet-nightjar. Look also for raptors such as Black-breasted Buzzard, Wedge-tailed Eagle and Black Falcon.

Victoria Hwy at 15°16’57”S and 131°34’43”E

This spot is located 4km east of the junction with Buntine Hwy (96). There is a creek crossing there with an ephemeral waterhole which can yield a large variety of birds. In particular, Star Finches are often reported. A pair of Black-breasted Buzzards have often been seen flying over the area. Red-browed Pardalotes call loudly from the creekline vegetation. In winter, masses of Masked Woodswallows feed in the flowering gums. Other birds at this site include Australian Bustard, Brolga, Varied Lorikeet, Apostlebird, Banded Honeyeater, White-quilled Honeyeater and Australian Hobby.

Brandy Bottle Creek

The name on the roadside sign actually says Bottle Brandy Creek, I guess somebody had a tad too much of it. The site is located 2.5km southwest of the junction with Buntine Hwy (96). GPS coordinates are 15°18’59”S and 131°33’35”E.

Sit at the waterhole and observe masses of Cockatiels, Budgerigars and Apostlebirds arriving for a sip of water. Brolgas, Black-necked Storks, White-necked Herons, Little Egrets and Nankeen Night-Herons often stand in the shallow water. In the bushland, search for Jackie Winter, White-throated Gerygone, Silver-backed Butcherbird, Great Bowerbird, Horsfield's Bronze-cuckoo and Green Oriole.

Horsfield's Bronze-cuckoo

It is also a good spot for raptors, where rarer species such as Square-tailed Kite, Little Eagle and Black-breasted Buzzard have been recorded.

Victoria Hwy at 15°25'52"S and 131°28'31"E

This spot is located 20km southwest of the Buntine Hwy junction. A small dam can be found on the north side of the road. It can be very productive at times. In the Wet, a variety of waterbirds is found here including Freckled Duck, Pink-eared Duck, Red-kneed Dotterel and Wood Sandpiper.

Pale-vented Bush-hens were recorded several times, including one with a small chick. Star Finches, Masked Finches and Long-tailed Finches regularly come for a drink. In grassy areas, look for Australian Bustard, Brown Quail and Red-chested Button-quail. The waterhole is often teeming with parrots such as Budgerigars, Cockatiels, Galahs and Red-tailed Black-Cockatoos.

Other birds recorded in the area include Tawny Grassbird, Golden-backed Honeyeater, Brush Cuckoo and Olive-backed Oriole.

Campbell Spring

Campbell Spring is located 40km past the Buntine Hwy junction. GPS coordinates are 15°29'42''S and 131°23'20''E. A creek runs along the south side of the road. Black Bittern is resident in the creekline vegetation. This spot is also good for finches; look for Gouldian Finch, Star Finch, Black-bellied Crimson Finch and Yellow-rumped Mannikin. The common Chestnut-breasted Mannikins arrive in huge flocks for a drink. Other birds include Banded Honeyeater, Yellow-tined Honeyeater, Azure Kingfisher, Red-browed Pardalote, Oriental Dollarbird and Australian Owlet-nightjar.

Dingo Creek

Dingo Creek site is located 20km east of Timber Creek at GPS coordinates of 15°44'07''S and 130°33'30''E. A short track runs to the creek about 100m west of the creek crossing. Turn into it and follow for about 50m to get to a small carparking place.

The area is very productive. Black Bittern can be flushed from the stands of pandanus along the creek edge. Nankeen Night-Herons roost there. Finches are abundant, with Pictorella Mannikin and Gouldian Finch recorded. Little Woodswallows often fly over the creek. Other birds in the area include Red-browed Pardalote, Northern Rosella, Grey-fronted Honeyeater, Banded Honeyeater, Tawny Grassbird, Horsfield's Bronze-cuckoo and Pheasant Coucal. Among the nocturnal birds are Spotted Nightjar and Australian Owlet-nightjar.

Durack Monument

Durack Monument commemorates the pioneering Durack family who established the cattle industry in the Kimberley-NT area. The memorial is located at the junction of Bullita Access Tk (on Google maps called just Bullita/Timber Ck), about 10km east of Timber Creek. GPS coordinates are 15°44'16''S and 130°30'28''E. The monument stands on the north side of the road, while on the other side you'll find a waterhole under the road bridge. This area is fantastic for finches, with 10 species recorded. These include Pictorella Mannikin, Yellow-rumped Mannikin, Star Finch and Gouldian Finch. Finches often forage on bare ground around the monument where they perhaps can easily see the wind-swept grass seeds.

When grevilleas are flowering around the monument, you can expect plenty of honeyeaters. Look for Grey-fronted Honeyeater, Golden-backed Honeyeater, Rufous-throated Honeyeater, Banded Honeyeater and Silver-crowned Friarbird.

In the grassy area around the monument, look for Horsfield's Bushlark, Brown Quail, Golden-headed Cisticola and Australian Bustard.

Small flocks of Spinifex Pigeons regularly arrive at the waterhole for a drink. In the vegetation surrounding the creek, look for Buff-sided Robin, Red-browed Pardalote, Black-tailed Treecreeper, Jacky Winter, Singing Honeyeater and Weebill.

Jacky Winter

East Baines River Crossing

This site is located 50km southwest of Timber Creek. GPS coordinates are 15°46'03''S and 130°01'35''E. This is another good spot for finches. You may come across Star Finch, Gouldian Finch and Pictorella Mannikin here. There are several channels/creek crossings in the area, check the ones that still hold some water.

In the wet season, the selection of waterbirds on the river includes White-necked Heron, Nankeen Night-Heron, Black Bittern, Great Egret, Pied Stilt and Black-fronted Dotterel. Occasionally, large flocks of Oriental Pratincoles are recorded.

Bushland birds include Masked Woodswallow, Shining Flycatcher, Paperbark Flycatcher, Rufous Songlark, Red-winged Parrot, Golden-backed Honeyeater, Rufous-throated Honeyeater and Striated Pardalote. At night, you may get Tawny Frogmouth, Southern Boobook and Bush Stone-curlew.

Saddle Creek Rest Area

This rest stop is located 60km east of the NT/WA border at GPS coordinates of 15°57’25’’S and 129°33’43’’E.

White-quilled Rock-Pigeons have been recorded in the rocks piled by the creek. Pictorella Mannikins come for a drink in large flocks. Other finches include Yellow-rumped Mannikin and Gouldian Finch. A Great Bowerbird’s bower is located at the entrance track to the rest area. Other birds at this site include Chestnut-backed Button-quail, Banded Honeyeater, White-quilled Honeyeater, Little Woodswallow, Olive-backed Oriole and Red-backed Fairy-wren.

Victoria River Roadhouse

This iconic roadhouse is located on the banks of Victoria River, 190km southwest of Katherine. It is surrounded by the magnificent escarpment of the Judbarra Gregory National Park. Stunning sunrises and sunsets are adding to the charm of the landscape. The roadhouse offers a variety of accommodation from cabins to spacious caravan sites with all facilities. There is also a restaurant and, most importantly, fuel available 24/7. Helicopter flights operate from the roadhouse, showcasing the breathtaking Outback scenery of the Victoria River Valley.

Over 150 bird species have been recorded around the Victoria River Roadhouse. **Key species** are Purple-crowned Fairy-wren, Gouldian Finch and Yellow-rumped Mannikin. Other birds of interest include Great Bowerbird, Little Corella, Grey-crowned Babbler, Banded Honeyeater, Golden-backed Honeyeater, Tree Martin, Masked Woodswallow, Shining Flycatcher and Barking Owl. Rarities include Oriental Plover, Little Curlew, Wood Sandpiper, Western Gerygone, Rufous Owl, Grey Falcon.

In search of birds, inspect the campground, an old bridge over the river and the boat ramp with the farmland and dam along the boat ramp access road.

Victoria River Roadhouse is the most accessible site in NT to see Purple-crowned Fairy-wren. Your best bet to find them is the boat ramp area. The birds demonstrate a preference to a narrow belt of pandanus and patches of cane grass along Victoria River. In the Wet, when the river is flowing high, the birds are moving to the eucalypts behind the pandanus. Because the birds are expected to dwell near the ground, birders may be surprised to observe Purple-crowned Fairy-wrens high in the gum trees at high water.

Purple-crowned Fairy-wren

To get to the boat ramp, from Victoria Hwy 500m west of the roadhouse turn into a farm road and drive 2.8km to the end of the road, where a carpark is provided. A short track leads to the concreted boat ramp. Focus your search first on the cane grasses around the carpark, later widen the scope and inspect the stands of pandanus 1km-2km along the waterholes in the riverbed.

The access road to the boat ramp runs through the farmland and is suitable for spotlighting. Nocturnal birds recorded here include Southern Boobook, Bush Stone-curlew and Spotted Nightjar. Look also for Red-chested Button-quails at night; they have been reported to pop out from the long grass onto the edge of the road. During the day, check out a small dam on the west side of the road. You may get Plumed Whistling-Duck, Hardhead, White-necked Heron, Azure Kingfisher, Common Sandpiper, Black-fronted Dotterel or an occasional Australian Pratincole, Little Curlew or Oriental Plover. However, we were not lucky; the only thing we spotted on this dam was a wallowing large water buffalo and Azure Kingfisher on a farm structure nearby.

The camping grounds were full of parrots. A large, noisy flock of Little Corellas was roosting in trees by the river. There were also Northern Rosellas, Red-winged Parrots, Red-tailed Black-Cockatoos and Cockatiels checking out the gums at the campsite. The grounds were ruled by Great Bowerbirds. The birds were tame and cheeky, always ready to snatch something from the campers to adorn their bowers. We located one bower under a shrub near the cabins. A pair of Masked Lapwings decided to nest in the middle of the caravan park, just where the rigs were turning. An Oriental Dollarbird had a tense face-off with an Australian Magpie over the water rights at a bird bath.

Oriental Dollarbird and Australian Magpie

The profusely flowering gum trees were bending under the load of Varied Lorikeets and Red-collared Lorikeets, accompanied by a variety of honeyeaters such as Banded Honeyeaters, Yellow-tinted Honeyeaters, White-quilled Honeyeaters, Golden-backed Honeyeaters and Rufous-throated Honeyeaters. One morning, a mixed group of finches and doves were foraging on the ground between the caravans. There were Gouldian Finches, Long-tailed Finches and Double-barred Finches in the group. At night, Barking Owls and Bush Stone-curlews were calling.

From the campsite, we took a walk on the old Victoria River Bridge which runs just underneath the new, high bridge. We observed a large group of Chestnut-breasted Mannikins with a few Yellow-rumped Mannikins in the mix, feeding in the long grasses near the bridge. In the riparian vegetation under the bridge, we sighted a couple of Purple-crowned Fairy-wrens. Common Sandpiper was perching on the stones in the middle of the river. Standing on the old bridge, we also spotted Nankeen Night-Heron, Channel-billed Cuckoo, Pheasant Coucal, Radjah Shelduck and Pied Heron. Black-breasted Buzzard was flying over the river and campgrounds.

Victoria River Roadhouse features a long list of raptors, including Peregrine Falcon, Black Falcon, Square-tailed Kite and Wedge-tailed Eagle. There are also several records of Grey Falcon.

Timber Creek

This small Outback town (population: 70) is situated on Victoria Hwy (1) halfway between Katherine and the Western Australia border. This is the only significant settlement along this route. It sits on the doorstep of the western section of the Judbarra Gregory National Park. The town is famous for great fishing, scenic escarpment and old boab trees. It is also the finch capital of Australia. In winter and spring, if waiting patiently at a good waterhole, you may get 10-11 finch species.

Accommodation is available in two places: Timber Creek Hotel and Wirib Store. Both offer caravan parks, fuel and basic supplies.

Over 170 bird species have been recorded within 20km radius of Timber Creek. **Key species** are Gouldian Finch, Pictorella Mannikin, Yellow-rumped Mannikin, Star Finch, Purple-crowned Fairy-wren, Buff-sided Robin, Chestnut-backed Button-quail and Black-breasted Buzzard. Other birds of interest include Spinifex Pigeon, Azure Kingfisher, Black-tailed Treecreeper, Bar-breasted Honeyeater, Banded Honeyeater, Grey-fronted Honeyeater, Horsfield's Bushlark, Budgerigar, Red-browed Pardalote and Barking Owl. Among the rarities are Hooded Robin, Painted Finch, Oriental Plover, Black Bittern, Grey Goshawk and Grey Falcon.

Timber Creek Caravan Parks

There are two adjacent small caravan parks in Timber Creek: Wirib Tourist Park and Timber Creek Roadhouse. They offer good facilities, spacious shady campsites and a water-filled creek at the back, lined with dense pandanus and paperbarks. A full set of finches can sometimes be found in these caravan parks, without much effort. When the sprinklers are working at the roadhouse's and Wirib fuel station's front yards, finches can be observed without entering the caravan park grounds, which are accessible only to guests.

Buff-sided Robins are resident in the area, just search the creekline. Black Bittern, Azure Kingfisher, Shining Flycatcher, Paperbark Flycatcher, Arafura Fantail and Black-bellied Crimson Finch can often be spotted in the pandanus thicket. When paperbarks are in bloom, honeyeaters become abundant. Look for Rufous-throated Honeyeater, Yellow-tinted Honeyeater, Bar-breasted Honeyeater, White-quilled Honeyeater, Banded Honeyeater and Grey-fronted Honeyeater. Large numbers of

Great Bowerbirds can be observed on both properties, front and back. Square-tailed Kites are often flying over the area. At night, you will hear or see the resident pair of Barking Owls and perhaps Southern Boobook and Tawny Frogmouth.

Buff-sided Robin on the grounds of Timber Creek Caravan Park

Hickey Beach Picnic Area

A track behind Timber Creek Council Office leads to a picnic area by a waterhole with a small beach. GPS coordinates are 15°39′28″S and 130°28′48″E. Finches may visit here for a drink, including Gouldian Finch, Star Finch, Black-bellied Crimson Finch and Yellow-rumped Mannikin. Purple-crowned Fairy-wrens live in the pandanus at the edge of the waterhole. Other birds at this site include Banded Honeyeater, Yellow-tinted Honeyeater, Silver-crowned Friarbird, Shining Flycatcher, White-bellied Cuckoo-shrike, Pacific Baza and Collared Sparrowhawk.

Policemans Point

This site can be very productive for finches and other birdlife. It is located 4km west of the Timber Creek Hotel. GPS coordinates for the Policemans Point are 15°37′53″S and 130°28′32″E. To get there, turn off Victoria Hwy at GPS coordinates of 15°37′56″S and 130°26′44″E. Follow an unsealed track for 2km to the river. The road forks out; it is worth checking both forks of the track. The right fork leads to the Point where you'll find two picnic tables.

Star Finches

This site is good for finches, in particular for Star Finch and Gouldian Finch but the rarer Pictorella Mannikin and Yellow-rumped Mannikin are also found there. When coming for a drink, the birds land on the bushes that line the water. As the observation point is higher, it is easy to watch and photograph them.

When we arrived there on an overcast, gloomy afternoon, two Black-necked Storks were wading in shallow water on the opposite bank of the river and a single Caspian Tern was hunting over the river. This bird is a long-staying visitor in the area, so far away from the coast, and it has been reported over the years by many birders. We flushed Black Bittern from the riverine vegetation. A continuous stream of Chestnut-breasted Mannikins mixed with Double-barred Finches and Black-bellied Crimson Finches was passing us by on their way to the water. Other thirsty arrivals included Cockatiels, Red-winged Parrots, Brown Honeyeaters, Yellow-tinted Honeyeaters, Rufous-throated Honeyeaters and a couple of Bar-breasted Honeyeaters. In the surrounding woodland, we ticked off Northern Rosella, Great Bowerbird, Masked Woodswallow, White-winged Triller and Jacky Winter.

On the drive along the left fork to the river, we flushed Chestnut-backed Button-quail and a flock of Brown Quails from the grass. Pandanus near the river yielded Purple-crowned Fairy-wrens. Radjah Shelducks, Black-fronted Dotterels and single Glossy Ibis and Common Sandpiper were foraging in the riverbed. Other birds in this spot included Pallid Cuckoo, Bush Stone-curlew, White-breasted Woodswallow, Shining Flycatcher, Australian Bustard and Spotted Harrier.

Timber Creek Airstrip

This a very good spot for finches, where all 11 Northern Territory species have been recorded. The site is located 6km west of the Timber Creek Hotel, signposted from Victoria Hwy with an obscure sign depicting a plane. GPS coordinates at the turnoff are 15°37'21''S and 130°26'44''E. The birds like to perch on the boundary fence of the airstrip, so check the fenceline thoroughly. Look in particular for Star Finches and Gouldian Finches, but Pictorella Mannikin, Yellow-rumped Mannikin or even Painted Finch haven been reported from this site.

Horsfield's Bushlark, Brown Songlark and Brown Quail are common on the airstrip. Edges of tall grasses may produce Red-chested Button-quails. In the Wet, the airstrip is regularly visited by Oriental Plovers.

In woodland around the airstrip, search for Black-tailed Treecreeper, Weebill, Varied Lorikeet, Varied Sittella, Buff-sided Robin, Brush Cuckoo, Northern Rosella, Masked Woodswallow and White-browed Woodswallow.

Nackeroo Lookout

Nackeroo Lookout's view of Victoria River

The turnoff to the Nackeroo Lookout is located opposite the Timber Creek Airstrip, about 10m west of Timber Creek. Perched on the escarpment, the lookout is a fantastic spot to watch the sunrise or sundown over the vast plains.

A single-line, steep, unsealed track winds up over the range, to reach two lookouts and a pleasant picnic area at the top. The plateau is sparsely covered in woodland, with spinifex on the ground. During our journey in June 2022, it was the best place to find Gouldian Finches in the Timber Creek area. The 10-40 strong flocks of Gouldian Finches were feeding alongside Long-tailed and Masked Finches in the freshly burnt areas. An occasional Star Finch and Pictorella Mannikin could be seen among them.

The cream-flowering woollybutts were covered with masses of Masked Woodswallows. Black-faced Woodswallows and Little Woodswallows were also present. Orange-flowering woollybutts were a magnet for honeyeaters. We got Banded Honeyeater, Yellow-tinted Honeyeater, Grey-fronted Honeyeater, Rufous-throated Honeyeater, Brown Honeyeater, White-throated Honeyeater, Golden-backed Honeyeater and Silver-crowned Friarbird.

Peregrine Falcon was flying along the escarpment. A pair of Bush Stone-curlews showed up at the picnic area. We also spotted a single Spinifex Pigeon there. The woodland habitat also produced Red-backed Kingfisher, Varied Sittella, Rainbow Bee-eater, Black-tailed Treecreeper, Horsfield's Bronze-cuckoo and Rufous Whistler. On our way down, we flushed a Chestnut-backed Button-quail from the roadside.

Bradshaw Bridge

This impressive bridge spans the Victoria River 8km west of Timber Creek. It gives access to the military training grounds. You cannot drive over the bridge, but you can walk to the other side for birding, and you can fish from the bridge.

A large rest area is provided by the river in front of the bridge. GPS coordinates are 15°36'50"S and 130°24'27"E. This is a well-known Purple-crowned Fairy-wren spot. Look for them in the cane grass along the river on the right side of the bridge. A large colony of Fairy Martins lives under the bridge. Azure Kingfishers may be hunting along the riverbanks. Finches come to drink here, including Star Finch, Gouldian Finch and Yellow-rumped Mannikin. If you are lucky, you may spot Spinifex Pigeons walking down to the water.

Other birds in the area include Jacky Winter, Banded Honeyeater, Bar-breasted Honeyeater, Little Woodswallow, Tawny Grassbird, Australian Owlet-nightjar and Black-breasted Buzzard.

Judbarra Gregory National Park

Judbarra Gregory National Park, formerly known as Gregory National Park, is the second largest (1,300,000ha) national park in the Northern Territory. It is located along Victoria Hwy (1) in the transitional region between the tropical and semi-arid zones, approximately 360km south of Darwin and 160km west of Katherine. It features spectacular scenery of deep gorges carved into a vast, rugged escarpment country. Striking limestone formations can be found in the western section, with stands of mighty boabs scattered among them. Vegetation consists mostly of grassy open woodland, with some areas of monsoon rainforest.

Escarpment of Judbarra Gregory National Park

The Park is split into two geographically separate sections: the eastern section around the Victoria River Roadhouse, and the western section, south of Timber Creek. The fabulous Jasper Gorge lies between the two sections but is not part of the National Park. Victoria River which flows through the Park is packed with the saltwater crocodiles, be very careful while approaching the water on foot. Crocodile-watching tours can be booked from Timber Creek.

The Park is accessed from Victoria Hwy (1). Accommodation is available at the Victoria River Roadhouse and in Timber Creek. Limited campgrounds are scattered through the Park. Facilities in these places are basic (pit toilets, fireplaces) so you need to be self-sufficient. 4WD vehicles with high clearance are recommended (the western section is the 4WD paradise). Further information is provided in the Park brochure, downloadable here: https://nt.gov.au/__data/assets/pdf_file/0009/278442/judbarra-gregory-national-park-fact-sheet-and-map.pdf.

Over 190 bird species have been recorded in the Judbarra Gregory National Park. **Key species** are Grey Falcon, Purple-crowned Fairy-wren, White-quilled Rock-Pigeon, Sandstone Shrike-thrush, Gouldian Finch, Pictorella Mannikin, Yellow-rumped Mannikin and Star Finch. Other birds of interest include Spinifex Pigeon, Chestnut-backed Button-quail, Banded Honeyeater, Grey-fronted Honeyeater, Helmeted Friarbird, Black-tailed Treecreeper, Buff-sided Robin, Spotted Nightjar and Black-breasted Buzzard. Among the rarities are Flock Pigeon, Ground Cuckoo-shrike, Hooded Robin and Fork-tailed Swift.

Sullivan Creek Campground

Apostlebird

This spacious campground is located on the banks of a permanent waterhole, 17km east of the Victoria River Roadhouse. Access is easy (100m) from Victoria Hwy (1). GPS coordinates at the turnoff are 15°35’14”S and 131°16’32”E. The site’s basic facilities include toilets, fireplaces and picnic tables. The place is known for its resident Black Bittern that often roosts in the clumps of pandanus. Around the water, look also for Azure Kingfisher, Pheasant Coucal, Oriental Dollarbird, Shining Flycatcher and Nankeen Night-Heron. Finches at this site include Gouldian Finch, Black-bellied Crimson Finch, Masked Finch and Long-tailed Finch.

Other birds around Sullivan Creek Campground include Apostlebird, Red-winged Parrot, Varied Lorikeet, Yellow-tinted Honeyeater, Banded Honeyeater, White-throated Gerygone, Spotted Nightjar and Tawny Frogmouth. Both Zitting and Golden-headed Cisticola have been recorded; the former is much rarer.

Joe Creek Picnic Area

This site is situated in the eastern section of the Park, 10km west of the Victoria River Roadhouse. Access is off Victoria Hwy (1) via a 2km-long unsealed track (often closed in the wet season). Facilities comprise a carpark, picnic tables and toilets. A 1.7km Nawulbinbin Circuit which starts from the carpark leads up and down the steep, rocky slopes to the base of the escarpment featuring the Aboriginal rock art. On your way, you'll pass many groups of striking Livingstonia palms growing on the scree slopes. While birding, stop every now and then and take in the view. The scenery of the surrounding foothills and the escarpment is simply spectacular.

The site is a natural amphitheatre. During our visit, we enjoyed a chorus of Blue-winged Kookaburras, echoing against the rock walls of the escarpment. As they finished, a Pied Butcherbird started its beautiful trill and each note echoed multiple times in the amphitheatre. Later, a duet of Pheasant Coucals joined in, providing the bass section. So, find a seat in the shade and listen to the concert of the day, perhaps even with the characteristic 'oomm, oomm' of White-quilled Rock-Pigeons.

As we explored the walk, we also recorded Spinifex Pigeon, Helmeted Friarbird, Grey-fronted Honeyeater, Little Woodswallow, Rufous Whistler, Western Gerygone and White-winged Triller.

Escarpment Walk

This site is located in the eastern part of the Judbarra Gregory National Park, just a few kilometres west of the Victoria River Roadhouse. A spacious carpark is provided by Victoria Hwy. Escarpment Walk is a 3km return trail, moderate with some steep sections. This is the place to look for the escarpment specialists such as White-quilled Rock-Pigeon and Sandstone Shrike-thrush. The former usually roost on rock ledges and in crevasses. Little Woodswallows and Peregrine Falcons are regularly seen flying along the cliffs.

Before heading uphill, check the grassy, flat areas by the carpark and the bushes lining the dry creek bed. Finches often forage on the ground between the tussocks of grass. Look for Black-bellied Crimson Finch, Star Finch, Gouldian Finch, Long-tailed Finch and Yellow-rumped Mannikin. The most numerous will be Chestnut-breasted Mannikins. Other birds here include Pheasant Coucal, Brown Quail, Golden-headed Cisticola, Northern Rosella and Rufous Whistler. In the flowering bushes by the creek, you may spot Banded Honeyeater, Northern Fantail, Weebill, Grey-crowned Babbler and Red-winged Parrot.

Northern Rosella in the rain

On the walk, besides the two escarpment specialists, look for Silver-backed Butcherbird, Red-backed Kingfisher, Spinifex Pigeon, Grey-fronted Honeyeater, Helmeted Friarbird, White-winged Triller, Black-faced Woodswallow, White-throated Gerygone, Weebill and raptors. Wedge-tailed Eagle is nearly guaranteed. You'll also have a good chance to sight Grey Falcon or Black-breasted Buzzard.

If you stop in the carpark in the evening, look for Spotted Nightjars; they like to hunt in this area.

Old Victoria River Crossing

This site is situated in the eastern section of the Park. Access is via a short track about 6km west of the Victoria River Roadhouse. The last section of the track is terrible, 4WD only, or just walk it instead, it's not far. GPS coordinates at the turnoff from Victoria Hwy are 15°35'21''S and 131°06'07''E. The road sign directing to the crossing is obscure.

This is another site to look for Purple-crowned Fairy-wrens. Also, good numbers of Red-browed Pardalotes live here and can be heard calling from the vegetation by the riverbed.

By the end of Dry, only small puddles remain in the riverbed. Flocks of finches come there to drink. You'll have a good chance to sight Star Finches and Yellow-rumped Mannikins. Black-fronted Dotterels and Common Sandpipers can often be seen feeding at the edges of the puddles.

In the woodland, look for Northern Rosella, Yellow-throated Miner, White-winged Triller, Leaden Flycatcher, White-bellied Cuckoo-shrike and Brown Quail. Black-breasted Buzzards were reported roosting in trees near the river.

Gregory's Tree

The historical Gregory's boab

The famous Gregory's boab grows in the Historical Reserve located about 15km west of Timber Creek. The old boab is a living monument to the exploration of the Australia's north. The north Australian expedition was led by Augustus Charles Gregory in 1855-56. The old boab marks the area of Gregory's camp and still bears the visible inscriptions noting the dates of arrival and departure from the camp.

To get there, turn north off Victoria Hwy (1) at the GPS position of 15°34'04''S and 130°21'60''E and follow an unsealed road for 4km. At the end of this road, you'll find a carpark, a picnic area and a start of a 500m walk to the monument tree.

Birds around the picnic area include Grey-crowned Babbler, Yellow-tinted Honeyeater, Rufous-throated Honeyeater, Grey-fronted Honeyeater, White-bellied Cuckoo-shrike and Weebill.

On the walk, look for Spinifex Pigeon, Buff-sided Robin, Long-tailed Finch, Budgerigar and Brown Goshawk. We spotted a Black-breasted Buzzard roosting in the famous boab. There were also a couple of Little Woodswallows there.

Big Horse Creek Camping Area

This beautiful camping area, adorned with scattered groups of old boabs, is located in the western section of the Park, about 10km west of Timber Creek. GPS coordinates for the turnoff to this site from Victoria Hwy (1) are 15°35'51''S and 130°21'21''E. Facilities here include toilets, picnic tables, fireplaces and a boat ramp. During our visit in June 2022, we found Purple-crowned Fairy-wrens near the boat ramp, as well as Paperbark Flycatchers, Australian Yellow White-eyes, Black-bellied Crimson Finches and White-breasted Woodswallows. Through the campsites, we met numerous cheeky Great Bowerbirds and Grey-crowned Babblers. The latter maintain several large nests there. Buff-sided Robins were visible in the campground. We also got Red-tailed Black-Cockatoo, Brown Quail, Bar-breasted Honeyeater, Golden-backed Honeyeater and Red-browed Finch.

Find access to the river, available from several camping sites, to observe finches coming to drink, including Gouldian Finch, Star Finch and Yellow-rumped Mannikin. Check the riverbanks; Great-billed Herons are occasionally reported from here.

Bullita Homestead Campground

This is the main campground in the western section of the Judbarra Gregory National Park, located 56km south of Timber Creek. To get there, about 10km east of Timber Creek turn south from Victoria Hwy (1) into an unsealed, rough Bullita Access Tk (on Google maps called just Bullita/Timber Ck); a 4WD will be needed. The road is closed Nov-Apr due to summer flooding. The turnoff is opposite the Durack Monument, at GPS coordinates of 15°44'16''S and 130°30'28''E.

The first 5km of this track can be very productive, particularly for finches that come to drink from a waterhole located near the turnoff from the highway. The next good stop is just 4km down the road, at the next creek crossing. You may get here finches again, often in large numbers, including Gouldian Finch, Star Finch, Masked Finch, Long-tailed Finch, Pictorella Mannikin and Yellow-rumped Mannikin. In the surrounding bushes, look for Black-tailed Treecreeper, Red-browed Pardalote, Budgerigar, Banded Honeyeater, Yellow-tinted Honeyeater, Jacky Winter, Varied

Sittella and Rufous Songlark. From time to time, Crested Bellbirds and Hooded Robins are recorded. Grassbirds along the first 5km of the track include Brown Quail, Red-chested Button-quail and Horsfield's Bushlark. Among the likely raptors are Spotted Harrier, Brown Goshawk, Black-shouldered Kite, Brown Falcon and Black Falcon. The latter likes to follow the roadside grassfires.

34km from Victoria Hwy, you'll see the turnoff to the Limestone Gorge, the main attraction of the western section of the National Park. This area is recommended only to the serious off-roaders, with proper 4WD equipment and experience. After an 8km drive, the landscape of unique limestone formations opens before you. Take a walk among them along the 0.6km return Calcite Flow Walk. Look for Sandstone Shrike-thrush, Spinifex Pigeon, Little Woodswallow, Buff-sided Robin, Grey-fronted Honeyeater, Black-tailed Treecreeper, Varied Sittella, Channel-billed Cuckoo and Wedge-tailed Eagle. Finches are found here in good numbers including Gouldian Finch, Long-tailed Finch, Pictorella Mannikin and Yellow-rumped Mannikin.

The Bullita Homestead Campground is situated 42km down the Bullita Access Tk on the banks of East Baines River near the historic Bullita Homestead. Site facilities consist of toilets, fireplaces and picnic tables. Birding is good along the riverbed. Among the common birds are Oriental Dollarbird, Great Bowerbird, Paperbark Flycatcher, Cockatiel, Shining Flycatcher and Olive-backed Oriole. A good selection of honeyeaters includes Yellow-tinted Honeyeater, Banded Honeyeater, White-gaped Honeyeater, White-quilled Honeyeater and Rufous-throated Honeyeater. Nocturnal birds include Bush Stone-curlew, Southern Boobook, Australian Owlet-nightjar and Nankeen Night-Heron.

Jasper Gorge

This beautiful gorge is not part of the Judbarra Gregory National Park however it is adjacent to the eastern border of its western section. It is reached via an unsealed Buchanan Hwy. The turnoff from Victoria Hwy (1) is located 62km west of Victora River Roadhouse and 27km east of Timber Creek. After 48km on a reasonable dirt road, you'll reach a permanent waterhole in the Gorge. Campsites are provided but there are no facilities. Be self-sufficient with everything.

Over 120 bird species have been recorded in Jasper Gorge. **Key species** are Gouldian Finch, Pictorella Mannikin, Yellow-rumped Mannikin, Star Finch, Sandstone Shrike-thrush, White-quilled Rock-Pigeon, Purple-crowned Fairy-wren and Spotted Nightjar. Other birds of interest include Grey-fronted Honeyeater, Golden-backed Honeyeater, Banded Honeyeater, Helmeted Friarbird, Red-browed Pardalote, Azure Kingfisher, Brush Cuckoo, Shining Flycatcher, White-throated Gerygone and Black-breasted Buzzard. Rarities include Ground Cuckoo-shrike, Crimson Chat, Grey Falcon and Square-tailed Kite.

The access road (Buchanan Hwy) is well-known for the presence of finches, particularly at the end of the Dry when only shallow waterholes are left at its multiple creek crossings and birds come in large flocks in search of water. Mind it, if you come too late in the Dry, there may be no water left and no birds. We experienced it at one of our visits there. Listed below are the most productive stops along the road.

Buchanan Hwy at 15°45'17''S and 130°38'50''E

This spot is a creek crossing about 1km south of the turnoff from Victoria Hwy. There are usually several waterholes there. Ten finch species have been recorded in this location, including Gouldian Finch, Star Finch, Pictorella Mannikin and Yellow-rumped Mannikin. Spinifex Pigeons regularly come for a drink. It is also a good spot for Red-browed Pardalotes.

Yellow-rumped Mannikin

Masked Woodswallows arrive in huge flocks in early winter when eucalypts start to bloom. Other birds here include Jacky Winter, Grey-fronted Honeyeater, Golden-backed Honeyeater, Banded Honeyeater, Australian Bustard, Horsfield's Bushlark, Budgerigar, Varied Lorikeet and Hooded Robin (rare). Several rare raptors have been reported from the area including Grey Falcon, Black Falcon, Square-tailed Kite and Black-breasted Buzzard. Brown Goshawks may sit motionlessly in the bushes near the water, waiting for their prey.

Buchanan Hwy at 15°46’48’’S and 130°39’17’’E

The site is located 4.5km from Victoria Hwy. The waterholes are on both sides of the road. Bird composition is similar to that of the previous site. Large flocks of Budgerigars favour this spot. Pictorella Mannikins were recorded in huge numbers (500-1,000 birds). A pair of Hooded Robins is nesting near the creek. Look also for Little Button-quail, Little Woodswallow, Black-tailed Treecreeper, Rufous Songlark, Australian Owlet-nightjar, Singing Honeyeater, Varied Lorikeet, Spotted Harrier and Brown Goshawk.

Buchanan Hwy at 15°50’42’’S and 130°38’21’’E

This site is called Skull Creek Crossing and is located 9km from Victoria Hwy. The creek bed is quite deep, allowing several waterholes to be formed in dry season. These are visible from the road. Ten species of finches have been recorded here, including Gouldian Finch, Star Finch, Pictorella Mannikin and Yellow-rumped Mannikin. Large numbers of Cockatiels, Diamond Doves and Bar-shouldered Doves come to drink. Other birds at this spot include Brolga, Red-browed Pardalote, Golden-backed Honeyeater, Jacky Winter, Pallid Cuckoo and Sacred Kingfisher.

Buchanan Hwy at Skull Creek crossing

Jasper Gorge Area

The gorge and its drainage lines support a variety of finches; remarkably all 11 NT species have been recorded here. Painted Finches regularly come to drink from the waterhole, as well as the other desirable species: Gouldian Finch, Star Finch, Pictorella Mannikin and Yellow-rumped Mannikin. Azure Kingfishers, Shining Flycatchers and Purple-crowned Fairy-wrens can be found along the watercourses. The flowering paperbark trees attract nectar-feeders such as Banded Honeyeater, Golden-backed Honeyeater, Yellow-tinted Honeyeater, Helmeted Friarbird, Silver-crowned Friarbird, Varied Lorikeet and Red-collared Lorikeet.

White-quilled Rock-Pigeon reaches its southern range limit here. Sandstone Shrike-thrush and Spinifex Pigeon can also be found in the area. Other birds include Red-winged Parrot, Great Bowerbird, Oriental Dollarbird, Grey-crowned Babbler, Little Button-quail, White-throated Gerygone and Pied Butcherbird. Nocturnal birds include Spotted Nightjar, Australian Owlet-nightjar, Southern Boobook and Tawny Frogmouth.

A large camp of little red flying-foxes live by the waterhole which is also home to several freshwater crocodiles.

Keep River National Park

The 57,000ha Keep River National Park sits off Victoria Hwy (1) right on the NT/WA border, 470km west of Katherine. It may be a small Park, but it contains a diversity of landscapes including sandstone ridges (reminiscent of the Bungle Bungle rock formations), so it is sometimes referred to as 'Baby Bungles National Park'. There are two camping sites in the Park, with facilities that include drinking water (usable after boiling), toilets, fireplaces and picnic tables. Several fantastic walks lead to magnificent lookouts and impressive Aboriginal art. A Visitor Centre operates at the Cockatoo Lagoon near the Park entrance. Further information and a site map can be downloaded here: https://nt.gov.au/__data/assets/pdf_file/0003/200100/keep-river-national-park-fact-sheet.pdf.

Over 170 bird species have been recorded in the Keep River National Park. **Key species** are White-quilled Rock-Pigeon, Sandstone Shrike-thrush, Gouldian Finch, Spinifex Pigeon and Little Woodswallow. Other birds of interest include Silver-backed Butcherbird, Banded Honeyeater, Golden-backed Honeyeater, White-quilled Honeyeater, Helmeted Friarbird, Channel-billed Cuckoo, Little Button-quail, Varied Lorikeet, Australian Bustard, Masked Finch and Square-tailed Kite. Rarities include Yellow Chat, Swinhoe's Snipe, Pictorella Mannikin, Hardhead and Grey Goshawk.

Rock formations at Keep River National Park

Cockatoo Lagoon

Masses of waterbirds congregate on this waterlily-covered lagoon during the Dry. The most common are Plumed Whistling-Ducks, Magpie Geese, Pacific Black Ducks and Hardheads. Look also for Brolga, Black-necked Stork, Azure Kingfisher, Nankeen Night-Heron, Pied Heron, Glossy Ibis and Baillon's Crake. A rarity at the Top End, Dusky Moorhen (first sighting in 2015), is breeding on the lagoon. Take a walk around the lagoon, looking for finches arriving for a drink. These may include Gouldian Finch, Star Finch, Long-tailed Finch, Yellow-rumped Mannikin and Pictorella Mannikin. A pair of Australian Hobbies have been nesting for years on a tower near the Visitor Centre. Other birds around this site include Spinifex Pigeon, Eastern Koel, Northern Rosella, Green Oriole, Oriental Dollarbird, Black-tailed Treecreeper, Brown Songlark, Bar-breasted Honeyeater and Black-breasted Buzzard.

Ginger's Hill Walk

This site is located 2km north of the Cockatoo Lagoon. The short walk, 200m return, leads to a stone structure typical for the Aboriginal works in this region. Along the trail, look for Silver-backed Butcherbird, Black-tailed Treecreeper, Grey-fronted Honeyeater, Little Woodswallow, Long-tailed Finch and Helmeted Friarbird.

Goorrandalng Campground

This place, also spelled Gurrandalng, is located 18km from the Park entrance at GPS coordinates of 15°52'27''S and 129°03'08''E. The basic site facilities include picnic tables, pit toilets and fire rings.

White-quilled Rock-Pigeon at the campsite

This is a very good spot for White-quilled Rock-Pigeons. They inhabit a big pile of rocks just in the middle of the camping area. You may even experience a Rock-Pigeon flying over your head to reach crevices in the rock.

A Great Bowerbird's bower is located in the camp. Look also for Lemon-bellied Flycatcher, Varied Sittella, Long-tailed Finch, White-quilled Honeyeater, Pied Butcherbird and Wedge-tailed Eagle. At night, you may hear Southern Boobook, Tawny Frogmouth and plenty of Bush Stone-curlews.

Check also the riverbed and the surrounding bushland a few hundred metres from the campground. Little Button-quails are often recorded there. If there are puddles of water, Gouldian Finches will come to drink. Other birds in this area include Nankeen Night-Heron, Rufous Whistler, Paperbark Flycatcher, Olive-backed Oriole and Bar-breasted Honeyeater.

A 2km-long return walk starts from this campsite and runs among the 'Baby Bungles' rocks. Look for White-quilled Rock-Pigeon, Spinifex Pigeon, Sandstone Shrike-thrush, Little Woodswallow, Peregrine Falcon, White-throated Gerygone, Dusky Honeyeater and Helmeted Friarbird.

Jarnem Campground

The campground is located in the northern part of the Park, 32km from the entrance. GPS coordinates are 15°45'43''S and 129°05'56''E. Basic facilities include picnic tables, pit toilets and fire rings. The site offers a 7km-long walk that will take you to the lookout revealing stunning views of the area. Along this trail, look for White-quilled Rock-Pigeons, Spinifex Pigeon and Little Woodswallow.

The flowering grevilleas around the campground may yield Banded Honeyeater, White-gaped Honeyeater, White-quilled Honeyeater and Silver-crowned Friarbird. At night, listen and look for Spotted Nightjar, Australian Owlet-nightjar, Southern Boobook and Tawny Frogmouth.

Other birds include Gouldian Finch, Masked Finch, Long-tailed Finch, Jacky Winter, Red-backed Kingfisher, Red-browed Pardalote, Purple-backed Fairy-wren and Red-backed Fairy-wren.

Northeastern NT

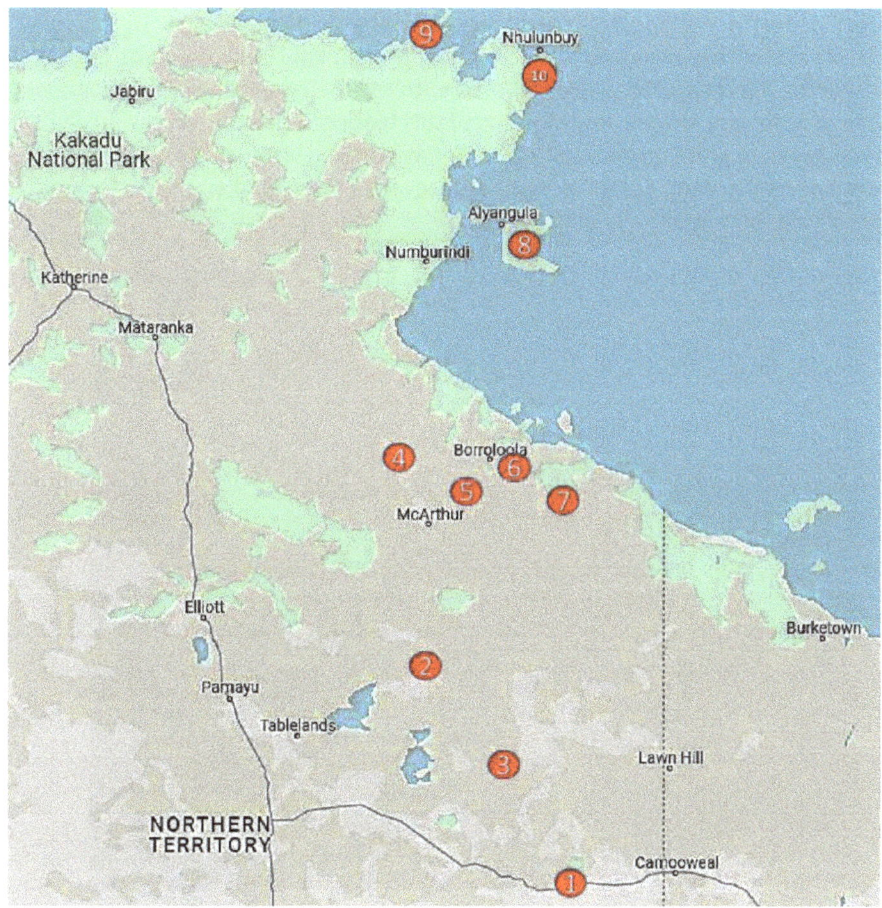

1 [Barkly Highway]
2 [Tablelands Highway]
3 [Connells Lagoon Conservation Reserve]
4 [Limmen National Park]
5 [Caranbirini Conservation Reserve]
6 [Borroloola]
7 [Carpentarian Grasswren Sites]
8 [Groote Eylandt]
9 [Elcho Island]
10 [Nhulunbuy]

Barkly Highway

Barkly Hwy (66) is the only sealed road between Queensland and Northern Territory. It begins in Cloncurry (QLD) and terminates at the junction with Stuart Hwy (A87) at the Threeways Roadhouse in NT. The 550km NT section runs through a monotonous, flat, black soil plains, covered with Mitchell grassland with small patches of with very low shrubs. Mounds of this black soil protrude occasionally from the Mitchell grass, usually with a broken windmill nearby, marking the presence of a farm dam. Flocks of Flock Bronzewings often land on these mounds when arriving for a drink.

Barkly Hwy plains

There are no towns or villages along Barkly Hwy in NT. The only accommodation, supplies and fuel is offered by the Barkly Homestead Roadhouse halfway through the distance. However, there are several rest stops along the road where you can break your journey and get some interesting birding.

Over 160 bird species have been recorded along the NT section of Barkly Highway. **Key species** are Grey Falcon, Black Falcon, Flock Bronzewing and Horsfield's Bushlark. Other birds of interest include Australian Bustard, Australian Pratincole, Brown Songlark, Chiming Wedgebill, Black-faced Woodswallow, Little Button-quail, Spotted Harrier and Black-breasted Buzzard. Rarities include Hooded Robin, Crested Bellbird, House Sparrow and Ground Cuckoo-shrike.

Barkly Hwy at 19°56'35"S and 137°51'11"E

This spot is located 15km west of the NT/QLD border at the Happy Creek crossing, which is usually dry. Search for Flock Bronzewings here.

Common birds at this site are Horsfield's Bushlark, Brown Songlark and Australasian Pipit. Other birds include Masked Woodswallow, Black-faced Woodswallow, Zebra Finch, Cockatiel, Rufous Songlark, and Red-backed Kingfisher. Check the raptors: Black Falcons have been observed here hunting Zebra Finches or Flock Bronzewings.

Soudan Bore Rest Area

This overnight rest area is located 125km east of Barkly Homestead at GPS coordinates of 20°04'25"S and 136°52'42"E. There is a small dam nearby, worth checking. Grass plains around the rest area often produce large numbers of Zebra Finches, Budgerigars, Diamond Doves and Horsfield's Bushlarks. These attract raptors; Spotted Harrier often hunts over the grass while Black-breasted Buzzard may hang around the waterhole, keeping an eye on the birds coming to drink.

Check the flowering bushes near the dam for the presence of Singing Honeyeater, Rufous-throated Honeyeater and Grey-headed Honeyeater. Even Black Honeyeater or Golden-backed Honeyeater are sometimes sighted.

Other birds at this site include Australian Bustard, Little Button-quail, Grey Shrike-thrush, Crimson Chat, Long-tailed Finch and Australian Raven.

Barkly Homestead

The roadhouse is located 260km west of the QLD/NT border and 190 km east of Stuart Hwy. This is the only airconditioned place along Barkly Hwy (66) to have a meal and a rest. Do some birding, too. A very productive dam is located just to the west of the roadhouse and the caravan area, where birds come to drink in good numbers. We observe large flocks of Zebra Finches, Diamond Doves, Budgerigars and Cockatiels. Raptors (Brown Goshawk, Whistling Kite and Australian Hobby) were perched nearby. In the water, a pair of Australasian Grebes were attending to three young chicks. A couple of Red-kneed Dotterels and a single Wood Sandpiper were foraging along the water edge. Several interesting records exist for this dam including Australian Painted-snipe, Latham's Snipe, Australian Spotted Crake, Common Sandpiper, Oriental Plover and Eastern Yellow Wagtail.

The dam at Barkly Homestead

Also on the western side of the roadhouse, about 500m away, is a rubbish tip surrounded by tall grasses and bushland. Look there for Purple-backed Fairy-wrens and Hooded Robins.

On the south side of the caravan park, you'll see a grassy area and a rubbish pile of disused machinery. We saw Hooded Robin and two Spotted Harriers perched on the protruding steel junk. Nankeen Kestrel was hovering over the area and a pair of Australian Bustards were crossing the field. Two House Sparrows were feeding on the ground.

Near the disused machinery, a solar power bank and a couple of wastewater ponds have been commissioned. We found several Glossy Ibises, Nankeen Night-Herons, Grey Teals, Hardheads and Black-fronted Dotterels as well as a single Common Sandpiper and Wood Sandpiper there. A pair of Australasian Grebes were breeding on one of the ponds. A flock of Little Corellas were using the solar farm as their playground, tearing out the rubber seals from the panels.

When the sprinklers were operating in the caravan park, we had the pleasure of watching the parrots coming down for a bath. These were Galahs, Budgerigars, Red-winged Parrots and Little Corellas. In the flowering trees, honeyeaters were plentiful including Yellow-throated Miner, Singing Honeyeater, Grey-fronted Honeyeater, Golden-backed Honeyeater and Spiny-cheeked Honeyeater.

The roadhouse surprised us with the variety of raptors. Besides those mentioned before, Collared Sparrowhawks were nesting in the campground, raising two chicks. Peregrine Falcon liked perching on the communications tower. Wedge-tailed Eagles were soaring high above the site. Also recorded at Barkly Homestead are Grey Falcon, Black Falcon, Little Eagle and Square-tailed Kite.

Barkly Hwy at 19°26'18''S and 135°26'20''E

The site is located 51km west of Barkly Homestead and 4km east of the Frewena Rest Area. This spot is a well-known Grey Falcon nesting site. The birds have their nest on a communications tower accessed by a 300m track south from the highway. You will not miss it as the roadside is carved with numerous wheel tracks of hopeful birders stopping there. For example, in January 2023, the pair raised two cheeks to adulthood.

Other birds there include Red-backed Kingfisher, Rufous Whistler, White-winged Triller, Rufous Songlark, Black-faced Woodswallow and Black Falcon.

Frewena Rest Area

Frewena after heavy rains

Frewena Rest Area is an overnight stop sitting on the verge of a large ephemeral wetland that at times overflows to the south side of the highway. The site is located 55km west of Barkly Homestead at GPS coordinates of 19°25'59"S and 135°24'04"E. The only facility is a couple of sheltered picnic tables. During our visit in March 2022, there was plenty of water and the area was full of life. The wetland was used by Pied Stilts for nesting. The colony, scattered widely in the wetland, had nests in various stages of breeding, from eggs to flying juveniles. Budgerigars and Diamond Doves were drinking from the puddles, Chiming Wedgebill and Singing Honeyeater were calling, and Black Falcon was roosting in a dead tree. We also ticked off Grey Teal, Pink-eared Duck, Hardhead, Hoary-headed Grebe, Glossy Ibis, Red-kneed Dotterel and Black-fronted Dotterel.

On the second visit, in July 2022, the water was nearly gone and so were the birds. A single White-necked Heron was standing far away among the cattle chomping on the drying swamp vegetation. A pair of Australian Bustard and a small flock of Diamond Doves and Zebra Finches completed the picture.

Grey Falcons are reported from this site from time to time. Australian Painted-snipe and Great Cormorant were also recorded.

41 Mile Bore Rest Area

This huge, leafy overnight rest stop offers plenty of private campsites for cars and caravans. It is located 116km west of Barkly Homestead and 70km east of Stuart Hwy at GPS coordinates of 19°19'17"S and 134°51'02"E.

An elongated ephemeral waterhole sits in the middle of the site. The site is praised for its glorious sunrises and sunsets.

When the shrubs are flowering, a good variety of honeyeaters can be found here including Grey-fronted Honeyeater, Grey-headed Honeyeater, Singing Honeyeater, Brown Honeyeater and even Black Honeyeater and Pied Honeyeater. Other birds reported from this site include Masked Woodswallow, Purple-backed Fairy-wren, Horsfield's Bronze-cuckoo, Major Mitchell's Cockatoo, White-winged Triller and Black-breasted Buzzard. A pair of Grey Falcons is observed from time to time, hunting in the area.

Our stop there was rewarded with a close, prolonged observation of an Australian Hobby that was methodically consuming a Galah sitting on a low branch in a tree next to our car. Plucking is really hard work.

Australian Hobby

Tablelands Highway

Tablelands Hwy (11) offers 380km of a remote, single-lane sealed road. The route runs through Barkly Tablelands between Barkly Homestead in the south and Cape Crawford on Carpentaria Hwy (1) in the north. The road is unfenced so watch you speed and beware of wandering stock. There are no towns or villages along the way, the first fuel is in the Heartbreak Hotel in Cape Crawford.

There are several rest areas along the road which can be used for birding. Barkly Tablelands offers the landscape of flat to gently undulating plains covered with Mitchell grass. There are some remnants of bushland dominated by acacias with the spinifex understory. There are also ephemeral swamps and lakes surrounded by a belt of bluebushes and coolibah trees.

Over 150 bird species have been recorded along the Tablelands Highway. **Key species** are Flock Bronzewing, Pictorella Mannikin, Yellow Chat, Oriental Plover, Red-chested Button-quail, Letter-winged Kite and Grey Falcon. Other birds of interest include Australian Bustard, Australian Pratincole, Oriental Pratincole, Ground Cuckoo-shrike, Brown Songlark, Horsfield's Bushlark, Spotted Nightjar, Black Falcon and Spotted Harrier. Rarities include Freckled Duck, Australasian Shoveler, Great Crested Grebe, Hooded Robin and Grey Butcherbird.

Playford River Crossing

This site is located at GPS coordinates of 19°17'20''S and 136°03'31''E approx. 50km north of Barkly Homestead and 1km north of the turnoff to Alroy Downs Station.

Playford River crossing

This is a well-known site to look for Yellow Chat and Flock Bronzewing. Yellow Chats appear in the area in good numbers, sometimes over 20 birds, particularly in summer, Dec-Mar. Towards the end of summer, waders that have gathered at the Playford River crossing include Oriental Plover, Sharp-tailed Sandpiper, Wood Sandpiper, Pied Stilt and Banded Lapwing. From March, at the start of dry season, huge numbers of birds concentrate around the waterhole formed at the crossing. These include Whiskered Terns, Australian Gull-billed Terns, Australian Pratincoles, Straw-necked Ibises, Black-tailed Native-hens and Brolgas. Raptors arrive too, such as Swamp Harriers, Black-breasted Buzzards and Brown Goshawks. Look also for the rarer species such as Grey Falcon, Black Falcon and Peregrine Falcon. A Grey Falcon nest is located on the communications tower less than 10km south of the crossing.

Birds fly in from the surrounding plains in large numbers for a drink. These include Crested Pigeon, Cockatiel, Budgerigar, Little Corella and Zebra Finch. Most spectacular is to see the landing of a 500-bird strong flock of Flock Bronzewings.

Other birds found in this area include Australian Bustard, Brown Songlark, Horsfield's Bushlark, Hooded Robin, Apostlebird, Crimson Chat, Orange Chat and Ground Cuckoo-shrike. At night, look for Spotted Nightjar (very common), Australian Owlet-nightjar and Southern Boobook.

Tablelands Hwy at 19°05'15''S and 136°04'32''E

This spot is located 80km north of Barkly Hwy and about 5km south of Kennedy Creek crossing. A large, shallow waterhole is located on the east side of the road; it quickly dries out in winter. In the Wet, waders are found here including Oriental Plover, Little Curlew, Common Greenshank, Sharp-tailed Sandpiper and Australian Pratincole. Waterbirds include Glossy Ibis, Royal Spoonbill, Pink-eared Duck, Hardhead and Brolga. Flock Bronzewing visit for a drink. Other birds in the area include White-winged Fairy-wren, Purple-backed Fairy-wren, Brown Songlark and Australian Bustard.

Kennedy Creek Crossing

This site is located approximately 85km north of Barkly Hwy at the GPS position of 19°02'48''S and 136°05'10''E. If there is water in the creek's waterholes, it is a place worth checking. Look for Yellow Chat, it is found here regularly, in particular in April-May. Flock Bronzewings are observed in numbers up to 5,000 birds. A long-lasting Black Falcon's nest is located on a communications tower north of the crossing. Oher raptors in the area include Spotted Harrier, Brown Falcon and Little Eagle.

Spotted Harrier patrolling the plains near the Kennedy Creek crossing

In the Wet, flocks of Oriental Pratincoles, Australian Pratincoles and Oriental Plovers are found here. The rare Freckled Ducks have been recorded several times. Look also for Red-chested Button-quails and Little Button-quails; these are sometimes seen at the edge of grass when spotlighting.

Other birds include Fairy Martin, Black-tailed Native-hen, Brolga, Golden-headed Cisticola, Red-backed Kingfisher, White-winged Triller and Horsfield's Bushlark.

Tablelands Hwy at 18°50'32"S and 136°04'15"E

The site is located at the White Hole Creek bridge, 120km north of Barkly Hwy. Check the 5km stretch of the road on either side of the bridge. Horsfield's Bushlarks are very common on the grassy plains. Diamond Doves and Flock Bronzewings visit the waterholes for a drink. Look also for Australian Bustard, Brolga, Little Curlew, White-necked Heron, Masked Woodswallow (often in large flocks), White-browed Woodswallow and Black-faced Woodswallow.

Grey Falcons nest in a tower in this area.

Brunette Downs Station

At the Brunette Downs Station, you'll find a large waterhole in Brunette Creek. Access is via Rockhampton/Brunette Downs track, turnoff from the main road is about 140km north of Barkly Hwy at GPS coordinates of 18°37'55"S and 136°01'47"E. Drive west for about 10km until you see the water. The birds to look for during this trip are Ground Cuckoo-shrike, Flock Pigeon, Pink-eared Duck, Freckled Duck, Australasian Shoveler, Great Crested Grebe, Glossy Ibis and Grey Falcon. Look also for Sharp-tailed Sandpiper, Black-fronted Dotterel, Australasian Darter and Brolga.

Brunette Downs Rest Area

The rest stop is located 145km north of Barkly Hwy at GPS coordinates of 18°28'27"S and 135°58'46"E. This is the place to look for Ground Cuckoo-shrikes, they like hanging out in this area. Flocks of Fork-tailed Swifts have been reported many times at the end of summer. Other birds here include Australian Pratincole, Oriental Pratincole, Yellow-throated Miner, Singing Honeyeater, Spinifex Pigeon, Flock Bronzewing and Horsfield's Bushlark. A good selection of raptors includes Brown Falcon, Black Falcon, Grey Falcon, Australian Hobby, Black-shouldered Kite and Spotted Harrier.

Australian Pratincole

Tablelands Hwy at 18°21'40''S and 135°53'48''E

This spot is located approximately 170km north of Barkly Hwy. Corella Creek Tk runs west just north of the creek. This is another spot to look for Ground Cuckoo-shrikes. You may also come across Red-browed Pardalote, Paperbark Flycatcher, Rufous-throated Honeyeater, Tree Martin and Masked Woodswallow.

Kiana Rest Area

The site is located in the area marked on Google maps as Creswell, at GPS coordinates of 17°31'42''S and 135°41'02''E. This overnight stop is good for spotlighting – look for Red-chested Button-quail, Little Button-quail, Spotted Nightjar, Tawny Frogmouth and Southern Boobook. During the day, you may get Grey-fronted Honeyeater, Singing Honeyeater, Long-tailed Finch, Masked Woodswallow and Brown Falcon.

Connells Lagoon Conservation Reserve

The 25,900ha reserve, also known as Dalgajini, is situated in the heart of Barkly Tablelands approximately 180km north of Barkly Hwy. The reserve was established to protect Mitchell grassland and its wildlife. The landscape is predominantly flat, the ground is covered by Mitchell grass with small stands of trees and bluebush in the wetter areas. The reserve is fenced to exclude cattle, with the Connells Lagoon located just outside the boundary fence.

Typical habitat at Connells Lagoon

To get there, turn north from Barkly Hwy (66) into Tablelands Hwy (11). Ater 130km turn into Ranken Rd that runs between Brunette Downs Station and Alexandria Station. GPS coordinates at the turnoff are 17°31'31''S and 136°00'11''E. Drive 57km on the gravel (accessible to 2WD vehicles); the main entry to the reserve is an obscure, overgrown track marked with a rusty drum carrying a hardly visible sign pointing to a bore. Another track further down, looking slightly more used, is not signposted and leads to Pictorella Swamp, usually dry. Tracks inside the reserve are 4WD only, the length is about 30km. There are no facilities. The site fact sheet with a map can be downloaded here: https://nt.gov.au/__data/assets/pdf_file/0014/200057/connells-lagoon-conservation-reserve-fact-sheet-and-map.pdf.

This site is seldom visited by birders so only 80 bird species are on the Connells Lagoon Conservation Reserve's birdlist, mostly of grassland variety. **Key species** are Flock Bronzewing, Pictorella Mannikin, Australian Bustard and Red-chested Button-quail. Other birds of interest include Australian Pratincole, Horsfield's Bushlark, Brown Songlark, Singing Honeyeater, Australian Owlet-nightjar and Spotted Harrier. Rarities include Yellow Chat, Little Curlew, Oriental Plover, Grey Falcon, Letter-winged Kite and Eastern Grass Owl.

Other wildlife in the reserve includes red kangaroo, dingo and long-haired rat (plague rat). The latter has found refuge here; normally it is rare but after heavy rains the population may reach plague proportions. Then, the rare Letter-winged Kites appear in good numbers and start breeding.

When driving on Ranken Rd, you'll pass a couple of spots worth stopping. First, stop 10km before the reserve where a large tower is situated – Grey Falcon has a nest there. Also, Black Falcon, Australian Pratincole and Horsfield's Bushlark were recorded in this area.

Another 5km down the road (52km from the turnoff), keep your eyes peeled for a broken windmill, cement water trough and a water tank. There is a small dam nearby. You may be rewarded with a view of Flock Bronzewings arriving in early morning or late afternoon (8am or 6pm) for a drink at the dam. Birds usually perch on the water trough before approaching the water. Raptors should be in attendance to hunt the pigeons. You may sight Black Falcon, Australian Hobby, Brown Goshawk, Swamp Harrier and Spotted Harrier.

There are several bores (Middle, West and Hidden) in the reserve that attract wildlife. These are the spots where you may get Flock Bronzewings. Horsfield's Bushlarks are the most common birds in the reserve, visible when flying over the plains and singing. Other grassland birds include Zebra Finch, Diamond Dove, Brown Songlark, Australasian Pipit, Australian Bustard, Budgerigar, Australian Pratincole, Red-backed Fairy-wren and Little Button-quail. At night, Australian Owlet-nightjars can be heard. Other birds include Black-faced Woodswallow, Yellow-throated Miner, Cockatiel and Singing Honeyeater.

The reserve is a good place for birds of prey such as Wedge-tailed Eagle, Nankeen Kestrel, Brown Falcon and Spotted Harrier.

Male Red-backed Fairy-wren

Limmen National Park

This wonderful, 937,000ha remote National Park, is located in the Carpentaria Gulf Region 280km southeast of Katherine and 65km from Borroloola, a small town on the Gulf of Carpentaria. The Park features spectacular sandstone formations, numerous rivers and associated wetlands. It preserves savannah country at the base of Arnhem Land. The Park sits at the edge of the Gulf, between Roper River and Cape Crawford on Carpentaria Hwy, and between wet tropics and arid zone, so bird diversity is truly enjoyable here. Most of the rainfall (800mm) falls between December and March and roads are impassable in this period. Several lagoons in the vicinity of Nathan River Rd are a birdwatcher's delight.

The main attractions of Limmen National Park are the 'lost cities', Western and Southern, – the rock formations resembling tall apartment blocks and pillars. These are a paradise to wildlife, especially to the escarpment specialists. The Park can be accessed from north and south:

- from Stuart Hwy (1) via Roper Hwy (20) with the turnoff 10km south of Mataranka. Roper Hwy is sealed only to the junction with Tablelands Hwy.
- from Barkly Hwy (66) via Tablelands Hwy (11) followed by Carpentaria Hwy (1). This route is sealed only to the junction with Carpentaria Hwy.

All roads in the Park are unsealed and closed in the Wet season (Nov-May) due to flooding. You'll need a high-clearance 4WD to conquer this Park. Camping sites with basic facilities (toilets, wood barbecues and picnic tables) are located at Towns River, Butterfly Falls, Southern Lost City, Didi Baba and Munbililla. You are also allowed to bush camp anywhere in the Park. Boat ramps are provided at Towns River and Munbililla. Ensure to have enough food, water and fuel for the duration of your journey. There are no services for 350km between the Roper Bar store and Cape Crawford. The Park's fact sheet and map is downloadable here: https://nt.gov.au/__data/assets/pdf_file/0005/200102/Limmen-National-Park-fact-sheet-and-map.pdf.

Over 160 bird species have been recorded in the Limmen National Park. **Key species** are Sandstone Shrike-thrush, Little Woodswallow, Buff-sided Robin, Gouldian Finch, Bar-breasted Honeyeater and Chestnut-backed Button-quail. Other birds of interest include waterbirds, waders, Azure Kingfisher, Apostlebird, Red-tailed Treecreeper, Red-backed Kingfisher, Northern Rosella, Australian Bustard, Jacky Winter, Long-tailed Finch and Masked Finch. Among the rarities are Grey Falcon, Black Falcon, Square-tailed Kite, Partridge Pigeon, Painted Honeyeater, Dusky Moorhen, Little Ringed Plover, Swinhoe's Snipe, Sarus Crane and Pictorella Mannikin.

Lomarieum Lagoon

This is a very productive birding site, located off Nathan River Rd south of Roper River. To get there, from Roper Hwy turn into Nathan River Rd before reaching Roper Bar. Pass the Munbililla (Tomato Island) campground and drive on until you see the lagoons on the left. GPS coordinates are 14°46'46"S and 134°53'10"E. Water is covered with waterlilies, it is a lovely spot so you can bush camp here and get close to nature. However, beware of roaming feral pigs, wild buffaloes and of course saltwater crocodiles.

The lagoon is often filled up to the brim with waterbirds such as Green Pygmy-geese Magpie Geese, Wandering Whistling-Ducks, Radjah Shelducks and Hardheads, with a few Black-necked Storks and Brolgas walking among them. In September 2022, a group of Sarus Cranes was sighted in the lagoon – this is the third record of this species in Northern Territory. Check the muddy edges of the lagoon for waders; Black-fronted Dotterel, Red-kneed Dotterel, Sharp-tailed Sandpiper and Common Greenshank are often reported. Little Ring Plover and Swinhoe's Snipe were also found here.

Sarus Crane

Finches come to drink, including Gouldian Finch, Long-tailed Finch, Black-bellied Crimson Finch and Pictorella Mannikin. Other birds in the area include White-throated Gerygone, Apostlebird, Sacred Kingfisher, Glossy Ibis, Australian Owlet-nightjar, Black-breasted Buzzard and White-bellied Sea-Eagle.

Western Lost City

Western Lost City is the main attraction of the Park. To get access, you need the gate code from the Nathan River Ranger Station. The station is not always manned so call the ranger in advance on (08) 8975 9940. The code, changed weekly, is also written on a whiteboard at the Ranger Station. The Lost City's fact sheet and map can be found here: https://nt.gov.au/__data/assets/pdf_file/0020/372080/limmen-national-park-lost-city.pdf.

From the locked gate to the City is 28km on a rough, poorly maintained track with several creek crossings. It will take at least 1.5hr in a sturdy 4WD to cover this distance. 2km down the track, look for Purple-crowned Fairy-wrens in the vegetation surrounding a creek crossing. 14km from the gate you'll came across a waterhole where a variety of waterbird species may be found. Look for Brolga, Black-necked Stork, Nankeen Night-Heron and Azure Kingfisher. Gouldian Finches, Long-tailed Finches and Masked Finches come to drink here.

When walking among the towering structures of Lost City, you'll have a good chance to sight Sandstone Shrike-thrush and Little Woodswallow. Black Falcon, Spotted Harrier and Little Eagle were recorded a few times. Other birds at this site include Brown Quail, Australian Bustard, Northern Fantail, White-gaped Honeyeater, Great Bowerbird and Sacred Kingfisher.

Little Woodswallow

Southern Lost City Campground

The campground is set among an amazing landscape of outlandish sandstone columns; you may be looking over your shoulder half expecting a Tyrannosaurus Rex to appear. It is located 3km south of the Nathan River Ranger Station at GPS coordinates of 15°48'34"S and 135°27'22"E. To get there, from Nathan River Rd take Southern Lost City Tk, heading north.

In the camping area, you'll be able to tick off Great Bowerbird, Apostlebird, Grey-crowned Babbler, Yellow-tinted Honeyeater, Paperbark Flycatcher and Rainbow Bee-eater. At night, Australian Owlet-nightjar, Tawny Frogmouth and Southern Boobook may be calling.

A 2.5km Southern Lost City loop starts from the campground. On this walk, look for Sandstone Shrike-thrush, Little Woodswallow, Northern Rosella, Long-tailed Finch, Little Bronze-cuckoo, Black-tailed Treecreeper, Little Button-quail and Varied Sittella. There is also abundance of honeyeaters such as White-quilled Honeyeater,

Banded Honeyeater, Rufous-throated Honeyeater, Grey-headed Honeyeater and Silver-crowned Friarbird. The rare Painted Honeyeater was recorded a few times.

Butterfly Falls Campground

Butterfly Falls is the only place in the Park considered safe for swimming although not suitable at the end of the Dry as the water turns stagnant and stinky. Facilities include toilets and shaded picnic tables. The site is accessed via a vehicular track 2km off Nathan River Rd. GPS coordinates are 15°37'36''S and 135°27'38''E.

Buff-sided Robins hop around the campsites. Look for the Great Bowerbird's bower, decorated in an elegant 'white and silver' style. The main choice are white snail shells but the bower is also adorned with silver metallic objects such as pieces of tinfoil and crushed coke cans.

A walking track that starts at the camp may produce Sandstone Shrike-thrush, Little Woodswallow, Chestnut-backed Button-quail, Azure Kingfisher, Australian Bustard, Banded Honeyeater, Bar-breasted Honeyeater, Grey-fronted Honeyeater, Nankeen Night-Heron, Red-winged Parrot and Pheasant Coucal. Among the rarer findings in the area are Partridge Pigeon, Grey Falcon and Square-tailed Kite.

Towns River Campground

Take Towns River Tk from Nathan River Rd and drive 2km to the camping area. In the vegetation along the banks of Towns River look for Purple-crowned Fairy-wren, Buff-sided Robin and Arafura Fantail. Purple-backed Fairy-wrens are found in thick lantana scrub adjacent to the camping area. When grevilleas are in bloom, plenty of nectar-feeders arrive, including Bar-breasted Honeyeaters, Banded Honeyeaters, White-gaped Honeyeaters, White-quilled Honeyeaters and Varied Lorikeets.

Square-tailed Kites inhabit the area. Other birds include Lemon-bellied Flycatcher, Black-bellied Crimson Finch, Long-tailed Finch, Little Woodswallow, Bush Stone-curlew, Northern Fantail and Collared Sparrowhawk.

Lorella Springs Wilderness Park

This site is surrounded by the Limmen National Park but it is a private property, not part of the Park. It offers a wide range of accommodation and safe swimming in the hot springs near the campground. The site is open in the Dry (Apr-Sep) and currently only to pre-booked organised tours. To get there, from Cape Crawford on Carpentaria Hwy (1) drive north for 45km towards Limmen National Park on Ryans Bend. Keep to the left at the Y-junction and take Nathan River Rd to drive 56km.

Next, turn right into Lorella and drive the final 30km to the Wilderness Park. All this route is unsealed.

Over 130 bird species have been recorded in the Lorella Springs Wilderness Park. **Key species** are Gouldian Finch, Sandstone Shrike-thrush, Buff-banded Rail, Little Woodswallow, Bar-breasted Honeyeater and Banded Honeyeater. Other birds of interest include Azure Kingfisher, Brolga, Green Pygmy-goose, Black-necked Stork, Nankeen Night-Heron, Black-tailed Treecreeper, Northern Fantail, Arafura Fantail, Varied Lorikeet, Jacky Winter and Barking Owl. Hooded Robin is the local rarity.

Good birding can be experienced near the campground where you may find Azure Kingfisher, Paperbark Flycatcher, Bar-breasted Honeyeater, Long-tailed Finch, Black-bellied Crimson Finch and Great Bowerbird. Look for Sandstone Shrike-thrushes on the Tawallah Falls Tk. Birds are usually calling from small caves near the top of the rockface. Search also for Little Woodswallow, Jacky Winter, Varied Sittella, Leaden Flycatcher and Common Bronzewing there.

Black-necked Stork, Green Pygmy-goose, Cattle Egret, Azure Kingfisher and Marsh Sandpiper have been reported from the Flying Fox Swamp. This is also a good place for finches. Look for Gouldian Finch and Masked Finch as well as Large-billed Gerygone and Paperbark Flycatcher.

Another good birding spot is the Scary Creek Swamp where a family of Barking Owls sometimes roost together in a tree at the edge of the swamp. Look also for Red-backed Button-quail, Silver-backed Butcherbird, Little Woodswallow, Brolga, Bush Stone-curlew and Nankeen Night-Heron.

Caranbirini Conservation Reserve

Caranbirini Conservation Reserve is a small, 1,200ha reserve, located on Carpentaria Hwy (1) 46km south of Borroloola and 700km southeast of Darwin. This remarkable place, sometimes referred to as 'mini Bungle Bungles National Park', protects a large range of habitats including a spectacular sandstone 'lost city', large waterholes surrounded by the riparian vegetation as well as areas of open woodland.

To get there, drive east from Cape Crawford on Carpentaria Hwy (1) for 64km, then turn right into a 500m access road to the carpark. Take short walks to points of interest in the reserve. Camping is not permitted; the closest accommodation can be found in Borroloola and in the Heartbreak Hotel in Cape Crawford. Facilities include shaded picnic tables, bird hide, lookouts and three walking trails: Caranbirini Waterhole Trail (300m return), Barrawulla Loop (2km loop through the Lost City) and a long Jagududgu Walk (7.5km loop). See the fact sheet with a site map here:

https://nt.gov.au/__data/assets/pdf_file/0016/200095/caranbirini-conservation-reserve-fact-sheet.pdf.

Yellow-tinted Honeyeater

Over 150 bird species have been recorded in the Caranbirini Conservation Reserve. **Key species** are Sandstone Shrike-thrush, Gouldian Finch and Purple-crowned Fairy-wren. Other birds of interest include Green Pygmy-goose, Little Woodswallow, Spinifex Pigeon, Banded Honeyeater, Yellow-tinted Honeyeater, Bar-breasted Honeyeater, Grey-headed Honeyeater, Jacky Winter, Paperbark Flycatcher and Peregrine Falcon. Rarities include Carpentarian Grasswren, Northern Shrike-tit, Pale-vented Bush-hen, Emu, Masked Owl, Red Goshawk and Little Eagle.

On the access road, look for Red-backed Button-quails that may be skulking at the road edge. A chatty flock of Apostlebirds may be using the road as their walking path to the water. Spinifex Pigeons like to sunbathe near the gate.

Caranbirini Waterhole

Purple-crowned Fairy-wrens are resident in the riverine vegetation. A substantial flock of Green Pygmy-geese is always present at the waterhole. Gouldian Finches regularly visit for a drink, particularly in the Dry. Bar-breasted Honeyeaters are also present in good numbers in winter. Look also for Yellow-tinted Honeyeater, White-throated Honeyeater, Grey-headed Honeyeater, Rufous-throated Honeyeater, Banded Honeyeater, White-plumed Honeyeater and Silver-crowned Friarbird. This is a good place to find Azure Kingfisher, Shining Flycatcher, Paperbark Flycatcher,

Jacky Winter and Northern Fantail. You also have a chance to come across Northern Shrike-tit. Raptors hanging around the waterhole include Australian Hobby, Brown Goshawk, Wedge-tailed Eagle and occasionally Black-breasted Buzzard or even Red Goshawk. At night, Tawny Frogmouth and Barking Owl may be calling.

Barrawulla Loop

Explore sandstone formations along the walk and search for Sandstone Shrike-thrushes on top of the rocks. Look also for Little Woodswallow, Black-faced Woodswallow, Silver-crowned Friarbird, Spinifex Pigeon, White-quilled Honeyeater, Rufous-throated Honeyeater and Peregrine Falcon. Gouldian Finches and Long-tailed Finches can be observed foraging on the ground. There are some old records (more than 30 years old) of Carpentarian Grasswren from the southern section of Jagududgu Walk, mainly from its intersection with Barrawulla Loop.

Borroloola

Borroloola is a small fishing town sitting on the banks of McArthur River 50km south of the river mouth. It is considered to be the gateway to the Gulf of Carpentaria and is famous for its excellent fishing. It can be reached via Carpentaria Hwy (1), a sealed one-lane road running for 380km from the Daly Waters Inn on Stuart Hwy (A87) to Borroloola. Carpentaria Hwy is part of Savannah Way which links Cairns in Northern Queensland with Broome in Western Australia. Sections of this route are unsealed, particularly from Borroloola in NT to Burketown in Qld, and subject to closures during the Wet. Savannah Way has several road names along its length but always the 'National 1' number.

Accommodation in town includes caravan park, motel and guest houses. There is also a fuel station, café, several small shops and an airstrip.

Over 150 bird species have been recorded in and around Borroloola. **Key species** are Purple-crowned Fairy-wren, Buff-sided Robin, White-breasted Whistler, Mangrove Golden Whistler, Great-billed Heron, Zitting Cisticola, Pictorella Mannikin and Beach Stone-curlew. Other birds of interest include waders, waterbirds, Azure Kingfisher, Orange-footed Scrubfowl, Grey-headed Honeyeater, Red-headed Honeyeater, Little Shrike-thrush, Brown Quail, Barking Owl and White-bellied Sea-Eagle. Rarities include Yellow Chat, Orange Chat, Star Finch, Ground Cuckoo-shrike, Sarus Crane, Square-tailed Kite and Little Eagle.

Check the Rodeo Showgrounds in town; Spotted Nightjar, Large-tailed Nightjar, Southern Boobook and Barking Owl may be calling at night.

In the McArthur River Caravan Park, you may come across Azure Kingfisher, Red-tailed Black-Cockatoo, Torresian Imperial-Pigeon, Green Oriole, Grey-crowned Babbler, White-bellied Cuckoo-shrike, Blue-winged Kookaburra and Barking Owl.

Azure Kingfisher

It may be a good idea to inspect the southern boat ramp. To get there, from Robinson Rd in town turn east into Boat Ramp Tk and drive 500m to the river. Search for Purple-crowned Fairy-wren and Buff-sided Robin. Buff-banded Rails are sometimes observed at the river edge. Also, look for Black-bellied Crimson Finch, Golden-headed Cisticola and Paperbark Flycatcher.

A walk along McArthur River 1km upstream from the bridge may produce Purple-crowned Fairy-wrens; they live in cane grass west of the bridge. Other birds near the river include Australian Reed-Warbler, Masked Finch, Long-tailed Finch, Silver-crowned Friarbird, Paperbark Flycatcher, Oriental Dollarbird, Buff-sided Robin and Tawny Grassbird.

Snipe Lagoon

This small lagoon is located along Carpentaria Hwy 5.7km east of the bridge, opposite Wandangula Rd. GPS coordinates are 16°03'56"S and 136°21'58"E. Swinhoe's Snipes are reported from there with some regularity. A pair of Sarus Cranes, extremely rare in NT, has been sighted once.

Other birds include Bar-breasted Honeyeater, Rufous-throated Honeyeater, Long-tailed Finch, Sharp-tailed Sandpiper, Black-fronted Dotterel, Pallid Cuckoo and Brolga.

Borroloola Wastewater Treatment Plant

To get there, from N1 turn south into an unnamed track south of the Rodeo Showgrounds and drive to the ponds. Approximate GPS coordinates are 16°05'45"S and 136°18'28"E. Look on the water for Pink-eared Duck, Australian Wood Duck, Radjah Shelduck, Hoary-headed Grebe, Australasian Grebe, Brolga and Pied Stilt. Waders reported from this site include Australian Pratincole, Swinhoe's Snipe and Black-fronted Dotterel. Masses of Fairy Martins are often observed hunting insects over the ponds.

In the long grass surrounding the ponds, look for Pictorella Mannikin, Chestnut-breasted Mannikin, Long-tailed Finch, Masked Finch, Black-bellied Crimson Finch and Star Finch. Other birds include Spotted Harrier, Red-backed Kingfisher, Red-tailed Black-Cockatoo, White-winged Triller and Grey-crowned Babbler.

King Ash Bay Boat Ramp

To get there, take Bing Bong Rd from N1, then turn right to Batten Rd which will take you to the boat ramp. The distance from Borroloola is about 40km.

Buff-sided Robin can be found near the river. Great-billed Herons occasionally visit the area. Expect to find Striated Heron, Pied Heron, Caspian Tern, Australian Gull-billed Tern, Australian Pelican, Common Greenshank and Eastern Reef Egret. A good range of mangrove specialists can be found here. Look for White-breasted Whistler, Mangrove Golden Whistler, Australian Yellow White-eye, Broad-billed Flycatcher, Mangrove Gerygone, Shining Flycatcher and Azure Kingfisher.

Caspian Terns with Australian Pelican, getting ready for takeoff

Other birds in the area include Little Bronze-cuckoo, Jacky Winter, Orange-footed Scrubfowl and Little Shrike-thrush.

Sir Edward Pellew Islands

Sir Edward Pellew Group is a cluster of barrier sandstone islands sitting at the mouth of McArthur River. The biggest are Vanderlin, North, West, Southwest and Centre Islands; with numerous smaller islands in between. Access is by boat only, vessels can be launched from the King Ash Bay Boat Ramp, then sail 35km down McArthur River and Carrington Channel to the Gulf. You need an experienced skipper because conditions in the Gulf can be dangerous. This is private Aboriginal land so permits will be needed.

The 5,400ha Barranyi National Park has been established on the North Island. Camping grounds are provided at Mud Bay and Paradice Bay. The latter has toilets and fire rings. Barranyi fact sheet and map can be downloaded here: https://nt.gov.au/__data/assets/pdf_file/0015/200094/barranyi-north-island-national-park-fact-sheet-and-map.pdf.

Four species of sea turtles nest on the West Island. The islands of the Group are also a refuge for the waders and seabirds. In particular, three small islets, Pearce, Urquhart and Harvey Island (a total of 9ha), are recognised as an Important Bird Area by Birdlife International thanks to breeding colonies of thousands of terns. The main species are Greater Crested Tern (50,000) and Roseate Tern (17,500). Bridled Terns, Little Terns and Black-naped Terns also breed in smaller numbers there.

Bing Bong Port

Osprey

This small mining industry harbour is located 57km north of Borroloola accessible via Bing Bong Rd from N1. A boat ramp with a small carpark is located east of the port at the end of an unsealed track. Both the harbour and boat ramp are worth checking for the presence of waders. Beach Stone-curlews are regularly found near the harbour. Waders on the birdlist include Greater Sand Plover, Lesser Sand Plover, Grey Plover, Great Knot, Ruddy Turnstone, Whimbrel, Far Eastern Curlew, Common Sandpiper and Australian Pied Oystercatcher. A good variety of terns includes Little Tern, Common Tern, White-winged Black Tern, Caspian Tern, Lesser Crested Tern and, the most numerous, Greater Crested Tern. Brown Boobies often perch on the channel markers. Other birds include Black-necked Stork, Eastern Reef Egret, Little Egret and Great Egret. There is also an Osprey nest in Bing Bong.

Check the mangroves north of the boat ramp. White-breasted Whistler and Mangrove Golden Whistler are relatively common there and quite easy to find.

Mangrove Gerygones are very common and singing all the time. This patch of the mangroves may also yield Collared Kingfisher, Australian Yellow White-eye, Red-headed Honeyeater, Broad-billed Flycatcher, Shining Flycatcher, Lemon-bellied Flycatcher, Purple-backed Fairy-wren, Brahminy Kite and White-bellied Sea-Eagle.

Inspect the grass plains adjacent to the river for the possible presence of Zitting Cisticola.

Carpentarian Grasswren Sites

Carpentarian Grasswren is a very rare and elusive species, mostly occurring in the Mount Isa region in Queensland. Isolated small populations are also found along Savannah Wy (N1) in NT near the Qld border. In particular, concentrate on the first 100km section of N1 (called Wollogorang Rd there) from the border as well as the northern part of Calvert Rd. Both roads are terrible, a 4WD vehicle is a must. Look for the birds in rocky areas covered with spinifex.

Wollogorang Road at 17°14'10"S and 137°50'21"E

The site is located approximately 15km west of NT/Qld border. Inspect the road both ways for about 1km. Before this book went to print, the grasswrens were last reported in October 2022, 200m south of the road, at the exact GPS coordinates of 17°13'33"S and 137°52'41"E. Look also for Little Woodswallow, Purple-backed Fairy-wren, Grey-fronted Honeyeater, Paperbark Flycatcher and Rainbow Bee-eater.

Wollogorang Road at 17°22'13"S and 137°44'60"E

Search for Carpentarian Grasswren in spinifex along the gorge about 20km west of NT/Qld border. Other birds in this location include Spinifex Pigeon, Jacky Winter, Common Bronzewing, Grey-fronted Honeyeater, White-throated Honeyeater and Golden-Backed Honeyeater.

Wollogorang Road at 16°56'02"S and 137°21'36"E

This site is located at the Calvert River crossing, about 100km west of NT/Qld border and 35km west of the junction with Calvert Rd. Look for Carpentarian Grasswren in the spinifex, then check the lush vegetation around the waterhole in the riverbed. Purple-crowned Fairy-wrens and Buff-sided Robins are resident there. Other birds include Nankeen Night-Heron, Lemon-bellied Flycatcher, Shining Flycatcher, Leaden Flycatcher, Northern Fantail, Arafura Fantail and White-throated Gerygone.

Calvert Road at 17°12'25"S and 137°22'11"E

From Wollogorang Rd turn south into Calvert Rd and drive for about 16km. A rocky area is situated near the road by the Little Calvert River. Look there for Carpentarian Grasswren and also for Sandstone Shrike-thrush. Check the waterhole in the riverbed where finches come to drink. You may get Gouldian Finch, Long-tailed Finch and Masked Finch. Azure Kingfishers often hunts at the waterhole. Other birds in this area include Budgerigar, Varied Lorikeet, Banded Honeyeater, White-necked Heron, Nankeen Night-Heron, Varied Sittella, Masked Woodswallow, Little Woodswallow, Apostlebird and Barking Owl.

Groote Eylandt

Groote Eylandt is the Gulf of Carpentaria's largest island and the 4th largest in Australia. It is 50km wide and 60km long. Groote Eylandt is part of the Groote Archipelago of 40 islands located approximately 50km offshore, 630km east of Darwin. Habitats of the archipelago include beaches, dense monsoon forest, mangroves and mudflats. In comparison with other islands in NT, the habitats are relatively pristine, with no feral animals. An unnamed 10ha islet off the northeastern coast of Groote Eylandt has been identified by Birdlife International as the IBA (Important Bird Area) because it supports over 1% of the world population of Roseate Terns – approx. 5,000 pairs. Bridled Terns and Black-naped Terns also breed on the islet.

As the Groote Eylandt is part of the Arnhem Land, permits are required from the Anindilyakwa Land Council. To obtain a recreation permit, call (08) 8987 4006, go to https://permits.anindilyakwa.com.au/, or email admin@alcnt.com.au. Processing of the application may take up to 5 days. There are 15 recreation spots where visitors are allowed to go, see the map on the page https://anindilyakwa.com.au/land-and-sea/recreation/.

Access to the island is possible with daily 1.5hr flights from Darwin. Accommodation is available at the Groote Eylandt Lodge in Alyangula where the airport is located, also offering car rental.

Over 220 bird species have been recorded on Groote Eylandt. **Key species** are Beach Stone-curlew, Chestnut Rail, Rainbow Pitta, Roseate Tern, Chestnut-backed Button-quail and Masked Owl. Other birds of interest include waders, seabirds, Australian Magpie, Barn Swallow, Azure Kingfisher, Mangrove Golden Whistler, Australian Yellow White-eye, Red-headed Honeyeater, Rufous-banded Honeyeater, Common Cicadabird, Orange-footed Scrubfowl, Brown Whistler, Green-backed Gerygone, and Large-tailed Nightjar. Rarities include Great-billed Heron, Swinhoe's Snipe and King Quail.

Alyangula

Alyangula is the largest township on Groote Eylandt, population of 880, mostly employees of the manganese ore-mining company GEMCO. You'll find here a resort, golf course, a café, fuel station and several small shops. The area around the town is good for seabirds, particularly for terns. Visit the town wharf and look for Greater Crested Tern, Lesser Crested Tern, Australian Gull-billed Tern, Bridled Tern, Black-naped Tern, White-winged Black Tern and Little Tern. During or after windy periods, Lesser Frigatebirds appear. Brahminy Kites and Ospreys are seen regularly along the shore. The latter have a nest in the port stockpile, easily viewed from the fuel station. Australian Hobby is nesting in the communications tower. Barn Swallows are often recorded in town in summer.

Take a walk from the GEMCO accommodation through the golf course and along the beach. Along the way you may encounter Rose-crowned Fruit-Dove, Orange-footed Scrubfowl, Blue-winged Kookaburra, Sacred Kingfisher and Torresian Imperial-Pigeon. Bush Stone-curlews are resident on the golf course. On the beach, look for Common Sandpiper, Little Egret, Striated Heron and Nankeen Night-Heron. Check the monsoon forest bordering the beach; it may yield Rainbow Pitta, Bar-breasted Honeyeater, Brown Honeyeater, Pheasant Coucal, Varied Triller and Little Bronze-cuckoo. The mangroves may produce Mangrove Golden Whistler, Australian Yellow White-eye, Arafura Fantail, Beach Stone-curlew and Mangrove Gerygone.

Australian Yellow White-eye

At night, you'll have a chance to see or hear Spotted Nightjar, Large-tailed Nightjar, Australian Owlet-nightjar, Tawny Frogmouth and Southern Boobook. The northern, much paler race of Masked Owl is sporadically reported.

Eningkirra Beach

This spot, locally known as Mission Landing, is located at the mouth of Angurugu Creek halfway along the west coast of Groote Eylandt. GPS coordinates are 13°58'07"S and 136°24'52"E. Inspect the beach as well as the islands and mangroves in the vicinity. Look for Beach Stone-curlew, Chestnut Rail and Great-billed Heron along the mudflats and adjacent mangroves. Other species at Eningkirra Beach include Eastern Reef Egret, Pacific Golden Plover, Grey Plover, Lesser Sand Plover and Grey-tailed Tattler. In some productive monsoon thickets nearby, search for Rainbow Pitta, Shining Flycatcher, Brown Whistler, Green-backed Gerygone, Northern Fantail and Arafura Fantail.

Salt Creek (Amudalya)

Whimbrel

Salt Creek recreation area is located in the southwest corner of the island. The approximate GPS coordinates are 14°07'52"S and 136°26'01"E. This is a great wader site; 23 species have been recorded. Beach Stone-curlews are breeding in this area. Common waders include Australian Pied Oystercatcher, Curlew Sandpiper,

Great Knot, Grey-tailed Tattler, Lesser Sand Plover, Greater Sand Plover, Grey Plover, Whimbrel and Ruddy Turnstone. Among the rarer species here are Terek Sandpiper, Marsh Sandpiper and Common Sandpiper.

Mangrove dwellers found in the creek mouth include Chestnut Rail, Mangrove Robin, Broad-billed Flycatcher, Shining Flycatcher and Mangrove Golden Whistler. Brown Quail and Chestnut-backed Button-quail live in the grassy area by the beach.

Angurugu Sewage Ponds

To get there, drive south on Rowell Hwy past the airport, cross Angurugu Creek, then turn east into Unknown Rd (*sic*!) to the ponds. Several ponds will be to your left, viewing is from the road. Approximate GPS coordinates are 13°58'51''S and 136°27'05''E. Large-flocks of Wandering Whistling-Ducks, Grey Teals and Australasian Grebes are often found on the ponds. Among 20 wader species, Swinhoe's Snipe is reported regularly. Other waders include Common Sandpiper, Black-tailed Godwit, Little Curlew, Pacific Golden Plover, Wood Sandpiper, Red-kneed Dotterel, Oriental Pratincole and Australian Pratincole.

Bush birds around the ponds include Forest Kingfisher, Green Oriole, Rufous Whistler, White-bellied Cuckoo-shrike, Rainbow Bee-eater, Red-winged Parrot, Silver-crowned Friarbird and Chestnut-breasted Mannikin.

Elcho Island

Elcho Island, also known as Galiwinku, part of Arnhem Land, is located 3km off the north shore of Australia, at the southern end of Wessel Islands Group. Galiwinku is also the name for the largest settlement on the island, population 2,200.

Elcho Island is a place of natural beauty, with beaches surrounded by the deep-red cliffs. Permit is required to enter for recreational activities. Permits can be obtained from Northern Land Council, apply here: https://www.nlc.org.au/apply-for-permit. Allow 10 working days for processing. Regular flights to Elcho Island are operated from Darwin. Accommodation is available in the Galiwinku Visiting Contractors Accommodation and Marthakal Motel.

Over 150 bird species have been recorded on Elcho Island. **Key species** are Beach Stone-curlew, Roseate Tern, Black-naped Tern, Red-headed Honeyeater, Bar-breasted Honeyeater and Broad-billed Flycatcher. Other birds of interest include waders, seabirds, Eastern Reef Egret, Black-necked Stork, White-browed Crake, Black Butcherbird, Collared Kingfisher, Azure Kingfisher, Lemon-bellied Flycatcher, Rufous-banded Honeyeater, Brown-capped Emerald-Dove, Arafura Fantail and

Large-tailed Nightjar. Rarities include Great-billed Heron, Fork-tailed Swift and Eurasian Hoopoe that appeared in February 2014 and put Elcho on the birding map.

Twenty wader species and ten tern species have been recorded on the island. These include Sooty Oystercatcher, Australian Pied Oystercatcher, Grey Plover, Greater Sand Plover, Lesser Sand Plover, Ruddy Turnstone, Grey-tailed Tattler, Common Sandpiper and Terek Sandpiper. The tern selection includes Common Tern, Little Tern, Lesser Crested Tern, Australian Gull-billed Tern, Roseate Tern, Sooty Tern and Brown Noddy. Other seabirds include Brown Booby, Great Frigatebird and Lesser Frigatebird.

Sooty Oystercatcher

In the monsoon thickets and mangroves around the island, look for Shining Flycatcher, Northern Fantail, Azure Kingfisher, Orange-footed Scrubfowl, Brown Whistler, Common Cicadabird, Bar-shouldered Dove, Brown-capped Emerald-Dove and Green-backed Gerygone.

Other birds on Elcho Island include Magpie Goose, Plumed Whistling-Duck, Radjah Shelduck, Australasian Grebe, Eastern Reef Egret, Pied Heron and Glossy Ibis.

Nhulunbuy

Nhulunbuy is a mining town on Gove Peninsula, 700km northeast from Katherine via Central Arnhem Rd. The Gove Peninsula is part of Arnhem Land and is famous for its spectacular beaches and fishing. Nhulunbuy is a deep-water port, suitable for exporting the mined bauxites to Asia, as the local alumina smelter closed in 2014.

There are many birding spots around the Gove Peninsula, mostly for waders and seabirds. The easiest and cheapest way to visit is to fly from Darwin to Gove Airport in Nhulunbuy. A visitor permit is needed from the Dhimurru Aboriginal Corporation if you intend to go outside of town to any recreation areas. See the detailed information and pay the fees at https://www.dhimurru.com.au/permits-information.html. Rent a car in Nhulunbuy to move around. The only other alternative is to drive your own 4WD for 700km on Central Arnhem Rd from Katherine. It will give you an opportunity to experience the untamed beauty of the land but it will be also a hard journey. The road is terrible and there are practically no fuel and supplies until you reach Nhulunbuy so prepare and pack well for the trip. An additional transit permit from the Northern Land Council is required to travel on this road, apply here: https://www.nlc.org.au/apply-for-permit.

Over 200 bird species have been recorded in the Nhulunbuy area. **Key species** are Beach Stone-curlew, Great-billed Heron, Roseate Tern, Silver-backed Butcherbird, Rainbow Pitta, Broad-billed Flycatcher and Large-tailed Nightjar. Other birds of interest include waders, seabirds, Rufous-banded Honeyeater, Banded Honeyeater, Red-headed Honeyeater, Brolga, Black-necked Stork, Azure Kingfisher, Collared Kingfisher, Orange-footed Scrubfowl and Common Cicadabird. Rarities include Little Kingfisher, Swinhoe's Snipe, Oriental Cuckoo, Eastern Yellow Wagtail, Barn Swallow, Freckled Duck, Black-headed Gull and Spectacled Monarch.

Nhulunbuy WTP

The ponds are located near the northern border of Town Lagoon, GPS coordinates are 12°09'54''S and 136°46'36''E. To get there, from Beagle Cct take Sewer Ponds and drive to the ponds. Twenty wader species are on this site's birdlist. This is the place to look for Swinhoe's Snipes; they are found here in small numbers every year. Other waders include Black-tailed Godwit, Pacific Golden Plover, Curlew Sandpiper, Common Sandpiper, Marsh Sandpiper, Wood Sandpiper and Red-kneed Dotterel. White-browed Crakes are resident. Brolgas are often recorded. Large numbers of waterbirds include Australasian Grebes, Radjah Shelducks, Wandering Whistling-Ducks and Green Pygmy-geese. Rarer ducks such as Chestnut Teal and Freckled Duck appear from time to time. In summer, look for Barn Swallow, Oriental Cuckoo and Eastern Yellow Wagtail. At night, Large-tailed Nightjars may be seen hunting over the ponds.

In the surrounding bush and mangroves, you may come across Forest Kingfisher, Sacred Kingfisher, Green Oriole, Silver-backed Butcherbird, Lemon-bellied Flycatcher, Bar-breasted Honeyeater and Green-backed Gerygone.

Nhulunbuy Town Lagoon

Town Lagoon is a pristine freshwater wetland that winds through a stunning paperbark forest and monsoon thicket. This is the most productive birding area in Nhulunbuy. Access is from Chesterfield Cre. A 3km Gaynaru Nature Walk will take you to the edge of the lagoon with viewing platforms and a bird hide. Follow Nhulunbuy Walk Trail Network signs to get there.

Over 160 bird species have been recorded around the Nhulunbuy Town Lagoon. **Key species** are Black Bittern, White-browed Crake, Rainbow Pitta, Bar-breasted Honeyeater, Red-headed Honeyeater, Silver-backed Butcherbird, Large-tailed Nightjar and Rufous Owl. Other birds of interest include Pied Heron, Green Pygmy-goose, Comb-crested Jacana, Glossy Ibis, Azure Kingfisher, Orange-footed Scrubfowl, Torresian Imperial-Pigeon, Northern Rosella, Little Bronze-cuckoo, Shining Flycatcher, Swamp Harrier and Osprey. Rarities include Spectacled Monarch, Oriental Cuckoo, Freckled Duck, Broad-billed Sandpiper and Eastern Yellow Wagtail.

Rainbow Pitta is often found in the monsoon forest. Look also for Northern Fantail, Lemon-bellied Flycatcher, Brown Whistler, Rufous-banded Honeyeater, Forest Kingfisher, Little Shrike-thrush, Green-backed Gerygone and Large-billed Gerygone. An unusual vagrant, Spectacled Monarch, was found here in July 2019.

Observe the wetland birds from the bird hide or a viewing platform. You may see White-browed Crakes, Green Pygmy-geese, Magpie Geese, Brolgas or flush a Black Bittern from the surrounding vegetation.

Nine species of cuckoos have been recorded at Town Lagoon including Oriental Cuckoo, Little Bronze-cuckoo, Brush Cuckoo and Channel-billed Cuckoo.

Nhulunbuy Saltpans

Access to this site is via Melville Bay Rd and Beagle Cct through the cemetery. These are tidal saltpans so are covered with seawater during high tide. They also get flooded in heavy rains. Approx. GPS coordinates are 12°10’48”S and 136°45’27”E. This is a good wader site; 23 species are using the area for feeding and roosting. Common species are Red-necked Stint, Grey-tailed Tattler, Lesser Sand Plover, Red-capped Plover, Sharp-tailed Sandpiper and Curlew Sandpiper. Among rarer species are Beach Stone-curlew, Terek Sandpiper, Oriental Plover and Red Knot.

Oriental Plover

Silver-backed Butcherbirds and Bush Stone-curlews are found regularly in the cemetery. Birds in the bush include Rainbow Bee-eater, Bar-breasted Honeyeater, Red-headed Honeyeater, Helmeted Friarbird, Shining Flycatcher, Oriental Dollarbird, Large-billed Gerygone and Black-bellied Crimson Finch.

Nhulunbuy Spit and Refinery

To get there, drive on Melville Bay Rd to the carpark at the end of the road, past the refinery and Gove Port. At high tide, a large, mixed flock of terns gathers on the spit. These are mostly Greater Crested Terns and Black-naped Terns but look also for Common Terns, Little Terns, Roseate Terns and Lesser Crested Terns. In March 2015, Black-headed Gull was recorded here. A pair of Beach Stone-curlews is resident in this area. Other waders here include Sooty Oystercatcher, Australian Pied Oystercatcher, Common Sandpiper, Great Knot, Pacific Golden Plover and Lesser Sand Plover.

Check the wharf, port structures and large refinery tanks for raptors. You may get Peregrine Falcon, Osprey or White-bellied Sea-Eagle. The former's favourite perching spots are rims of the refinery fuel tanks. Also, Brown Boobies often roost on the wharf.

Galuru (East Woody Beach)

This is a good wader site. To get there, from Beagle Cct in Nhulunbuy take Gove Golf Club Rd and drive north. Turn west into East Woody Point just before reaching the beach and drive to the end of the road. Approx. GPS coordinates are 12°09'51''S and 136°45'17''E. Galuru is a beautiful, squeaky clean, white beach. At the end of the spit is East Woody Island that can be reached on foot except for the high tide. The walk will reward you with a 360° view, so you can watch both the sunrise and sunset from the same spot.

Twenty-two wader species are using this site. Beach Stone-curlews are found here regularly. Look for Terek Sandpiper, Common Sandpiper, Marsh Sandpiper, Sooty Oystercatcher and Sanderling among the more common species. Great-billed Herons are seen occasionally in the tidal creek. Black-naped Tern, Little Tern, Lesser Crested Tern and Roseate Tern are the less common terns recorded here.

Common Sandpiper

Seach the mangroves for Mangrove Robin, Collared Kingfisher, Azure Kingfisher, Mangrove Gerygone, Green-backed Gerygone, Australian Yellow White-eye, Shining Flycatcher, Broad-billed Flycatcher and Red-headed Honeyeater.

Lombuy (Crocodile Creek)

This wader site is located 3km west of Galuru. Drive Melville Bay Rd in the westerly direction and take a track to Lombuy Beach 3km before Birritjimi Beach. GPS coordinates are 12°10'45''S and 136°43'46''E. Bird composition is similar to that of Galuru site. Rocky outcrops in the water are visible from the beach. Observe roosting terns there including Roseate Terns and Bridled Terns, while Black-naped Terns and Greater Crested Terns will be roosting on the beach.

Bushes near the beach may yield Rose-crowned Fruit-Dove, Varied Lorikeet, Bar-breasted Honeyeater, Red-headed Honeyeater, Varied Triller and Green-backed Gerygone.

Drimmie Head Road

From Melville Bay Rd take Drimmie Head Rd and drive to the Gove Boat Club and check the mudflats and sandspit before the bridge that allows access to the island. GPS coordinates here are 12°12'02''S and 136°42'33''E.

Striated Heron

Great-billed Herons visit the mudflats in front of the mangroves. Terek Sandpipers, Common Sandpipers, Grey-tailed Tattlers, Whimbrels, Far Eastern Curlews, Little Egrets, Striated Herons and Eastern Reef Egrets may also be feeding there. The mangroves may produce Little Kingfisher, Arafura Fantail, Little Bronze-cuckoo, Mangrove Gerygone, Australian Yellow White-eye, Brahminy Kite and Osprey.

Rainbow Cliffs

The native name of Rainbow Cliffs is Banambarrnga. It is a popular tourist destination just south of Nhulunbuy. Drive from town on Melville Bay Rd, then take a track to the left past the Telecom tower. GPS coordinates for Rainbow Cliffs are 12°12’36’’S and 136°49’45’’E. There is a campground there.

This spot is popular with the birders thanks to the resident Peregrine Falcons. They often perch on the cliffs. On the beach, look for Sooty Oystercatcher, Beach Stone-curlew, Common Sandpiper and Eastern Reef Egret.

In the flowering woollybutts (in winter), you should get plenty of nectar-feeding birds such as Varied Lorikeet, Red-collared Lorikeet, Red-headed Honeyeater, Banded Honeyeater, White-gaped Honeyeater and Silver-crowned Friarbird.

In the campground, look for Leaden Flycatcher, Great Bowerbird, White-bellied Cuckoo-shrike, Spangled Drongo and Large-billed Gerygone.

Tennant Creek & Central Deserts

1 [Threeways Roadhouse]
2 [Tennant Creek WTP]
3 [The Pebbles]
4 [Mary Ann Dam]
5 [Karlu Karlu (Devils Marbles)]
6 [Iytwelepenty National Park]
7 [Barrow Creek]
8 [Gemtree Roadhouse]
9 [Other birding sites on Stuart Hwy]
10 [Newhaven Wildlife Sanctuary]

Threeways Roadhouse

This famous roadhouse is located just north of the junction of Stuart Hwy (A87) and Barkley Hwy (66), and about 25km north of Tennant Creek. It offers a welcome break in your long journey through the Australian Outback. You'll find here toilets, shop, fuel station, an airconditioned restaurant and a variety of accommodation including a large caravan park.

The birds take full advantage of leaking water taps and the sprinklers operating on the grounds. You can use this to your benefit, too. Several rare species, such as Painted Honeyeater, Golden-backed Honeyeater and Black Falcon, were recorded here. A pair of Black-breasted Buzzard nests in the area and is often seen flying over the roadhouse.

Common birds here include Apostlebird, White-breasted Woodswallow, Black-faced Woodswallow, Rufous-throated Honeyeater, Zebra Finch and Galah. You may also spot Australian Ringneck, Pallid Cuckoo, Jacky Winter, Grey-headed Honeyeater, Grey-fronted Honeyeater and Brown Falcon.

Gregarious Zebra Finches

Tennant Creek WTP

This site is located south of Tennant Creek, which, at 3,000 residents as of 2021, is one of the biggest towns in Northern Territory. The wastewater treatment plant utilises several freshwater ponds and is surrounded by sparse bushland. The land around Tennent Creek is very dry and little water is available throughout much of the year. Not surprisingly, the ponds are a magnet for a variety of birds. Waterbirds congregate here in large numbers.

The site is reached via Fazaldeen Rd. Approximate GPS coordinates are 19°40'14''S and 134°10'20''E. To get there, turn west into this road from Stuart Hwy (A87) 2km south of the city centre and then turn into an unnamed track first to the left. This track will lead you to the ponds which are fenced but birds are visible. The fence is supported by numerous termite mounds. An interesting accent of the site is an old sign prohibiting duck shooting. The sign was shot at many times.

Over 180 bird species have been recorded around the Tennant Creek treatment ponds. **Key species** are Black-breasted Buzzard, Black Falcon, Red-necked Avocet, Red-kneed Dotterel, Little Button-quail, Budgerigar, Diamond Dove and Crimson Chat. Other birds of interest include waders and waterbirds, Spinifex Pigeon, White-rumped Swallow, Red-backed Kingfisher, Australian Ringneck, Rufous Songlark, Grey-crowned Babbler, Cockatiel and Pallid Cuckoo. Rarities include Grey Falcon, Square-tailed Kite, Blue-billed Duck, Great Crested Grebe, Ruff, Long-toed Stint, Pectoral Sandpiper, Latham's Snipe, Pied Heron, Flock Bronzewing, Stubble Quail, Eastern Yellow Wagtail, Painted Honeyeater, Yellow Chat, Pictorella Mannikin, Painted Finch, House Sparrow, Major Mitchell's Cockatoo and Common Myna.

A pair of Black-breasted Buzzards nest at this site and can sometimes be observed drinking water from the ponds.

During our visit, about 100 Black Kites were roosting on the fences or circling overheads. On the water, we found large flocks of waterbirds including Pink-eared Ducks, Grey Teals, Hardheads, Eurasian Coots, Australasian Grebes and Hoary-headed Grebes. On the banks were Plumed Whistling-Ducks, Wood Sandpipers, Black-fronted Dotterels, Red-kneed Dotterels, Pied Stilts and plenty of Straw-necked Ibises. Pied Stilts were breeding; we saw three birds sitting on the nests. Huge numbers of Tree Martins and Fairy Martins were flying over the water. We also spotted a couple of White-rumped Swallows.

Straw-necked Ibis

Red-backed Kingfishers and Sacred Kingfishers were sitting on the fences which also served as a stopover for Zebra Finches arriving to quench their thirst. A steady stream of Budgerigars, Cockatiels and Diamond Doves was also landing for a drink of water. We also ticked off Spinifex Pigeon, Australian Ringneck, White-winged Triller and Yellow-throated Miner.

In the surrounding bush, we got Weebill, Mistletoebird, Rufous Songlark, Singing Honeyeater, White-plumed Honeyeater, Grey-headed Honeyeater, Pallid Cuckoo, Spotted Harrier and plenty of woodswallows including Little Woodswallow, White-browed Woodswallow and Black-faced Woodswallow.

Fazaldeen Rd also proved to be worthwhile, particularly near the rubbish tip where we observed hundreds of Black Kites, Little Corellas and Galahs. We also found Brown Quails, Red-chested Button-quails, Spinifex Pigeons, Red-browed Pardalotes and Little Crows along this road.

The Pebbles

The Pebbles is an outcrop of granite boulders situated 11km north of Tennant Creek. It is known to the Aboriginal people as Kunjarra, a sacred women's site for dancing and healing. Access is from Stuart Hwy (A87) just past Tenant Creek

Telegraph Station when travelling north. Turn west into Pebbles Quarry Rd, followed by turning left into Devil Pebbles Rd which will take you to the carpark. The length of travel from Stuart Hwy is 6km on a dirt road, a 4WD vehicle is advisable. Approximate GPS coordinates are 19°32'02"S and 134°10'48"E.

The site is open for day-use only, no camping is allowed. You'll find here a picnic area with toilets and a walking track that facilitates birding. The Pebbles site is not as spectacular as Devils Marbles but is still worth a visit.

About 60 bird species have been recorded at The Pebbles. **Key species** are Spinifex Pigeon, Spinifexbird, Painted Finch, Orange Chat, Crested Bellbird and Little Woodswallow. Other birds of interest include Grey-headed Honeyeater, Singing Honeyeater, Red-browed Pardalote, Little Button-quail, Diamond Dove, Grey-crowned Babbler and Spotted Nightjar. Grey-crowned Cuckoo-shrike is a rarity.

Crested Bellbird

The walking trail is particularly good for Spinifexbird which may come up to the grass tips to sing. Water tends to accumulate in rockholes and cervices of the rocky areas. Search there for Painted Finch, Grey-headed Honeyeater and Zebra Finch, seeking drinking water.

Mary Ann Dam

This site, also called Tingkkarli or Lake Mary Ann, is situated 5km northeast of Tennant Creek. It is reached from Stuart Hwy (A87) via Mary Ann Dr, a 1.6km sealed road. It is a man-made dam surrounded by grassland on one side and natural bushland on the other side. Mary Ann is a recreational dam for local residents who come here for swimming and canoeing. It has a nice picnic area and 1.6km of walking and cycling paths. Day-use only, no camping.

Over 140 bird species have been recorded around the Mary Ann Dam. **Key species** are Dusky Grasswren, Spinifexbird, Spinifex Pigeon, Painted Finch, Glossy Ibis and Black-breasted Buzzard. Other birds of interest include waders, waterbirds, Grey-fronted Honeyeater, Grey-headed Honeyeater, Red-backed Kingfisher, Little Woodswallow, Black-faced Woodswallow, Masked Woodswallow, Indian Peafowl, Budgerigar and Purple-backed Fairy-wren. Rarities include Freckled Duck, Great Crested Grebe, Swinhoe's Snipe, Black Honeyeater, Fork-tailed Swift, Dusky Moorhen, Pictorella Mannikin and Eastern Yellow Wagtail.

Dusky Grasswren and Spinifexbird are the main purpose of a visit; both are reasonably easy to find during a walk through the spinifex-cladded hills. Look also for Painted Finches which, in some years, are abundant here. Drying mud at the dam edge may in summer yield waders such as Common Sandpiper, Wood Sandpiper, Sharp-tailed Sandpiper, Marsh Sandpiper and Common Greenshank. Swinhoe's Snipes were sighted a few times in sparse vegetation at the lake verge near a small creek. Waterbirds at this site include Pink-eared Duck, Hardhead, White-necked Heron, Great Crested Grebe, Black-tailed Native-hen and Glossy Ibis.

Occasionally, large flocks of Masked Woodswallows and White-browed Woodswallows appear at the lake. Little Woodswallows and Black-faced Woodswallows are here year-round. Other bush birds in the area include Cockatiel, Budgerigar, White-winged Triller, Rufous Whistler, Singing Honeyeater, Yellow-throated Miner, White-winged Fairy-wren and Channel-billed Cuckoo.

Black-breasted Buzzards are observed regularly over the lake. Other raptors include Swamp Harrier, Spotted Harrier, Black Kite, White-bellied Sea-Eagle and Wedge-tailed Eagle.

Karlu Karlu (Devils Marbles) CR

Karlu Karlu, formerly known as Devil Marbles, is a well-known, small (1,800ha) Conservation Reserve that extends on both sides of Stuart Hwy (A87) about 100km south of Tennant Creek and 400km north of Alice Springs. This famous tourist attraction features stacks of rounded giant granite boulders, precariously balancing on top of one another. The gigantic marbles are scattered along the valley that forms the reserve. These marbles have become internationally recognised as the symbol of Australian Outback, similarly to the Uluru Rock. They look particularly spectacular when the setting sun highlights their deep red colour.

Massive boulders at Karlu Karlu

The vegetation consists mostly of spinifex, with scattered groups of stunted-growth trees and shrubs. The Conservation Reserve has a small camping area near the boulders, with picnic tables, barbecues and toilets, accessed via a sealed road. Several walking tracks are useful for birding. The map and further information is downloadable here: https://nt.gov.au/__data/assets/pdf_file/0016/200059/karlu-karlu-devils-marbles-fact-sheet-and-map.pdf.

Over 80 bird species have been recorded in the Devils Marbles Conservation Reserve. **Key species** are Spinifexbird, Little Button-quail, Painted Finch, Ground Cuckoo-shrike, Hooded Robin and Black-breasted Buzzard. Other birds of interest include Red-browed Pardalote, Grey-fronted Honeyeater, Grey-headed Honeyeater,

Budgerigar, Diamond Dove, Rufous Songlark, Masked Woodswallow, Pallid Cuckoo, Grey-crowned Babbler, White-winged Fairy-wren, White-backed Swallow and Australian Raven. Rarities include Grey Falcon, Pictorella Mannikin, Mulga Parrot, Black Honeyeater, Fork-tailed Swift, Grey Butcherbird and Major Mitchell's Cockatoo.

We stopped there in March 2022 for a quick lunch and sighted a Little Button-quail with a small chick hiding in the tall dry grass literally next to our picnic table.

Fairy Martins breed in the reserve; multiple colonies of bottle-shaped nests are glued to the boulders. At the time of our visit, the most common birds in the area were Budgerigars, Zebra Finches, White-breasted Woodswallows and Singing Honeyeaters. Two small flocks of Painted Finches were drinking water accumulated in small hollows in the granite rocks. A pair of White-backed Swallows were flying over the picnic area. On the Karlu Karlu Walk, we encountered Spinifexbird, Pied Butcherbird, Horsfield's Bronze-cuckoo, Black-faced Woodswallow, Spinifex Pigeon, Rufous Whistler and Grey-crowned Babbler. A pair of Australian Ravens were walking around the picnic area. Raptor sightings on that day included Wedge-tailed Eagle, Brown Falcon, Black-shouldered Kite and Black-breasted Buzzard.

Iytwelepenty National Park

This 112,000ha park, formerly known as Davenport Ranges National Park, is situated about 150km southeast of Tennant Creek and 500km north of Alice Springs. It protects an example of the environmental zone between the Top End and Central Australia. It is an important refuge for wildlife, especially for the waterbirds, due to its extensive network of waterholes. It offers beautiful swimming spots, stunning scenery and satisfying birdwatching.

The Park can be reached via two separate unsealed routes from Stuart Hwy (A87):

- near Bonney Well turnoff via Kurundi / Epenarra Rd
- from the Taylor Creek turnoff onto Murray Downs / Hatches Creek Rd (more difficult, so a slower route but nicer views).

Both routes are prone to flooding in the summer months (Dec-Mar) so a 4WD vehicle is needed, with high clearance for the Murray Downs route. Only two basic camping grounds are provided: at Whistleduck Creek and Old Police Station Waterhole. Facilities included toilets, fire pits and picnic tables. A site map and more information can be found in the Fact Sheet downloadable here: https://nt.gov.au/__data/assets/pdf_file/0015/200058/iytwelepenty-davenport-ranges-national-park-fact-sheet-and-map.pdf.

Over 100 bird species have been recorded in the Iytwelepenty National Park. **Key species** are Spinifex Pigeon, Spinifexbird, Western Bowerbird, Golden-backed Honeyeater, Painted Finch, Little Button-quail and Red-backed Kingfisher. Other birds of interest include Budgerigar, Cockatiel, Common Sandpiper, Brolga, White-necked Heron, Grey-crowned Babbler, White-winged Triller, White-plumed Honeyeater, Grey-fronted Honeyeater, Rufous Songlark and Spotted Nightjar. Rarities include Dusky Moorhen, Hooded Robin, Black Honeyeater, Crested Bellbird, Pictorella Mannikin and Major Mitchell's Cockatoo.

Whistleduck Creek Campground

The campground is located approximately 80km from Stuart Hwy via Kurundi / Epenarra Rd. It is a closer and more accessible location from Tennant Creek. The area is teeming with honeyeaters, particularly in spring (September) when many bushes and trees are flowering. Look for Grey-fronted Honeyeater, Spiny-cheeked Honeyeater, Golden-backed Honeyeater, Brown Honeyeater and White-plumed Honeyeater. Occasionally, Black Honeyeater can be sighted.

Whistling Kites are nesting near the campsite. Little Eagles can sometimes be seen. Other birds here include Little Button-quail, Brown Quail, Red-browed Pardalote, Little Woodswallow, Crimson Chat, Australian Ringneck and Painted Finch. You may hear Southern Boobook, Tawny Frogmouth and Spotted Nightjar During the night.

Old Police Station Waterhole

This campground is located further down along Kurundi / Epenarra Rd, 160km from Tennant Creek. It can also be reached via Murray Downs but that road is more challenging. This is the place where you can find a good selection of waterbird species in this dry area, including Black Swan, Grey Teal, Australasian Grebe, Brolga, Royal Spoonbill, Common Sandpiper and White-necked Heron.

Western Bowerbirds are regularly seen in the campground; look for a bower nearby. Bush birds coming to drink at the waterhole include Diamond Doves, Budgerigars, Cockatiels, Australian Ringnecks, Grey-crowned Babblers and Spinifex Pigeons. Other birds in the area include Grey-headed Honeyeater, Singing Honeyeater, Weebill, Rufous Songlark, Red-browed Pardalote and Red-backed Kingfisher.

A good selection of raptors can be found around the waterhole, such as Little Eagle, Black-breasted Buzzard, Australian Hobby, Brown Goshawk and Brown Falcon. Nocturnal birds include Australian Owlet-nightjar, Southern Boobook and Barn Owl.

Barrow Creek

The tiny settlement of Barrow Creek (population 4 as of 2023) is the famous roadhouse with the pub and camping area. The roadhouse was built in 1932 so is as old as the Sydney Harbour Bridge. It is located on Stuart Hwy (A87) about 220km south of Tennant Creek and 290km north of Alice Springs. The place has a unique atmosphere of an old Outback pub and is worth stopping for refuelling, meal and rest. The place is not well-known as a birding spot but if you explore up to 10km north and south along Stuart Hwy, you may find amazing birds there.

Over 100 bird species have been recorded in Barrow Creek. **Key species** are Grey Falcon, Black Falcon, Dusky Grasswren, Rufous-crowned Emu-wren, Spinifexbird, Ground Cuckoo-shrike and Painted Finch. Other birds of interest include Budgerigar, Cockatiel, Diamond Dove, Zebra Finch, Red-browed Pardalote, Hooded Robin, Australian Ringneck, White-backed Swallow, Little Button-quail and Black-breasted Buzzard. Rarities include Flock Bronzewing, Slaty-backed Thornbill, Orange Chat, Major Mitchell's Cockatoo, Black Honeyeater and Golden-backed Honeyeater.

A thousand-strong flock of Budgerigars at Barrow Creek waterhole

In May 2022, we spent two hours at a small waterhole just south of the roadhouse, observing a breathtaking spectacle of 100,000+ of Budgerigars coming in big flocks for a drink of water. They were moving in swift, shimmering green clouds that covered the whole sky. There were also huge numbers of Zebra Finches, Cockatiels, Diamond Doves and Galahs around the waterhole. The birds were often flushed into the air by raptors perching quietly in the surrounding bushes. However, the raptors looked well-fed and not very interested in hunting. Suddenly, Grey Falcon appeared from nowhere, expertly caught a Diamond Dove, then was gone over a mesa. Seeing hundreds of thousands of Budgerigars in the Outback was one of the ticks on our bucket list and we were totally satisfied with the experience.

Other birds around the dam included Hooded Robin, White-winged Fairy-wren, Singing Honeyeater and Grey-fronted Honeyeater. As we were returning into the coolness of the pub, our eyes met with the big eyes of two Bush Stone-curlews, resting in the shade next to the sculptures placed on the ground by the entrance door. After we sat at an outside bar table, a friendly Western Bowerbird approached us, looking for a morsel.

Stuart Hwy at 21°33’51”S and 133°49’24”E

The site is located approximately 8km south of the Barrow Creek Roadhouse. There is a low plateau rising above the plain here, with an extensive cover of spinifex and a small creekline, usually dry.

About 1km north of the creek, look for an obscure track running west. Dusky Grasswrens were found along this track, hopping on the rocks. Look also for Rufous-crowned Emu-wren, Spinifexbird, Ground Cuckoo-shrike and Black-breasted Buzzard. Little Button-quails can be sometimes found here in large numbers.

The area around the creekline may also yield Purple-back Fairy-wren, Splendid Fairy-wren, Spiny-cheeked Honeyeater, Singing Honeyeater, Western Gerygone, Slaty-backed Thornbill, Black-faced Woodswallow, Hooded Robin, Crested Bellbird and Little Crow.

Barrow Creek Bridge

This stopping bay is located 5km north of the Roadhouse, on the northwestern side of Stuart Hwy (A87). GPS coordinates are 21°29’18”S and 133°54’47”E. Birds here include Black-breasted Buzzard, Australian Hobby, Peregrine Falcon, Pallid Cuckoo, Crimson Chat, Yellow-throated Miner, White-fronted Honeyeater, White-winged Triller, Crested Bellbird, Hooded Robin, Common Bronzewing and Red-backed Kingfisher.

Gemtree Roadhouse

This property is located on the sealed section of Plenty Hwy (12), 140km northeast of Alice Springs. This place is very popular with fossickers. To get there, turn off Stuart Hwy (A87) 70km north of Alice and continue east for another 70km until you arrive at the roadhouse just past Gilles Creek. GPS coordinates are 22°58'06''S and 134°14'35''E. The roadhouse offers good facilities including a bar and a swimming pool. There is a splendid caravan park here with plenty of shady trees and a 3.5km-long walking track for birding.

About 80 bird species have been recorded around the Gemtree Roadhouse. **Key species** are Western Bowerbird, Slaty-backed Thornbill, Mulga Parrot, Major Mitchell's Cockatoo, Hooded Robin and Black-breasted Buzzard. Other birds of interest include Grey Butcherbird, Common Bronzewing, Diamond Dove, Red-backed Kingfisher, White-browed Babbler, Spiny-cheeked Honeyeater, Little Button-quail, Red-capped Robin, Crimson Chat, Inland Thornbill, Chestnut-rumped Thornbill and Spotted Harrier. Rarities include Ground Cuckoo-shrike, Bourke's Parrot and Pied Honeyeater.

Splendid Fairy-wrens are common around the roadhouse. Grey Butcherbirds are constantly singing melodiously, and a Western Bowerbird walks around, inspecting the grounds. At night, Southern Boobook and Spotted Nightjar can be heard.

Splendid Fairy-wren

On the walking trail, look for Crested Bellbird, Australian Ringneck, White-plumed Honeyeater, Rufous Whistler, White-winged Fairy-wren, Splendid Fairy-wren, Common Bronzewing, Horsfield's Bronze-cuckoo and Southern Whiteface.

Other Birding Sites on Stuart Highway

Birding in this vast arid country between Tennant Creek and Alice Springs is mainly conducted along Stuart Hwy.

Stuart Hwy at 19°36'08"S and 134°11'28"E

These coordinates refer to a short track to the west, located 300m north of the intersection of Stuart Hwy with Mary Ann Dr, about 5km north of Tennant Creek. This track that runs to the west through the gully and then turns south, leading through the hills back to Stuart Hwy. This is a fantastic birding site, where you may spot Dusky Grasswren, Spinifexbird, Spinifex Pigeon, Painted Finch and, if you are really lucky, Rufous-crowned Emu-wren.

Look for Dusky Grasswren in the old grove of spinifex on the southern side of the track along the creekline. Check the stands of trees and shrubs for Grey-headed Honeyeater, Grey-fronted Honeyeater, Weebill, White-winged Triller, Black-faced Woodswallow, Little Woodswallow and Red-backed Kingfisher. Other birds in the area include White-winged Fairy-wren, Rufous Songlark, Spotted Harrier, Black-breasted Buzzard and Brown Goshawk.

Stuart Hwy at 20°11'03"S and 134°13'11"E

The site is an overnight camping area situated beside a large man-made dam, 100m west of Stuart Hwy, 65km south of Tennant Creek. This spot can be very productive when masses of Budgerigars, Cockatiels and Zebra Finches gather for a drink. Sometimes, a large flock of Flock Bronzewings may appear. At times of plenty, raptors such as Black Falcon, Little Eagle, Australian Hobby, Peregrine Falcon, Spotted Harrier and others, are reported from this area.

Look for Red-necked Avocet, Red-kneed Dotterel, Black-fronted Dotterel and Great Egret on the water. Other birds in the area include Common Bronzewing, Black-faced Woodswallow, Singing Honeyeater, Spiny-cheeked Honeyeater and White-plumed Honeyeater.

Bonney Creek Rest Area

This site is located on the west side of Stuart Hwy, north of Bonney Creek and 500m south of the junction with Kurundi Rd, approximately 90km south of Tennant Creek. GPS coordinates are 20°25'49''S and 134°14'47''E.

The bridge over Bonney Creek is home to a large colony of Fairy Martins. A permanent waterhole east of the highway attracts a good variety of birds, especially in the dry periods. The site is good for raptors; Black Falcon, Spotted Harrier and Black-breasted Buzzard are regularly recorded. White-necked Herons are often seen feeding at the edges of the waterhole.

Bushland around the campground may yield Red-capped Robin, Red-backed Kingfisher, White-winged Fairy-wren, Red-browed Pardalote, Yellow-rumped Thornbill, Rufous Whistler and Grey-crowned Babbler.

Red-capped Robin

Wycliffe Well Roadhouse

This is a quirky Outback place, known as the UFO capital of Australia. It is located on Stuart Hwy (A87) about 130km south of Tennant Creek and 380km north of Alice Springs. It has fuel, restaurant, caravan park and plenty of UFO memorabilia. A big sign at the front announces 'Earthlings are also welcome' however toilets are reserved only for 'Maliens' and 'Femaliens'.

A man-made lake is located nearby, with a track leading to it. The place is good for waterbirds; typical sightings include Black-tailed Native-hen, Red-kneed Dotterel, Black-fronted Dotterel, Hoary-headed Grebe, Pink-eared Duck, Hardhead, Nankeen Night-Heron, White-necked Heron and Yellow-billed Spoonbill. Many birds come to drink at the lake, particularly large flocks of Budgerigars and Diamond Doves.

A pair of Little Eagles is often recorded near the roadhouse. Other raptors include Black-breasted Buzzard, Spotted Harrier, Black Falcon, Brown Falcon and Whistling Kite. Fairy Martins are nesting in the outbuildings. You may also come across Little Button-quail, Common Bronzewing, Weebill, Rufous Songlark, Crimson Chat, Red-browed Pardalote, Rainbow Bee-eater, Yellow-throated Miner, Singing Honeyeater and Banded Honeyeater. Occasionally, Major Mitchell's Cockatoo is recorded.

Taylors Creek Rest Area

This large overnight rest stop is located 180km south of Tennant Creek. It has good facilities including sheltered picnic tables, toilets, fire pits and a large water tank which, when dripping water, attracts birds seeking a drink. Taylor Creek is nearby.

Grey Falcon was recorded here several times. Other raptors include Black-breasted Buzzard, Australian Hobby, Black Kite, Whistling Kite (nesting near the creek), Brown Goshawk and Collared Sparrowhawk.

The place is known for the repetitive appearances of flocks of Major Mitchell's Cockatoos, favouring this location as their watering hole. You may also encounter Crested Bellbird, Little Button-quail, Budgerigar, Crested Pigeon, Grey-crowned Babbler and Weebill. Mulga Parrot is an occasional visitor.

Stuart Hwy at 21°57'37''S and 133°29'48''E

The John McDouall Stuart Monument is placed in this rest area. The cairn marks a century from the discovery of the centre of Australia by John Stuart in 1860. The site is located 20km north of the Ti-Tree Roadhouse. Stands of mulga surround it, where Red-capped Robins and Hooded Robins can be found. If you spend more time exploring, you have a chance to find White-browed Treecreeper here.

Masses of Zebra Finches nest in the trees. Other birds at this rest stop include Crested Bellbird, Inland Thornbill, Rufous Whistler, Purple-backed Fairy-wren, Splendid Fairy-wren, Little Crow, Spiny-cheeked Honeyeater, Horsfield's Bronze-cuckoo and Black-breasted Buzzard (occasional sightings).

Aileron Roadhouse

The roadhouse is located on Stuart Hwy (A87) about 135km north of Alice Springs. It is home of the striking giant sculpture of the 'Anmatjere Man'. At 17m high and 8 tonnes weight, it stands prominently on top of a hill near the roadhouse.

We stayed at Aileron in May 2022 and enjoyed watching birds coming to drink from the sprinklers. These included Major Mitchell's Cockatoos, Galahs, Budgerigars, Australian Ringnecks, Zebra Finches, Yellow-throated Miners and White-plumed Honeyeaters. A Little Eagle and several Black Kites were flying overhead. Flocks of Grey-crowned Babblers were moving through the grounds. In the bushland around the roadhouse, we found Crested Bellbird, Rufous Songlark, Brown Songlark, Singing Honeyeater, Spiny-cheeked Honeyeater, Red-capped Robin and Southern Whiteface.

Major Mitchell's Cockatoos drinking from leaking sprinklers at Aileron RH

Prowse Gap Rest Area

This large overnight rest stop is located on Stuart Hwy (A87) about 130km north of Alice Springs, not far from the Aileron Roadhouse. Facilities include sealed surface, toilets, sheltered picnic tables and a large rainwater tank which, if not empty, leaks and attracts a variety of bush birds. The site is surrounded by mulga and is fenced but there is a large gap in the fence to an informal camping ground among the mulga trees. This opening give access to birding.

Prowse Gap is good for Hooded Robin, Red-capped Robin, Crested Bellbird, Chestnut-rumped Thornbill, Inland Thornbill and Western Gerygone. There is also a chance to come across White-browed Treecreeper or Slaty-backed Thornbill here.

Other birds in the area include Splendid Fairy-wren, Purple-backed Fairy-wren, Spiny-cheeked Honeyeater, White-browed Babbler, Major Mitchell's Cockatoo and White-backed Swallow.

Ryan Well Historical Reserve

The reserve is located about 125km north of Alice Springs and 10km south of Aileron Roadhouse. The well was dug in 1899 to supply water for stock animals. The site is situated on both sides of Stuart Hwy (A87) at GPS coordinates of 22°43'09"S and 133°22'59"E. You can bush camp here overnight. Look here for Bourke's Parrot, Mulga Parrot, Little Button-quail, Crested Bellbird, Splendid Fairy-wren, Hooded Robin and Rufous Songlark. Occasional finds include Slaty-backed Thornbill, Pied Honeyeater and Black-breasted Buzzard.

Native Gap Conservation Reserve

This tiny (11ha) roadside reserve is located on the western side of Stuart Hwy (A87) about 115km north of Alice Springs. GPS coordinates are 22°48'01"S and 133°25'00"E. The main feature of the reserve is a rocky outcrop of the Hann Range that protrudes about 30m above the surrounding plains. The low areas are covered by woodland dominated by desert bloodwood and ironwood, with an understory of spinifex and other grasses. The outcrop is cladded in spinifex and a variety of sparse trees such as white cypress pine, ghost gum and fig trees.

Access to the reserve is via an unsealed service track leading to a Telstra tower. Further information and a site map can be found in the Fact Sheet, downloadable here: https://nt.gov.au/__data/assets/pdf_file/0008/200042/native-gap-conservation-reserve.pdf.

Dusky Grasswrens are found here from time to time, foraging on the ledges near the top of the outcrop. Woodland at its base may produce Crested Bellbird, Grey-crowned Babbler, Grey-fronted Honeyeater, Pallid Cuckoo, Western Bowerbird, Masked Woodswallow, Inland Thornbill and Red-browed Pardalote. There are also a few records of the rare Grey Honeyeater.

Connors Well Rest Area

Connors Well rest stop is located on the western side of Stuart Hwy (A87) about 95km north of Alice Springs. It is a very spacious caravan rest area but no toilets, just a large water tank and picnic tables. The place is surrounded by grassland with scattered small shrubs and sparse small trees. Australian Bustard, Rufous Songlark and Brown Songlark are often found there. Chiming Wedgebills are occasionally seen singing from the bushtops. Budgerigars, Diamond Doves and Zebra Finches often form mixed flocks feeding of the seeds blown by the wind onto the bare ground of the rest area. Occasionally, you can spot Bourke's Parrots or Australian Ringnecks among them.

Other birds include Black-faced Woodswallow, Little Crow, Red-capped Robin, Chestnut-rumped Thornbill, Crimson Chat, Rufous Whistler, Crested Bellbird, Hooded Robin, Australian Hobby and Wedge-tailed Eagle.

Chestnut-rumped Thornbill

Tropic of Capricorn Rest Area

This site is located at GPS coordinates of 23°26'16''S and 133°46'52''E on the western side of Stuart Hwy (A87). Bush surrounding the rest area is the place to look for Slaty-backed Thornbill which was recorded here many times. Other birds include Western Gerygone, Southern Whiteface, White-browed Babbler, Mulga Parrot, Rufous Whistler and Little Button-quail.

Newhaven Wildlife Sanctuary

This is Australia's largest (262,000ha) non-government protected area. It is owned and run by the Australian Wildlife Conservancy (AWC). The site is located 350km northwest of Alice Springs. This is a world-famous, key arid-zone birdwatching destination. The landscape of the Sanctuary is spectacular; there are extensive sand dunes, sand plains and saltmarshes here, overlooked by the rugged ranges that rise 800m above the ground. Spinifex-covered sand plains dominate the scenery, broken by the shimmering salt lakes. The property also features bloodwood woodland, dunes dotted with desert oaks and grassland with beautiful ghost gums. In wetter years, ephemeral lakes fill up with water, attracting waterbirds. The Sanctuary has a 9,450ha area protected with a predator-proof fence. A reintroduction programme is undertaken there by AWC for about 30 species of endangered small marsupials such as greater bilby, golden bandicoot, mala and burrowing bettong. There are plans to extend the predator-free area to 100,000ha (1/3 of the property).

To get there, from Stuart Hwy (A87) north of Alice Springs turn west into Tanami Rd and drive approximately 200km to Tilmouth Roadhouse. The road is a sealed one-lane but the surface is quite damaged by the road trains which use this route extensively. That doesn't make the travel in a smaller car pleasant. About 25km past the roadhouse, turn left into Newhaven Property Access and drive 136km on a dirt road to the Sanctuary. The last fuel and food supplies are at Tilmouth Roadhouse, you need to get enough for a return trip.

The Sanctuary is open to public only in the cooler months (Apr-Sep). You can camp here; the 10 available sites are unpowered but there are toilets and showers and also drinking water. Bookings are essential, go to https://www.australianwildlife.org/where-we-work/newhaven/visiting-newhaven-wildlife-sanctuary/. For further information call (08) 8964 6000. A substantial part of the property is off-limits to tourists due to the continuing conservation work. The best option for exploring and birdwatching is the 300km of self-guided driving tracks. All roads and tracks are unsealed and often in a bad condition, so you need a high clearance 4WD. Self-guided tours are specifically designed for visitors. Each tour has a different feel and often different bird species. There are also short birdwatching walks and several escarpment lookouts. Fact sheets and maps for the tours are available at the Homestead.

Over 180 bird species have been recorded in the Newhaven Wildlife Sanctuary. **Key species** are Grey Falcon, Grey Honeyeater, Ground Cuckoo-shrike, Dusky Grasswren, Rufous-crowned Emu-wren and Slaty-backed Thornbill. Other birds of interest include Spinifex Pigeon, Spinifexbird, Painted Finch, Banded Whiteface, Black Honeyeater, Pied Honeyeater, White-fronted Honeyeater, Red-backed Kingfisher, White-backed Swallow, Crimson Chat, Splendid Fairy-wren and Barn Owl. Rarities include Night Parrot, Princess Parrot, Bourke's Parrot, Freckled Duck, Fork-tailed Swift and Western Bowerbird.

An incredible sighting of a pair of Night Parrots was reported in 1996 from the Camel Bore. Princess Parrot is another rare and sought-after bird. In 2012, as many as 50 individuals were recorded in the Sanctuary, including near the Homestead and the Camelot. The best chance to spot them is after a good rainfall; look for them in the southeastern part of the property where in the heat of the day they may roost in dense foliage of desert oaks or desert bloodwoods.

Tilmouth Well Roadhouse

This is an oasis on the Tanami Desert, providing a refreshing break on your way to the Newhaven Sanctuary. In this area you can many common birds such as Budgerigars, Galahs, Diamond Doves, Zebra Finches and Yellow-throated Miners. Western Bowerbird has a bower in the caravan park. A lonely Emu moves occasionally across the tree-less grounds.

A great variety of raptors can be seen on Tanami Rd along the last 20km stretch before the turnoff to the Sanctuary. You have a chance to find there Black-breasted Buzzard, Black Falcon, Brown Falcon, Spotted Harrier, Australian Hobby, Black-shouldered Kite, Square-tailed Kite, Black Kite and Whistling Kite.

Black-shouldered Kite

Newhaven Homestead

Expect to see a good variety of birds around the house and the camping area. Common species include Diamond Dove, Ground Cuckoo-shrike, Crimson Chat, Crested Bellbird, Australian Ringneck, Rufous Whistler, Black-faced Cuckoo-shrike and Western Gerygone. Common honeyeaters include Spiny-cheeked Honeyeater, Grey-headed Honeyeater, Singing Honeyeater, White-plumed Honeyeater, Golden-backed Honeyeater and Brown Honeyeater. Zebra Finches are abundant; they come to drink from the waterhole near the campsite. Pallid Cuckoos are regularly calling around the Homestead. Major Mitchell's Cockatoos visit frequently. Other birds in the area include Chestnut-rumped Thornbill, Inland Thornbill, Red-capped Robin, Grey Fantail and Black-breasted Buzzard.

Potato Creek Gorge Tour

Rufous-crowned Emu-wren

This 15km tour includes an extensive area of mature spinifex. Rufous-crowned Emu-wren and Spinifexbird can be found there with some effort. In the flowering ghost gums and holly grevilleas, look for Grey-fronted Honeyeater, Grey-headed Honeyeater and Yellow-throated Miner. The rarer White-fronted Honeyeater, Black Honeyeater and Pied Honeyeater were also recorded.

Numerous bores provide water for the wildlife. Zebra Finches, Painted Finches, Diamond Doves and Crested Pigeons are nearly always present.

Dusky Grasswrens inhabit the rocky escarpment areas in the gorge.

The Airstrip

Rufous-crowned Emu-wrens can be found in the spinifex on the southwestern side of the airstrip. Other birds in the area include Crested Bellbird, Australasian Pipit, Yellow-rumped Thornbill, Black-shouldered Kite and Nankeen Kestrel.

The Lakes Tour

This 50km route passes the airstrip and then a series of small wetlands, continuing on towards the northern shores of Lake Bennett. This lake, a saltpan surrounded by the saltmarshes, is the major feature of Newhaven. Rainfall determines the state of Lake Bennett and other wetlands, and the selection of wildlife than can be seen there at a given time.

Passing the airstrip, you'll get to several areas of mature spinifex, where Rufous-crowned Emu-wrens may be present. Further down the road, you'll be driving through shrub-covered plains where Banded Whitefaces is found. This habitat also supports Purple-backed Fairy-wrens, White-winged Fairy-wrens, Splendid Fairy-wrens, Red-capped Robins, Hooded Robins, Inland Thornbills, Crested Bellbirds, Black-faced Woodswallows, Little Woodswallows and Singing Honeyeaters.

The area surrounding Lake Bennett may prove to be productive for Crimson Chat, Orange Chat and Australian Bustard. When freshwater is present on the surface, some waders and waterbirds arrive, including Red-capped Plover, Curlew Sandpiper, Common Greenshank, Black-fronted Dotterel, Hoary-headed Grebe, Grey Teal, Pink-eared Duck and Yellow-billed Spoonbill. Zebra Finches and various honeyeaters visit then for a drink of water. Check the saltbushes at the edges of the saltpan - it is a good area where you may find Brown Songlark, White-winged Triller, Black Honeyeater, Pied Honeyeater, Crimson Chat and Horsfield's Bushlark.

The smaller wetlands can also be productive; in particular, check Swan Lake, located north of Lake Bennett, where Grey Falcon, Black-breasted Buzzard and Inland Dotterel were recorded. Look also for Banded Lapwing, Banded Whiteface, Hooded Robin, Australasian Pipit and Orange Chat.

At Suzie's Lake, look for White-browed Babbler, Chestnut-rumped Thornbill, Red-capped Robin, Hooded Robin and Spotted Harrier.

Bottleneck Lakes can yield White-winged Fairy-wren, Splendid Fairy-wren, White-backed Swallow, Orange Chat, Hooded Robin, Brown Falcon, White-browed Babbler and Singing Honeyeater.

Male White-winged Fairy-wren

The Dunes Tour

This long, 80km tour heads southwest from the Homestead. The first good place to stop is in the desert oak woodland about 13km down the road. Look here for Weebill, Chestnut-rumped Thornbill, Yellow-rumped Thornbill, Western Gerygone, Masked Woodswallow, Singing Honeyeater, Red-capped Robin, Hooded Robin and Crested Bellbird. Also, Banded Whiteface was reported from this spot. Black-breasted Buzzard or Spotted Harrier may be flying over the dunes. Other raptors in the area include Brown Falcon, Black Kite and Nankeen Kestrel.

About half-way through the tour, check the stands of mature spinifex for Rufous-crowned Emu-wren and Spinifexbird.

It is also worth stopping at the Camel Bore where in 1996 the Night Parrot was sighted. And while it will likely be a disappointment, you may still observe Zebra Finches and honeyeaters visiting the bore for a drink of water. Bourke's Parrots were recorded along Camel Bore Rd.

This route finally reaches the shores of Lake Bennet.

Hillside Drive Tour

This 50km route will allow you to visit the Freshwater Bore where a variety of birds gather for a drink including Zebra Finches, Diamond Doves, Singing Honeyeaters, Budgerigars, Australian Ringnecks, Major Mitchell's Cockatoos and Mulga Parrots. Grey Honeyeaters are occasionally recorded during this tour. Other birds along the route include Australian Bustard, Chestnut-rumped Thornbill, Yellow-rumped Thornbill, Pallid Cuckoo, Crimson Chat, Black-faced Woodswallow, Little Woodswallow and Australian Hobby.

Black-faced Woodswallow, race melanops

Alice Springs Area

1 Ilparpa Ponds
2 Ilparpa Swamp Wildlife Protected Area
3 Alice Springs Desert Park
4 John Flynn's Grave Historical Reserve
5 Olive Pink Botanic Garden
6 Alice Springs Telegraph Station
7 Kunoth Bore

Ilparpa Ponds

The site, formerly called Alice Springs Waste Stabilisation Ponds, is located 5km south of Alice Springs CBD. This isolated stretch of permanent water in the otherwise bone-dry country is a magnet for birds of all kinds. It is one of the best birding sites in Northern Territory. Some of the 20+ ponds om site are inaccessible to public, but the ponds labelled EP are, under strict conditions. A bird hide has been constructed on the embankment of EP10. About 5km of walking tracks run on the pond levees. An area of dense vegetation, mostly saltbushes and bluebushes, extends south of the EP ponds. Reeds and bulrushes border the levees of larger ponds. Dense weeds and grasses grow along the water edges, providing nesting habitat for many waterbirds.

Black Swans at Ilparpa Ponds

Access to this site is restricted. To get there, a special procedure must be followed, as described below. It may look overly complicated, but if you do it in advance, you'll have a fantastic time at this site, shared with a knowledgeable guide willing to devote his/her personal time to you.

- Online completion of a safety induction for the Ilparpa Ponds and singing of an indemnity form. Go to https://www.powerwater.com.au/about/community/bird-watching
- Print your induction certificate and carry it with you onsite.

- Contact Tourism Central Australia to arrange a guided tour with an official bird guide. This can be done by visiting the Alice Springs Visitor information Centre (on the corner Todd Mall and Parsons Street). Alternatively, contact Tourism Central Australia on 8952 5800, 1800 645 199 or via email at info@discoverca.com.au.
- You will receive a list of current bird guides to contact by mobile phone or email. You'll need to find a guide who will have time to accompany you at a mutually convenient time. These guides will have keys to the gate. Wilson Security must be called before and after the visit.
- Compulsory on site are: enclosed shoes, hi-viz vest, personal ID and the induction certificate.
- A minimum of two fully inducted visitors are required per visit unless arranged otherwise. The walk around the site takes at least 4hrs, bring a lot of water and some snacks.

To get there, from Stuart Hwy (A87) south of the Heavitree Gap roundabout turn west into Commonage Rd. Drive up to the gate of the recycling plant that blocks the road and turn left into a drive along the fence to get to the carpark. Birdwatchers enter through a small pedestrian gate to the right of main gate. The guide will have a key to this gate.

Over 230 bird species have been recorded around the Ilparpa Ponds. **Key species** are Orange Chat, Black Falcon, as well as waders and waterbirds including Freckled Duck, Australian Spotted Crake, Spotless Crake and Glossy Ibis. Other birds of interest include Black-tailed Native-hen, Little Grassbird, White-winged Fairy-wren, Splendid Fairy-wren, Crimson Chat, Major Mitchell's Cockatoo, Budgerigar, Red-backed Kingfisher, Little Pied Cormorant, Southern Whiteface, Rufous Songlark and Zebra Finch. Rarities include Grey Falcon, Yellow Chat, Bourke's Parrot, Grey Wagtail, Eastern Yellow Wagtail, Fork-tailed Swift, Australian Shelduck, Blue-billed Duck, Musk Duck, Black-necked Stork, White-fronted Honeyeater, Pied Honeyeater, Ground Cuckoo-shrike and many rare waders, listed below.

In total, 42 wader species are on this site's birdlist. Regularly found here are: Wood Sandpiper, Sharp-tailed Sandpiper, Common Sandpiper, Marsh Sandpiper, Long-toed Stint and Latham's Snipe. Some native waders are resident and breeding on the ponds, mostly Red-capped Plovers, Pied Stilts, Red-kneed Dotterels and Black-fronted Dotterels. Rarer natives, such Banded Lapwing, Inland Dotterel and Banded Stilt, visit the ponds from time to time. The absolute native rarity, Australian Painted-Snipe, has also been recorded. Rare migratory vagrant waders sighted here include Ruff, Pectoral Sandpiper, Broad-billed Sandpiper, Terek Sandpiper, Red-necked Phalarope, Oriental Plover and Little Curlew. So, nearly each visit here may bring something new, something exciting.

Male Musk Duck

We were lucky to get a fantastic bird guide named Dorothy. She, although still recovering from a painful surgery, walked us all around the ponds, pointing out rarities and recalling previous findings. Thanks to her, our time on the ponds was spent efficiently and enjoyably.

The ponds were crowded with Grey Teals, some still nesting on the banks (we found a couple of nests, full of eggs), others with numerous cute ducklings in tow. Swamp Harrier unsuccessfully attempted to snatch one from its mother. Several other raptors hanged around the ponds including Whistling Kite, Black Kite, Brown Falcon and Spotted Harrier.

Rarer ducks on the water included Chestnut Teal, Australasian Shoveler, Freckled Duck and Blue-billed Duck. As we progressed along the levees, we had to back away a few times from the nests of Red-capped Plovers on the levee, seeing the female displaying the 'injured bird' behaviour.

A pair of Black-fronted Dotterels were feeding their small, fluffy chick on the mudbanks. A single Ruff, a continuing bird, was still present at its usual spot, in the far corner of EP7. We also sighted Red-necked Avocets, Wood Sandpipers, Marsh Sandpipers, Common Sandpipers, Curlew Sandpipers and small groups of Bar-tailed and Black-tailed Godwits. We flushed a single Latham's Snipe near EP7.

A large group of Black-tailed Native-hens were skirting around the water edge. In the floating vegetation in front of the bird hide were a couple of Australian Spotted Crakes. On the water were Australasian Grebes and Hoary-headed Grebes. A couple of Whiskered Terns and a single Australian Gull-billed Tern were flying over the ponds. A large flock of Tree Martins was hawking insects over the ponds, among them were a couple of White-backed Swallows. A White-necked Heron was standing on the levee of one of the far ponds. A single Rock Dove walked past the heron. Little Grassbirds and Golden-headed Cisticolas were calling constantly from the wetland vegetation. The saltbushes-bluebushes yielded plenty of White-winged Fairy-wrens and Purple-backed Fairy-wrens. A small covey of Brown Quails was running in front of us at the vegetation edge. We also sighted Splendid Fairy-wren, Singing Honeyeater and Inland Thornbill.

Bush birds coming to drink from the ponds included Budgerigars, Cockatiels, Australian Ringnecks, Yellow-throated Miners, Spinifex Pigeons, White-plumed Honeyeaters and Zebra Finches.

In the trees around the carpark, we noticed a pair of Long-billed Corellas as well as several Red-tailed Black-Cockatoos and a large, noisy murder of Little Crows.

Ilparpa Swamp Wildlife Protected Area

This 1,800ha reserve borders the Alice Springs Waste Stabilisation Ponds (Ilparpa Ponds) from the south. To get there, from Stuart Hwy (A87) south of the Heavitree Gap roundabout turn west into Ilparpa Rd. The Wildlife Protected Area starts about 500m from the turnoff and extends north and west up to the spinifex-covered hills west of Ilparpa Ponds. Birding is conducted mostly off Ilparpa Rd.

The swamp only holds water in very wet years, otherwise it is dry, overgrown with wet grasses and low shrubs, mainly chenopods, and some higher bushes. When the reserve is flooded with shallow water, crakes arrive to breed there. These include Australian Spotted Crake, Spotless Crake, Baillon's Crake and Buff-banded Rail. Waders are also in attendance, including Wood Sandpiper, Marsh Sandpiper, Common Greenshank and Red-kneed Dotterel. They all disappear when water recedes, mostly relocating to the Ilparpa Ponds next door.

Buff-banded Rail

At dry times, grassland birds move in, such as Stubble Quail, Brown Quail, Little Button-quail, Red-chested Button-quail, Brown Songlark and Golden-headed Cisticola. In the low bluebushes and saltbushes, you may find White-winged Fairy-wren, Purple-backed Fairy-wren, Splendid Fairy-wren, Southern Whiteface and Zebra Finch. Patches of bushland may produce Inland Thornbill, Western Gerygone, Rufous Songlark, Western Bowerbird, Red-capped Robin, Hooded Robin, Spiny-cheeked Honeyeater, Yellow-throated Miner, Australian Ringneck, Budgerigar and Pallid Cuckoo. Check the mulga stands for the occasional presence of Black Honeyeater, Pied Honeyeater, White-fronted Honeyeater and Mulga Parrot.

Along the northern edge of the site, you'll find areas covered by spinifex. Spinifexbirds are relatively common here. Search also for Rufous Emu-wren and Dusky Grasswren.

Ilparpa Claypans

Ilparpa Claypans are located to the west of Ilparpa Swamp. They comprise several interconnected ephemeral wetlands in the Roe Creek's catchment. They tend to dry out last in the area and are well utilised by the local population for recreation.

To get there, continue on Ilparpa Rd for 9.5km from the turnoff from Stuart Hwy. An obscure entrance track is located behind a large board announcing 'No littering, No camping... (*No nothing*)'. GPS coordinates there are 23°45'20''S and 133°47'42''E. If you get to Temple Bar Caravan Park, you are too far, go back.

Over 120 bird species have been recorded around the Ilparpa Claypans. **Key species** are Hooded Robin, Australian Ringneck, Western Bowerbird, Red-kneed Dotterel, Crimson Chat and Black-breasted Buzzard. Other birds of interest include Red-capped Robin, Red-backed Kingfisher, Rufous Songlark, Mulga Parrot, Budgerigar, Grey-headed Honeyeater, Little Button-quail and Spotted Harrier. Rarities include Grey Falcon, Redthroat, Australasian Shoveler, Banded Lapwing and Painted Finch.

During our visit in April 2022, Black-fronted Dotterels and Red-kneed Dotterels were breeding, with small chicks running behind them. We flushed Latham's Snipe from the short grass. There were also small numbers of Black-tailed Godwits, Common Greenshanks and Red-necked Avocets. Large flocks of Budgerigars, Cockatiels and Diamond Doves were coming to drink. A couple of Pink-eared Ducks and a few Grey Teals and Black Swans were paddling lazily in the shallow water. A single juvenile Nankeen Night-Heron was hunting at the water edge. Swamp Harrier was flying over the claypans.

A scan of surrounding bushland yielded Major Mitchell's Cockatoo, White-winged Triller, Pied Butcherbird, Grey Shrike-thrush, Black-faced Woodswallow, Weebill and Horsfield's Bronze-cuckoo.

Alice Springs Desert Park

This important Northern Territory wildlife park is undoubtedly the best bird park in the country. This unique educational facility maintains a chain of fantastic walk-through aviaries, housing over 60 bird species native to the deserts of Central Australia. Among some of the more exciting species on display are Rufus-crowned Emu-wren, Dusky Grasswren, Eyrean Grasswren, Inland Dotterel, Cinnamon Quail-thrush, Orange Chat, Redthroat, Princess Parrot, Bourke's Parrot and Chiming Wedgebill. The aviaries are scattered along a 2km trail running through three different habitats: Desert Rivers, Sand Country and Woodlands, matching each habitat bird selection.

There is also a Nocturnal House, Natural Theatre with a flying bird show, and many benches along the trail for a rest. The Visitor Center at the entrance has a kiosk and toilets. Everything is surrounded by 1,600ha of native bush and grassland and framed by the hills of McDonnell Ranges. There are plenty of wild birds in this peaceful natural haven, and it is sometimes confusing to see whether a bird is free-flying or captive, particularly in the case of honeyeaters.

To get there, from Stuart Hwy (A87) in Alice, turn west into Larapinta Dr (B6) and drive 7km, then turn left into Desert Park Entrance drive. Opening hours are 7:30am to 6pm, last entry is 4:30pm. You'll need 3-4 hours to explore the site. For further information, map and bookings see https://alicespringsdesertpark.com.au/.

Over 120 bird species have been recorded in the Alice Springs Desert Park (free-flying). **Key species** are Grey Honeyeater, Western Bowerbird, Redthroat, Crested Bellbird, Hooded Robin, White-backed Swallow and Little Eagle. Other birds of interest include Mulga Parrot, Grey-crowned Babbler, White-browed Babbler, Splendid Fairy-wren, Red-backed Kingfisher, Red-capped Robin, Red-browed Pardalote, Spinifex Pigeon, Western Gerygone and Black-shouldered Kite. Rarities include Scarlet-chested Parrot, Princess Parrot, Major Mitchell's Cockatoo, Bush Stone-curlew, Pied Honeyeater, Black Honeyeater, Golden-backed Honeyeater, Slaty-backed Thornbill, Rainbow Lorikeet and Black Falcon.

A very productive birding area is the mulga scrub around the carparks and along the entrance drive. In recent years (early 2020') Grey Honeyeaters were recorded here in winter and early spring, coinciding with grevillea and mulga flowering times.

When we arrived there in April 2022, we were welcomed in the carpark by a Western Bowerbird that was calling from the top of a tall tree, imitating a butcherbird's song. A flock of White-browed Babblers and a couple of Little Button-quails were on the ground. Crested Bellbird was picking up seeds from the soil. White-backed Swallows were flying over the Park's Visitor Centre. Grey Shrike-thrushes were calling loudly from the low shrubbery. We also spotted Mulga Parrot, Australian Ringneck, Red-backed Kingfisher and Red-capped Robin. And that was all before we even entered the Park!

Bush Stone-curlew

A family of Purple-backed Fairy-wrens sat in a bush near the Nocturnal House and a pair of Bush Stone-curlews were nodding off in the morning heat near the Visitor Centre. Flowering yellow grevilleas attracted plenty of honeyeaters including White-plumed Honeyeaters, Spiny-cheeked Honeyeaters, Singing Honeyeaters and a single Pied Honeyeater. Mulga Parrots were inspecting hollows, and a pair of Tawny Frogmouths were quietly roosting near the Visitor Centre.

Along the circular walk between the aviaries, we came across Hooded Robin, Jacky Winter, Splendid Fairy-wren (plenty), Rufous Whistler, Horsfield's Bronze-cuckoo, Western Gerygone, Spinifex Pigeon, Grey-crowned Babbler, Whistling Kite and Wedge-tailed Eagle.

Landscape of the circular walk in the Desert Park

John Flynn's Grave Historical Reserve

This tiny, 3.4ha reserve is the resting place of Rev. John Flynn, the founder of the Royal Flying Doctors and a highly revered, meritorious person of the Outback Region. The Reserve is located at 623 Larapinta Dr, 7km west of Alice Springs CBD, at the base of Mt Giller of the MacDonnell Ranges just past the entrance to the Alice Springs Desert Park. The grave is a monument marked with a huge boulder. This is the second stone; the first was brought from Devils Marbles but in 1999 had to be returned after local Indigenous protests (as it could bring bad luck from the Devil's place). The large, round stone on the John Flynn's grave weighs 8 tonnes and is well visible from the road.

The facilities include a carpark, information shelter with benches and a short walking track to the grave site. The second walking option here is a 2.5km track to the Desert Park. Another track, running to the Mr Giller summit, starts in the carpark and leads to an important Dusky Grasswren habitat. However, Mt Giller was registered as an Aboriginal sacred site in 2021 and access to the track was closed to the public, what a pity.

Over 100 bird species have been recorded in the John Flynn's Grave Historical Reserve. **Key species** are Dusky Grasswren, Spinifex Pigeon, Painted Finch, Slaty-backed Thornbill and Peregrine Falcon. Other birds of interest include Spinifexbird, Little Woodswallow, Hooded Robin, White-backed Swallow, Grey-headed Honeyeater and Splendid Fairy-wren. Rarities include Bourke's Parrot, Rufous Emu-wren and Grey Honeyeater.

Grey Honeyeaters were recorded several times in the bush near the grave. Red-browed Pardalotes are common, you'll hear their calls. Groups of White-browed Babblers are often seen on the ground. In the mulga near the grave, you may get Chestnut-rumped Thornbill, Inland Thornbill, Yellow-rumped Thornbill, Rufous Whistler, Budgerigar, Mulga Parrot, Yellow-throated Miner and Spiny-cheeked Honeyeater. Tawny Frogmouths often roost in trees near the carpark.

White-browed Babbler

The track to Desert Park may produce Grey Honeyeater (rare), Western Bowerbird, Red-backed Kingfisher, Hooded Robin, Western Gerygone, Splendid Fairy-wren, Weebill, Black-eared Cuckoo, Grey-crowned Babbler and Australian Owlet-nightjar.

Olive Pink Botanic Garden

This small, 16ha native botanic garden is a short drive from the Alice Springs CBD on the easter banks of the nearly always dry Todd River at 27 Tuncks Rd.

The regatta boat races, the biggest Alice Springs attraction, take place in the dry sand in the bed of Todd River every October. Occasionally, Todd River can be full of water; then the boat races have to be postponed. Only in Australia...

The Garden was created in the 1950' by a fascinating local character, Miss Olive Pink. She and her gardener planted masses of native trees and shrubs, turning a feral goat-infested wasteland into a bird paradise. The Garden offers a network of short walks through the native vegetation and a longer path to the Annie Meyers Hill, where at dusk you may encounter black-footed rock-wallabies.

With time, the garden has become one of the best attractions of Alice Springs. It is open from 8am to 6pm. Sit and relax in the site's cosy café and observe plenty of local birds.

Over 110 bird species have been recorded in the Olive Pink Botanic Garden. **Key species** are Western Bowerbird, Australian Ringneck, Major Mitchell's Cockatoo, Red-browed Pardalote and Red-capped Robin. Other birds of interest include Grey-crowned Babbler, Red-backed Kingfisher, Grey-headed Honeyeater, Yellow-throated Miner, Splendid Fairy-wren, Inland Thornbill, Western Gerygone, Channel-billed Cuckoo and Rainbow Bee-eater. Rarities include Grey Honeyeater, Bourke's Parrot, Jacky Winter, Ground Cuckoo-shrike, Rainbow Lorikeet, Rosy-faced Lovebird, Rock Dove, Spotted Dove, Spotted Nightjar and Peregrine Falcon.

The Garden is famous for its resident Western Bowerbirds. The birds are often seen around the café. A well-known bower is located under a dense small bush, 20m from the carpark, near a large information board about the bowerbirds which was overgrown by foliage. GPS coordinates for the bower are 23°42'23''S and 133°52'19''E. We visited the garden just after the covid pandemic and found a discarded blue facemask adorning the bower. See photo.

Western Bowerbird's bower in the Olive Pink Botanic Garden

Another sought-after species in the garden is Grey Honeyeater. It used to be the regular in the area, particularly in the mulga stands in spring, but since 2015, sightings of this rare bird have become sporadic.

A small, growing population of escapee Rainbow Lorikeets established themselves in Alice Springs; they are regularly visiting the Garden.

Café grounds are productive for Rainbow Bee-eater, Western Gerygone, White-plumed Honeyeater, Spiny-cheeked Honeyeater, Mistletoebird, Australian Ringneck, Budgerigar, Rufous Whistler and Zebra Finch. A family of Grey-crowned Babblers is usually moving between the tables. Noisy corvids are around; take time to differentiate between Little Crow, Torresian Crow and Australian Raven.

Check a small wetland near the café – Australian Reed-Warbler can be found there. Occasionally, White-necked Heron or Black-tailed Native-hen are recorded.

Walking through the garden, especially when gum trees are flowering, can be very rewarding. Honeyeater selection includes Singing Honeyeater, Grey-headed Honeyeater, White-plumed Honeyeater and an occasional White-fronted Honeyeater, Black Honeyeater or Pied Honeyeater. In the shrubs along your walk, search for Red-capped Robin, Zebra Finch, Inland Thornbill, Chestnut-rumped Thornbill, Grey Shrike-thrush, Splendid Fairy-wren, Purple-backed Fairy-wren, Black-eared Cuckoo and Weebill. Listen to the calls of Red-browed Pardalote, Western Gerygone and Grey Butcherbird.

When walking to the top of Annie Meyers Hill, check the skies for raptors. You may be lucky to observe Black Falcon, Peregrine Falcon, Black-breasted Buzzard, Little Eagle and Wedge-tailed Eagle. There is also a chance to sight a flying White-backed Swallow or Little Woodswallow. Fairy Martins are always there.

Alice Springs Telegraph Station

This 450ha Historical Reserve features the buildings of old Telegraph Station which was built in 1872 along the Overland Telegraph Line to relay messages between Adelaide and Darwin. It also marks the original site of the first European settlement in Alice Springs.

Vegetation in the Reserve consists mostly of native grassland with scattered stands of bushes. Dry creeks are lined with huge river red gums. Large gums also provide shade around the picnic areas and carparks.

To get there, 4km north of Alice Springs turn east into Herbert Heritage Dr. The Reserve is open every day from 8am to 9pm. A café is located in the historical precinct. Other facilities include several picnic areas, shaded picnic tables and public toilets. There is also a network of short walking trails offering scenic views. Camping is not permitted. Further information and a map can be found in the Alice Springs Telegraph Station fact sheet, downloadable here: https://nt.gov.au/__data/assets/pdf_file/0008/200033/alice-springs-telegraph-station-fact-sheet-and-map.pdf.

Over 120 bird species have been recorded in the Alice Springs Telegraph Station Historical Reserve. **Key species** are Red-browed Pardalote, Redthroat, Western Bowerbird, Spinifexbird and White-backed Swallow. Other birds of interest include Australian Ringneck, Cockatiel, Splendid Fairy-wren, Rainbow Bee-eater, Hooded Robin, Grey-headed Honeyeater, Spiny-cheeked Honeyeater, Little Crow, Grey Butcherbird, Common Bronzewing and Zebra Finch. Rarities include Grey Falcon, Little Eagle, Grey Honeyeater, Black Honeyeater, Slaty-backed Thornbill, Banded Whiteface, Ground Cuckoo-shrike and Pheasant Coucal.

Red-browed Pardalote is the main reason for visiting this site. Search for them on the Riverside Walk where the birds could be picking insects from the foliage. Red-browed Pardalotes are also often found in the gums of the historic precinct and near the main carpark. Listen to their characteristic calls when trying to locate them. Remember, Striated Pardalotes also reside in the area.

The Riverside Walk runs along Todd River. Besides Red-browed Pardalotes, look for White-backed Swallows here. Occasionally, Welcome Swallows can be found in the area. After the rains, there is a chance to see Painted Finches coming to drink from the puddles in the riverbed, and an occasional White-necked Heron or White-faced Heron standing near the water. Inspect the gum trees along the riverbed for White-winged Triller, Western Gerygone, Singing Honeyeater, Yellow-throated Miner, Rufous Whistler, Sacred Kingfisher, Weebill and Brown Goshawk. Whistling Kites and Black Kites are nesting along the river.

Birding around the historical precinct can be quite productive. Rainbow Bee-eaters regularly nest in hollows dug in the sand between the buildings. Families of Grey-crowned Babblers often roam on the café grounds. Even White-browed Babblers sometimes appear. Be on the lookout for a long-term resident pair of Long-billed Corellas. Other birds in this area include Spotted Dove, Weebill, Western Bowerbird, Black-faced Woodswallow, Australian Ringneck, Common Bronzewing and Australian Magpie. In the breeding season, you may notice a pair of crows laboriously feeding a giant Channel-billed Cuckoo chick.

The Bradshaw Walk is good for the ground-foraging species such as Little Button-quail, Rufous Songlark, Redthroat, Yellow-rumped Thornbill, Chestnut-rumped Thornbill, Diamond Dove, Peaceful Dove and Red-capped Robin. Reported occasionally are Ground Cuckoo-shrike and Spinifex Pigeon.

We found Red-browed Pardalotes in this gum tree near the carpark

The famous Larapinta Trail starts in this Reserve. If you have time, the first few kilometres are worth the birdwatcher's time. Ground Cuckoo-shrikes can occasionally be sighted here. Look also for Southern Whiteface, Banded Whiteface (rare), Inland Thornbill, Slaty-backed Thornbill, Hooded Robin, Crested Bellbird and Splendid Fairy-wren.

Altogether, 16 raptor species have been recorded in the Reserve, including Wedge-tailed Eagle, Black-shouldered Kite, Collared Sparrowhawk, Swamp Harrier, Australian Hobby and Peregrine Falcon. Southern Boobook is common, and you may also encounter Tawny Frogmouth and Barn Owl.

Kunoth Bore

This a popular birding site, good for searching for Grey Honeyeaters. It is located approximately 50km northwest of Alice Springs. To get there, first drive 20km on Stuart Hwy (A87) in the northerly direction. Next, turn west into Tanami Rd (5) to cover the remaining 30km. The site is Aboriginal land, leased to the Hamilton Downs Station. There are two birding places to check out there: a large farm dam called Kunoth Bore, close to Tanami Rd, and a mulga scrub along Hamilton Downs Youth Camp Track.

Over 150 bird species have been recorded around the Kunoth Bore site. **Key species** are Grey Honeyeater, Bourke's Parrot, Slaty-backed Thornbill, Major Mitchell's Cockatoo, Black Honeyeater, Pied Honeyeater, Hooded Robin, Black-eared Cuckoo and Black-breasted Buzzard. Other birds of interest include Budgerigar, Cockatiel, Diamond Dove, Zebra Finch, Banded Lapwing, Mulga Parrot, Red-backed Kingfisher, Western Bowerbird, Red-capped Robin, Splendid Fairy-wren, White-browed Babbler, White-backed Swallow, Brown Goshawk and Spotted Harrier. Rarities include Grey Falcon, Oriental Plover, Flock Bronzewing, White-fronted Honeyeater, Ground Cuckoo-shrike, Banded Whiteface, Stubble Quail, Red-chested Button-quail and Common Starling.

Kunoth Bore Dam

Getting to the dam is quite tricky. Drive 29km along West Tanami Rd and stop near the farm gate at the GPS coordinates of 23°30'44''S and 133°35'05''E. There is a yellow flood sign in this spot. Turn left into an overgrown vehicular track and drive through the gate. Drive past an old windmill, go through the second gate and drive to the dam wall (about 500m from the main road). Find a shady vantage point on the levee and enjoy the birds. A picnic basket is recommended as you are sure to spend a few hours there.

We visited the dam twice in March 2022 and it was pure magic for us. A period of heavy downpours happened a few weeks earlier, and everything around was lush and green. Thousands of birds were landing at the dam verges for a drink. Thick streams of Budgerigars, Cockatiels, Diamond Doves, Crested Pigeons and Zebra Finches were arriving nearly continuously. Among them, we found three Bourke's Parrots. There were also Major Mitchell's Cockatoos, Mulga Parrots and Australian Ringnecks. Small flocks of honeyeaters were stopping in the dense dead finish bushes, checking out the safety status before plunging into the water. That was a wise behaviour as literally dozens of raptors were roosting on bushtops and treetops around the dam, too lazy in the morning heat to even harass the birds. These were Brown Falcons, Whistling Kites, Black Kites, Australian Hobbies, Brown Goshawks and Black-shouldered Kites. However, when a pair of Black-breasted Buzzards flew over the dam, it startled all the small birds in the air. A Brown Goshawk caught an Australian Ringneck just in front of us, but the injured bird managed to flee and hide in a dead finish bush at the dam verge. The raptor tried to extract its would-be-pray for an hour but was unsuccessful.

Bourke's Parrot visiting Kunoth Bore in the company of Crested Pigeons

In the surrounding grassland and bushes, we spotted Brown Songlark, Little Button-quail, Singing Honeyeater, Black-faced Woodswallow, White-browed Babbler, Tree Martin, Jacky Winter and Hooded Robin. Several White-backed Swallows were flying over the water.

Hamilton Downs Youth Camp Track

Mulga at Hamilton Downs Youth Camp Track

To get there, take the first turnoff to the left from Tanami Rd after the previous site, about 1km past the Kunoth Bore Dam. Beware, the track is deep sand, drivable only for the experienced 4-wheel drivers. Search for Grey Honeyeater in the mulga scrub along the first 5km from the turnoff. The mulga may also produce Slaty-backed Thornbills and Bourke's Parrots. The latter sometimes feed along the road in substantial numbers, up to 20 birds. Other birds recorded along this track include Redthroat (rare), Western Gerygone, Yellow-rumped Thornbill, Inland Thornbill, Red-capped Robin, Masked Woodswallow, Spiny-cheeked Honeyeater, Splendid Fairy-wren, White-winged Fairy-wren and Crested Bellbird.

Look for the patches of eremophilas, they usually bloom in winter (Jun-Aug). In this time period, you'll have a chance to sight nomadic honeyeaters such as White-fronted Honeyeater, Black Honeyeater and Pied Honeyeater.

MacDonnell Ranges

1 [Yeperenye Nature Park]
2 [Corroboree Rock Conservation Reserve]
3 [Trephina Gorge Nature Park]
4 [N'Dhala Gorge Nature Park]
5 [Arltunga Historical Reserve]
6 [Santa Teresa Road]
7 [West MacDonnell Ranges National Park]
8 [Finke Gorge National Park]
9 [Owen Springs Reserve]

Yeperenye Nature Park

This small park, also known as Emily and Jessie Gaps, is located along Ross Hwy (8, sealed) at the Heavitree Range just 10km east of Alice Springs. The waterholes at the gaps are popular picnicking destinations. The gaps are usually dry, but any significant rain will fill the creek and river, with the flow filling the gaps and the waterholes. A 7km-long walking and cycling Yeperenye Trail was constructed in 2021 to join both Gaps. The trail runs along the foothills of the Range and provides good access to birding. Additionally, short tracks lead to both Emily and Jessie Gaps off Ross Hwy.

Facilities in the park include fire pits, toilets, picnic tables and information boards. No camping is allowed. Further information can be found in the Yeperenye Nature Park fact sheet, downloadable here: https://nt.gov.au/__data/assets/pdf_file/0012/200055/yeperenye-emily-jessie-gaps-nature-park.pdf.

Over 100 bird species have been recorded in the Yeperenye Nature Park. **Key species** are Dusky Grasswren, Redthroat, Painted Finch, Little Woodswallow, Major Mitchell's Cockatoo, Hooded Robin and Peregrine Falcon. Other birds of interest include Budgerigar, Australian Ringneck, White-backed Swallow, Red-capped Robin, Western Bowerbird, Red-browed Pardalote, Grey-headed Honeyeater, White-browed Babbler, Little Button-quail and Wedge-tailed Eagle. Rarities include Grey Honeyeater, Princess Parrot, Grey Falcon, Golden-backed Honeyeater, White-fronted Honeyeater, Pied Honeyeater and Black Honeyeater.

Emily Gap

The scenic Emily Gap comes first on your route along Ross Hwy. The area around the carpark is home to resident Hooded Robins and Western Bowerbirds. Look also for Black-shouldered Kite, Major Mitchell's Cockatoo, Channel-billed Cuckoo, White-plumed Honeyeater, Varied Sittella and Sacred Kingfisher. At night, Southern Boobook and Australian Owlet-nightjar can be heard.

Along the first 1.5km of the Yeperenye Trail, look for Dusky Grasswrens on the rocks and for a flying Peregrine Falcon or Little Woodswallows.

Jessie Gap

Jessie Gap, the waterhole by Ross Highway

The waterhole by the road can be truly productive if there is some water in it. We took out our folding chairs, sat under a gum tree and the birds soon came. We spotted several Painted Finches among masses of Zebra Finches, Diamond Doves, Budgerigars and Cockatiels arriving for a drink of water. A conveniently horizontal large branch served as a launching pad for several small species such as Grey-headed Honeyeater, White-plumed Honeyeater, Brown Honeyeater and Yellow-throated Miner. The air was filled with calls of Red-browed Pardalotes. A flock of Red-tailed Black-Cockatoos landed in the tree above us, annoying a pair of Major Mitchell's Cockatoos quietly dosing in the foliage.

After walking to the picnic area in the Gap, we found a bower of Western Bowerbird near a picnic table. It was tastefully decorated with green fruit and green glass shards. Peregrine Falcon was flying along the cliffs.

If you walk on the Yeperenye Trail, check the grassy areas for Stubble Quail, Splendid Fairy-wren, Purple-backed Fairy-wren, Redthroat and Hooded Robin. Look also for Dusky Grasswren. Other birds reported from the trail include Crested Bellbird, Little Crow, Chestnut-rumped Thornbill, Grey-headed Honeyeater, Little Woodswallow, Pied Butcherbird and Grey Fantail.

Corroboree Rock CR

Corroboree Rock in the foreground

This important Aboriginal site is located 42km east of Alice Springs, off Ross Hwy (8) in the East McDonnell Ranges. The rock is a fascinating, huge, dark-grey slab of dolomite protruding from the surrounding bushland. It is an easy rest stop on your way to other East McDonnell birding sites such as Trephina Gorge. Facilities include a carpark, toilets, picnic tables and a short walk at the base of the rock. No camping is allowed in the reserve.

About 80 bird species have been recorded around the Corroboree Rock. **Key species** are Hooded Robin, Grey-headed Honeyeater, Little Woodswallow, Mulga Parot and White-backed Swallow. Other birds of interest include Red-browed Pardalote, Budgerigar, Cockatiel, Crested Bellbird, Splendid Fairy-wren, Western Bowerbird, Black-faced Woodswallow and Redthroat. Rarities include Grey Falcon, Grey Honeyeater and Rufous-crowned Emu-wren.

During our visit, Hooded Robins were visible around the carpark. Purple-back Fairy-wrens were numerous in grassy areas. A pair of Grey Shrike-thrushes were building a nest. On the walk to the rock, we also came across Rainbow Bee-eater, Chiming Wedgebill, Spinifexbird, Western Gerygone, Little Button-quail and Australian Owlet-nightjar.

Trephina Gorge Nature Park

This small, 1,800ha park is located in the East MacDonnell Ranges, 85km east of Alice Springs. There are two gorges in the park: Trephina Gorge and John Hayes Rockhole. The former is an incredible place with stunning sheer cliff faces, and the latter a skinny rocky gorge with steep walls and several semi-permanent waterfalls. The waterfalls attract a variety of birds that come there for a drink and a bath. The park is also home to the largest ghost gums in Australia.

To get there, take Ross Hwy (8) from Alice Springs. Drive nearly 80km on a sealed road to the park entrance. From there, you'll have another 9km (with 4km sealed) to the carpark at the gorge. The park offers four camping grounds with barbecues, toilets, drinking water and shaded picnic areas. John Hayes Rockhole campground is a 4WD access only, the other three are easily reached from the gorge access road. There are several walking trails, mostly easy hikes of 1-4km long. Further information and maps can be found in the Fact Sheet downloadable here: https://nt.gov.au/__data/assets/pdf_file/0010/200053/Trephina-gorge-fact-sheet.pdf.

Painted Finch

Over 120 bird species have been recorded in the Trephina Gorge Nature Park. **Key species** are Painted Finch, Little Woodswallow, Dusky Grasswren, Spinifexbird, Spinifex Pigeon and Western Bowerbird. Other birds of interest include Grey-headed Honeyeater, Grey-fronted Honeyeater, Budgerigar, Mulga Parrot, Crimson Chat, Hooded Robin, Jacky Winter and White-browed Babbler. Rarities include White-fronted Honeyeater, Golden-backed Honeyeater, White-backed Swallow, Major Mitchell's Cockatoo, Spotted Dove, Little Eagle and Letter-winged Kite.

It is worth making a few stops on the 9km access road to the carpark to encounter a diversity of bush birds such as Western Gerygone, Mulga Parrot, Rufous Songlark, Cockatiel, Budgerigar, Hooded Robin, Diamond Dove, Peaceful Dove, Crimson Chat, Common Bronzewing, Spinifexbird and the ubiquitous Zebra Finches. Be careful if driving in the evening; Spotted Nightjars often roost in the middle of the road. Look for their reddish-orange eyes shining in the headlights.

Around the carpark, you may get Purple-backed Fairy-wren, Hooded Robin, Crested Bellbird and Australian Owlet-nightjar.

Bluff Campground

This is the place to look for Hooded Robin, Weebill, Black-faced Woodswallow and the honeyeaters. Little Eagles are regularly seen here. The noisy calls of Grey Butcherbirds are often heard in the area. Other birds include Horsfield's Bronze-cuckoo, Black-eared Cuckoo, Grey-crowned Babbler, Splendid Fairy-wren and Spotted Harrier.

Panorama Campground

This campground is suitable for caravans and larger vehicles. Large flocks of Budgerigars often come to roost at night. Western Bowerbirds are resident. Other bird species here include Diamond Dove, Yellow-throated Miner, Little Woodswallow and Red-backed Kingfisher.

Gorge Campground

The campground and its picnic area can be very productive. Check the flowering gums with plenty of mistletoes for the honeyeaters such as Spiny-cheeked Honeyeater, Grey-headed Honeyeater, White-plumed Honeyeater and Singing Honeyeater. Usually, plenty of Mistletoebirds hang around. Other finds may include Western Bowerbird, Red-backed Kingfisher, Red-browed Pardalote, Splendid Fairy-wren and Australian Ringneck. Hooded Robins are resident in the area.

The trailhead for Trephina Gorge starts at the campground. Look for Painted Finches in the gully at the creek crossing. Other birds along the walk include Red-browed Pardalote, Little Woodswallow, Grey-headed Honeyeater, Grey Shrike-thrush and

Spinifexbird. Spinifex Pigeons are often seen atop the gorge walk. Look also for Dusky Grasswrens there. Check the rock ledges for Peregrine Falcons.

Take a short walk from the campground to a waterhole to look for Painted Finches taking a bath there. A pair of Little Eagles are the regulars around the waterhole. Red-browed Pardalotes call intensely from the gum trees there.

Rockhole Campground

To get there, you'll need a high clearance 4WD vehicle. From the Trephina Gorge access road turn into John Hayes Rockhole Tk (signposted) and drive 4km to the campground with a small waterhole nearby. While on that road, look for Dusky Grasswren, Ground Cuckoo-shrike, Crested Bellbird, Western Gerygone, Inland Thornbill, Slaty-backed Thornbill and Black-shouldered Kite. The sought-after Slaty-backed Thornbills are generally encountered near the camping area. You can also find Western Bowerbird and Grey Butcherbird there.

A 3.5km return Chain of the Ponds Walk is worth a try. Dusky Grasswren may be found there. You'll also have a chance to spot Redthroat, Splendid Fairy-wren, Purple-backed Fairy-wren, Inland Thornbill, Painted Finch, Spinifex Pigeon, Grey Fantail, Hooded Robin and Spiny-cheeked Honeyeater.

N'Dhala Gorge Nature Park

This 500ha park is located less than 100km east of Alice Springs via Ross Hwy (8). The park is arid, red and spectacular, so the visit is worth the effort. The landscape includes areas of low sand dunes, rocky outcrops and the stunning gorge known for its 6,000 Aboriginal rock carvings.

To get there, drive 90km on sealed Ross Hwy towards the Ross River Homestead. The turnoff to the gorge is 500m before the Homestead. You'll then face 11km of a terrible 4WD track to reach the park. The track crosses the dry bed of Ross River several times, with some very steep banks. The river crossings become immediately impassable after the rains. Facilities in the park include a small campground with toilets, picnic tables and fire rings. A 2km return, marked walking tracks leads to the gorge. The track is often overgrown, and you'll be walking over stones and boulders. Besides the camping site, accommodation can be found in the Ross River Resort at the Homestead. A fact sheet with the map can be downloadable here: https://nt.gov.au/__data/assets/pdf_file/0009/200043/ndhala-gorge-factsheet-map.pdf.

About 80 bird species have been recorded in the N'Dhala Gorge Nature Park. **Key species** are Western Bowerbird, Hooded Robin and Painted Finch. Other birds of interest include Red-browed Pardalote, Grey-headed Honeyeater, White-backed Swallow, Little Woodswallow, Little Crow, Purple-backed Fairy-wren, Splendid Fairy-wren, Budgerigar, Diamond Dove, Zebra Finch, Spinifex Pigeon and Grey-crowned Babbler. Rarities include Redthroat, Slaty-backed Thornbill and Bush Stone-curlew.

The star attraction of the park is Painted Finch. Look for them along the gorge walk; they would be coming for a drink to the waterhole. There will also be Budgerigars, Zebra Finches, Diamond Doves and a variety of honeyeaters such as Grey-headed Honeyeater, Singing Honeyeater, White-plumed Honeyeater and Brown Honeyeater. Rarer species occasionally recorded there include Grey-fronted Honeyeater, White-fronted Honeyeater, Golden-backed Honeyeater and Black Honeyeater.

Singing Honeyeater

On the gorge walk, you may also encounter Red-tailed Black-Cockatoo, Australian Ringneck, Mulga Parrot, Pallid Cuckoo, Common Bronzewing, Rufous Songlark, Rufous Whistler, White-winged Fairy-wren, Splendid Fairy-wren, Little Woodswallow, Black-fronted Dotterel and White-necked Heron.

A pair of Peregrine Falcons are resident in the gorge and are often seen of the cliff ledges. Other raptors include Brown Falcon, Brown Goshawk, Australian Hobby, Collared Sparrowhawk and Wedge-tailed Eagle.

Ross River Resort

This is a good place to stay while visiting the N'Dhala Gorge Nature Park. It offers a variety of accommodation, from powered and unpowered camping sites to cabins and bunkhouses. Ther is fuel, general store, swimming pool and bar. Sunset camel tours and hot air ballooning can be organised there.

Plenty of birdlife can be seen on the resort grounds. A family of Bush Stone-curlews, rare in the region, is resident here. The most visible are pigeons and parrots, including Spinifex Pigeon, Diamond Dove, Galah, Red-tailed Black-Cockatoo and Australian Ringneck. Common birds also include Western Bowerbird, Grey-crowned Babbler, White-browed Babbler, Pied Butcherbird, Little Crow and Torresian Crow. You may also come across Crested Bellbird, Hooded Robin, Striated Pardalote, Purple-backed Fairy-wren, Yellow-rumped Thornbill, Black-faced Woodswallow, Southern Boobook and Australian Hobby. At night, Southern Boobook may be calling.

Southern Boobook

Arltunga Historical Reserve

The reserve can be reached via Ross Hwy (8) 110km east of Alice Springs. The first 77km on the Ross Hwy is sealed, then the remaining 33km is a gravel track. Arltunga was officially the first town of Central Australia. It was built in 1887during the gold rush and once supported 300 people who all came there on foot from the Oodnadatta railhead, a 600km walk. You can learn about the colourful history of this place in the Visitor Centre. The reserve is today a well-known gold fossicking site. Picnic facilities with barbecues, shaded picnic tables and toilets are located at the Visitor Centre and Police Station Precinct. Camping is not permitted; to camp go to the Trephina Gorge nearby. Self-guided walks are provided through the reserve. Further information and maps can be found in the Fact Sheet downloadable here: https://nt.gov.au/__data/assets/pdf_file/0006/199986/arltunga-historical-reserve-fact-sheet-and-map.pdf.

About 80 bird species have been recorded in the Arltunga Historical Reserve. **Key species** are Dusky Grasswren, Spinifex Pigeon, Redthroat, Western Bowerbird, Hooded Robin and Painted Finch. Other birds of interest include Budgerigar, Mulga Parrot, Grey-headed Honeyeater, Crested Bellbird, Western Gerygone, Splendid Fairy-wren and Southern Boobook. Ground Cuckoo-shrike is the rarity.

Birding is usually conducted on the 10km-long network of tracks through the site. Painted Finches can be observed feeding in small flocks on the grounds of the Police Station Precinct. White-backed Swallows may be flying overhead. Expect to find Little Button-quail, Purple-backed Fairy-wren, Inland Thornbill, Yellow-rumped Thornbill, Chestnut-rumped Thornbill, Weebill, Grey-crowned Babbler, Rufous Whistler, Varied Sittella, Australasian Pipit, Australian Hobby and Brown Falcon.

Santa Teresa Road

This unsealed, often very corrugated road starts at the roundabout near the Alice Springs Airport and runs southeast for 70km to the Santa Teresa township. Only the first 13km are sealed but conventional vehicles can by driven to Santa Teresa. Past the township, you'll get to the Old Andado Tk, part of Binn's Tk that runs through the Simpson Desert. Take a 4WD there.

Along the first 100km section of the road, there are several good areas of spinifex-cladded, low limestone hills that have become popular among the birdwatchers as a reasonably accessible location from Alice Springs to find Dusky Grasswren and Rufous-crowned Emu-wren as well as other arid country bird species. Rufous-crowned Emu-wrens prefer the habitat of dense, long, mature unburnt spinifex that develops into large clumps. Such habitat usually occurs along narrow drainage lines at the base of slopes. Listen to their high-pitch, insect-like calls. Dusky Grasswrens prefer rocky escarpment and scree country, covered with large, but lower clumps of mature spinifex. These birds seldom fly, just bounce over the boulders with their tails cocked. The main foe of this species is burning of their habitat, which destroys their homes and kills the birds. Unfortunately, prescribed burning is religiously executed in Australia, ignoring the survival needs of species such as grasswrens.

About 100 bird species have been recorded along Santa Teresa Road. **Key species** are Rufous-crowned Emu-wren, Dusky Grasswren, Spinifexbird, Bourke's Parrot, Cinnamon Quail-thrush, Ground Cuckoo-shrike and Pied Honeyeater. Other birds of interest include Painted Finch, Grey-fronted Honeyeater, Red-backed Kingfisher, Crested Bellbird, Hooded Robin, White-winged Fairy-wren, Chiming Wedgebill and Western Bowerbird. Rarities include Slaty-backed Thornbill, Inland Dotterel, Grey Falcon, Black Falcon and Peregrine Falcon.

Tyre in the Pole

This is the most productive site for both Rufous-crowned Emu-wren and Dusky Grasswren. It is located 31.5km from the airport roundabout. GPS coordinates are 24°00'53''S and 134°04'43''E. The prominent landmark in this monotonous landscape is a power pole with a car tyre wedged into it, very easily recognizable (see photo).

Santa Teresa Road – tyre in the pole landmark

Spinifex grows on both sides of the road up to the ridge. It is however severely burnt in some spots so look for patches of undisturbed habitat. Check the old growth on both sides of the road for Rufous-crowned Emu-wren and Spinifexbird, while the rocky gullies and hills for Dusky Grasswren. We saw a single Dusky Grasswren on the hill on the right side of the road (when facing Santa Teresa). Spinifexbird was just on the road verge on the top of a very dense clump of spinifex. We had no luck with Emu-wrens there. Cinnamon Quail-thrush was moving among the sparse vegetation of spinifex and small shrubs on a rocky scree. Other birds at this site were Singing Honeyeater, Zebra Finch, Black-faced Woodswallow, Grey-headed Honeyeater, Nankeen Kestrel and Black-shouldered Kite.

Other Stops along Santa Teresa Road

Santa Teresa Rd at 23°51’56’’S and 133°59’10’’E

This spot is located at the end of sealed section of Santa Teresa Rd, 13km from the airport roundabout. You’ll find here a small dam, a creek crossing and extensive grassland with stands of mulga.

Check the mulga for White-browed Treecreepers; they have been reported repeatedly from this location. Grey Falcons and Little Eagles were recorded several times. Cockatiels and Budgerigars often visit the dam for a drink. Banded Whitefaces, Southern Whitefaces and Painted Finches have also been observed. Grassland birds found here include Little Button-quail, Red-chested Button-quail, Rufous Songlark, Brown Songlark, Little Grassbird, Zebra Finch and Australasian Pipit. Other birds at this site include White-backed Swallow, Varied Sittella, White-winged Triller, Australian Pratincole, Western Gerygone, Barn Owl and Spotted Nightjar.

Santa Teresa Rd at 23°58’41’’S and 134°03’15’’E

The site is located 26.5km from the airport roundabout. This is another area worth checking for Rufous-crowned Emu-wren and Dusky Grasswren. Look for the latter on the clifftop edges of flat-topped hills. You have also a chance to find Red-backed Kingfisher (on the power lines), Hooded Robin, Red-browed Pardalote, Weebill, Little Button-quail, White-winged Fairy-wren, Crested Bellbird, Chiming Wedgebill, Crimson Chat, Grey-fronted Honeyeater and Grey-headed Honeyeater. Look for Bourke’s Parrots in the patches of mulga and for Painted Finches in the rocky areas.

Santa Teresa Rd at 23°59'39"S and 134°03'54"E

This site is known as the Bourke's Parrot Swamp. It is located north of the turnoff to Deep Well Tk. This spot is sometimes very productive for Bourke's Parrot. Look also for Mulga Parrot, Australian Ringneck, Banded Whiteface and Grey Fantail. Also, Grey Falcon was reported from this area.

Santa Teresa Rd at 23°58'59"S and 134°03'40"E

This spot is called Gidgee Patch and is located 29km from the airport roundabout. Check the area of gidgee along Santa Teresa Rd for the presence of Red-chested Button-quail, Little Button-quail and Rufous Songlark. White-browed Treecreepers have been observed repeatedly on the trunks of gidgee. Search for Spinifexbird in the spinifex clumps.

Substantial flocks of Crimson Chats were seen in this area. Other birds here include Splendid Fairy-wren, White-browed Babbler, Pied Honeyeater, White-fronted Honeyeater, Masked Woodswallow, Red-backed Kingfisher, Southern Whiteface, Budgerigar, Pallid Cuckoo and Black-shouldered Kite.

Santa Teresa Sewage Treatment Plant

Several ponds are located south of Santa Teresa along Allambi Rd, off Santa Teresa Rd. GPS coordinates are 24°08'40"S and 134°22'00"E. Waterbirds congregating here include Grey Teal, Pink-eared Duck, Hoary-headed Grebe, Black-tailed Native-hen, Eurasian Coot as well some waders such as Wood Sandpiper, Red-necked Avocet, Banded Lapwing, Black-fronted Dotterel and Red-kneed Dotterel. Flock Bronzewings are occasional visitors. Other birds in this area include Budgerigar, Cockatiel, Tree Martin, Singing Honeyeater, Australasian Pipit and Brown Falcon.

West McDonnell Ranges National Park

The strange, undulating shapes of West McDonnell Ranges

This large, 207,000ha spectacular National Park, with the Indigenous name of Tjoritja, is situated west of Alice Springs. It is a linear park with easy access to its many attractions from Larapinta Dr (B6) and Namatjira Dr (B7). The park spans the distance of 160km along the West McDonnell Ranges. Its most famous attractions are Ormiston Gorge, Ellery Creek Big Hole, Glen Helen Gorge, Simpsons Gap, Standley Chasm and Redbank Gorge.

To get there, take Larapinta Dr in Alice Springs and then continue west on Namatjira Dr. Both roads are sealed, as are the access drives to the side, so the trip can be conveniently undertaken in a 2WD vehicle. The attractions are well signposted from the main roads. Facilities include carparks, picnic areas with barbecues and toilets, swimming waterholes and numerous marked walking tracks. The longest, Larapinta Trail, runs parallel to the main roads. Further information with a map can be found in the Park's fact sheet, downloadable here: https://nt.gov.au/__data/assets/pdf_file/0008/200051/tjoritja-west-macs-fact-sheet-and-map.pdf.

Simpsons Gap

This is one of the most prominent gaps in the West McDonnell Ranges. The turnoff to the Gap is located off Larapinta Dr 18km west of Alice Springs. Drive on sealed Darken Dr for 6km to get to the Gap's carpark.

You will find here a narrow gorge with towering cliffs and a permanent waterhole. Several short walks pass through mulga woodland, large ghost gums and grassland. Particularly good for birding are the 200m-long Ghost Gum Walk and 1.8km Cassia Hill Walk. Further information with a map can be found in the Simpsons Gap fact sheet here: https://nt.gov.au/__data/assets/pdf_file/0007/200050/simpsons-gap-fact-sheet-and-map.pdf.

Simpsons Gap

Over 140 bird species have been recorded around the Simpsons Gap. **Key species** are Painted Finch, Major Mitchell's Cockatoo, Banded Whiteface, Red-backed Kingfisher, Western Bowerbird and Peregrine Falcon. Other birds of interest include Grey-headed Honeyeater, Splendid Fairy-wren, Little Woodswallow, Little Button-quail, Mulga Parrot, Australian Ringneck, Chestnut-rumped Thornbill, Hooded Robin, Spotted Nightjar and Spotted Harrier. Rarities include White-fronted Honeyeater, Grey Honeyeater, Pied Honeyeater, Dusky Grasswren, Redthroat, Grey Wagtail and Black Falcon.

Stop at the Ranger Station (Visitor Centre) to kick off birdwatching in the area. We admired for a while a flock of Major Mitchell's Cockatoos with a wailing chick in tow. Grey-crowned Babblers were foraging under the deck of the house. We also ticked off Western Bowerbird, Australian Ringneck, Yellow-throated Miner, Pallid Cuckoo, Spinifex Pigeon and Collared Sparrowhawk.

On the Ghost Gum Walk near the Visitor Centre, we came across a mixed flock of honeyeaters feeding in the flowering bushes, including White-plumed Honeyeater, Brown Honeyeater, Grey-headed Honeyeater, Singing Honeyeater and a single Pied Honeyeater. Other birds on the walk included Rufous Songlark, Mulga Parrot, Purple-backed Fairy-wren, Sacred Kingfisher, Tree Martin, Red-browed Pardalote, Nankeen Kestrel, Black-shouldered Kite and Spotted Harrier.

Tree Martin

Cassia Hill got its name from the low shrubs covering the hillside. Cassia Hill Walk starts from the carpark near Darken Dr and runs to the top of Cassia Hill. Look here for Redthroats; they are often singing from tops of cassia bushes. In grassy areas, search for Little Button-quail, Spinifex Pigeon, Brown Songlark, Southern Whiteface and Yellow-rumped Thornbill. There are plenty of Splendid Fairy-wrens, White-winged Fairy-wrens and Zebra Finches around. Other birds on the walk may include Red-backed Kingfisher, Masked Woodswallow, Hooded Robin, Crested Bellbird, Red-capped Robin, Weebill, Wedge-tailed Eagle and Black-shouldered Kite.

Woodland Trail is much longer, 17km return, starting off Darken Dr midway to the gorge. Grey Honeyeater was recorded several times at the entrance to this walk from Darken Rd. Emus, otherwise rare in this National Park, can be spotted here. Chiming Wedgebill was reported. Look also for Hooded Robin, Sacred Kingfisher, Rufous Whistler, Little Woodswallow, White-browed Woodswallow, Black-faced Woodswallow, Western Gerygone, Horsfield's Bronze-cuckoo, Purple-backed Fairy-wren, Chestnut-rumped Thornbill, Striated Pardalote, Brown Falcon, Brown Goshawk and Australian Hobby.

Birds coming for a drink at the waterhole in the Gap include Painted Finches, Australian Ringnecks, Mulga Parrots and masses of Budgerigars. Look for Peregrine Falcon perched on the cliff and Little Woodswallows circling over the ridge. Sometimes, waterbirds visit the waterhole, including White-necked Heron, Australasian Grebe and Black-fronted Dotterel.

Dusky Grasswrens are occasionally found on the spinifex-cladded slopes to the left (when facing Simpsons Gap).

Standley Chasm

This magnificent gorge is located 50km west of Alice Springs. The turnoff is well signposted from Larapinta Dr. The whole route is sealed.

The Chasm is only 3m wide but 80m high, so it is a stunning structure. The site is privately owned and surrounded by the West McDonnell Ranges National Park. A natural spring nearby attracts a lot of wildlife. Facilities include a camping area with powered and unpowered sites, toilets, barbecues, kitchen and carpark. There is also a kiosk with good coffee and food, and a gift shop. Opening hours are from 8am to 5pm Mon-Sat and 8am to 2pm on Sundays. An easy 2.4km walk from the reception runs though the Chasm. Access to the West McDonnell Ranges' section of the Larapinta Trail is located 1km down the walk. This steep trail will take you to the top of the ridge. On your way, look for Dusky Grasswrens on the rocky slopes. There should be also plenty of Spinifex Pigeons and Splendid Fairy-wrens. In the reeds near the spring, look for Australian Reed-Warbler. Occasionally, Black-breasted Buzzards are flying over the gorge.

Other birds at this site include Crested Bellbird, Western Bowerbird, Sacred Kingfisher, Horsfield's Bronze-cuckoo, Singing Honeyeater, Spiny-cheeked Honeyeater, Inland Thornbill and Little Button-quail. At night, you may hear Southern Boobook, Barn Owl and Australian Owlet-nightjar.

Corner or Larapinta and Namatjira Drives

This spot is located about 5km further west from the Standley Chasm's turnoff. GPS coordinates are 23°49'21''S and 133°28'24''E. Major Mitchell's Cockatoos breed here. Look also for Peregrine Falcon. After heavy rains, every bush will be flowering, producing plenty of grass seeds and insects. Populations of Zebra Finches, Diamond Doves and Budgerigars are exploding at such times. Nomadic honeyeaters (White-fronted Honeyeater, Black Honeyeater and Pied Honeyeater) appear to feed on the nectar. Flocks of Masked Woodswallow gorge on both nectar and insects. Other bush birds in the area include Redthroat, Weebill, Slaty-backed Thornbill, Inland Thornbill, Crested Bellbird, Hooded Robin and Red-capped Robin.

Namatjira Drive at 23°48'40''S and 133°23'07''E

This place is located 9.5km west of the Larapinta Dr junction. A track runs north for about 1km to a bush camp on the banks of Hugh River. Birds along the track include Dusky Grasswren, Spinifexbird, Painted Finch, Slaty-backed Thornbill, Black-eared Cuckoo, Splendid Fairy-wren, Hooded Robin and Little Button-quail. From time to time, Bourke's Parrots are recorded. There is also a chance to come across Crested Bellbird, Major Mitchell's Cockatoo and Spotted Harrier.

Namatjira Drive at 23°48'15''S and 133°10'34''E

The landscape of West McDonnell Ranges along Namatjira Drive near the Point Howard Lookout

Point Howard Lookout, with a steep access off Namatjira Dr, is located at these coordinates. It is a good stop to search for raptors soaring in the sky. Often seen here are Black-breasted Buzzard, Australian Hobby, Wedge-tailed Eagle, Whistling Kite and Black Kite.

As we arrived there, Little Button-quail was feeding in sparse grass near the carpark. A small flock of Zebra Finches with a couple of Painted Finches in the mix was picking seeds from the ground.

Ellery Creek Big Hole

This picturesque waterhole is formed in the Ellery Creek which runs through the gorge in the West McDonnell Ranges National Park. It is located 80km west of Alice Springs, off Namatjira Dr. The 2km access road and carpark are unsealed. The site is well signposted from the main road. This is a popular destination for swimming (water is always very cold), camping and birdwatching. Facilities include picnic tables, barbecues, toilets and walking tracks. The Dolomite Walk is a loop that starts at the carpark to meander through spinifex-dominated habitat, so good for birding. The walk is generally easy, with a few steeper sections.

Further information with a map can be found in the site's fact sheet, downloadable here: https://nt.gov.au/__data/assets/pdf_file/0011/200036/ellery-creek-big-hole-fact-sheet-and-map.pdf.

Over 130 bird species have been recorded around the Ellery Creek Big Hole. **Key species** are Spinifexbird, Spinifex Pigeon, Painted Finch, Black Honeyeater and Major Mitchell's Cockatoo. Other birds of interest include Budgerigar, Western Bowerbird, Hooded Robin, Sacred Kingfisher, Red-backed Kingfisher, Little Woodswallow, Grey-headed Honeyeater, Golden-backed Honeyeater and Red-browed Pardalote. Rarities include Rufous-crowned Emu-wren, Princess Parrot, Bourke's Parrot, Ground Cuckoo-shrike and Little Eagle.

Check the spinifex-covered plains along the access track, 500m from the main road. Spinifexbirds are usually there. It used to be a good spot for Rufous-crowned Emu-wren but this coveted species has disappeared from this location after a severe fire. Other birds along the access track include Major Mitchell's Cockatoo, White-winged Triller, Crimson Chat, Grey-headed Honeyeater, Hooded Robin, Red-backed Kingfisher and an occasional Black-breasted Buzzard.

Rufous-crowned Emu-wrens can sometimes be found on the Dolomite Walk (1.5hrs return). In winter, the flowering bushes (mostly mallee) attract the rare White-fronted Honeyeaters and Black Honeyeaters. Grey-headed Honeyeaters are regular visitors, as are Spiny-cheeked Honeyeaters, Singing Honeyeaters and Brown

Honeyeaters. The walk is also good for Spinifexbird, often found on tops of the long, dense, unburnt spinifex. Slaty-backed Thornbills are found infrequently along the walk. Look also for Spinifex Pigeon, Sacred Kingfisher, Black-eared Cuckoo, Red-capped Robin, Hooded Robin, Rainbow Bee-eater, Peregrine Falcon and Little Eagle.

The Big Hole supports a variety of waterbirds but in small numbers. Regularly found here are Black-fronted Dotterel, Australasian Grebe, Nankeen Night-Heron, White-necked Heron, Grey Teal, Pink-eared Duck and Hardhead. Some rarer species, such as Black-tailed Native-hen, Dusky Moorhen, Hoary-headed Grebe, Australian Wood Duck and Black Swan, are reported occasionally. At dusk, Spotted Nightjars can be seen hawking insects over the waterhole.

Dusky Moorhen, rare in NT

At the east junction of the Dolomite Walk with the Larapinta Trail, along the first kilometre from the turnoff going west, you have a slight chance of a sighting of Dusky Grasswren. Other birds here include Purple-backed Fairy-wren, White-winged Fairy-wren, Black-eared Cuckoo, Redthroat, Spinifex Pigeon, Inland Thornbill and Southern Whiteface.

Serpentine Gorge

Serpentine Gorge is a narrow gap in the West McDonnell Ranges, situated 100km west of Alice Springs, half-way between the Ellery Creek Big Hole and Ormiston Gorge. It is well signposted from Namatjira Dr, accessible via an unsealed 4km-long

Serpentine Gorge Tk. Facilities include carpark, shaded shelters, picnic tables, toilets and a well-marked 2.5km return walking track to the gorge. Camping is not allowed.

Over 100 bird species have been recorded in the Serpentine Gorge. **Key species** are Painted Finch, Spinifex Pigeon, Dusky Grasswren, Major Mitchell's Cockatoo, Slaty-backed Thornbill, Little Woodswallow and Black-breasted Buzzard. Other birds of interest include Red-browed Pardalote, Red-backed Kingfisher, Black-eared Cuckoo, Hooded Robin, Red-capped Robin, Budgerigar, White-browed Babbler, Western Bowerbird and Peregrine Falcon. Rarities include Grey Honeyeater, Ground Cuckoo-shrike, White-browed Treecreeper, White-browed Woodswallow and Letter-winged Kite.

Most of the time, the dry weather causes most of the waterholes in the area to dry out, and the waterhole in the Serpentine Gorge is the only one still holding water. Waterbirds and other birdlife gather at this location as there is not much choice otherwise. Large flocks (about 20 birds) of Major Mitchell's Cockatoos come for a drink at dusk. Other birds here include Diamond Doves, Painted Finches, Common Bronzewings, Australian Ringnecks, Golden-backed Honeyeaters, Grey-headed Honeyeaters and Brown Honeyeaters.

On the walk to the gorge, be on the lookout for Slaty-backed Thornbill, Splendid Fairy-wren, Spinifex Pigeon, Grey Butcherbird, Little Button-quail, Rufous Whistler and Western Bowerbird. At night, Australian Owlet-nightjars are calling around the picnic area.

Ochre Pits

This colourful outcrop of ochre on the banks of a sandy creek is located 120km west of Alice Springs. It is an old ochre mining site, used to be mined over thousands of years by Aboriginal people, to be traded among tribes all over Australia. The turnoff to the site is well signposted from Namatjira Dr. A short vehicular track leads to the pits with a carpark, unmanned information centre, picnic tables, barbecues, toilets and a short walking track to the pits.

A mosaic of mulga, mallee woodlands and riverine vegetation create favourable conditions for Grey Honeyeater. This rare species has been recorded here several times in winter and spring. If mallee species are flowering profusely, a huge influx of honeyeaters is observed, including Brown Honeyeater, Golden-backed Honeyeater, White-plumed Honeyeater and even Pied Black and White-fronted Honeyeater.

Patches of mulga may produce the rare Slaty-backed Thornbill. Painted Finches and Little Button-quails were reported feeding at the edge of spinifex. Near the carpark, search for Red-capped Robin, Golden-backed Honeyeater, Crested Bellbird, Yellow-rumped Thornbill, Western Bowerbird and Purple-backed Fairy-wren.

Ormiston Gorge

Ormiston Gorge is one of the most popular and most photographed tourist destinations in the whole Red Centre of Australia. It is located 135km west of Alice Springs and reached via an 8k-long sealed road off Namatjira Dr. It is known for its towering red walls surrounding a permanent waterhole, good for swimming but water is always cold. The adjacent breathtaking landscape incudes rivers, panoramic lookouts, and mountains with amazing rocky formations. A comfortable campground is provided near the gorge. Facilities include Visitor Centre with a kiosk and general store, barbecues and toilets. There is also a network of walking tracks, such as a 200m walk to the waterhole, 2.5km Ghost Gum Walk (loop to the lookout) and 8.5km loop called Ormiston Pound Walk. Larapinta Trail runs past the site. Further information with a site map can be found in the Ormiston Gorge fact sheet here: https://nt.gov.au/__data/assets/pdf_file/0010/200044/ormiston-gorge-fact-sheet-and-map.pdf.

Ormiston Gorge waterhole

Over 150 bird species have been recorded in the Ormiston Gorge. **Key species** are Grey Honeyeater, Dusky Grasswren, Rufous-crowned Emu-wren, Spinifexbird, Spinifex Pigeon, Painted Finch, Peregrine Falcon, Black-breasted Buzzard and Little Eagle. Other birds of interest include Major Mitchell's Cockatoo, Budgerigar, Little Woodswallow, Red-browed Pardalote, Western Bowerbird, Golden-backed Honeyeater, Grey-headed Honeyeater, White-fronted Honeyeater, Black

Honeyeater, Hooded Robin, Crested Bellbird, White-backed Swallow and Southern Whiteface. Rarities include Grey Falcon, Australian Bustard, Ground Cuckoo-shrike and Square-tailed Kite.

The first place to stop is a stony area of a white drainage line on both sides of access road about 200m from the turnoff from Namatjira Dr. A large patch of long, dense spinifex grows under small mallee tree on the west side. This is a good place to search for Spinifexbird. It is often seen singing from low-hanging mallee branches. Look also for Rufous-crowned Emu-wren in the clumps of dense spinifex, but this species is much more difficult to find here. When eremophilas, grevilleas and mallee are in bloom, honeyeaters appear in abundance. Common species include Singing Honeyeater, Spiny-cheeked Honeyeater and Grey-headed Honeyeater. There is also a chance to spot the nomadic species: White-fronted Honeyeater, Pied Honeyeater and Black Honeyeater.

In the rocky areas, search for Painted Finches on the ground. When walking through the spinifex, inspect the scattered bushes, looking for White-winged Fairy-wren, Red-backed Kingfisher, Crested Bellbird, Hooded Robin and Weebill. Looking up, you may spot Little Woodswallow and White-backed Swallow in flight. It is also a good place for raptors. Common species include Wedge-tailed Eagle, Brown Falcon and Whistling Kite, while Black-breasted Buzzards are recurring visitors.

Visitor Centre and Campground

This site is worth checking for Grey Honeyeater. They appear irregularly but sometimes stay for a couple of months. The best spot are the trees and bushes around the ranger quarters. Spinifex Pigeons are common, often feeding under the tables at the kiosk. Other birds hanging around the cafe include Grey Shrike-thrushes, Pied Butcherbirds, Zebra Finches, Yellow-rumped Thornbills and Western Bowerbirds. The latter often cause confusion by mimicking the beautiful calls of Pied Butcherbird or even whistling like a Whistling Kite, causing all the birds to scatter.

Other birds around the campground include Major Mitchell's Cockatoo, Grey-headed Honeyeater, Red-browed Pardalote, Australian Ringneck, Collared Sparrowhawk, Grey-crowned Babbler and Rufous Whistler.

Spotted Nightjars have been observed flying over the Visitor Centre after dusk. Other nocturnal birds here include Southern Boobook, usually roosting in the creek area east of the kiosk, Australian Owlet-nightjar and Barn Owl.

The famous waterhole is only 200m from the campground. Look there for White-necked Heron, White-faced Heron, Nankeen Night-Heron and Black-fronted Dotterel. A pair of Major Mitchell's Cockatoos nest in the river red gums near the waterhole. Zebra Finches and Painted Finches regularly come for a drink. In the gum trees surrounding the waterhole, you may spot Channel-billed Cuckoo, Striated Pardalote, Red-browed Pardalote, Australian Ringneck and White-plumed Honeyeater.

Ghost Gum Lookout Walk

This 2.5km loop starts from the carpark and takes you to the Ghost Gum Lookout with a platform offering stunning views over the gorge. From there, you may continue on the loop along the gorge wall to descend to the waterhole, or come back a shorter distance to the carpark. Both options can be productive for birding. Dusky Grasswrens are occasionally found at the lookout platform or along the walk to the waterhole. A good spot for Spinifexbird is just 50m past the lookout. Peregrine Falcons nest on the gorge wall, often surveying their territory and catching Budgerigars arriving at the waterhole for a drink.

Dusky Grasswren

Other birds along the walk include Hooded Robin, Spinifex Pigeon, Grey-headed Honeyeater, Horsfield's Bronze-cuckoo, Masked Woodswallow, Splendid Fairy-wren and Purple-backed Fairy-wren.

Ormiston Gorge Pound Walk

The Pound is a ring of mountains dominated by Mt Giles. Its western boundary is formed by Ormiston Gorge. This long walk is probably the best birding option in this section of the National Park. It will take approximately 5hrs to complete, and walkers need to be fit to attempt it, mainly because there is nearly no shade when crossing the Pound. The walk starts at the roadside 500m from the Visitor Centre. The path meanders across the scenic slopes up to the ridge line. Follow the ridges, next drop down to the Pound. Return to the campsite along the waterhole.

Your first stop is at the Ormiston Creek crossing not far from trailhead, where you should inspect the river red gums fringing the creek bed. A large flock of Major Mitchell's Cockatoos often roosts there for the night. Listen to the calls of Red-browed Pardalotes. Other birds here include Western Bowerbird, Sacred Kingfisher, Rainbow Bee-eater, Weebill, Golden-backed Honeyeater, Grey-headed Honeyeater and Yellow-throated Miner. When water is present in the creek, Black-fronted Dotterels will be feeding at its edges. Occasionally, other waterbirds may appear, such as White-necked Heron, Grey Teal and Australasian Grebe. Black-breasted Buzzard and Little Eagle have been recorded near the creek several times.

For about 1km past the creek crossing, look for Spinifex Pigeon, Rufous Whistler, Splendid Fairy-wren, Western Gerygone and Grey-crowned Babbler.

Spinifex Pigeon

Next, you'll get into a hilly country where you should inspect any rocky habitat covered with mature spinifex The main sought-after species over there is Dusky Grasswren.

When you descend into the Pound, you'll walk through the treeless flat covered with spinifex. Check the patches of taller and denser spinifex. Spinifexbird is quite commonly sighted there while Rufous-crowned Emu-wren is possible, but more difficult to find. Look also for Jacky Winter, Little Button-quail, Purple-backed Fairy-wren, White-winged Fairy-wren, Inland Thornbill, Horsfield's Bronze-cuckoo, Black-faced Woodswallow, Diamond Dove, Budgerigar, White-winged Triller, Rufous Whistler and Hooded Robin. You'll pass several small rocky outcrops where Painted Finches and Spinifex Pigeons can be found.

The walk is good for the raptors. Nankeen Kestrel, Brown Falcon, Brown Goshawk, Whistling Kite and Australian Hobby are common. Peregrine Falcons can be spotted in the gorge. Little Eagle and Black-breasted Buzzard appear occasionally at the start of the walk.

Glen Helen Gorge

This spectacular gorge is located on Finke River about 130km from Alice Springs. A large permanent waterhole there is an important summer refuge for fish and waterbirds. Access is from Namatjira Dr via a short, sealed track leading to the Glen Helen Resort. As signposted at the start of the track, the resort is still closed, but you can drive up part of the way and take a walk along Finke River to the gorge.

Over 130 bird species have been recorded in Glen Helen Gorge. **Key species** are Little Woodswallow, Spinifex Pigeon, Painted Finch, Western Bowerbird and Australian Reed-Warbler. Other birds of interest include waterbirds, Common Bronzewing, Grey-headed Honeyeater, Australian Ringneck, Budgerigar, Rufous Songlark, Hooded Robin, Purple-backed Fairy-wren, Red-browed Pardalote and Red-backed Kingfisher. Rarities include Australian Spotted Crake, Pied Heron, Red-tailed Black-Cockatoo and Little Grassbird.

On the walk along Finke River, search for Crimson Chat, Painted Finch, Brown Songlark, White-winged Fairy-wren and Black-shouldered Kite.

Black-fronted Dotterels breed near the waterhole. A wide selection of waterbirds there includes White-necked Heron, Nankeen Night-Heron, Hardhead, Black Swan, Dusky Moorhen, Eurasian Coot, Black-tailed Native-hen, Whiskered Tern and cormorants. Australian Reed-Warblers may be calling from the reeds. With luck, you may spot Buff-banded Rail popping out of the reeds or hear the call of Little Grassbird.

Other birds around Glen Helen Gorge include Pied Butcherbird, Spiny-cheeked Honeyeater, Singing Honeyeater, Black-faced Woodswallow and Mulga Parrot.

Finke River 2 Mile Bush Camp

Access to the site, which is situated on the eastern side of Finke River, is 200m past the turnoff to Glen Helen Gorge. On the other side on the river is the Mount Sonder Lookout. The campground is accessible by a short track off Namatjira Dr, only by 4WD vehicles. No facilities are provided so you must be self-sufficient.

View of Finke River from the camp

This spot is a birding gem in the West McDonnell Ranges National Park. In the campsite, you may encounter Major Mitchell's Cockatoos, Red-tailed Black-Cockatoos, Zebra Finches and several raptors. Plenty of Budgerigars nest in trees along Finke River. At night, listen to Southern Boobook, Barn Owl and Australian Owlet-nightjar.

This site is good for waterbirds, particularly for rails and crakes. Baillon's Crake, Australian Spotted Crake and Buff-banded Rail have been recorded here. Rarer wetland birds include Australian Wood Duck, Plumed Whistling-Duck, Plumed Egret, Common Sandpiper, Red-kneed Dotterel and Little Grassbird. Regularly seen bush birds include Spinifex Pigeon, Crested Bellbird, White-backed Swallow, Red-browed Pardalote, Sacred Kingfisher, Western Bowerbird and Purple-backed Fairy-wren.

Mount Sonder Lookout

The lookout is located on the western side of Finke River, about 500m from the Glen Helen turnoff. GPs coordinates are 23°40'38''S and 132°40'09''E. Spinifex Pigeons, Painted Finches and Zebra Finches are often feeding in grassy patches around the lookout. Occasional records exist of Dusky Grasswren sighted in rocky areas near the lookout. You may see some waterbirds in the distance, flying over the river. These include White-faced Heron, White-necked Heron and Purple Swamphen.

This site may also produce Black-shouldered Kite, Australian Magpie, Budgerigar, Brown Songlark and Singing Honeyeater.

Redbank Gorge

The stunning gorge, chasm and a permanent waterhole are located at the base of Mount Sonder, 160km west of Alice Springs. To get there, turn north from Namatjira Dr into a 5km-long Redbank Gorge Access. This road section is unsealed and a 4WD vehicle is required. The site offers two basic camping areas: Woodland Camp and Ridgetop Camp, both equipped with toilets, picnic tables and fire pits. Gas barbecues are at Woodland only. A 2km return walking track runs from the carpark to Redbank Gorge. It is unmarked and for the part of the route running in a dry creek bed. Larapinta Trail runs through the site and can be used to get to the Mount Sonder Lookout. Further information and a site map can be found in the Redbank Gorge fact sheet here: https://nt.gov.au/__data/assets/pdf_file/0019/370414/redbank-gorge-fact-sheet-and-map.pdf.

About 90 bird species have been recorded in the Redbank Gorge. **Key species** are Dusky Grasswren, Rufous-crowned Emu-wren, Spinifexbird, Spinifex Pigeon, Major Mitchell's Cockatoo, Crested Bellbird, Golden-backed Honeyeater and Peregrine Falcon. Other birds of interest include Red-browed Pardalote, Budgerigar, Grey-headed Honeyeater, Little Woodswallow, Masked Woodswallow, Inland Thornbill, Splendid Fairy-wren, Jacky Winter, Hooded Robin and Wedge-tailed Eagle. Rarities include Pied Honeyeater, Slaty-backed Thornbill, Little Grassbird, White-browed Woodswallow, Red-tailed Black-Cockatoo and Black Falcon.

The 5km return Mt Sonder Walk (part of Larapinta Trail) can be productive for Dusky Grasswren. Other birds on this walk include Peregrine Falcon, Spinifexbird, Spinifex Pigeon, White-fronted Honeyeater, Grey-headed Honeyeater and Rufous-crowned Emu-wren.

At the Ridgetop Campground, you may come across Hooded Robin, Crested Bellbird, Splendid Fairy-wren, Red-browed Pardalote and Black-faced Woodswallow. The Woodland Campground may produce Little Button-quail, Hooded Robin, Varied Sittella, Grey Butcherbird, Little Woodswallow, Major Mitchell's Cockatoo, Mulga Parrot, Chestnut-rumped Thornbill, Spinifexbird and Grey-headed Honeyeater. Nocturnal birds can be found in both camps, including Australian Owlet-nightjar, Spotted Nightjar, Tawny Frogmouth, Southern Boobook and Barn Owl.

Australian Owlet-nightjar

Around the Redbank Gorge site, check patches of mallee, mulga and eremophila with the spinifex understory for the presence of Hooded Robin, Red-capped Robin, Mulga Parrot, Inland Thornbill, Zebra Finch, Splendid Fairy-wren and Varied Sittella. On the Redbank Gorge Walk, look for Painted Finch, Sacred Kingfisher, Grey-headed Honeyeater, Western Gerygone, Major Mitchell's Cockatoo, Wedge-tailed Eagle and Peregrine Falcon.

Tnorala Conservation Reserve

This small, 480ha reserve, previously known as Gosse Bluff, is located off Larapinta Dr 175km west of Alice Springs. A 4WD vehicle is recommended for the last leg of the route, a 5km access road. The main feature of the reserve is a huge crater that was created 140mln years ago, when a huge comet struck central Australia and formed a crater of 25km in diameter, believed to be the largest in the world. After enduring millions of years of erosion, the outer ring structure has nearly disappeared. Today, only the inner ring remains, protruding 100m above the plains. Its diameter is 5km and the structure is still impressive and worth visiting.

To get there, be on the lookout for a small sign to Gosse Bluff to turn west off Larapinta Dr. An unsealed access track will take you to the middle of the crater. You'll find there a picnic area with a shelter, picnic tables and toilets. A short, easy walk leads to a lookout on the crater wall. No camping is allowed. Further information and a site map can be found in the Tnorala Conservation Reserve fact sheet here: https://nt.gov.au/__data/assets/pdf_file/0009/200052/tnorala-conservation-reserve-fact-sheet-and-map.pdf.

About 80 bird species have been recorded in the Tnorala Conservation Reserve. **Key species** are Dusky Grasswren, Western Bowerbird, Hooded Robin, Golden-backed Honeyeater, Peregrine Falcon and Wedge-tailed Eagle. Other birds of interest include Crested Bellbird, Red-browed Pardalote, Splendid Fairy-wren, Grey-headed Honeyeater, Jacky Winter, Varied Sittella, Pallid Cuckoo, Budgerigar and Inland Thornbill. Rarities include Rufous-crowned Emu-wren, Grey Falcon, Ground Cuckoo-shrike, Slaty-backed Thornbill, Pied Honeyeater and Black Honeyeater.

Picnic area is a good birding spot, featuring a friendly Western Bowerbird. Its bower is nearby. Regularly seen around the picnic area are Hooded Robin, Red-capped Robin, Jacky Winter, Crested Bellbird, Little Button-quail and plenty of Diamond Doves and Budgerigars. On the walk to the lookout, search for Dusky Grasswrens; they may be hopping on the rocks. Also expect to find Little Woodswallow, Black-faced Woodswallow, Grey-headed Honeyeater, Singing Honeyeater, Crimson Chat, Purple-backed Fairy-wren, Splendid Fairy-wren and Red-browed Pardalote.

The site offers a small chance of sighting of Rufous-crowned Emu-wren. Search any clumps of long, dense spinifex in any direction 50m from the carpark.

Finke Gorge National Park

Finke Gorge National Park covers 46,000ha. It is located 140km west of Alice Springs, on the southern side of Larapinta Dr. It is known for its breathtaking landscapes and the impressive Palm Valley. The very rare red cabbage palms, restricted only to this national park, are protected there. Only 3,000 trees are surviving. The Park is dissected by Finke River, considered to be the oldest river in the world. It is one of the rivers of the Lake Eyre Basin.

This remote Park can be enjoyed only by experienced 4WDrivers. To get there:

- Go west from Alice Springs on Larapinta Dr and just after passing Hermannsburg turn south onto the track to Palm Valley, well signposted. A significant part of this 16km-long track runs in the sandy bed of Finke River so a high clearance 4WD is a must. Any rain makes this route impassable.

- In Hermannsburg, take the Finke 4WD route (a.k.a. Boggy Hole Access). It runs south through the Boggy Hole section of the Finke Gorge National Park to the Kings Canyon National Park. This route is very difficult so careful planning and lots of off-road experience are needed.

View of McDonnell Ranges from Larapinta Dr near Hermannsburg

Facilities can be found only in the Palm Valley section of the Park, where camping grounds are provided with toilets, showers and gas barbecues. A picnic area with sheltered picnic tables is available for day visitors. Several short walks meander along Finke River and across the plateau. Further information and a site map can be found in the Finke Gorge National Park fact sheet, downloadable here: https://nt.gov.au/__data/assets/pdf_file/0012/200037/finke-gorge-national-park-fact-sheet-and-map.pdf.

Over 130 bird species have been recorded in the Finke Gorge National Park. **Key species** are Painted Finch, Dusky Grasswren, Spinifexbird, Redthroat, Spinifex Pigeon, Pied Honeyeater, Western Bowerbird, White-backed Swallow and Peregrine Falcon. Other birds of interest include Crested Bellbird, Hooded Robin, Red-capped Robin, Weebill, Grey Fantail, Splendid Fairy-wren, Grey-headed Honeyeater, Spiny-cheeked Honeyeater, Major Mitchell's Cockatoo, Red-browed Pardalote, Chestnut-rumped Thornbill and Inland Thornbill. Rarities include Bourke's Parrot, Letter-winged Kite, Slaty-backed Thornbill, Baillon's Crake and Buff-banded Rail.

Western Bowerbird

Productive birding can be expected in the Finke Gorge Campground. A pond with patches of reeds is located nearby. You may be able to see wetland birds there such as Black-tailed Native-hen, Grey Teal, White-faced Heron, Black-fronted Dotterel, Australian Reed-Warbler or even Baillon's Crake or Buff-banded Rail. Tawny Frogmouths roost in the campground. Major Mitchell's Cockatoos, Mulga Parrots and Australian Ringnecks visit the site. Sometimes you may hear sweet tinkling of Redthroats or constant calling of Pallid Cuckoos.

Other birds in the area include Yellow-throated Miner, Brown Honeyeater, Brown Goshawk, Western Gerygone, Red-browed Pardalote, Western Bowerbird and Zebra Finch.

A 5km return Mpulungkinya Tk wanders in the riverbed along the lush palm oasis, to return to the carpark across the plateau. There are usually plenty of Western Bowerbirds around - check the fruiting fig trees growing in the crevices along this walk. Other birds likely to be found here include Hooded Robin, Red-capped Robin, Spinifexbird, Slaty-backed Thornbill, Crested Bellbird, Brown Honeyeater, Weebill, Splendid Fairy-wren, Western Gerygone, Horsfield's Bronze-cuckoo, Pallid Cuckoo, Rufous Whistler and an occasional Little Eagle.

Mpaara Walk is another interesting walking track. It is a 5km loop starting at the Kalarranga carpark and leads to a lookout with unforgettable views of the crater grounds. Common birds along the walk include Spinifex Pigeon, Painted Finch, Zebra Finch, Purple-backed Fairy-wren, Splendid Fairy-wren, Chestnut-rumped Thornbill and Striated Pardalote. There is a chance of a glimpse of Dusky Grasswren. Other birds in the area include Hooded Robin, Major Mitchell's Cockatoo, Australian Ringneck, Grey-crowned Babbler, Singing Honeyeater and Australian Hobby.

Owen Springs Reserve

This 157,000ha property is located 40km southwest of Alice Springs. A former cattle station, it was open to the public in 2000 and quickly became a favourite destination for 4WD visitors, seeking quiet bush camping and challenging 4WD tracks. The site holds a vivid memory of the explorer John McDouall Stuart, who was first to cross Australia from Adelaide to Timor Sea. Today, Stuart Hwy is named after him. The main track through the reserve follows the route that John Stuart took.

The landscape includes rocky gorges, sand dunes and Hugh River. The river is lined on its broad banks with the shady river red gums. In many places, large waterholes remain long after the rains, attracting the birdlife. The most important to the birders is the Redbank Waterhole.

The reserve can be accessed from Alice Springs via one of the two routes:

- via Larapinta Dr (6). After 50km turn south into Owen Springs Homestead Rd, a terrible 4WD track.
- via Stuart Hwy (A89). This is the route preferably used by the birders. Drive 66km south from Alice Springs, then turn west into a 4km track to Redbank Waterhole. GPS coordinates at the turnoff to that track are 24°09'11"S and 133°30'41"E.

Bush camping is allowed along the Hugh River, mostly near the Redbank Waterhole. No other facilities are provided except for a few information signs. A fact sheet with the map can be downloaded here:
https://nt.gov.au/__data/assets/pdf_file/0011/200045/owen-springs-reserve-fact-sheet-and-map.pdf.

Over 120 bird species have been recorded in the Owen Springs Reserve. **Key species** are Major Mitchell's Cockatoo, Mulga Parrot, Red-backed Kingfisher, Red-browed Pardalote, Southern Whiteface and Australian Bustard. Other birds of interest include waterbirds (if water is present), Budgerigar, Cockatiel, Australian Ringneck, Western Bowerbird, Sacred Kingfisher, Crested Bellbird, White-backed Swallow, White-browed Babbler, Hooded Robin, Australian Owlet-nightjar and Australian Hobby. Rarities include Little Eagle, Black Falcon, Sulphur-crested Cockatoo, Ground Cuckoo-shrike, Slaty-backed Thornbill, Pied Honeyeater, Great Crested Grebe and Australian Pelican.

Redbank Waterhole is the main destination. Fortunately for this difficult park, it sits only 4km from Stuart Hwy. The waterhole is a good place to look for waterbirds and waders in this otherwise bone-dry country. Regular finds include Australian Wood Duck, Hardhead, Australasian Grebe, White-necked Heron, Black-fronted Dotterel, Australasian Darter and Royal Spoonbill. Among the rarer species are Common Greenshank, Sharp-tailed Sandpiper, Red-kneed Dotterel, Black-tailed Native-hen and Freckled Duck.

Sharp-tailed Sandpiper

The old river red gums lining the banks of the waterhole provide nesting hollows for many birds. Budgerigars breed here in large numbers. The hollows are also utilised by Little Corellas, Australian Ringnecks, Major Mitchell's Cockatoos, Australian Owlet-nightjars and Red-backed Kingfishers.

Striated Pardalotes and Rainbow Bee-eaters nest in the burrows in the banks of the waterhole. Large communal nests of Grey-crowned Babblers are scattered in the gum trees around the waterhole. A pair of Pied Butcherbirds nest near the water and sing beautifully in the campground. During the night, you may hear Southern Boobook, Barn Owl and Australian Owlet-nightjar. Raptors nesting around the waterhole include Nankeen Kestrel, Whistling Kite, Black Kite, Australian Hobby and Collared Sparrowhawk. Black-breasted Buzzard is a frequent visitor.

Other birds in the area include Splendid Fairy-wren, White-backed Swallow, Yellow-throated Miner, Weebill, Southern Whiteface, Sacred Kingfisher, Common Bronzewing and White-winged Triller.

When driving to the Homestead, be on the lookout for Australian Bustards; they often wander across the land. Flocks of Crimson Chats appear near the Homestead in summer. Occasionally, Ground Cuckoo-shrikes can be observed along the track to the Homestead. Other birds in the area include Hooded Robin, Southern Whiteface, Mulga Parrot, Black-faced Woodswallow, Masked Woodswallow, Australasian Pipit and Splendid Fairy-wren.

Southern Whiteface

Southern NT

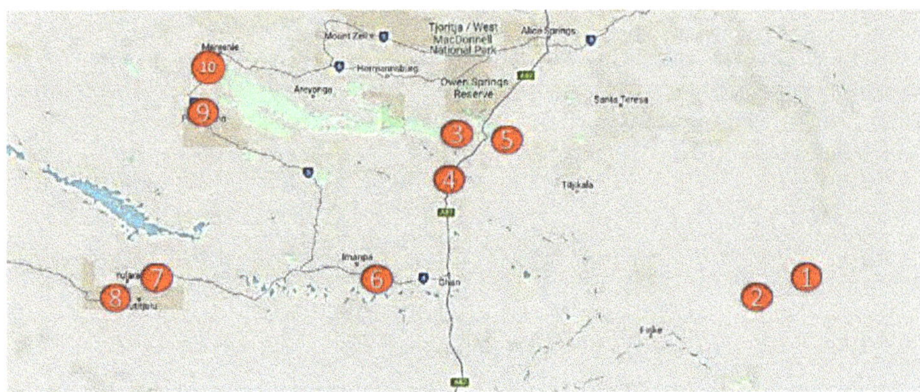

1 [Mac Clark Conservation Reserve]
2 [Old Andado Homestead]
3 [Henbury Meteorites Conservation Reserve]
4 [Stuart Hwy from Alice Springs to SA Border]
5 [Rainbow Valley Conservation Reserve]
6 [Lasseter Highway]
7 [Yulara]
8 [Uluru-Kata Tjuta National Park]
9 [Watarrka (Kings Canyon) National Park]
10 [Mereenie Loop Road]

Mac Clark Conservation Reserve

The reserve protects stands of waddywood (*Acacia peuce*), one of the rarest and most striking trees that grow in the Australian arid zone. It survives on a stony plain with the annual rainfall of less than 150mm. About 1,000 mature trees are fenced off from the cattle in this reserve. Only a few trees still survive outside the Mac Clark Reserve, in Boulia and Birdsville.

The Reserve is situated approximately 290km southeast of Alice Springs via Santa Teresa Rd. Get to the Alice Springs Airport roundabout and drive on Santa Teresa Rd for 266km. Next, turn left into Mac Clark Park, then after 8km turn right into Madigan Line, from which after about 2km you turn off to the reserve. On some maps, the road after Santa Teresa is called Old Andado Tk. There are no facilities in the reserve and no signposting. GPS coordinates are 25°07'36"S and 135°26'45"E. If you reach the Old Andado Homestead, you have overshot the turnoff to the reserve by 36km and are still on Santa Teresa Rd. Further information and maps can be found in the Fact Sheet downloadable here: https://nt.gov.au/__data/assets/pdf_file/0007/200041/mac-clarke-conservation-reserve-fact-sheet-and-map.pdf.

About 90 bird species have been recorded in the Mac Clark Conservation Reserve. **Key species** are Letter-winged Kite, Inland Dotterel, Gibberbird, Black-breasted Buzzard, Banded Whiteface and Eyrean Grasswren. Other birds of interest include Australian Pratincole, Orange Chat, Crimson Chat, Budgerigar, Flock Bronzewing, Brown Songlark, Singing Honeyeater, Hooded Robin and White-backed Swallow. Rarities include Eastern Grass Owl, Cinnamon Quail-thrush and Black Falcon.

Letter-winged Kites and Eastern Grass Owls breed in the reserve in very wet years when the hairy-tailed rat population explodes.

As you are approaching the site, stop 20km before the turnoff to the reserve. GPS coordinates are 24°51'26"S and 135°21'26"E. If there was a heavy rain before, you may experience incredible birding there. In the flowering eremophila bushes, you'll have a good chance to find Pied Honeyeater and Black Honeyeater. Other birds here could be Cinnamon Quail-thrush, Banded Whiteface, Southern Whiteface, Crested Bellbird, Crimson Chat and White-browed Babbler.

At the turnoff from Santa Teresa Rd to Mac Clark Park, at the GPS coordinates of 25°06'36"S and 135°25'37"E, you'll see large dunes that are home to Eyrean Grasswrens. The birds aren't too hard to find; the key is to sit patiently and wait until they come out of the spinifex.

The gibber plains inside the reserve can yield some interesting species, especially after the rain. Look for Inland Dotterel, Gibberbird, Orange Chat and Australian Pratincole. Inland Dotterel can be here in large numbers, particularly along Mac Clark Park.

Inland Dotterel

Also found in the reserve are Australian Bustard, Banded Lapwing, Australian Raven, Little Corella and several raptor species such as Brown Falcon, Spotted Harrier, Australian Hobby, Peregrine Falcon, Nankeen Kestrel and Black-shouldered Kite. Of course, Letter-winged Kite is the star attraction.

Old Andado Homestead

Old Andado Homestead is located at the edge of Simpson Desert, approximately 330km southeast of Alice Springs. It is surrounded by one of the largest cattle stations in Australia (Old Andado Station, not associated now with the Homestead). This is an extremely remote property. GPS coordinates are 25°22’49’’S and 135°26’30’’E. Santa Teresa Rd and Old Andado Tk are badly corrugated, with sections of deep sand or sharp rocks, so a high-clearance 4WD vehicle is a must, together with full supplies for the return journey. The route is impassable after a heavy rain.

Old Andado Homestead is a reminder of how life used to be before the modern amenities. The Homestead and its outbuildings (the meat house and saddle house) are maintained by the volunteer caretakers as the longed-for rest stop for about 1,000 travellers crossing the Simpson Desert every year. You'll find here unpowered camping sites, water, toilets and donkey hot showers. There is no fuel or food. Further information about the site can be accessed here: https://www.oldandado.com.au/.

About 100 bird species have been recorded around the Old Andado Homestead. **Key species** are Eyrean Grasswren, Gibberbird, Inland Dotterel, Banded Whiteface, Cinnamon Quail-thrush, Letter-winged Kite and Grey Falcon. Other birds of interest include Orange Chat, Crimson Chat, Black Honeyeater, Pied Honeyeater, Chiming Wedgebill, Crested Bellbird, Banded Lapwing, Little Button-quail, Flock Bronzewing, Budgerigar, Major Mitchell's Cockatoo, White-backed Swallow, White-winged Fairy-wren, Australian Raven and Spotted Harrier. Rarities include Grey Honeyeater, Bourke's Parrot and Eastern Grass Owl.

There are only a few trees around the Homestead, so they are extensively used by birds for roosting. You may see Galahs, Cockatiels, Budgerigars, Major Mitchell's Cockatoos, Little Corellas, Yellow-throated Miners, Rainbow Bee-eaters and more. This place is excellent for Eyrean Grasswren. They can be found in cane grass on the red sand dunes near the camping ground and near the airstrip. In the same habitat, look for White-winged Fairy-wren, Singing Honeyeater, White-backed Swallow, Chiming Wedgebill, Rufous Songlark and Spotted Harrier.

Nankeen Kestrels are sometimes seen here in large numbers, feeding on abundant grasshoppers after a heavy rain.

Check the patches of gibber along the access road to the Homestead. Gibberbirds and Banded Whitefaces have been recorded there. Patches of eremophila are also worth inspecting, especially when flowering. They are visited by White-fronted Honeyeaters, Spiny-cheeked Honeyeaters, Black Honeyeaters, Pied Honeyeaters, Singing Honeyeaters, White-plumed Honeyeaters, Yellow-throated Miners and Masked Woodswallows. Check the samphire patches for Orange Chats.

Another good habitat are the creeklines with mulga. The rare Grey Honeyeaters are occasionally reported from there. Search for Bourke's Parrots and Ground Cuckoo-shrikes. Other birds include Tree Martin, Orange Chat, Crimson Chat, White-winged Triller, Red-backed Kingfisher, Little Crow, Red-browed Pardalote, Pied Butcherbird, Mistletoebird and Zebra Finch.

Male Orange Chat

Raptors give the biggest joy to a birder along the road and around the property. Sixteen species are on the site list including the rarest finds such as Grey Falcon, Black Falcon and Letter-winged Kite. The latter breed at the property in wet years when there is abundance of native rats. You should also come across Spotted Harrier, Swamp Harrier, Black-breasted Buzzard, Wedge-tailed Eagle, Whistling Kite, Black Kite and Brown Falcon.

The lowland around the Homestead turns in the rainy years into a large swamp that attract large numbers of waterbirds and waders including Grey Teals, Pink-eared Ducks, Hoary-headed Grebes, Australian Gull-billed Terns, Whiskered Terns, White-necked Herons, Banded Lapwings, Red-necked Avocets and Pied Stilts. Many will be breeding. At such times, Eastern Grass Owls are seen, hunting over the swamp.

When driving on Old Andado Tk, stop at the GPS coordinates of 25°15’54”S and 135°24’10”E, in the area of parallel sand dunes with swales in between. Eyrean Grasswren can be found on the dunes. Also, flocks of Banded Whitefaces have been observed foraging atop the dunes. In the swales, look for Inland Dotterel, Little Button-quail, Chiming Wedgebill, Cinnamon Quail-thrush, White-winged Fairy-wren, Black-faced Woodswallow, Budgerigar and Brown Falcon. Occasionally, Flock Bronzewings can be found near the track.

Henbury Meteorites CR

This interesting reserve, located 145km southwest of Alice Springs, preserves the site of 12 craters ranging from 7 to 180m in diameter. They were formed by fragmented meteorites that hit the Earth surface. It happened very recently, about 4,700 years ago, when the area was populated. The story of a fiery devil running away from the sun is still repeated in the local folklore. Aboriginal people still hold a tabu over drinking rainwater from the craters. It would have been full of heavy metals at the beginning. Over 500kg of meteorite fragments were found in the previous century, with the biggest piece weighing 100kg.

To get there, turn off Stuart Hwy (A87) 132km south of Alice Springs onto Ernest Giles Rd. It is well signposted. Continue west for 8km. Turn north onto Henbury Craters Tourist Access and drive 5km to the site entrance. The access is on a good gravel track but it can become impassable after the rains.

A picnic area is provided in the reserve, with shaded picnic tables, toilets and barbecues. There is also a small camping area adjacent to the carpark and a self-guided, short walking track along a crater. Searching for and collecting meteorite fragments is illegal these days and stiff fines apply. Further information with a site map can be downloaded here:
https://nt.gov.au/__data/assets/pdf_file/0014/200039/henbury-meteorites-conservation-reserve-fact-sheet-and-map.pdf.

About 70 bird species have been recorded in the Henbury Meteorites Conservation Reserve. **Key species** are Cinnamon Quail-thrush, Ground Cuckoo-shrike, Bourke's Parrot, Mulga Parrot and Pied Honeyeater. Other birds of interest include Major Mitchell's Cockatoo, Australian Ringneck, Western Bowerbird, White-browed Babbler, Southern Whiteface, Hooded Robin, White-backed Swallow, Spotted Harrier and Black-shouldered Kite. Rarities include White-fronted Honeyeater, Black Honeyeater, Slaty-backed Thornbill and Black-breasted Buzzard.

This is a good place to look for Cinnamon Quail-thrushes. Search for them inside the gates, foraging in the open on the field of gravel. Check the vegetated wash at the northeastern end of the fenced area. The quail-thrushes are surprisingly tame here.

Male Cinnamon Quail-thrush

Australian Hobbies are nesting on site and are often seen flying over the area. Walk to the crater wall, looking for Ground Cuckoo-shrike, Mulga Parrot, Crimson Chat, Australasian Pipit, Pied Honeyeater, Singing Honeyeater and Black-shouldered Kite.

Rainbow Valley CR

This small (250ha), beautiful reserve is located about 100km south of Alice Springs. The reserve protects a large, colourful sandstone bluff. Sandstone layers in the bluff resemble rainbow stripes; the place is popular with photo-takers who often snatch spectacular shots here. At the base of the bluff are sand dunes covered with cane grass and spinifex, with scattered clusters of grevillea and eremophila bushes. Mulga trees grow close to the rock, while desert oaks occur on the eastern side of the reserve.

To get there, drive 75km south from Alice Springs on Stuart Hwy (A87). Turn east onto a well signposted Rainbow Valley track, a 22km dirt road with sections of terrible corrugations and deep sand. A 4WD vehicle is a must. Camping is allowed in two designated areas only. Facilities include gas barbecues, fire pits, picnic tables and toilets. There are two short, easy walking tracks: 1km circular Mushroom Rock Walk and 1.6km circular Claypan Walk. The latter meanders along the edge of a mostly dry claypan, with several viewing platforms allowing views over the valley and the bluff. Further information and a site map can be downloaded here:

https://nt.gov.au/__data/assets/pdf_file/0013/200047/rainbow-valley-conservation-reserve-fact-sheet-and-map.pdf.

About 100 bird species have been recorded in the Rainbow Valley Conservation Reserve. **Key species** are Pied Honeyeater, Black Honeyeater, Cinnamon Quail-thrush, Bourke's Parrot, Orange Chat, Major Mitchell's Cockatoo, Little Woodswallow and Peregrine Falcon. Other birds of interest include Budgerigar, Mulga Parrot, Hooded Robin, Rainbow Bee-eater, Singing Honeyeater, White-winged Fairy-wren, Chiming Wedgebill, Fairy Martin, Southern Whiteface, Crimson Chat, Red-browed Pardalote and White-backed Swallow. Rarities include Scarlet-chested Parrot, Grey Falcon, Australian Bustard, Inland Dotterel, Banded Whiteface, White-fronted Honeyeater and Red-tailed Black-Cockatoo.

Migratory Black and Pied Honeyeaters breed in this reserve, utilising the flowering grevilleas and eremophilas.

Female Pied Honeyeater

Along the access road, search for Cinnamon Quail-thrush, Banded Whiteface and Inland Dotterel. Around the camping areas, Chiming Wedgebills are often singing. Look also for Purple-backed Fairy-wren, White-winged Fairy-wren, Chestnut-rumped Thornbill and Hooded Robin.

On the Mushroom Rock Walk, you'll see large breeding colonies of Fairy Martins on the upper rock walls. Claypan Walk may occasionally produce foraging Crimson Chats and Orange Chats. Other birds along this walk include Singing Honeyeater,

Spiny-cheeked Honeyeater, Masked Woodswallow, Crested Bellbird, Red-capped Robin and Red-backed Kingfisher.

On the dunes, search for White-winged Fairy-wrens and Redthroats (rare).

Nankeen Kestrels can nearly always be found perching on the bluff. Southern Whitefaces and Budgerigars come to drink the water pooling in the rocky hollows.

Stuart Hwy South of Alice Springs

This approximately 300km section of the main throughfare has several birding spots worth checking.

Typical landscape along Stuart Highway

Stuart Hwy at 23°47'27''S and 133°52'40''E

This small patch of mulga woodland is known to the local birders as Corner Reserve. It is located at the corner of Stuart Hwy and Roger Vale Dr, which is the road leading the Alice Springs Airport.

This site is a popular location to tick off White-browed Treecreeper and Redthroat, just after you land at the airport. If you are in luck, Grey Honeyeater can also be present. Other birds here include Budgerigar, Spinifex Pigeon, Splendid Fairy-wren, White-winged Fairy-wren, Chestnut-rumped Thornbill, Hooded Robin, Red-capped Robin, Grey-crowned Babbler and Grey Butcherbird.

The rarities at this site include Ground Cuckoo-shrike, Banded Lapwing, Black-eared Cuckoo and Spotted Harrier.

Stuart Hwy at 23°53'23''S and 133°46'47''E

This site is a patch of mulga on the eastern side of the highway, located approximately 20km south of Alice Springs. Bourke's Parrots and White-browed Treecreepers have been recorded here. Look also for Mulga Parrot, Hooded Robin, Crested Bellbird and Black-breasted Buzzard.

There are a couple of records of Princess Parrot and Grey Honeyeater from this location.

Stuart Hwy at 23°57'08''S and 133°43'10''E

This is mulga woodland on both sides off the highway, located some 40km south of Alice Springs. White-browed Treecreeper, Slaty-backed Thornbill and Black-breasted Buzzard were recorded here. Other birds in the area include Crimson Chat, Mulga Parrot, Major Mitchell's Cockatoo, Hooded Robin and Little Eagle.

Stuarts Well Roadhouse

This roadhouse, also known as Jims Place, is located 90km south of Alice Springs. GPS coordinates are 24°20'16''S and 133°27'49''E. It is a good rest stop after exploring the Henbury meteorite site or Rainbow Valley. The charming Outback roadhouse offers fuel, a variety of accommodation, mini-shop, restaurant and pub. It is also next door to a camel farm where a camel safari can be arranged. The pub may seem quiet during the day, but it turns into an entertainment hub at night. Where else would see a singing and piano playing dingo (called Dinki); he was so famous before it retired that was even featuring as a question of the Trivial Pursuit.

Birding can be done 1-2km both ways along the highway, in the campground and along the walk to the hills.

About 100 bird species have been recorded around the Stuarts Well Roadhouse. **Key species** are Bourke's Parrot, Major Mitchell's Cockatoo, Pied Honeyeater, White-fronted Honeyeater, Spinifex Pigeon, Chiming Wedgebill and Barn Owl. Other birds of interest include White-backed Swallow, Rainbow Bee-eater, Rufous Songlark, Masked Woodswallow, Red-tailed Black-Cockatoo, Red-backed Kingfisher, White-browed Babbler, Crested Bellbird, Crimson Chat, Varied Sittella and Wedge-tailed Eagle. Rarities include Australian Bustard, Painted Finch and Little Eagle.

Pied Honeyeaters regularly nest in this area. Australian Bustards can occasionally be seen in the green lucerne fields; their absolute favourite fodder. In the vegetation along the highway, Bourke's Parrot, Mulga Parrot and Australian Ringneck are recorded occasionally.

The campground may produce Hooded Robin, Western Bowerbird, Little Corella, Yellow-throated Miner, Crested Pigeon, Rufous Songlark and Red-backed Kingfisher. Painted Finches and Zebra Finches appear regularly to drink from the sprinklers. At night, Barn Owls are calling. On the walk to the hills, you may encounter Brown Songlark, White-backed Swallow, Striated Pardalote, Chiming Wedgebill, Little Crow, Budgerigar and Varied Sittella.

Male Hooded Robin

Cannonball Run Monument

The site is located on Stuart Hwy, 97km south of Alice Springs. GPS coordinates are 24°22'25''S and 133°25'11''E. A small monument commemorates four people who died here in the tragic accident in 1994 during the inaugural NT Cannonball Run car race. The Japanese team mowed down two judges and perished themselves.

The monument's carpark is surrounded by vast gibberland with patches of small bushes. Bourke's Parrots are regularly recorded, sometimes feeding at the edge of the carpark. It is also a good spot for Cinnamon Quail-thrush, Inland Dotterel, Chiming Wedgebill, White-winged Fairy-wren and White-backed Swallow. Banded Whiteface is sighted occasionally.

Other birds include Budgerigar, Major Mitchell's Cockatoo, Crimson Chat, Redthroat, Little Button-quail, Black-breasted Buzzard and Little Eagle.

Finke River Bridge Rest Area

The site is located 125km south of Alice Springs. GPS coordinates are 24°33'04''S and 133°14'20''E. Facilities include toilets, shaded picnic tables and fire pits. The riverbed is worth exploring, especially if you are lucky to get there after the rain. The water attracts hundreds of birds. Look for Budgerigars, Cockatiels, Mulga Parrots and Diamond Doves. Search also for Black-fronted Dotterels; they will be feeding at the water edge. Also recorded here in wet years are Sharp-tailed Sandpiper, Common Greenshank, Yellow-billed Spoonbill, Grey Teal and Pacific Black Duck. Occasionally, a single Australian Pelican may land on the water.

You can also walk along obscure 'tracks' around the rest area. These may produce Rufous Songlarks (calling from the tops of small trees), Weebills, Red-browed Pardalotes, White-winged Fairy-wrens, Splendid Fairy-wrens, Black-shouldered Kites and Whistling Kites.

Around the rest area, look for Grey-crowned Babblers, Red-capped Robins and Little Crows. The site is good for raptors, with Little Eagle recorded several times. You also have a chance to see Black-breasted Buzzard, Brown Falcon and Wedge-tailed Eagle.

Grey-crowned Babbler

Desert Oaks Rest Area

Desert Oaks site is located on the western side of the road 170km south of Alice Springs and 33km north of Erldunda Roadhouse. GPS coordinates are 24°54'18''S and 133°11'46''E. Stands of desert oaks and mulga grow around the rest area. An old, obscure track runs west from there. Along that track, look for Slaty-backed Thornbill, Inland Thornbill, White-winged Triller, Splendid Fairy-wren, White-winged Fairy-wren, White-backed Swallow and Nankeen Kestrel. Occasionally, Little Eagle and Grey Falcon were sighted in this location.

A family of Tawny Frogmouths often rest in trees at Desert Oaks. Little Crows are nesting there. Look also for Pallid Cuckoo, Chiming Wedgebill, Mulga Parrot, Crested Pigeon, Southern Whiteface, Banded Whiteface and Major Mitchell's Cockatoo.

Stuart Hwy at 25°00'39''S and 133°11'59''E

This fantastic birding spot may offer you a chance of sighting the rare Banded Whiteface. It is located 21km north of Erldunda Roadhouse. There are extensive areas of gibberland here, with scattered patches of low shrubland. Further away from Stuart Hwy, on both sides of the road, are stands of mulga and eremophila mixed with corkwood.

About 80 bird species have been recorded in this Stuart Hwy location. **Key species** are Banded Whiteface, Inland Dotterel, Banded Lapwing, Cinnamon Quail-thrush, Chiming Wedgebill, Bourke's Parrot, Black Honeyeater and Pied Honeyeater. Other birds of interest include Southern Whiteface, White-browed Babbler, Crested Bellbird, Inland Thornbill, White-winged Fairy-wren, Crimson Chat, Orange Chat, Major Mitchell's Cockatoo and Little Button-quail. Rarities include Flock Bronzewing, Redthroat and White-fronted Honeyeater.

The star attraction of the site is Banded Whiteface. The birds favour stony areas with sparse low bushes. They may be found feeding with mixed flocks of Zebra Finches, Yellow-rumped Thornbills and Southern Whitefaces. Another sought-after species here is Inland Dotterel. In some years, they are spotted in the gibberland in good numbers. Search also for Cinnamon Quail-thrushes. They favour rocky ground in the open, between stands of mulga or eremophila.

Grassy areas are good places to look for Budgerigar, Brown Songlark, Rufous Songlark, Australasian Pipit, Banded Lapwing and Little Button-quail.

Small flocks of Bourke's Parrots are occasionally found among the mulga. Other birds in this habitat include Chestnut-rumped Thornbill, Red-capped Robin, White-browed Babbler, Chiming Wedgebill, Mulga Parrot, Splendid Fairy-wren, Western Gerygone and Weebill.

Nomadic honeyeaters (such as Pied Honeyeater, Black Honeyeater and White-fronted Honeyeater) usually appear in winter and spring to feed on the eremophila blossoms.

Other birds observed in this section of Stuart Hwy include Grey Butcherbird, Black-faced Woodswallow, Torresian Crow, Grey-headed Honeyeater, Brown Honeyeater and Rufous Whistler. Fourteen raptor species on the birdlist include Wedge-tailed Eagle, Little Eagle, Brown Falcon, Black-breasted Buzzard, Nankeen Kestrel and Spotted Harrier.

Erldunda Roadhouse

This is an important roadhouse, strategically located at the junction of Stuart Hwy (A87) and Lasseter Hwy (A4) about 200km south of Alice Springs. Besides fuel, it offers camping, hotel, pub, restaurant and general store. Three small wastewater ponds located at the northern border of the property are a magnet for birds. Next to the campground is a paddock with kept Emus. Some of their wild brethren can often be found on the outside of the enclosure.

Plenty of parrots utilise the roadhouse grounds including a large flock of Galahs. There are also Major Mitchell's Cockatoos and Australian Ringnecks. They regularly roost during the night on trees behind the roadhouse. Torresian Crows, Little Crows and Australian Ravens are here together, just to give you a headache identifying them. You can also expect to find Grey Butcherbird, Pied Butcherbird, Rufous Whistler, Western Bowerbird, White-breasted Woodswallow, Singing Honeyeater, Yellow-throated Miner, Rainbow Bee-eater, Pallid Cuckoo and Zebra Finch. Occasional recordings at Erldunda Roadhouse include White-backed Swallow, Black Honeyeater, Pied Honeyeater and Crimson Chat.

Male Crimson Chat

Sixteen species of raptors have been reported from the area. Resident species are Black Kite, Whistling Kite and Australian Hobby. Among infrequent findings are Little Eagle, Black-breasted Buzzard, Spotted Harrier and Peregrine Falcon. Rare species that were sighted here include Common Starling and Pheasant Coucal.

Stuart Hwy at 25°40'02''S and 133°13'58''E

The site is located 20km north of Kulgera Roadhouse. Look for Cinnamon Quail-thrush in this area. Search through the sparse low bushes near the highway. You may also be lucky to sight Bourke's Parrot, Inland Dotterel, Orange Chat or Banded Whiteface. Other birds here include White-winged Fairy-wren, Brown Songlark, Pallid Cuckoo, Grey-headed Honeyeater, Crested Bellbird and Black-faced Woodswallow.

Kulgera Roadhouse

Kulgera Roadhouse is located 275km south of Alice Springs and 21km north od SA border. It features a beautiful Outback pub that the owners advertise as 'the first and last pub in the Northern Territory' and 'the most central pub in Australia'. The roadhouse also provides a restaurant, accommodation, fuel and basic supplies in a general store.

A resident pair of Australian Hobbies have their nest on a communication tower. Birds around the campground include White-backed Swallow, Yellow-throated Miner, Rainbow Bee-eater, Little Crow, White-winged Fairy-wren, Purple-backed Fairy-wren, Little Corella and Australian Magpie. On one occasion when we stopped at the roadhouse, a flock of Emus was calmly walking past the fuel pumps among the refuelling cars.

Search for Banded Whiteface, White-winged Triller, Crested Bellbird, Chiming Wedgebill, Cockatiel and Budgerigar at the surrounding farm.

Rarer birds recorded at the Kulgera Roadhouse include Square-tailed Kite, Peregrine Falcon, Australian Bustard, Banded Lapwing, Welcome Swallow and Australian Pratincoles.

Lasseter Highway

Lasseter Hwy (A4) is a fully sealed, 245km-long thoroughfare that connects the iconic Australian tourist destinations, Kata Tjuta and Uluru, with Stuart Hwy at Erldunda. It is worth making several short stops on your way there; you'll never know what you may find. Raptors may prove to be particularly rewarding; even the rare Black-breasted Buzzard and Little Eagle are often reported.

Lasseter Hwy at 25°11'28''S and 132°43'34''E

This spot is located 5km east of the Mt Ebenezer Roadhouse ruins and approximately 54km from Erldunda Roadhouse. A small dam is situated on the northern side of the highway, connected to it with an obscure short track. Parrots flock there for a drink of water, with Red-tailed Black-Cockatoos the most spectacular among them. A few Major Mitchell's Cockatoos and Mulga Parrots usually hang around with them.

Search for Banded Lapwing and Black-fronted Dotterel around the water. Bush birds in the area include Slaty-backed Thornbill, Inland Thornbill, Rainbow Bee-eater, Cockatiel, Black-faced Woodswallow, Brown Songlark and Common Bronzewing. Grey Falcon was recorded a couple of times. Other raptors include Black-shouldered Kite, Brown Falcon, Whistling Kite and Black-breasted Buzzard.

Mt Ebenezer Roadhouse Ruins

The ruins of the abandoned Mt Ebenezer Roadhouse are located approximately 50km west of Erldunda Roadhouse. It was a very well-situated, beautiful place, where we stayed overnight during our first trip to Uluru. It was sadly closed down in 2012, and today only devastated remains of a couple of buildings are still standing, surrounded by a few large trees and stands of bushes. These are eagerly used by various birds for roosting and nesting in this nearly treeless plain. Parrots, mostly Galahs, Little Corellas and Red-tailed Black-Cockatoos, like roosting on the leafless treetops. Galahs shine like baubles in the setting sun. Bushes are filled with huge nests of Zebra Finches.

Chiming Wedgebill are singing around. Look for a Black-shouldered Kite's nest nearby. Other birds in the area include Hooded Robin, Singing Honeyeater, Pallid Cuckoo, Red-backed Kingfisher, Masked Woodswallow, Black Honeyeater (rare) and Wedge-tailed Eagle.

Wedge-tailed Eagle

Kernot Range Rest Area

This rest area is located at the GPS position of 25°10'37''S and 132°15'06''E, 7km east of the Luritja Rd (3) turnoff. It is a large free campsite, surrounded by dense bushes and grassland. This spot is good for parrots; regularly seen here are Major Mitchell's Cockatoo, Mulga Parrot, Australian Ringneck, Budgerigar and Cockatiel. Search for Little Button-quails, often seen at the grass edge.

Other birds here include Crimson Chat, Rufous Songlark, Crested Bellbird, Little Woodswallow, Black-faced Woodswallow, White-winged Triller and Australian Raven. Black-breasted Buzzard and Wedge-tailed Eagle have also been recorded.

Lasseter Hwy at 25°10'19''S and 132°10'48''E

This spot marks the intersection with Luritja Rd (3). Search for Bourke's Parrots, reported from this area several times. If you miss out, your consolation prize may be a flock of Major Mitchell's Cockatoo, Mulga Parrots or Budgerigars.

In the bushes, look also for Redthroat, Slaty-backed Thornbill, Splendid Fairy-wren, Crimson Chat, Red-capped Robin and White-winged Triller. If you are lucky, you may be rewarded with a sight of Australian Bustard or Emu walking through the grassland. An occasional raptor may include Little Eagle, Spotted Harrier or Black-breasted Buzzard.

Lasseter Hwy at 25°20'54''S and 131°51'14''E

This site is located 10km east of the Curtin Springs Roadhouse. A small dam can be found 600m north of the highway, accessed by a track which starts at the GPS location of 25°20'51''S and 13°50'40''E. Observations are done from a distance, at the farm fence. Waterbirds may be difficult to identify without a scope. Species reported from the dam include Freckled Duck, Glossy Ibis, Australian Wood Duck, Pink-eared Duck, Pied Stilt and White-necked Heron. This is a nesting site of White-backed Swallows, and they are regularly found here.

There would be plenty of Diamond Doves, Budgerigars and Zebra Finches coming to quench their thirst. Other birds in the area include Chiming Wedgebill, Red-backed Kingfisher, Purple-backed Fairy-wren, Rufous Songlark, Black-shouldered Kite, Wedge-tailed Eagle and an occasional Peregrine Falcon or Black-breasted Buzzard.

Curtin Springs Station

Curtin Springs Roadhouse is located on the Lasseter Hwy (4) 84km east of Uluru on the 416,000ha (1 million acres) pastoral property. Seen in the distance, the majestic Mt Conner dominates the stunning landscape. The mountain is also called the 'false Uluru' as its shape often fools the first-time visitors, convinced that they just had the first glimpse of the world-famous landmark.

Curtin Springs is both a working cattle station and an incredible tourist destination, just 85km away from Yulara, the gateway to Uluru. The roadhouse offers fuel and a variety of accommodation. There is a restaurant and a pub, too. Guided walks on the Station and safari tours on desert dunes to the Salt Lakes and to Mt Conner can be arranged. If the Yulara Resort is too crowded, this is an excellent alternative.

Mt Conner seen from Lasseter Hwy

Parrots and raptors draw the birdwatchers to the Station. Major Mitchell's Cockatoos are visible through the area, and particularly in the trees around the roadhouse. Common species also include Cockatiel, Budgerigar, Mulga Parrot and Little Corella. There are also records of Bourke's Parrot and Princess Parrot from the Station. Among the fourteen species of raptors observed here, the star attractions are Black-breasted Buzzard, Little Eagle and Black Falcon. Even Grey Falcon has sometimes been sighted.

The flowering bushes welcome nomadic honeyeaters (Black Honeyeater, Pied Honeyeater and White-fronted Honeyeater). Orange Chats and Oriental Plovers can sometimes be seen near the Salt Lakes.

Other birds at the Station include Cinnamon Quail-thrush, Brown Songlark, White-browed Babbler, White-backed Swallow, Splendid Fairy-wren, Red-capped Robin, Crimson Chat, Emu and Southern Whiteface.

Sandy View Rest Area

This spot is located 29km east of the Yulara turnoff at GPS coordinates of 25°13'14''S and 131°13'42''E. This is one of the places where you can see Uluru for the first time.

A camping ground is located off the rest area. Check the surrounding dunes covered with old spinifex. Rufous Grasswrens were sighted there several times. Banded Whitefaces come to feed among the sparse vegetation at the campground.

Major Mitchell's Cockatoos are regularly seen in the area. Spotted Harrier may be observed when hunting over the dunes. Other birds include White-winged Fairy-wren, Splendid Fairy-wren, Singing Honeyeater, Crimson Chat, Jacky Winter, Crested Bellbird, White-winged Triller and Black-breasted Buzzard.

Lasseter Hwy at 25°13'21''S and 131°05'00''E

This site is located 12km east of the Yulara turnoff. This is the place to look for Rufous Grasswren among the dunes near the highway. Look also for White-backed Swallow, Little Button-quail, Inland Thornbill, Splendid Fairy-wren, Red-capped Robin and Black-breasted Buzzard. Rarer species in the area include Little Eagle, Cinnamon Quail-thrush, Redthroat, Emu, Pied Honeyeater and White-fronted Honeyeater.

Yulara

The tourist township of Yulara (pop. about 1,000 staff plus up to 250,000 visitors per year) is located outside the Uluru-Kata Tjuta National Park, about 15km from the Park's entry station. Most of the township is made up by the Ayers Rock Resort, currently an Aboriginal-owned enterprise. Accommodation is also provided in a large caravan park. Yulara offers restaurants, shops, fuel, art galleries and conference facilities. There is an airport on site, car hire and various tour operations, including camel rides.

The township is surrounded by spinifex-covered dunes, with scattered stands of low bushland and desert oaks. Several lookouts and viewing points allow a view of Uluru in the distance. A network of connecting walking tracks run in the dunes outside the township. These can be very productive as birding walks. Also, be on the lookout for the watering sprinklers and active overflow from pumps and facilities in Yulara - they compellingly attract birdlife in this bone-dry country.

Over 150 bird species have been recorded in the Yulara area. **Key species** are Rufous Grasswren, Princess Parrot, Banded Whiteface, Bourke's Parrot, Redthroat and White-fronted Honeyeater. Other birds of interest include Major Mitchell's Cockatoo, Mulga Parrot, Australian Ringneck, Red-backed Kingfisher, White-backed Swallow, Masked Woodswallow, White-browed Babbler, Crimson Chat, Crested Bellbird, Purple-backed Fairy-wren, Little Eagle and Black-breasted Buzzard. Rarities include Ground Cuckoo-shrike, Slaty-backed Thornbill, White-browed Woodswallow, Fork-tailed Swift, Black Honeyeater and Letter-winged Kite.

Australian Ringneck (Port Lincoln ssp.)

The rare Rufous Grasswren is one of the most sought-after species in the area. It is probably easier to find around Yulara than in the Uluru-Kata Tjuta National Park. The species favours mature spinifex growing on sand dunes; the habitat typical to Yulara. Having said that, the elusive, secretive Rufous Grasswren is notoriously difficult to find, so you'll need a lot of patience walking through the spinifex, preferably in the early morning. Listed below in the descending priority order are recommended search locations for Rufous Grasswren:

- Dunefield east of Yulara Airport (the most productive site) along Coote Rd off Lasseter Hwy.
- Dunes along Lasseter Hwy at 25°13'24''S and 130°59'47''E. Search spinifex on the northern side of the road, starting approximately 400m east from the Red Centre Way information bay.
- Dunes at 25°13'47''S and 130°59'12''E. Search the dunes at the corner of Lasseter Hwy and Harney Pl, in particular near the Yulara Power Station.
- Dunes near the Ayers Rock Campground at 25°12'55''S and 130°59'15''E.

Banded Whiteface is another coveted species found in Yulara. Look for them in the similar sites to Rufous Grasswren's, but Banded Whiteface prefers a slightly different habitat of sparse low shrubs with patches of bare ground, where it likes foraging. They are often found in areas recovering after the fires. Banded Whiteface is much easier to spot due it its habit of landing on bushes or on fences. Listed below in the descending priority order are recommended search locations for Banded Whiteface:

- Dunefield east of Yulara Airport (the most productive site) along Coote Rd off Lasseter Hwy;
- Yulara WTP at 25°14'37''S and 130°58'30''E;
- 5km east of Yulara turnoff at 25°13'03''S and 131°01'10''E;
- 10km east of Yulara turnoff at 25°13'26''S and 131°04'16''E.

The third valuable species in Yulara is the extremely rare Princess Parrot. Most recently, a small flock appeared in the area in October 2023 and stayed for several weeks, visiting sprinklers and other pooling water, flying over the township and roosting in the desert oaks.

Dunefields east of Yulara Airport

These dunefields are the most reliable site for Rufous Grasswren in the area. To get there, take Coote Rd off Lasseter Hwy (A4) north of Yulara. The most common advice is to explore the dunes on the eastern side of Coote Rd. Actually, after a long search, we got them on the other side of the road, on a dune slope.

About 70 bird species have been recorded along Coote Rd. **Key species** are Rufous Grasswren, Banded Whiteface, Little Eagle, White-fronted Honeyeater and Chiming Wedgebill. Other birds of interest include Budgerigar, Major Mitchell's Cockatoo, Little Button-quail, White-winged Fairy-wren, Purple-backed Fairy-wren, Masked Woodswallow, White-backed Swallow, Rufous Songlark, Red-backed Kingfisher and Black-shouldered Kite. Rarities include Princess Parrot, Grey Honeyeater, Black Honeyeater and Swamp Harrier.

The Rufous Grasswren site along Coote Road

During our visit, Budgerigars were everywhere, landing in the spinifex growing on the dunes. While searching for the grasswrens, we came across Banded Whiteface, Black-faced Woodswallow, Masked Woodswallow, Crimson Chat, Purple-backed Fairy-wren, Little Button-quail, Singing Honeyeater, Brown Songlark and Brown Falcon. We flushed Spotted Nightjar which was roosting on the ground.

Yulara Wastewater Treatment Plant

To get there, from Lasseter Hwy (A4) 300m north of the Yulara turnoff, turn west into an obscure track. After 500m you'll reach the WTP pond at the end of Mala Rd. If this shortcut is impassable after the rain, drive north on Lasseter Hwy for 2km, turn west into Giles St, then left into Mala Rd and drive to the end of this road to the WTP. The pond is fenced but gaps in the shrubbery enable to scan the water.

Banded Whitefaces come to drink here, often landing on the fence.

Many rarities have been reported from this spot, such as Buff-banded Rail, Freckled Duck, Wood Sandpiper, Common Sandpiper, Dusky Moorhen, Nankeen Night-Heron, Plumed Egret, Australian Bustard, Black Honeyeater and Welcome Swallow. Common wetland birds include Grey Teal, Pink-eared Duck, Black-tailed Native-hen, White-necked Heron, Australasian Grebe, Black-fronted Dotterel and Red-kneed Dotterel.

Australian Bustard

In the surrounding area, look for Masked Woodswallow, Little Button-quail, Rufous Songlark, Hooded Robin, White-backed Swallow, White-winged Fairy-wren, Emu, Little Eagle, Black-breasted Buzzard and Brown Goshawk.

Yulara Rubbish Tip

To get there, drive north on Lasseter Hwy for about 2km, turn west into Giles St, then left into Mala Rd and then right into Rubbish Dump Tk. The tip is at the end of this track. Redthroats are regularly found in low bushland around the rubbish tip.

The access track may yield White-backed Swallow, Red-capped Robin, Singing Honeyeater, Purple-backed Fairy-wren, Little Button-quail, Zebra Finch, Budgerigar, Nankeen Kestrel, Australian Hobby and occasionally Little Eagle. Bourke's Parrots are observed from time to time along the Rubbish Dump Track.

Dunes at 25°15'20"S and 130°59'21"E

This site is located behind the Uluru Camel Tours and Coach Campground. To get there, turn south as signposted from Yulara Dr into Napala Rd near the turnoff from Lasseter Hwy. Turn right into Kunia St and follow the signs to the Uluru Camel Tours. Take the track leading into the dunes behind the Camel Tours.

This is another spot to look for Rufous Grasswrens. Princess Parrots occasionally are reported from this area, most recently in 2019. Other rarer species sighted here include Black Honeyeater, Redthroat and Square-tailed Kite.

Red-capped Robins are visible around the site. Look also for White-winged Triller, Common Bronzewing, Inland Thornbill, Splendid Fairy-wren, White-winged Fairy-wren, Grey-headed Honeyeater, Masked Woodswallow and Little Button-quail. Regular sightings of Spotted Harrier occur in this area. Australian Owlet-nightjars are calling at night.

Check the Yulara Coach Campground and the surrounding bushland. Redthroat and Little Eagle were reported from there several times. More commonly recorded are Australian Ringneck, Singing Honeyeater, Western Bowerbird, Rainbow Bee-eater, Black-faced Woodswallow and White-winged Fairy-wren. A family of White-browed Babblers may be foraging between the parked buses.

Yulara Caravan Park

Red-backed Kingfisher

This large caravan park with the separate camping area has a lot of trees and bushes that attract huge numbers of birds when in bloom. The grounds are framed by extensive sand dunes. Rufous Grasswren is sighted there from time to time. At the back of the caravan park is Naninga Lookout, easily accessible and perfect for admiring sunrises and sunsets over the Uluru rock. A small flock of Major Mitchell's

Cockatoos is resident in the caravan park; it was pure joy to watch their antics while resting by our caravan after a stint of intense birding.

Birds common around the caravan park include Diamond Dove, Budgerigar, Singing Honeyeater, Zebra Finch, Yellow-throated Miner, Western Bowerbird and Little Crow. You may also spot Red-backed Kingfisher, Grey-headed Honeyeater, Red-capped Robin, Hooded Robin, White-backed Swallow and Mistletoebird.

Raptors include Wedge-tailed Eagle, Whistling Kite and an occasional Little Eagle. At night, you may see or hear Southern Boobook or Spotted Nightjar. The latter favour roosting on the path leading to the Naninga Lookout.

Uluru-Kata Tjuta National Park

The Australian most famous National Park sprawls over 133,000ha and is UNESCO World Heritage-listed for its natural and cultural values. The Uluru rock (formerly Ayers Rock), one of the world's most striking landscapes, protrudes 348m over the surrounding Outback plain. The rock is located in the very middle of Australia. The Park also features Kata Tjuta (formerly The Olgas), situated 40km west of Uluru. These rocks rise 546m over the plain. There also Mt Conner, the last of the Big Three, located outside the National Park on the Curtin Springs Station, which is the tallest at 859m. This is that 'false Uluru' which you'd not miss to see on your way to Yulara. The locals also call Mt Conner the 'Fool-uru'.

In this arid country, the low mulga woodland with an understory of spinifex and small bushes dominates the landscape of the National Park. Stands of desert oaks are scattered across the spinifex-covered plains. River red gums line the usually dry creek beds. Patches of blue mallee and an extensive carpet of small shrubs grow on the slopes of sand dunes.

The Park is located 440km southwest of Alice Springs via Stuart Hwy (A87) and Lasseter Hwy (A4), sealed all the way. You can also fly to Yulara which has a small airport. It is called Ayers Rock Airport but also Connellan Airport or Yulara Airport. Regular flights schedule is serviced from Alice Springs. Directs flights are also offered four times a week from Sydney and a limited schedule from Brisbane. Car rental is available at the airport. Over the years, we took flights to Uluru from both Sydney and Brisbane and found them very convenient for people with little time to spare.

No camping is allowed in the National Park. An extensive range of accommodation is available in Yulara, 15km away (see above). For those without a car, there is a regular shuttle bus service around Uluru. Park facilities include the Cultural Centre with a café (if open), Aboriginal art galleries and a souvenir shop, carparks, sunset and sunrise viewing platforms, barbecues, drinking water stations, shaded picnic areas and toilets. There is also an excellent network of walking trails. Vehicular routes are all sealed. A good Visitor Guide with a site map can be downloaded here: https://parksaustralia.gov.au/uluru/pub/visitor-guide.pdf. You can also pick up a copy of this Visitor Guide and maps at the Cultural Centre, if open.

Over 180 bird species have been recorded in the Uluru-Kata Tjuta National Park. **Key species** are Rufous Grasswren, Banded Whiteface, Redthroat, Pied Honeyeater, White-fronted Honeyeater, Black Honeyeater, Little Woodswallow, Fairy Martin and Peregrine Falcon. Other birds of interest include Budgerigar, Crimson Chat, Black-eared Cuckoo, Grey-headed Honeyeater, Red-browed Pardalote, Red-capped Robin, Hooded Robin, Masked Woodswallow, Western Bowerbird, White-browed Babbler, Grey Butcherbird and White-winged Fairy-wren. Rarities include Princess Parrot, Red-necked Phalarope, Ground Cuckoo-shrike, Grey Honeyeater, Oriental Plover, Dusky Grasswren, Pictorella Mannikin, White-browed Treecreeper, Slaty-backed Thornbill, Orange Chat, Grey Falcon, Black Falcon, Square-tailed Kite and Letter-winged Kite.

Sunset Viewing Area

Uluru sunset with moonrise

The sunset viewing area for cars (there is also a separate viewing spot for tour buses) is a must stop to take the obligatory Uluru photo, with the setting sun behind you. The rock transforms in front of your eyes from pinkish to bright orange and then dark crimson, fading to brown. The sky photos at sunset come out magnificent, with an amazing mix of deep-coloured layers. And then the moon rises, turning the whole scene out of this world.

This is the best spot in the whole National Park to search for Rufous Grasswren. Just walk straight north from the Sunset carpark for about 500m and listen to their high-pitched calls. Be there very early in the morning or before the sunset to avoid the crowds. The birds have been occasionally observed scurrying through the carpark, even with people present.

Banded Whitefaces are sporadically recorded feeding at the edge of the carpark. Be also on the lookout for Redthroat and Slaty-backed Thornbill hiding in small bushes. In winter, large numbers of nomadic honeyeaters (Pied, Black and White-fronted Honeyeaters) are sometimes recorded in the flowering grevilleas. In some years, Little Button-quails are abundant in this spot.

Other birds found there include Budgerigar, Crimson Chat, Brown Songlark, Crested Bellbird, Masked Woodswallow, Hooded Robin and Black-shouldered Kite. When people desert the carpark after the sun is gone, Spotted Nightjar may be seen hawking insects over the area.

Cultural Centre

The Cultural Centre is located on a large roundabout near the Park Headquarters. It is a comfortable place to rest and have a bite. Bush around the Centre may produce Redthroat, Southern Whiteface and White-backed Swallow. A nagging pair of Australian Magpies is always there. Zebra Finches are nesting under the thatched roofs and in the surrounding small bushes.

If you follow a cultural tour path, the small bushes on your way may yield Splendid Fairy-wren, Chestnut-rumped Thornbill, Rufous Whistler, Western Gerygone, Red-capped Robin and Grey-headed Honeyeater. Raptors in the area include Australian Hobby, Brown Goshawk, Black-breasted Buzzard and Black-shouldered Kite.

Liru Walk

This 4km return walk winds through the shrubland and connects the Mala carpark with the Cultural Centre. You may come across some good birds along this walk such as Slaty-backed Thornbill, Banded Whiteface, Chiming Wedgebill, Redthroat and White-backed Swallow. Other birds include Black-eared Cuckoo, Horsfield's Bronze-cuckoo, Red-capped Robin, Hooded Robin, Grey-headed Honeyeater, Major Mitchell's Cockatoo, Jacky Winter, Masked Woodswallow and, when eremophilas are flowering, the nomadic honeyeaters.

Mutitjulu Waterhole

Kuniya Walk to the Mutitjulu Waterhole (with blooming bloodwood)

A 1km return Kuniya Walk runs from the carpark to the waterhole. The presence of permanent water means in this dry country that the area will be lush and full of wildlife. During the rains, a magical waterfall forms. We observed masses of small birds arrive in for a drink, mostly Zebra Finches, Grey-headed Honeyeaters, Brown Honeyeaters and Diamond Doves. Rainbow Bee-eaters were hunting insects over the water. Fairy Martins, nesting in large colonies on the rockfaces all over Uluru, were flying overhead. Tawny Frogmouths were roosting in a tree by the waterhole.

This is a good place for raptors, such as Nankeen Kestrel, Swamp Harrier, Peregrine Falcon, Wedge-tailed Eagle and Little Eagle. The resident pair of Black-breasted Buzzards nests in this area. In October 2023, Grey Falcon was recorded here.

Other birds in this spot include Redthroat, White-fronted Honeyeater, Major Mitchell's Cockatoo, Common Bronzewing, Red-browed Pardalote, Black-eared cuckoo, Masked Woodswallow, Little Woodswallow and Australian Owlet-nightjar.

Talinguru Sunrise Platform

This site, located to the southeast of the Uluru, provides dramatic views of the Uluru rock in the rising sun. A shorth path leads to the viewing platform from a large carpark. Birding starts along the 2km access road to the carpark. Rufous Grasswren was recorded here a few times. Other birds include White-winged Fairy-wren, Common Bronzewing, Spiny-cheeked Honeyeater, Singing Honeyeater, Black-faced Woodswallow, Crested Bellbird, Inland Thornbill, Pallid Cuckoo, Black-shouldered Kite and Nankeen Kestrel.

In the bushes around the carpark, look for Major Mitchell's Cockatoo, Australian Ringneck, Grey Butcherbird, White-browed Babbler and Singing Honeyeater. Little Button-quails and Brown Songlarks were observed along the path to the platform.

Raptors include Black-breasted Buzzard, Australian Hobby, Wedge-tailed Eagle and Peregrine Falcon. When we stopped at the carpark, we stumbled upon a Brown Goshawk that just caught a Yellow-throated Miner and started the plucking job.

Mala Walk

This 2km return walk is one of the most popular walks in the Park. It connects the Mala carpark with caves containing Aboriginal art in the Kantju Gorge.

Pallid Cuckoo

You'll be walking in the open mulga woodland and spinifex grassland in the shade of the Uluru mass. Starting in the carpark, look for Little Button-quails and Western Bowerbirds. Check the rock for the presence of Peregrine Falcons; a pair is resident in this area. Common birds along the walk include Rainbow Bee-eater, Budgerigar, Masked Woodswallow, Black-faced Woodswallow, Little Woodswallow, Black-faced Cuckoo-shrike, Singing Honeyeater and Grey-headed Honeyeater. Rarer birds include Hooded Robin, Chiming Wedgebill, Black-eared Cuckoo, Pallid Cuckoo and White-browed Babbler. There is an abundance of fairy-wrens: Splendid Fairy-wren, Purple-backed Fairy-wren and White-winged Fairy-wren. Sporadically seen are Redthroats and Ground Cuckoo-shrikes.

Sixteen raptor species are on the birdlist including Spotted Harrier, Black-breasted Buzzard, Little Eagle and Australian Hobby, as well as a few records of Grey Falcon.

Lungkata Walk

This 4km-long track runs next to the Uluru rock, connecting Kuniya Walk with the Mala carpark. This one of the most impressive sections of the whole Uluru Base Walk.

When at the Mala carpark, look at the multitude of Fairy Martin nests in the small depressions and overhangs in the rock, easily recognisable by the white trail of bird droppings. This is however present only in their breeding season. Nankeen Kestrels and Little Woodswallows may be perched high on the rockface.

The walk may produce Redthroat and Little Woodswallow. Other birds there include Sacred Kingfisher, Red-backed Kingfisher, Red-browed Pardalote, Hooded Robin, Jacky Winter and Yellow-rumped Thornbill. Black Falcon and Peregrine Falcon have also been recorded in the area.

Mutitjulu Sewage Ponds

Mutitjulu is a closed Aboriginal community of the Anangu people. Access is only with a permit or by permission of the local Anangu people. Mutitjulu Mala Rangers work in various capacities in the Park and may take you to this area if asked. The permit or permission must be organised in advance through the Mutitjulu Community Aboriginal Corporation (MCAC).

To get there, if you secured a permit, from Uluru Rd in the National Park turn into Petermann Rd (unsealed), then near the Police Station turn left into Mutitjulu Rd, and then left again into Sewage Ponds Access.

The ponds are known for several records of rare species such as Red-necked Phalarope (2017), Freckled Duck, Wood Sandpiper, Common Sandpiper, Oriental Plover, Yellow Chat, Black Honeyeater and Grey Falcon.

Common waterbirds on the ponds include Grey Teal, Pink-eared Duck, Hardhead, Australasian Grebe, Black-fronted Dotterel and Red-kneed Dotterel. Among the bush birds, you may get Crimson Chat, White-winged Triller, Major Mitchell's Cockatoo and Red-capped Robin.

The ponds are a magnet for raptors including Australian Hobby, Brown Goshawk and Black-breasted Buzzard.

Kata Tjuta - Walpa Gorge Walk

Entrance to the Walpa Gorge Walk

This spectacular gorge trek is approximately 2.6km long and runs through the Kata Tjuta's tallest domes.

Huge flocks of Zebra Finches, up to 5,000 birds, come to drink from a honeycomb of little rockholes that hold water. Among them are usually a few Painted Finches. Budgerigar flocks are not far behind the finches to approach the water.

Common birds along the walk include Spiny-cheeked Honeyeater, Singing Honeyeater, Grey-headed Honeyeater, White-plumed Honeyeater, Common Bronzewing, Peaceful Dove, Purple-backed Fairy-wren and Hooded Robin. Check the rock fig trees on the way; Western Bowerbirds feed in them when fruiting. In the gorge, look for Little Woodswallows and Peregrine Falcons flying along the cliffs. Other raptors in the area include Little Eagle, Black-breasted Buzzard, Wedge-tailed Eagle, Collared Sparrowhawk and Brown Falcon. From time to time, Grey Falcons are sighted along the walk.

Kata Tjuta - Valley of the Winds

This 3-4 hour-long circular walk starts from a large sunset-viewing carpark. Look there for Western Bowerbird and Hooded Robin.

The walk allows the visitors to immerse in the mysterious land of Kata Tjuta domes. The walk is rocky and steep, so quite difficult at places. At the start of the walk, the water holding rock depressions attract Zebra Finches and Painted Finches. Check the rocky slopes for Dusky Grasswren; this bird is rare in the Park but is sometimes sighted at the entrance to the valley. In this area, look also for raptors; they often roost in low shrubs near the water, intensely watching the flocks of small birds arriving for a drink. These may include Black-breasted Buzzard, Spotted Harrier, Brown Falcon, Brown Goshawk and Australian Hobby.

Brown Goshawk

Spinifex Pigeons are common along the walk. You may also come across Red-backed Kingfisher, Rufous Whistler, Crimson Chat, Varied Sittella, Redthroat, Australian Ringneck, Splendid Fairy-wren, Fairy Martin, Sacred Kingfisher and Rufous Songlark. Grey-headed Honeyeaters, Pied Honeyeaters and Singing Honeyeaters can be abundant at times. Also, the rare Grey Honeyeater and Black Honeyeaters have been reported from this area.

Watarrka (Kings Canyon) NP

This large, 105,200ha National Park is located at the western edge of the George Gill Ranges, 450km southwest of Alice Springs (if you take the easier, sealed route). The main feature of the National Park is Kings Canyon, boasting the spectacular red walls that rise a 100m above the surrounding landscape. Pockets of lush, green forest in the canyon have palms, ferns and cycads as well as river red gums, grevilleas and gidgee. This Outback oasis is often called the Garden of Eden.

Watarrka National Park can be reached by two routes:

- The best, 450km-long all sealed route is via Stuart Hwy, turning west into Lasseter Hwy (A4) and then north into Luritja Rd (3). This route will take you to Kings Canyon Resort.
- The alternative, 330km-long route is via Larapinta Dr through West McDonnell Ranges (sealed), followed by Mereenie Loop Rd (a dirt track, often terrible). A travel pass is required to drive on Mereenie Loop Rd, available from Alice Springs Visitor Centre, Standley Chasm shop, Kings Canyon Resort reception and Kings Creek Station reception. You cannot get it online.

The only accommodation options are:

- Kings Canyon Resort and Caravan Park, for bookings call (08) 8956 7446. Facilities include a restaurant, fuel station and shops.
- Kings Creek Station, for bookings call (08) 8956 7474.

There are several walking tracks in the park, including the 2.6km return Kings Creek Walk, 6km loop Kings Canyon Rim Walk and 2.6km return Kathleen Springs Walk. All these walks can be productive for birding. On your way to the canyon, you'll first get to a shady picnic site (Sunset Viewing Area) with shelters, barbecues and toilets, then to a spacious carpark with toilets just before a short path leading to the Rim Walk trailhead. Further information and a site map can be downloaded here: https://nt.gov.au/__data/assets/pdf_file/0011/200054/watarrka-national-park-fact-sheet-and-map.pdf.

Over 140 bird species have been recorded in the Kings Canyon National Park. **Key species** are Dusky Grasswren, Spinifex Pigeon, Painted Finch, White-fronted Honeyeater, Redthroat, Western Bowerbird, Little Woodswallow and Peregrine Falcon. Other birds of interest include Hooded Robin, Red-capped Robin, Major Mitchell's Cockatoo, Common Bronzewing, Red-browed Pardalote, Rufous Songlark, Grey-headed Honeyeater, Sacred Kingfisher, White-winged Fairy-wren and White-backed Swallow. Rarities include Ground Cuckoo-shrike, Princess Parrot, Grey Falcon, White-browed Treecreeper, Slaty-backed Thornbill and Banded Whiteface.

Kings Canyon Approach

First, you drive by the Sunset Viewing Picnic Area located 2km before the entrance to the Rim Walk. A carpark and several barbecues with shaded shelters are provided. We had a fantastic birding there. Hooded Robins were everywhere, singing in the bushes and intensely watching all humas in case they were preparing to throw some snags on a barbie. The birds are quite tame there. A pair of Mulga Parrots were sitting in a mulga bush and White-fronted Honeyeater was feeding in the mistletoe. Red-browed Pardalotes were attending to their chicks in the hollow dug out in a sandy heap. Zebra Finches were breeding in a large nest in a gum tree.

White-fronted Honeyeater

In the surrounding mulga, we came across Western Gerygone, Rufous Whistler, White-winged Triller, Budgerigar, Spiny-cheeked Honeyeater, Singing Honeyeater and Grey-headed Honeyeater.

Next, you arrive at a very spacious carpark with toilets at the entrance to the canyon. A waterhole is lining the south side of the carpark area. We found there a flock of Spinifex Pigeons busy drinking water and a large number of Magpie Larks feeding at the edges. We also got White-necked Heron, White-faced Heron and a couple of Black-fronted Dotterels. As we kept watching the waterhole, more flocks of various birds were arriving, such as Zebra Finches, Cockatiels, Budgerigars, Crested Pigeons and Diamond Doves. Among them were Painted Finches, Australian Ringnecks and a single Mulga Parrot. Honeyeaters were darting from the branches for a quick gulp of water. Among Yellow-throated Miners were a few Grey-fronted Honeyeaters and Grey-headed Honeyeaters.

In the surrounding trees and bushes, we got Little Woodswallow, Pied Butcherbird, Rainbow Bee-eater, Hooded Robin, Brown Falcon and Brown Goshawk. Common Bronzewings and Little Button-quails were feeding on the ground in the carpark.

Princess Parrots were reported from the waterhole in 2018.

Kings Creek Walk

This walk meanders on the side and inside the dry bed of Kings Creek. Half-way through the walk, you'll get to the Garden of Eden. It is a delightful area of cool waterhole with riverine vegetation. At the end of the walk, you'll find a platform facilitating spectacular views of canyon walls towering above you.

During our visit in March 2022, we met Spinifex Pigeons at the start of the track, hiding in the spinifex. Little Woodswallows and Peregrine Falcons were flying along the cliffs. A flock of Budgerigars and Zebra Finches landed on the ground to feed on the grasses. A male Common Bronzewing came out on the track and performed a whole singing and dancing routine in front of Alex, as if wooing her. We had to wait until he finished before we could continue on our way.

Male Common Bronzewing showing off on the Kings Creek Walk

A large puddle in the creek was visited by Painted Finches, Zebra Finches, Grey-headed Honeyeaters, White-plumed Honeyeaters and a single Grey Shrike-thrush. There was a lot of movement at a large rock fig at the creek edge as a dozen of Western Bowerbirds were gorging on the ripe figs. Red-browed Pardalotes were calling while gleaning through the leaves in the canopy of river red gums.

Other birds we encountered along this walk included Rainbow Bee-eater, Inland Thornbill, Rufous Whistler, Red-capped Robin, Brown Honeyeater, Red-backed Kingfisher and Pallid Cuckoo. We also got a glimpse of a Dusky Grasswren on a rocky slope cladded in spinifex, about 30m above the creek bed.

The Rim Walk

This 6km-long loop runs on the top of the canyon. It is regarded as one of the best walking tracks in Central Australia, but it is difficult. Even if you are fit and healthy, you are not allowed to attempt it when the air temperatures go over 35°C. Therefore, enter at the first light. A steep climb at the start is challenging, but you'll be rewarded with the most magical view once on top. That view was made world-famous in the Australian movie *Priscilla, Queen of the Desert*.

The Rim Walk trailhead

The star attraction of the walk is Dusky Grasswren, moderately common there in the areas of mature spinifex. Spinifex Pigeons are very common, perching on rocks or feeding in the spinifex. Small flocks of Painted Finches are often encountered along the walk.

When bushes are in bloom, expect to see a good variety of honeyeaters including Grey-headed Honeyeater, Grey-fronted Honeyeater, Golden-backed Honeyeater, Black Honeyeater, Pied Honeyeater, White-fronted Honeyeater, Brown Honeyeater, and White-plumed Honeyeater. Other birds on the walk include Hooded Robin, Red-capped Robin, Inland Thornbill, Chestnut-rumped Thornbill, Major Mitchell's Cockatoo, Australian Ringneck and Western Bowerbird.

Raptors can give you serious thrill during this walk. Look for Black-breasted Buzzard, Wedge-tailed Eagle, Little Eagle and Peregrine Falcon. Keep your eyes peeled for Grey Falcon; it was recorded there several times.

Kathleen Springs Walk

Kathleen Springs Walk is an easy stroll that leads to a small, spring-fed waterhole at the head of Kathleen Gorge. This is a cool, moist place to sit and enjoy in the heat of the Outback afternoon.

To get there, from Luritja Rd midway between Kings Creek Station and Kings Canyon Resort, turn east into a short, sealed road leading to a carpark, well signposted from Luritja Rd. The track, marked from the carpark, meanders down to the gorge and the waterhole.

We observed a couple of Emus walking past a flock of Straw-necked Ibises along the access road to the carpark. We also got Rufous Songlark, White-winged Fairy-wren, Black-faced Woodswallow, Crimson Chat and the raptors: Black-shouldered Kite and Nankeen Kestrel.

Birds along the walk included Spinifex Pigeon, Western Bowerbird, Hooded Robin, Varied Sittella, White-backed Swallow, Tree Martin, White-winged Triller, Grey-headed Honeyeater and Crested Bellbird. A pair of Black-breasted Buzzards nests in the area and we saw them circling overhead. Huge flocks of Budgerigars, Zebra Finches and Diamond Doves were arriving at the waterhole, panting from thirst. Peregrine Falcons and Little Woodswallows were flying along the creek.

Kings Canyon Resort

The resort is not part of the National Park but most of the visitors to the area stay there, as it offers a comfortable gateway for exploration of the Park. It is also worth paying attention to its birdlife. The rare Grey Honeyeaters have been sighted on the grounds several times.

When staying in the caravan park, we enjoyed Western Bowerbirds flying between the campers. Common birds on the grounds included White-plumed Honeyeater, Grey-headed Honeyeater, Yellow-throated Miner, White-winged Fairy-wren, Red-capped Robin, Zebra Finch, Rainbow Bee-eater and Brown Goshawk. There were plenty of parrot species including Major Mitchell's Cockatoo, Red-tailed Black-Cockatoo, Australian Ringneck, Galah and Cockatiel. The highlight of our stay was a pair of Ground Cuckoo-shrikes. During the night, Spotted Nightjar was flying near our the camp and Southern Boobook was calling. Also, a dingo was marauding around the campground, howling at night and sneaking in to steal the food.

It is worth to locate the resort's wastewater ponds, hidden behind the bushes on the eastern side of the campground. We got there Red-kneed Dotterel, Black-fronted Dotterel, White-necked Heron, Australasian Grebe, Pacific Black Duck and Hardhead. Hollows in a sandy levee were attended to by Red-browed Pardalotes. A small flock of Southern Whitefaces was feeding on the ground.

Luritja Road

The 165km-long Luritja Rd provides a comfortable, sealed access to the Watarrka National Park. While driving along the road, be on the lookout for good birds. In particular, there is a good chance to see Black-breasted Buzzard. We spotted two of them eating roadkill at the edge of the road. A few stops along the road are recommended below.

Salt Creek Rest Area

Desert oaks habitat

This spot is located 50km from the Lasseter Rd turnoff, at GPS coordinates of 24°46'22''S and 132°18'26''E. Beautiful desert oaks grow here. Desert oaks are the favourite daytime roosting places for Princess Parrots. Indeed, these parrots were recorded here several times. This site is anyway known for the surprising rarities. In 2022, Grey Falcon was observed. Other records include Bourke's Parrot, Little Eagle, Orange Chat, Banded Whiteface and Australian Bustard.

We stopped at this rest area for lunch and watched a flock of 15 Major Mitchell's Cockatoos roosting overhead in an oak tree. There two terrible youngsters with them, constantly and loudly screeching at their parents, pestering them for food. A pair of resident Australian Magpies were closely watching our picnic table, waiting for titbits. A male Red-capped Robin was shining bright-red from the branches. Varied Sittellas were climbing down the desert oak trunks. Flocks of Budgerigars and Zebra Finches were landing at the edge of spinifex.

Other birds recorded in this area include Common Bronzewing, Australian Ringneck, Crimson Chat, Mulga Parrot, Brown Falcon and Spotted Harrier.

Luritja Road at 24°38'39''S and 132°19'01''E

The site is located at the junction of Luritja Rd and Ernes Giles Rd. This is a good spot for raptors. Black-breasted Buzzard is found here regularly. Look also for Wedge-tailed Eagle, Little Eagle, Brown Goshawk and Australian Hobby. White-backed Swallows are sometimes seen flying here. You may also come across Australasian Pipit, Crimson Chat, Rufous Songlark, Southern Whiteface, Black-faced Woodswallow and Hooded Robin.

Luritja Road at 24°16'23''S and 131°32'42''E

Black-breasted Buzzard near a roadkill

This site is situated near the turnoff to Kings Canyon Access. Black-breasted Buzzards are resident here. Other birds in the area include Spinifex Pigeon, Hooded Robin, Grey-headed Honeyeater, Black Honeyeater, Brown Falcon and Little Eagle.

Mereenie Loop Road

This is the 197km-long, unsealed section of Red Centre Way which links Alice Springs with Kings Canyon. It begins at the western junction of Larapinta Dr and Namatjira Dr and ends a few kilometres north of Kings Canyon Resort where the sealed road commences. Mereenie is a terrible, corrugated track, for 4WD vehicles only. A permit is required beforehand to travel on this road as it runs through the Aboriginal land. The permit is only available from Alice Springs Visitor Centre, Standley Chasm shop, Kings Canyon Resort reception and Kings Creek Station reception.

The site is known for its sightings of the rare Princess Parrot. Small flocks can occasionally be seen feeding by the road or flying over. They breed in the hollows of river red gums growing along the dry creek beds. The Aboriginal land around Mereenie Loop is their stronghold, especially Haasts Bluff and Mt Winter. However, neither of these areas are accessible to the public. Birding records from the Mereenie Loop include:

- Morris Pass Lookout at 24°03'37"S and 131°24'35"E (start of the dirt road from the south);
- 35km north of Kings Canyon Resort;
- 1km from the intersection with Larapinta Dr at 23°57'46"S and 131°30'17"E.

Scarlet-chested Parrot, another rare species, was recorded in 2022 in the mallee-mulga habitat 2km north of the Santos gas plant. Bourke's Parrots are occasionally seen by the roadside, sometimes in good numbers. Other parrots are plentiful, especially Budgerigars and Cockatiels. You should also see some Major Mitchell's Cockatoos, Mulga Parrots and Australian Ringnecks.

The road passes through extensive areas of sand dunes, covered with spinifex mixed with eremophilas, grevilleas and upside-down shrubs. Winter brings blooms to the shrubbery, attracting hordes of honeyeaters including the rarer nomadic species.

Along Mereenie Loop, be on the lookout for raptors, especially Black-breasted Buzzard, Spotted Harrier and Little Eagle. Other birds reported from the road include Spinifexbird, Crested Bellbird, White-backed Swallow, Little Woodswallow, Masked Woodswallow, Splendid Fairy-wren, Hooded Robin, Western Gerygone, Little Button-quail, Brown Songlark, Rufous Songlark, Crimson Chat and Red-backed Kingfisher.

Further reading

Birdlife. *Working List of Australian Birds* v.4.3, dated October 2023

Les Christidis and Walter E. Boles, *Systematics and Taxonomy of Australian Birds*, CSIRO Publishing, 2008

Tim Dolby, Rohan Clarke (Ed.) *Finding Australian Birds*. CSIRO Publishing, 2014

Explore Australia's National Parks. Explore Australia Publishing, 2007

Andrew Geering, Lindsay Agnew, Sandra Harding. *Shorebirds of Australia*. CSIRO Publishing, 2007

Denise Lawungkurr Goodfellow. *Birds of Australia's Top End*. Reed New Holland, 2nd Ed, 2005

Nick Leseberg, Iain Campbell. *Birds & Animals of Australia's Top End*. Princeton University Press, 2015

Niven McCree, Richard Noske. *Birds of the Darwin Region*. CSIRO Publishing, 2015

Peter Menkhorst (Ed.) *The Australian Bird Guide*. CSIRO Publishing, 2017

Graham Pizzey and Frank Knight. *The Field Guide to Birds of Australia*, 9th Ed. Harper Collins, 2012

Richard Thomas, Sarah Thomas, David Andrew, Alan McBride. *The complete guide to finding the birds of Australia*. 2nd Ed. CSIRO Publishing, 2011

Bird index

Because of the numerous, recently introduced changes to taxonomy, which are recorded in Birdlife's *Working List of Australian Birds*, the latest version (v.4.3, dated October 2023) has been followed in this book for any changes. Otherwise, nomenclature follows *Systematics and Taxonomy of Australian Birds* by Les Christidis and Walter E. Boles, CSIRO Publishing, 2008.

Abundance scores and other symbols used in Bird Index:

A – abundant (seen daily in good numbers in suitable habitats and seasons or locally in large flocks)
C – common (frequently observed in suitable habitats and seasons)
M – moderately common (a reasonable chance to find)
U – uncommon (infrequently observed or hard to find)
R – rare (rarely present or very hard to find)
V – vagrant (less than 20 records)
I – introduced
S – summer migrant
W – winter migrant
P – passage migrant, autumn and spring
E – NT endemic

Genus	**English Name** *Latin Name*	Code	Where found
Apostlebird	**Apostlebird** *Struthidea cinerea*	M	Woodland, dry country, roadsides. Only southern Top End. Mataranka, Nitmiluk, Renner Springs, Victoria Hwy
Avocet	**Red-necked Avocet** *Recurvirostra novaehollandiae*	R	Wetlands, sewage ponds. Renner Springs, Corroboree Billabong, Tennant Creek WTP, Ilparpa Ponds.
Babbler	**Grey-crowned Babbler** *Pomatostomus temporalis*	M	Open forest, woodland, near watercourses. Casuarina CR, Kakadu, Pine Creek, Timber Creek, Elsey NP.
	White-browed Babbler *Pomatostomus superciliosus*	U	Dry woodland, mallee, open forest with dense understory. Only in South NT. Newhaven, Olive Pink BG, Alice Springs Desert Park, Kunoth Bore, Yulara, Uluru-Kata Tjuta NP.
Baza	**Pacific Baza** *Aviceda subscristata*	M	Monsoon forest, riparian forest, mangroves.
Bee-eater	**Rainbow Bee-eater** *Merops ornatus*	C	Lightly timbered areas, coastal scrub. Abundant in the Dry due to migration influx from the south.
Bellbird	**Crested Bellbird** *Oreoica gutturalis*	U	Mulga, arid and semi-arid scrub. The Pebbles, Newhaven, Alice Springs Desert Park, Santa Teresa Rd, West

			McDonnell Ranges, Uluru-Kata Tjuta NP, Watarrka NP.
Bittern	**Australian Little Bittern** *Ixobrychus dubius*	R	Wetlands. Palmerston Golf Course, Fogg Dam.
	Black Bittern *Ixobrychus flavicollis*	U	Estuaries, riverine vegetation, mangroves, paperbarks. Howard Springs, Mary R Wetland, Kakadu NP, Nitmiluk NP, Elsey NP, Timber Creek.
Black-Cockatoo	**Red-tailed Black-Cockatoo** *Calyptorhynchus banksii*	C	Dry woodland, coastal parks. Often feeding at newly burnt areas.
Boobook	**Southern Boobook** *Ninox boobook*	M	Woodland, dry open forest, parkland.
Booby	**Brown Booby** *Sula leucogaster*	U	Offshore waters. Buoys in Darwin Harbour, Bicentennial Park, East Pt, Nightcliff coast, Tiwi Is., Elcho Is.
	Masked Booby *Sula dactylatra*	V	Offshore waters. Bicentennial Park's coast.
Bowerbird	**Great Bowerbird** *Chlamydera nuchalis*	C	Woodland, parkland, urban areas, open forest. Top End only.
	Western Bowerbird *Chlamydera guttata*	M	Thickets, riverine woodland, rock figs in gorges, homesteads. Olive Pink BG, Ormiston Gorge, Uluru-Kata Tjuta NP, Watarrka NP, Finke Gorge NP.
Brolga	**Brolga** *Antigone rubicunda*	M	Wetlands, farmland, savannah. Locally common.
Bronze-Cuckoo	**Horsfield's Bronze-Cuckoo** *Chalcites basalis*	M	Woodland, often near wetlands.
	Little Bronze-Cuckoo *Chalcites minutillus*	C, S	Mangroves, monsoon forest, gardens. Common on the coast.
Bronzewing	**Common Bronzewing** *Phaps chalcoptera*	M	Woodland, forest, rocky outcrops, roadsides.
	Flock Bronzewing *Phaps histrionica*	U	Grassy plains, watercourses in dry country. Locally common, forming large flocks. Tablelands Hwy, Barkly Hwy, Connells Lagoon, Mac Clark CR.
Budgerigar	**Budgerigar** *Melopsittacus undulatus*	A	Open arid plains, grassy woodland, watercourses.
Bush-hen	**Pale-vented Bush-hen** *Amaurornis moluccana*	U	Monsoon forest, floodplains, swamps, dense, wet tall grass. Palmerston, Leanyer WTP, Holmes Jungle, Fogg Dam, Yellow Waters, Victoria Hwy.
Bushlark	**Horsfield's Bushlark** *Mirafra javanica*	M, S	Grassland, savannah, farmland. Barkly Hwy, Tablelands Hwy, Katherine WTP, Knuckey Lagoon, Fogg Dam, Timber C.
Bustard	**Australian Bustard** *Ardeotis australis*	U	Grassland, open plains, floodplains, savannah. Barkly Hwy, Tablelands Hwy, Renner Springs, Limmen NP, Manbulloo Homestead, Victoria Hwy.
Butcherbird	**Black Butcherbird** *Melloria quoyi*	M	Mangroves, coastal scrub, monsoon forest. Buffalo Cr., Bicentennial Park, East Pt, Orchard Rd, Palmerston WTP.
	Grey Butcherbird *Cracticus torquatus*	R	Woodland, urban areas, watercourses. Newhaven, West McDonnell Ranges, Arltunga, Uluru-Kata Tjuta NP, Karlu Karlu, Tablelands Hwy.

	Pied Butcherbird *Cracticus nigrogularis*	C	Urban areas, farmland, bushland, powerlines.
	Silver-backed Butcherbird *Cracticus argenteus*	U	Riverine forest, wooded gullies. Top End only. East Pt, Berry Springs, Arnhem Hwy, Litchfield NP, Kakadu NP, Nitmiluk NP, Keep River NP.
Button-quail	**Chestnut-backed Button-quail** *Turnix castanotus*	U	Monsoon forest, open woodland, thicket edges. Top End only. Chinaman Creek, Timber Creek, Nitmiluk NP, Kakadu NP, Marrakai Rd, Tiwi Is.
	Little Button-quail *Turnix velox*	M	Dry grassland, spinifex, inland floodplains. Nomadic, abundant in some years. Newhaven, West McDonnell Ranges, Karlu Karlu, Uluru-Kata Tjuta NP, Watarrka NP.
	Red-backed Button-quail *Turnix maculosus*	M	Floodplains, riverine forest, wetter grassy woodland, swamps. Top End only. Knuckey Lagoons, Palmerston WTP, Kakadu, Cutta Cutta, Tiwi Is.
	Red-chested Button-quail *Turnix pyrrhothorax*	U	Native grassland, grassy woodland, floodplains. Nomadic, dry season visitor to coast. Holmes Jungle, Jim Jim Falls, Chinaman Creek, Katherine WTP, Cutta Cutta Caves, Tablelands Hwy, Santa Teresa Rd, Ilparpa Swamp.
Buzzard	**Black-breasted Buzzard** *Hamirostra melanosternon*	U	Inland plains, waterholes, woodland edges, escarpment. Luritja Rd, Karlu Karlu, Lasseter Hwy, Uluru-Kata Tjuta NP, Newhaven, Kakadu NP, Barkly Hwy, Marrakai Rd, Threeways RH.
Chat	**Crimson Chat** *Epthianura tricolor*	U	Inland dry scrub, savannah. Nomadic and gregarious. Newhaven, Santa Teresa Rd, Barkly Hwy, Tablelands Hwy, Mac Clark, Stuart Hwy, Yulara.
	Orange Chat *Epthianura aurifrons*	R	Open plains, saltmarshes, floodplains. Nomadic. Playford R, Borroloola, Old Andado, Newhaven, Ilparpa Ponds.
	Yellow Chat *Epthianura crocea*	R	Saltmarshes, saline lagoons, sewage ponds. Nomadic. Playford R, Kennedy Cr, Newcastle Waters, Ilparpa Ponds, Borroloola, Leanyer, Katherine WTP.
Cicadabird	**Common Cicadabird** *Edolisoma tenuirostre*	U	Rainforest, paperbarks, mangroves, monsoon forest. Top End only. Kakadu NP, Leanyer WTP, Palmerston WTP, Buffalo Creek, Knuckey Lagoons, Howard Springs, McMinns Lagoon, Litchfield NP, Tiwi Is.
Cisticola	**Golden-headed Cisticola** *Cisticola exilis*	C	Tall rank grasses, roadsides, wetlands, pandanus scrub. Holmes Jungle, Lee Pt, Buffalo Creek, Kakadu, Fogg Dam.
	Zitting Cisticola *Cisticola juncidis*	U	Coastal marshes, floodplains, tidal flats. Leanyer WTP, Holmes Jungle, Knuckey Lagoons, Fogg Dam, South Alligator boat ramp, Bamurru Plains.

Cockatiel	**Cockatiel** *Nymphicus hollandicus*	A	Inland arid bushland, open plains, farmland, watercourses. Nomadic.
Cockatoo	**Major Mitchell's Cockatoo** *Cacatua leadbeateri*	U	Inland bushland, arid and semi-arid woodland, mulga, mallee. Barrow Cr, Newhaven, Alice Springs Desert Park, West McDonnell Ranges, Aileron, Luritja Rd, Yulara, Uluru-Kata Tjuta NP, Watarrka NP.
	Sulphur-crested Cockatoo *Cacatua galerita*	C	Woodland, forest, parkland, farmland, urban areas, near watercourses.
Coot	**Eurasian Coot** *Fulica atra*	C	Wetlands. Kakadu NP, Leanyer WTP, Newcastle Waters, Ilparpa Ponds, Tennant Creek WTP.
Corella	**Little Corella** *Cacatua sanguinea*	A	Woodland, farmland, urban areas, roadsides, wetlands, watercourses.
	Long-billed Corella *Cacatua tenuirostris*	R, I	Near human dwellings, mostly escapees. Ilparpa Ponds, Nightcliff.
Cormorant	**Great Cormorant** *Phalacrocorax carbo*	R	Freshwater wetlands. Yellow Waters, Newcastle Waters, Renner Springs, Frewena.
	Little Black Cormorant *Phalacrocorax sulcirostris*	A	Fresh- and saltwaters. Forms large fishing rafts.
	Little Pied Cormorant *Microcarbo melanoleucos*	M	Wetlands, estuaries, inshore waters. Yellow Waters, Knuckey Lagoons, Fogg Dam, Ilparpa Ponds.
	Great Pied Cormorant *Phalacrocorax varius*	M	Mostly in coastal waters, sometimes freshwater wetlands. Buffalo Creek, Dundee Beach, Newcastle Waters.
Coucal	**Pheasant Coucal** *Centropus phasianinus*	M	Savannah woodland, monsoon forest, pandanus, paperbarks, wetlands, gardens, parkland. Mostly in Top End.
Crake	**Australian Spotted Crake** *Porzana fluminea*	R	Wetlands, sewage ponds. Newcastle Waters, Barkly Homestead, Ilparpa Ponds, Finke R 2 Mile.
	Baillon's Crake *Zapornia pusilla*	R	Wetlands, sewage ponds. Fogg Dam, Katherine WTP, Keep R NP, Ilparpa Swamp, Finke R 2 Mile, Finke Gorge.
	Spotless Crake *Zapornia tabuensis*	R	Wetlands, mangroves, sewage ponds. Fogg Dam, Ilparpa Ponds, Ilparpa Swamp.
	White-browed Crake *Amaurornis cinerea*	M	Reedy swamps, mangroves, sewage ponds. Fogg Dam, Knuckey Lagoons, Buffalo Creek, Holmes Jungle, Kakadu NP, Ilparpa Ponds, Nhulumbuy.
Crane	**Sarus Crane** *Antigone antigone*	V	Swamps, farmland, grassland. Yellow Waters, Lomarieum Lag, Borroloola.
Crow	**Little Crow** *Corvus bennetti*	M	Inland woodland and shrubland. Often in large flocks on roadkill.
	Torresian Crow *Corvus orru*	C	Roadsides, open woodland, paddocks, rubbish tips, rural and urban areas.
Cuckoo	**Black-eared Cuckoo** *Chalcites osculans*	U	Open woodland, riverine forest, mulga, shrubland, saltmarshes. Bicentennial Park, Kakadu, Nitmiluk NP, Muirhead Bushland, Olive Pink BG, Kunoth Bore, West McDonnell Ranges.

	Brush Cuckoo *Cacomantis variolosus*	C	Mangroves, monsoon forest, woodland. Top End only. Buffalo Cr, Howard Springs, McMinns Lagoon, Kakadu NP, Marrakai Rd, Pine Creek, Timber Creek.
	Channel-billed Cuckoo *Scythrops novaehollandiae*	M, S, P	Closed forest, riverine forest, large fig trees, urban areas. Darwin BG, East Pt, Casuarina CR, Kakadu NP, Elsey NP, Keep R NP, Olive Pink BG, Emily Gap.
	Oriental Cuckoo *Cuculus obtatus*	U, S	Monsoon forest edges, bamboo thicket, riverine forest, mangroves. Tiwi Is., Kakadu, McMinns Lagoon, Fogg Dam, Darwin BG, Casuarina CR, East Pt, Knuckey Lagoons, Nhulumbuy.
	Pallid Cuckoo *Heteroscenes pallidus*	M, P	Sparsely wooded country, woodland, mangrove edges. Fogg Dam, Central Arnhem Rd, Timber Creek, Newhaven, Stuart Hwy, Lasseter Hwy, Uluru-Kata Tjuta NP.
Cuckoo-shrike	**Black-faced Cuckoo-shrike** *Coracina novaehollandiae*	C, W	Farmland, open forest, urban areas. Numbers increase sharply in winter.
	Ground Cuckoo-shrike *Coracina maxima*	U	Woodland, shrubland without groundcover, savannah. Tablelands Hwy, Barkly Hwy, Chinaman Creek, Borroloola, Karlu Karlu, Barrow Creek, Newhaven, Santa Teresa Rd.
	White-belled Cuckoo-shrike *Coracina papuensis*	C	Mangroves, monsoon forest, riverine forest, closed forest at escarpment, urban areas.
Curlew	**Far Eastern Curlew** *Numenius madagascariensis*	M, S	Estuaries, coastal wetlands. Buffalo Cr, Ludmilla Creek mouth, off Aralia St, Wagait Beach, Bing Bong Port, Tiwi Is.
	Little Curlew *Numenius minutus*	C, S	Inland wetlands, short grassland, lawns, floodplains, sewage ponds. Darwin BG, Leanyer WTP, Rapid Creek, Katherine WTP, Fogg Dam, Knuckey Lagoons, Kakadu NP, Newcastle Waters, Tablelands Hwy.
Darter	**Australasian Darter** *Anhinga novaehollandiae*	C	Inland waters, estuaries.
Dollarbird	**Oriental Dollarbird** *Eurystomus orientalis*	M, S	Open forest, woodland, near water.
Dotterel	**Black-fronted Dotterel** *Elseyornis melanops*	C	Freshwater wetlands.
	Inland Dotterel *Peltohyas australis*	R	Sparsely vegetated inland plains, gibberland, claypans. Erldunda, Stuart Hwy, Old Andado, Newhaven, Mac Clark CR, Cannonball Run Monument, Rainbow Valley.
	Red-kneed Dotterel *Erythrogonys cinctus*	M	Freshwater wetlands, prefers open mud and shallow water with sparse, short vegetation. Leanyer WTP, Fogg Dam, McMinns Lagoon, Kakadu NP, Katherine WTP, Newhaven.

Dove	**Bar-shouldered Dove** *Geopelia humeralis*	A	Gardens, parkland, gardens, coastal scrub.
	Diamond Dove *Geopelia cuneata*	A	Grassy woodland, spinifex and other grasslands, roadsides. Often abundant near waterholes.
	Peaceful Dove *Geopelia placida*	A	Open habitats, woodland, coastal scrub, farmland, parkland.
	Rock Dove *Columba livia*	R, I	Urban areas, parkland. Mataranka, Olive Pink BG, Ilparpa Ponds.
	Spotted Dove *Streptopelia chinensis*	R, I	Urban areas, parkland. A small population survives in Alice Springs. Olive Pink BG, AS Telegraph Station, Trephina Gorge.
Dowitcher	**Asian Dowitcher** *Limnodromus semipalmatus*	V, S	Estuaries, tidal flats, freshwater wetlands. Knuckey Lagoons, Holmes Jungle, Buffalo Creek.
Drongo	**Spangled Drongo** *Dicrurus bracteatus*	M	Monsoon forest, mangroves, coastal scrub, gardens. Top End only. East Pt.
Duck	**Australian Wood Duck** *Chenonetta jubata*	U	Parkland, wetlands, farmland, sewage ponds. Leaning Tree Lagoon, Jabiru, Borroloola, Ellery Creek Big Hole.
	Blue-billed Duck *Oxyura australis*	V	Wetlands, sewage ponds. Ilparpa Ponds, Tennant Creek WTP.
	Freckled Duck *Stictonetta naevosa*	R	Wetlands, sewage ponds. Ilparpa Ponds, Tennant Creek WTP, Leanyer WTP, Yulara WTP, Knuckey Lagoons, Tablelands Hwy, Newhaven, Renner S.
	Musk Duck *Biziura lobata*	V	Wetlands, sewage ponds. Ilparpa Ponds.
	Pacific Black Duck *Anas supercilosa*	C	Wetlands, sewage ponds.
	Pink-eared Duck *Malacorhynchus membranaceus*	M	Inland shallow lakes, sewage ponds, swamps. Leanyer WTP, Bird Billabong, Kakadu NP, Tablelands Hwy, Frewena, Tennant Creek WTP
Eagle	**Little Eagle** *Hieraaetus morphnoides*	U	Open forest, woodland, near waterholes. Litchfield NP, Nitmiluk NP, Newcastle Waters, Wycliffe Well, Trephina Gorge, Kakadu NP, Ormiston Gorge, Watarrka NP, Lasseter Hwy.
	Wedge-tailed Eagle *Aquila audax*	M	Rocky outcrops, plains, woodland, open forest, on roadkill on roads.
Egret	**Cattle Egret** *Bubulcus ibis*	C	Grassland near livestock, wetlands. Large breeding colonies. Mostly Top End.
	Great Egret *Ardea alba*	C	Wetlands, rivers, estuaries. Locally in large flocks.
	Eastern Reef Egret *Egretta sacra*	M	Rocky coasts, estuaries, reefs, inshore and offshore islands. Buffalo Creek, East Pt, Stokes Hill Wharf.
	Little Egret *Egretta garzetta*	C	Fresh- and saltwaters, more common in coastal areas.
	Plumed Egret *Ardea plumifera*	C	**Split from Intermediate Egret.** Wetlands, floodplains, waterholes, flooded grassy fields.

Emerald-Dove	**Brown-capped Emerald-Dove** *Chalcophaps indica*	M	**Split from Emerald Dove**. Monsoon forest, mangrove edges, gardens, wooded gullies, paperbark forest. Casuarina CR, East Pt, Howard Springs, Berry Springs, Kakadu NP, Murray R NP, Dundee Beach, Tiwi Is.
Emu	**Emu** *Dromaius novaehollandiae*	U	Open plains, grassy woodland. Yulara, Litchfield NP, Kakadu NP, Newhaven, West McDonnell Ranges, Watarrka.
Emu-wren	**Rufous-crowned Emu-wren** *Stipiturus ruficeps*	R	Woodland with tall unburnt spinifex on plains and rocky hills. Barrow Cr, Santa Teresa Rd, Newhaven, Ormiston Gorge, Redband Gorge, Ellery Creek Big Hole, Corroboree Rock.
Fairy-wren	**Purple-backed Fairy-wren** *Malurus assimilis*	M	Arid tall scrub with understory of thicket, spinifex or acacia. Nitmiluk NP, Fogg Dam, Kakadu NP, Alice Springs Desert Park, Newhaven, Barkly Hwy, West McDonnell Ranges.
	Purple-crowned Fairy-wren *Malurus coronatus*	R	5-10m strip of riverine vegetation such as pandanus, bamboo, cane grass. Finds refuge at the tops of gums and paperbarks during floods. Victoria River RH, Timber Creek, Judbarra Gregory NP, Limmen NP, Borroloola, Caranbirini CR.
	Red-backed Fairy-wren *Malurus melanocephalus*	C	Open forest, woodland with spear grass and low shrubs. Top End only.
	Splendid Fairy-wren *Malurus splendens*	M	Shrubland and woodland of the arid and semi-arid zones. Newhaven, Ilparpa Ponds, Alice Springs Desert Park, Kunoth Bore, N'Dhala Gorge, Yulara, Uluru-Kata Tjuta NP.
	White-winged Fairy-wren *Malurus leucopterus*	M	Arid plains, low open shrubland, with patches of bare ground and little tree cover. Karlu Karlu, Newhaven, Kunoth Bore, Santa Teresa Rd, Old Andado, West McDonnell Ranges, Uluru-Kata Tjuta NP, Watarrka NP.
Falcon	**Black Falcon** *Falco subniger*	U	Savannah, grassland, floodplains, sewage ponds. Barkly Hwy, Tablelands Hwy, Tennant Creek WTP, Barrow Creek, Shady Camp, Leanyer WTP.
	Brown Falcon *Falco berigora*	C	Woodland, open plains, along main roads.
	Grey Falcon *Falco hypoleucos*	R	Arid plains, woodland. Barkly Hwy, Tablelands Hwy, Top Springs, Judbarra Gregory NP, Barrow Creek, Taylors Creek, Newhaven, Old Andado, Watarrka NP, Central Arnhem Rd.
	Peregrine Falcon *Falco peregrinus*	U	Escarpment, ranges, gorges, rocky coast, open forest. Litchfield NP, Kakadu NP, Nitmiluk NP, Judbarra Gregory NP, Timber Creek, West

			McDonnell Ranges, Watarrka NP, Uluru-Kata Tjuta NP, Yeperenye.
Fantail	**Arafura Fantail** *Rhipidura dryas*	U	Riverine forest, mangroves, vine thicket, bamboo. East Pt, Casuarina CR, Howard Springs, Adelaide R, Fogg Dam, Kakadu, Elsey NP, Nitmiluk NP.
	Grey Fantail *Rhipidura albiscapa*	U, W	Woodland, open forest. Muirhead Bushland, Howard Springs, Berry Springs, Litchfield NP, Yeperenye.
	Mangrove Fantail *Rhipidura phasiana*	R	Mangroves and adjoining forest. Palmerston WTP, Dundee Beach, Orchard Rd, Buffalo Creek, Charles Darwin University, Tiwi Is.
	Northern Fantail *Rhipidura isura*	M	Monsoon forest, paperbarks, gardens, mangroves. East Pt, Buffalo Creek, Berry Springs, Victoria Hwy, Kakadu NP, Mary R NP, Nitmiluk.
Figbird	**Australasian Figbird** *Sphecotheres vieilloti*	A	Monsoon forest, gardens, anywhere with fruiting trees. Top End only.
Finch	**Black-bellied Crimson Finch** *Neochmia phaeton*	C	**Split from Crimson Finch**. Tall wet grasses, pandanus and paperbark swamps. Holmes Jungle, Fogg Dam, Howard Springs, Leanyer WTP, Casuarina CR, Adelaide River, Kakadu NP, Pine Creek, Timber Creek.
	Double-barred Finch *Taeniophygia bichenovii*	A	Open forest, riverine forest, grassy woodland, shrubland, parkland, gardens.
	Gouldian Finch *Chloebia gouldiae*	U	Savannah, never far from water. In 2022-23, their numbers increased exponentially. Timber Creek, Victoria Hwy, Nackeroo Lookout, Judbarra Gregory NP, Muirhead Bushland, Casuarina CR, Marrakai Rd, Kakadu NP, Edith Falls Rd, Alexander Forrest Monument RA, Central Arnhem Rd.
	Long-tailed Finch *Poephila acuticauda*	C	Savannah, near watercourses. Casuarina CR, Muirhead Bushland, East Pt, Adelaide River, Kakadu NP, Pine Creek, Victoria Hwy, Edith Falls Rd, Timber Creek, Keep R NP, Alexander Forrest Monument RA.
	Masked Finch *Poephila personata*	C	Savannah, near watercourses. Casuarina CR, Muirhead Bushland, East Pt, Pine Creek, Timber Creek, Buchanan Hwy, Kakadu, Fogg Dam.
	Painted Finch *Emblema pictum*	U	Gorges, rocky outcrops, spinifex-covered hills. Jasper Gorge, Karlu Karlu, Mary Ann Dam, Watarrka NP, West McDonnell Ranges, Yeperenye, Trephina Gorge, Santa Teresa Rd.
	Star Finch *Neochmia ruficauda*	M	Riverine forest, woodland, pandanus, reedbeds. Victoria Hwy, Policemans Pt, Timber Creek, Jasper Gorge, Buchanan Hwy, Buntine Hwy, Manbulloo H, Muirhead Bushland.

	Zebra Finch *Taeniopygia castanotis*	A	Arid and semi-arid grassland, open plains, farmland, savannah.
Flycatcher	**Broad-billed Flycatcher** *Myiagra ruficollis*	U	Mangroves, paperbark swamp, monsoon forest. Buffalo Creek, off Aralia St, Kakadu NP, S Alligator boat ramp, Borroloola, Elcho Is, Tiwi Is.
	Leaden Flycatcher *Myiagra rubecula*	M,W	Coastal scrub, dry forest, paperbark forest, gardens. East Pt, Casuarina CR, Nitmiluk NP, Kakadu NP, Elsey NP.
	Lemon-bellied Flycatcher *Microeca flavigaster*	C	Monsoon forest, paperbarks, bamboo, parks. East Pt, Casuarina CR, Mary R NP, Kakadu, Nitmiluk NP, Fogg Dam.
	Paperbark Flycatcher *Myiagra nana*	M	Paperbark woodland, riverine forest, monsoon forest. East Pt, Fogg Dam, Arnhem Hwy, Kakadu NP, Elsey NP, Timber Creek, Batchelor, Mary R NP.
	Shining Flycatcher *Myiagra alecto*	C	Paperbark forest, mangroves, monsoon forest, riverine forest. East Pt, Buffalo Creek, Howard Springs, Berry Springs, Kakadu NP, Tiwi Is.
Friarbird	**Helmeted Friarbird** *Philemon buceroides*	C	Monsoon forest, mangroves, gardens, vine ticket, escarpment.
	Little Friarbird *Philemon citreogularis*	A	Open forest, woodland, gardens, parks. Nomadic. Darwin BG, East Pt, Holmes Jungle, Kakadu NP, Tiwi Is, Judbarra Gregory NP, Keep R NP.
	Silver-crowned Friarbird *Philemon argenticeps*	M	Open forest, savannah, gardens, parks. East Pt, Wagait Beach, Kakadu, Litchfield, Timber Creek, Carabnirini.
Frigatebird	**Christmas Island Frigatebird** *Fregata andrewsi*	V	Offshore waters. Off Aralia St.
	Great Frigatebird *Fregata minor*	R	Offshore waters, islands. East Pt, White Rocks, Tiwi Is, Elcho Is.
	Lesser Frigatebird *Fregata ariel*	U	Offshore waters, islands. Darwin Harbour, White Rocks, off Aralia St, Dundee Beach, Groote Eylandt.
Frogmouth	**Tawny Frogmouth** *Podargus strigoides*	M	Woodland, forest, parks, urban areas. Bicentennial Park, Rapid Creek, Bowali Visitor Centre, Litchfield, Cutta Cutta, Keep R NP, Desert Oaks RA, Tiwi Is.
Fruit-Dove	**Black-banded Fruit-Dove** *Ptilinopus alligator*	U, E	**Split from Banded Fruit-Dove**. Monsoon forest, escarpment, gullies, fig trees. Nourlangie Rock, Gubarra, Ubirr, Mirrai Lookout, Jim Jim Falls, Maguk, Nawurlandja Lookout.
	Rose-crowned Fruit-Dove *Ptilinopus regina*	M	Coastal scrub, mangroves, monsoon forest. Darwin BG, East Pt, Buffalo Creek, Fogg Dam, Kakadu, Litchfield NP, Dundee Beach, Tiwi Is.
Galah	**Galah** *Eolophus roseicapilla*	A	Parkland, farmland, woodland, open plains, roadsides.
Garganey	**Garganey** *Spatula querquedula*	R, S	Sewage ponds, wetlands. Leanyer WTP, Knuckey Lagoons, McMinns Lag.

Gerygone	**Green-backed Gerygone** *Gerygone chloronota*	C	Monsoon, riverine and paperbark forest, mangroves, bamboo, gardens. Darwin BG, Buffalo Creek, Berry Springs, Dundee Beach, Fogg Dam, Kakadu NP, Elsey NP, Groote Eylandt.
	Large-billed Gerygone *Gerygone magnirostris*	M	Monsoon forest, mangroves, islands. Darwin BG, East Pt, Buffalo Creek, Holmes Jungle, Howard Springs, Tree Pt CR, Knuckey Lagoons, Nhulunbuy.
	Mangrove Gerygone *Gerygone levigaster*	C	Mangroves, islands. Leanyer WTP, Ludmilla Creek, Dundee Beach, off Aralia St, off Orchard Rd, Borroloola, Nhulunbuy, Tiwi Is.
	Western Gerygone *Gerygone fusca*	M	Mulga woodland, arid and semi-arid zones. Victoria R RH, West McDonnell Ranges, Newhaven, Olive Pink BG, Stuart Hwy, Arltunga, Uluru-Kata Tjuta NP, Watarrka NP.
	White-throated Gerygone *Gerygone olivacea*	U	Eucalypt forest, paperbark swamp, inland riverine vegetation. Adelaide R, Leaning Tree Lagoon, Mary R NP, Leach Lagoon, Elsey NP, Jasper Gorge.
Gibberbird	**Gibberbird** *Ashbyia lovensis*	R	Arid stony plains (gibberland) with sparse short grasses and herbs. Mac Clark CR, Old Andado Homestead.
Godwit	**Bar-tailed Godwit** *Limosa lapponica*	C, S	Estuaries, coastal wetlands, sewage points.
	Black-tailed Godwit *Limosa limosa*	M, S	Estuaries, coastal and freshwater wetlands, sewage ponds. Off Aralia St, Leanyer WTP, Palmerston WTP, Shady Camp, Bird Billabong, Ilparpa Ponds, Katherine WTP, Tiwi Is.
Goose	**Magpie Goose** *Anseranas semipalmata*	A	Wetlands, farmland, flooded grassland. Gregarious.
Goshawk	**Brown Goshawk** *Accipiter fasciatus*	C	Woodland, mulga, parkland, gardens, open forest, paperbark forest, monsoon forest.
	Grey Goshawk *Accipiter novaehollandiae*	U	Mangroves, riverine and paperbark forest, parkland, monsoon forest. East Pt, Tiger Brennan Dr, Leanyer WTP, Fogg Dam, Dundee Beach, Tiwi Is, Kakadu NP, Daly R.
	Red Goshawk *Erythrotriorchis radiatus*	R	Woodland, riverine forest, edges of paperbark swamp, monsoon forest. Population in decline. Tiwi Is (stronghold), Mataranka, Elsey NP, Litchfield NP, Mary R Wilderness Retreat, Kakadu NP.
Grassbird	**Little Grassbird** *Poodytes gramineus*	U	Mostly inland wetlands. Ilparpa Ponds, Finke R 2 Camp, Redbank Gorge, Glen Helen Gorge, Leach Lagoon.
	Tawny Grassbird *Cincloramphus timoriensis*	M	Dense wetland vegetation, long grasses. Katherine Showgrounds, Lee Pt, Manbulloo Homestead, Tenant Creek WTP, Fogg Dam, Holmes Jungle.

Grasswren	**Carpentarian Grasswren** *Amytornis dorotheae*	R	Spinifex-covered hills with few trees and patches of bare ground. Calvert Rd, Caranbirini CR, Wollogorang Rd.
	Dusky Grasswren *Amytornis purnelli*	U	Open woodland with spinifex groundcover on rocky slopes and ridges. Barrow Creek, Newhaven, Santa Teresa Rd, West McDonnell Ranges, Yeperenye, Trephina Gorge, Watarrka NP, Mereenie Loop.
	Eyrean Grasswren *Amytornis goyderi*	R	Cane grass on slopes and crests of sand dunes in Simpson Desert. Old Andado Homestead, Mac Clark CR.
	Rufous Grasswren *Amytornis oweni*	R	**Split from Striated Grasswren. Formed from Sandhill and Pilbara ssp.** Prefers old, dense spinifex hummocks on sand dunes with sparse small bushes. Yulara, Uluru-Kata Tjuta NP, Lasseter Hwy, Curtin Springs St.
	White-throated Grasswren *Amytornis woodwardi*	U, E	High plateau, sandstone country with mature spinifex, sparse bushes and boulders. Arnhem Land plateau only. Jim Jim Falls, Barrk Malan Walk, Yurmikmik Walks, Koolpin Gorge, Gunlom Falls.
Grebe	**Australasian Grebe** *Tachybaptus novaehollandiae*	C	Wetlands, rivers, sewage ponds.
	Great Crested Grebe *Podiceps cristatus*	R	Wetlands, sewage ponds. L Bennett, Jabiru, Tablelands Hwy, Mary Ann Dam, Tennant Creek WTP.
	Hoary-headed Grebe *Poliocephalus poliocephalus*	M	Fresh and brackish waters, sewage ponds. Ilparpa Ponds, Jabiru WTP, Katherine WTP, Tennant Creek WTP, Frewena, Borroloola, Santa Teresa Rd.
	Little Grebe *Tachybaptus ruficollis*	V	Sewage ponds. Leanyer WTP.
Greenshank	**Common Greenshank** *Tringa nebularia*	M, S	Coastal and inland wetlands.
Gull	**Black-headed Gull** *Larus ridibundus*	V	Coastal waters, beaches, sewage ponds. Darwin Harbor, Buffalo Creek, Leanyer WTP, Nhulunbuy.
	Black-tailed Gull *Larus crassirostris*	V	Beaches, coastal waters. Darwin Harbour.
	Franklin's Gull *Larus pipixcan*	V	Beaches, coastal waters. Darwin Harbour, Buffalo Creek.
	Lesser Black-backed Gull *Larus fuscus*	V	Beaches, coastal waters. Darwin Harbour, Buffalo Creek.
	Silver Gull *Larus novaehollandiae*	C	Beaches, estuaries, parklands.
Hardhead	**Hardhead** *Aythya australis*	M	Deep freshwater wetlands, sewage ponds.
Harrier	**Spotted Harrier** *Circus assimilis*	M	Dry floodplains, open country, farmland, savannah. Knuckey Lagoons, Buchanan Hwy, Stuart Hwy, Barkly

			Hwy, Tablelands Hwy, Fogg Dam, Marrakai Rd, Newhaven.
	Swamp Harrier *Circus approximans*	U	Floodplains, grassland, wetlands and adjacent open country. Leanyer WTP, Holmes Jungle, McMinns Lagoon, Fogg Dam, Playford R, Kakadu, Newcastle Waters, Ilparpa Ponds.
Heron	**Great-billed Heron** *Ardea sumatrana*	R	Mangroves, estuaries, tidal rivers and creeks. Buffalo Creek, Channel Is, Mary R Wilderness Retreat, Kakadu NP, Shady Camp, Bamurru Plains, Donkey Camp Weir, Nitmiluk NP, Daly R, Bing Bong Port, Nhulunbuy.
	Javan Pond Heron *Ardeola speciosa*	V	Estuaries, beaches. Rapid Creek estuary.
	Pied Heron *Egretta picata*	A	Wetlands, paperbark swamps, flooded grassy plains. Leanyer WTP, Fogg Dam, McMinns Lagoon, Kakadu, Adelaide R NP, Adelaide R Jumping Crocodiles.
	Striated Heron *Butorides striata*	C	Estuaries, mangroves, rocky walls, mudflats, islands.
	White-faced Heron *Egretta novaehollandiae*	C	Freshwater and coastal wetlands, estuaries.
	White-necked Heron *Ardea pacifica*	M	Freshwater wetlands, farm dams, flooded grassland, sewage ponds.
Hobby	**Australian Hobby** *Falco longipennis*	M	Urban areas, open country, woodland. Holmes Jungle, Kakadu, Tennant Creek WTP, Newhaven, Barkly Hwy, Ilparpa Ponds, Yulara, Erldunda RH, Barrow C.
Honeyeater	**Banded Honeyeater** *Cissomela pectoralis*	M	Savannah, mangroves, paperbarks. Nomadic. Holmes Jungle, Litchfield NP, Kakadu NP, Adelaide River, Elsey NP, Chainman Creek, Victoria Hwy.
	Bar-breasted Honeyeater *Ramsayornis fasciatus*	M	Paperbark swamps, riverine vegetation. Fogg Dam, Litchfield NP, Kakadu, Howard Springs, Pine Creek, Dundee Beach, Nitmiluk NP, Limmen NP, Timber Creek, Caranbirini CR.
	Black Honeyeater *Sugomel nigrum*	U	Woodland, arid shrubland, eremophila bushes. Nomadic. Barkly Hwy, West McDonnell Ranges, Newhaven, Old Andado, Stuart Hwy, Olive Pink BG, Uluru-Kata Tjuta NP, Watarrka NP.
	Brown Honeyeater *Lichmera indistincta*	A	Urban areas, wet forest, coastal scrub, woodland.
	Dusky Honeyeater *Myzomela obscura*	C	Mangroves, monsoon and riverine forest, coastal scrub, gardens. Darwin BG, Litchfield NP, Adelaide River, Fogg Dam, Kakadu NP, Pine Creek, Nitmiluk NP, Elsey NP.
	Golden-backed Honeyeater *Melithreptus laetior*	U	**Split from Black-chinned Honeyeater**. Riverine vegetation in dry areas, desert scrub. Newhaven, Victoria Hwy, West McDonnell Ranges, Keep R NP, Barkly Hwy, Central Arnhem Rd, Warloch Ponds.

	Grey Honeyeater *Conopophila whitei*	R	Mulga woodland and shrubland, dunes with flowering shrubs. Kunoth Bore, Alice Springs Desert Park, Olive Pink BG, Newhaven, Stuart Hwy, Simpsons Gap, Ochre Pits, Ormiston Gorge, Yulara, Uluru-Kata Tjuta NP.
	Grey-fronted Honeyeater *Ptilotula plumula*	U	Rocky woodland, spinifex-covered hills, arid shrubland. Renner Springs, Victora Hwy, Judbarra Gregory NP, Timber Creek, Santa Teresa Rd, Trephina Gorge.
	Grey-headed Honeyeater *Ptilotula keartlandi*	C	Arid woodland, especially on hills near waterholes. Uluru-Kata Tjuta NP, Watarrka NP, Stuart Hwy, West McDonnell Ranges, Trephina Gorge, Olive Pink BG, Newhaven, Mary Ann Dam, Barkly Hwy.
	Painted Honeyeater *Grantiella picta*	R	Inland woodland and forest infested with mistletoes. Nomadic. Threeways RH, Tennant Creek WTP, Limmen NP.
	Pied Honeyeater *Certhionyx variegatus*	U	Woodland, arid shrubland, eremophila bushes. Nomadic. Newhaven, Ryan Well, Alice Springs Desert Park, Santa Teresa Rd, West McDonnell Ranges, Rainbow Valley, Uluru-Kata Tjuta NP.
	Red-headed Honeyeater *Myzomela erythrocephala*	C	Mangroves, monsoon and riverine forests, parks, gardens, islands. East Pt, Charles Darwin NP, Buffalo Creek, Dundee Beach, Borroloola, Tiwi Is.
	Rufous-banded Honeyeater *Conopophila albogularis*	C	Gardens parks, monsoon forest, paperbark swamp, mangroves. Abundant in Darwin.
	Rufous-throated Honeyeater *Conopophila rufogularis*	C	Paperbark swamps, riverine forest, inland along watercourses, urban areas.
	Singing Honeyeater *Gavicalis virescens*	M	Arid low bushland, coastal scrub, dry wooded habitats. Marrakai Rd, Barkly Hwy, Newhaven, West McDonnell Ranges, Stuart Hwy, Uluru-Kata Tjuta NP, Watarrka NP.
	Spiny-cheeked Honeyeater *Acanthagenys rufogularis*	M	Inland woodland, arid and semi-arid habitats. Barkly Hwy, Barrow Creek, Newhaven, West McDonnell Ranges, Trephina Gorge, Uluru-Kata Tjuta NP, Watarrka NP, Olive Pink BG.
	White-fronted Honeyeater *Purnella albifrons*	R	Highly nomadic, appears wherever desert bushes are in bloom. Uluru-Kata Tjuta NP, Watarrka NP, Yulara, Kunoth Bore, Newhaven, West McDonnell Ranges, Stuart Hwy.
	White-gaped Honeyeater *Stomiopera unicolor*	C	Urban areas, parks, riverine forest, monsoon forest, mangroves, islands.
	White-lined Honeyeater *Microptilotis albilineatus*	U, E	Sandstone escarpment, base of gorges. Nourlangie Rock, Gubarra, Ubirr, Mirrai Lookout, Jim Jim Falls,

			Maguk, Gunlom Falls, Border Creek Walk, Nitmiluk NP.
	White-quilled Honeyeater *Entomyzon albipennis*	C	**Split from Blue-faced Honeyeater**. Urban areas, gardens, orchards, pandanus, wetlands, rural RHs. Holmes Jungle, Kakadu, Arnhem Hwy, Litchfield NP, Pine Creek, Victoria R RH, Mataranka Homestead, Timber Cr.
	White-plumed Honeyeater *Ptilotula penicillata*	C	Inland riverine forest, woodland. West McDonnell Ranges, Watarrka NP, Yeperenye, Newhaven, Tennant Creek
	White-throated Honeyeater *Melithreptus albogularis*	M	Wet forest, coastal scrub, gardens, paperbark woodland, open forest. Charles Darwin NP, East Pt, Litchfield NP, Fogg Dam, Kakadu NP, Elsey NP.
	Yellow-tinted Honeyeater *Ptilotula flavescens*	C	Rocky savannah, riverine forest, open forest, riparian thicket, mangroves, gardens. East Pt, Tiwi Is, Pine Creek, Kakadu NP, Judbarra Gregory NP, Elsey NP, Renner Springs, Alexander Forrest Monument.
Honey-buzzard	**Oriental Honey-buzzard** *Pernis ptilorhynchus*	V, S	Monsoon forest, woodland. Kakadu NP, Litchfield NP, Nitmiluk NP.
Hoopoe	**Eurasian Hoopoe** *Upupa epops*	V	Elcho Island, on the resort lawn, Feb-2014.
Ibis	**Australian White Ibis** *Threskiornis moluccus*	A	Wetlands, estuaries, parks, urban areas.
	Glossy Ibis *Plegadis falcinellus*	M	Wetlands, flooded grassland. Nomadic. Leanyer WTP, Mary R NP, Kakadu NP, Knuckey Lagoons, Katherine WTP, Newcastle Waters, Tablelands Hwy, Tennant Creek WTP, Ilparpa Ponds.
	Straw-necked Ibis *Threskiornis spinicollis*	C, W	Grassland, paddocks, flooded pastures. Nomadic.
Imperial-Pigeon	**Elegant Imperial-Pigeon** *Ducula concinna*	V	Parks, gardens. Off Aralia St.
	Torresian Imperial-Pigeon *Ducula spilorrhoa*	A, S	Parks, mangroves, monsoon forest, offshore islands. Penetrates the drier interior along rivers. Most are summer migrants from PNG, Sep-Apr.
Jacana	**Comb-crested Jacana** *Irediparra gallinacea*	C	Wetlands with floating vegetation.
Jacky Winter	**Jacky Winter** *Microeca fascinans*	U	Savannah, inland stony hills, near watercourses. Litchfield NP, Timber Creek, Buchanan Hwy, Marrakai Rd, Edith Falls Rd, Kunoth Bore, Ormiston.
Jaeger	**Pomarine Jaeger** *Stercorarius pomarinus*	V	Offshore and inshore waters. Buffalo Creek.
Kestrel	**Nankeen Kestrel** *Falco cenchroides*	C	Woodland, farmland, open plains, grassland, floodplains.
Kingfisher	**Azure Kingfisher** *Ceyx azureus*	M	Well-vegetated watercourses, mangroves, estuaries, paperbark swamps. Kakadu NP, Buffalo Creek, Berry Springs, Howard Springs, Mary R

			NP, Litchfield, NP, Elsey NP, Fogg Dam, Channel Is.
	Collared Kingfisher *Todiramphus chloris*	U	Estuaries, mangroves. Tiger Brennan Dr, East Pt, Ludmilla Creek, Channel Is, Tiwi Is, Bing Bong Port, Elcho Is.
	Forest Kingfisher *Todiramphus macleayii*	C	Woodland, open forest, parkland, coastal scrub. Adelaide River, Fogg Dam, Casuarina CR, Holmes Jungle, Kakadu NP, Darwin BG, Corroboree Billabong, Tiwi Is.
	Little Kingfisher *Ceyx pusillus*	U	Mangroves, monsoon forest, islands, wetlands. Buffalo Creek, Middle Arm, Fogg Dam, Howard Springs, Shady Camp, Corroboree Billabong, Yellow Waters, Daly R. Tiwi Is.
	Red-backed Kingfisher *Todiramphus pyrrhopygius*	M	Savannah, grassland, floodplains, mulga, lightly wooded arid habitats. Adelaide R, Fogg Dam, Central Arnhem Rd, Victoria Hwy, Barrow Creek, West McDonnell Ranges, Olive Pink BG.
	Sacred Kingfisher *Todiramphus sanctus*	M, P	Woodland, estuaries, wetlands, parklands, power lines, mangroves, gardens.
Kite	**Black Kite** *Milvus migrans*	A	Inland open plains, roadsides, water courses.
	Black-shouldered Kite *Elanus axillaris*	M	Open country, woodland, grassland, savannah. Uluru-Kata Tjuta NP, Karlu Karlu, Lasseter Hwy, West McDonnell Ranges, Newhaven.
	Brahminy Kite *Haliastur indus*	M	Mangroves, beaches, estuaries, floodplains, monsoon forest. Darwin Harbour, Buffalo Creek, Channel Is, Bing Bong Port, Tiwi Is.
	Letter-winged Kite *Elanus scriptus*	R	Open semi-arid and arid country, grassland. Mac Clark, Old Andado, Connells Lagoon, Tablelands Hwy.
	Square-tailed Kite *Lophoictinia isura*	R	Open forest, woodland. Berry Springs, Litchfield NP, Nitmiluk NP, Victoria R RH, Timber Creek, Elsey NP.
	Whistling Kite *Haliastur sphenurus*	C	Open plains, woodland, estuaries, roadsides.
Knot	**Great Knot** *Calidris tenuirostris*	C, S	Estuaries, mudflats, beaches.
	Red Knot *Calidris canutus*	M, S	Estuaries, mudflats, beaches, islands. East Pt, off Aralia St, Nhulunbuy, Tree Pt CR, Buffalo Creek.
Koel	**Eastern Koel** *Eudnamys orientalis*	M, S	Monsoon forest, gardens, parks.
Kookaburra	**Blue-winged Kookaburra** *Dacelo leachii*	M	Forest, woodland, paperbark swamps, parks, gardens.
Lapwing	**Banded Lapwing** *Vanellus tricolor*	R	Open plains, farmland, gibberland. Playford R, Newhaven, Kunoth Bore, Ilparpa Claypans, Santa Teresa Rd, Mac Clark, Stuart Hwy, Lasseter Hwy.

	Masked Lapwing *Vanellus miles*	A	Farmland, wetlands, parks, urban areas.
Lorikeet	**Rainbow Lorikeet** *Trichoglossus moluccanus*	R, I	Urban areas; a small, increasing population established from escapees in Alice Springs. Olive Pink BG.
	Red-collared Lorikeet *Trichoglossus rubritorquis*	A	Forest, gardens, orchards, woodland.
	Varied Lorikeet *Psitteuteles versicolor*	C	Nomadic, follows flowering gums and paperbarks. Casuarina CR, Litchfield NP, Adelaide R, Marrakai Rd, Kakadu NP, Katherine, Elsey NP, Keep R NP.
Lovebird	**Rosy-faced Lovebird** *Agaponis roseicollis*	R, I	Several pairs observed in Alice Springs. Olive Pink BG.
Magpie	**Australian Magpie** *Gymnorhina tibicen*	M	Urban areas, woodland, forest, farmland, roadsides, roadhouses.
Magpie-lark	**Magpie-lark** *Grallina cyanoleuca*	A	Urban areas, open plains, wetlands, floodplains, parklands.
Mannikin	**Chestnut-breasted Mannikin** *Lonchura castaneothorax*	A	Grassland (long grass), sedgeland, bamboo thicket, gardens.
	Pictorella Mannikin *Heteromunia pectoralis*	U	Semi-arid grassland, mostly with spinifex, woodland near water. Occasionally in large numbers. Buchanan Hwy, Renner Springs, Jasper Gorge, Tablelands Hwy, Buntine Hwy, Top Springs, Victoria Hwy, Timber Creek, Borroloola.
	Yellow-rumped Mannikin *Lonchura pravipyrmna*	R	Long grass grassland, bamboo, trees near water. Buffalo Creek, Pine Creek, Katherine Showgrounds, Victoria R RH, Judbarra Gregory NP, Buntine Hwy, Jasper Gorge, Timber Creek.
Martin	**Fairy Martin** *Petrochelidon ariel*	C	Dry open country, gorges, escarpment.
	Tree Martin *Petrochelidon nigricans*	A, W	Open forest, mangrove, open plains. Huge flocks in winter.
Miner	**Yellow-throated Miner** *Manorina flavigula*	C	Inland dry woodland. Scarce on the coast.
Mistletoebird	**Mistletoebird** *Dicaeum hirundinaceum*	C	Wooded habitats infected with mistletoe. Nomadic.
Monarch	**Spectacled Monarch** *Symposiachrus trivirgatus*	V	Coastal scrub. Nhulunbuy Town Lagoon.
Moorhen	**Dusky Moorhen** *Gallinula tenebrosa*	R	Freshwater wetlands. Glen Helen Gorge, Yulara, Bird Billabong, Jabiru L, Yellow Waters, Elsey NP, Lomarieum Lagoon, Mary Ann Dam.
Myna	**Common Myna** *Acridotheres tristis*	V, I	Near the roadhouse in Top Springs.
Native-hen	**Black-tailed Native-hen** *Trybonix ventralis*	U	Inland wetlands, mainly with flooded vegetation. Playford R, Redbank Waterhole, Renner Springs, Ilparpa Ponds, Glen Helen Gorge, Yulara WTP.
Needletail	**White-throated Needletail** *Hirundapus caudacutus*	R, S	Aerial over any habitat. Off Aralia St.
Night-Heron	**Nankeen Night-Heron** *Nycticorax caledonicus*	M	Wetlands, mangroves, gallery forest with pandanus. Roosts in trees near

			water. Buffalo Creek, Holmes Jungle, Fogg Dam, Kakadu NP, Mary R NP.
Nightjar	**Large-tailed Nightjar** *Caprimulgus macrurus*	M	Monsoon forest, mangroves, coastal scrub. East Pt, Berry Springs, Kakadu, Dundee Beach, Buffalo Creek, Daly R.
	Spotted Nightjar *Eurostopodus aurus*	M	Open forest, dry woodland inland. Roosts on the ground. Trephina Gorge, Tablelands Hwy, Newhaven, Kakadu, Jasper Gorge, Victoria R RH, Yulara.
Noddy	**Black Noddy** *Anous minutus*	V	Offshore waters. White Rocks, Casuarina Cr.
	Brown Noddy *Anous stolidus*	R	Offshore waters. Darwin Harbour, Dundee Beach, off Aralia St, Buffalo Creek, Elcho Is.
Oriole	**Green Oriole** *Oriolus flavocinctus*	C	Coastal gardens and parks, monsoon and riverine forest, mangroves. Darwin BG, Holmes Jungle, Howard Springs, Fogg Dam, Litchfield NP, Pine Creek, Elsey NP, Daly R.
	Olive-backed Oriole *Oriolus sagittatus*	M	Savannah, open forest, regular dry season visitor to the coast. Holmes Jungle, East Pt, Litchfield NP, Kakadu NP, Pine Creek, Chainman Creek, Elsey, NP, Tiwi Is.
Osprey	**Osprey** *Pandion haliaetus*	M	Coastal cliffs, inshore waters, estuaries, mangroves. Muirhead Bushland, Charles Darwin University, off Aralia St, Channel Is, Dundee Beach, Nitmiluk NP, Bing Bong Port.
Owl	**Barking Owl** *Ninox connivens*	M	Open forest, paperbark swamp, pandanus, urban areas. Darwin BG, Fogg Dam, Bicentennial Park, Kakadu, Pine Creek, Timber Creek, Victoria R RH, Elsey NP, Corroboree Park Tavern.
	Barn Owl *Tyto alba*	M	Urban areas, rural areas, parkland, savannah, grassland. Anzac Pde, Marrakai Rd, Litchfield NP, S Alligator boat ramp, Manbulloo Homestead.
	Eastern Grass Owl *Tyto longimembris*	U	Sedgeland, tall grassland, floodplain, saltmarshes, mangroves. Holmes Jungle, Anzac Pde, Daly R, Manbulloo Homestead, Mac Clark CR.
	Masked Owl *Tyto novaehollandiae*	R	Forest near water, paperbark swamp, monsoon forest. Tiwi Is (stronghold), Merl Camp, Nourlangie, Groote Eylandt, Daly R.
	Rufous Owl *Ninox rufa*	U	Tall paperbark forest, monsoon and riverine forest, parkland. Darwin BG, East Pt, Moth Block, Rapid Creek, Charles Darvin University, Holmes Jungle, Elsey NP, Berry Springs, Kakadu
Owlet-nightjar	**Australian Owlet-nightjar** *Aegotheles cristatus*	M	Woodland, dry forest. Casuarina CR, Litchfield NP, Kakadu NP, Limmen NP, Victoria Hwy, Keep R NP, Trephina G.

Oystercatcher	**Australian Pied Oystercatcher** *Haematopus longirostris*	C	Beaches, estuaries, mudflats, islands.
	Sooty Oystercatcher *Haematopus fuliginosus*	U	Beaches, rocky shores, reefs. East Pt, off Aralia St, Buffalo Creek, Nhulunbuy, Elcho Is.
Painted-snipe	**Australian Painted-snipe** *Rostratula australis*	R	Wetlands. Nomadic. Yellow Waters, Renner Springs, Barkly Homestead, Frewena, Ilparpa Ponds.
Parakeet	**Rose-ringed Parakeet** (aka Indian Ringneck) *Psitaculla krameria*	R, I	Urban areas, probably escapees. Rapid Creek estuary, off Aralia Rd.
Pardalote	**Red-browed Pardalote** *Pardalotus rubricatus*	M	Inland woodland and riverine forest. Victoria Hwy, Timber Creek, Judbarra Gregory NP, Alice Springs Telegraph Station, Yeperenye, West McDonnell Ranges, Uluru-Kata Tjuta NP, Watarrka
	Striated Pardalote *Pardalotus striatus*	M	Woodland, forest, parkland, urban areas.
Parrot	**Bourke's Parrot** *Neopsephotus bourkii*	U	Mulga and other arid shrubland, near watercourses. Kunoth Bore, Ryan Well, Santa Teresa Rd, Old Andado, Henbury Meteorites CR, Rainbow Valley, Stuarts Well, Yulara.
	Hooded Parrot *Psephotellus dissimilis*	U, E	Savannah woodland with termite mounds along watercourses. Lazy Lizard Caravan Park, Pine Creek Water Gardens, Pussy Cat Flats RV, Edith Falls Rd, Fergusson R, Chinaman Creek, Manbulloo Homestead.
	Mulga Parrot *Psephotellus varius*	M	Semi-arid woodland and shrubland. Watarrka NP, Uluru-Kata Tjuta NP, Stuart Hwy, West McDonnell Ranges, Newhaven, Trephina Gorge, Gemtree RH, Arltunga.
	Night Parrot *Pezoporus occidentalis*	R	Inland dry country with spinifex and other native grassland. Sighting of two birds in 1996 at Camel Bore in Newhaven.
	Princess Parrot *Polytelis alexandrae*	R	Mostly sand dune country cladded with spinifex and sparse trees. Nomadic. Mereenie Loop Rd (stronghold), Luritja Rd, Newhaven, Uluru-Kata Tjuta NP.
	Red-winged Parrot *Aprosmictus erythopterus*	C	Dry woodland, shrubland, farmland, open forest, islands. Muirhead Bushland, Wagait Beach, Litchfield NP, Kakadu NP, Timber Creek, Pine Creek, Victoria R RH, Elsey NP, Barkly H.
	Scarlet-chested Parrot *Neophema splendida*	V	Arid acacia woodland with low shrub understory. Nomadic. Alice Springs Desert Park, Rainbow Valey, Mereenie Loop Rd.
Peafowl	**Indian Peafowl** *Pavo cristatus*	U, I	Parkland, roadhouses, grassy woodland. Mataranka Homestead, Mary Ann Dam, Mt Bundy Station.

Pelican	**Australian Pelican** *Pelecanus conspicillatus*	C	Inland and coastal wetlands.
Phalarope	**Red Phalarope** *Phalaropus fulicarius*	V, S	Estuaries, mudflats, wetlands. Leanyer WTP.
	Red-necked Phalarope *Phalaropus lobatus*	V, S	Sewage ponds, estuaries, mudflats, wetlands. Leanyer WTP, Palmerston WTP, Ilparpa Ponds, Mutitjulu WTP.
Pheasant	**Common Pheasant** *Phasianus colchicus*	V, I	Grassland, roadsides. Fogg Dam.
Pigeon	**Crested Pigeon** *Ocyphaps lophotes*	A	Woodland, parkland, farmland, open plains, urban areas.
	Partridge Pigeon *Geophaps smithii*	U	Open forest with grassy understory, roadsides, freshly burnt areas. Kakadu, Litchfield NP, Tiwi Is, Bark Hut Inn, Djukbinj NP, Marrakai Rd, Pine Creek, Umbrawarra Gorge, Copperfield Dam.
	Spinifex Pigeon *Geophaps plumifera*	C	Arid rocky ranges, spinifex-covered hills. West McDonnell Ranges, Judbarra Gregory NP, Trephina Gorge, Mary Ann Dam, Uluru-Kata Tjuta NP, Watarrka NP, Renner Springs.
Pintail	**Northern Pintail** *Anas acuta*	V	Wetlands. Leanyer WTP, Knuckey Lagoons.
Pipit	**Australasian Pipit** *Anthus novaeseelandiae*	M	Open plains, dunes, farmland, coastal wetlands, floodplains.
Pitta	**Rainbow Pitta** *Pitta iris*	M	Monsoon forest, vine thicket, bamboo, mangroves, gardens. Kakadu NP, Fogg Dam, Holmes Jungle, Howard Springs, Berry Springs, Dundee Beach, Daly R, Channel Is, Tiwi Is.
Plover	**Common Ringed Plover** *Charadrius hiaticula*	V, S	Beaches, coastal wetlands. Casuarina CR.
	Greater Sand Plover *Charadrius leschenaultia*	C, S	Beaches, coastal wetlands. Buffalo Creek, off Aralia St, East Pt, Middle Arm, Wagait Beach, Dundee Beach, Bing Bong Port, Elcho Is.
	Grey Plover *Pluvialis squatarola*	M, S	Beaches, coastal wetlands. Buffalo Creek, off Aralia St, Ludmilla Creek, Far End Shores, Bing Bong Port, Groote Eylandt, Channel Is.
	Kentish Plover *Charadrius alexandrinus*	V, S	Beaches, coastal wetlands. Casuarina CR.
	Lesser Sand Plover *Charadrius mongolus*	C, S	Beaches, coastal wetlands. Buffalo Creek, off Aralia St, Bicentennial Park, East Pt, Dundee Beach, South Alligator boat ramp. Bing Bong Port.
	Little Ringed Plover *Charadrius dubius*	R, S	Freshwater wetlands, beaches. Leanyer WTP, East Pt, Buffalo Creek, Holmes Jungle, Anbangbang Billabong, Fogg Dam, Lomarieum Lagoon.
	Oriental Plover *Charadrius veredus*	U, S	Open areas, short grassland, sewage ponds. Leanyer WTP, Buffalo Creek, Palmerston WTP, Knuckey Lagoons,

			Katherine WTP, Tablelands Hwy, Victoria R RH, Tiwi Is.
	Pacific Golden Plover *Pluvialis fulva*	C, S	Beaches, reefs, coastal flats. Buffalo Creek, off Aralia St, Far End Shores, Shady Camp, Katherine WTP.
	Red-capped Plover *Charadrius ruficapillus*	C	Beaches and coastal and freshwater wetlands.
Pratincole	**Australian Pratincole** *Stiltia isabella*	C, W	Arid and semi-arid plains, grassland, claypans, lawns, airstrips, ovals, sewage ponds.
	Oriental Pratincole *Glareola maldivarum*	M, S	Plains with sparse or burnt grass, sewage ponds. Leanyer WTP, Holmes Jungle, Mamukala Wetlands, Leach Lagoon, Katherine WTP, Newcastle Waters, Top Springs.
Pygmy-goose	**Green Pygmy-goose** *Nettapus pulchellus*	M	Wetlands with waterlilies, paperbark swamps. Kakadu, Manton Dam, Fogg Dam, Leaning Tree Lagoon, Knuckey Lagoons, Mary R NP, Lomarieum Lag.
Quail	**Brown Quail** *Synoicus ypsilophorus*	C	Open grassland, woodland.
	King Quail *Synoicus chinensis*	U	Swampy grassland, dense vegetation on riverbanks. Holmes Jungle, Knuckey Lagoons, McMinns Lagoon, Fogg Dam, Pine Creek WTP, Groote Eylandt.
	Stubble Quail *Coturnix pectoralis*	R	Grassland, crops, pasture, shrubland. Tennant Creek WTP, Ilparpa Swamp, Kunoth Bore, Yeperenye.
Quail-thrush	**Cinnamon Quail-thrush** *Cinclosoma cinnamomeum*	R	Arid open country with stony patches and sparse low shrubs. Henbury Meteorites CR, Rainbow Valley, Stuart Hwy, Santa Teresa Rd, Mac Clark CR, Old Andado, Lasseter Hwy.
Rail	**Buff-banded Rail** *Hypotaenidia philippensis*	U	Wetlands, estuaries, sewage ponds, islands. Buffalo Creek, off Aralia St, Leanyer WTP, Fogg Dam, McMinns Lagoon, Yellow Waters, Borroloola, Finke R 2 Camp.
	Chestnut Rail *Eulabeornis castaneoventris*	U	Intact mangroves, mudflats, estuaries. Buffalo Creek, Charles Darwin NP, Tiger Brennan Dr, Channel Is, Ludmilla Creek, Shady Camp, Tiwi Is.
Raven	**Australian Raven** *Corvus coronoides*	U	Roadhouses, open plains, woodland. Barkly Hwy, Karlu Karlu, Olive Pink BG, Erldunda RH, Renner Springs.
Redshank	**Common Redshank** *Tringa totanus*	V, S	Beaches, mudflats, estuaries. Buffalo Creek, Leanyer WTP, Palmerston WTP.
Redthroat	**Redthroat** *Pyrrholaemus brunneus*	U	Low grassy bushland with stands of acacia, mallee or chenopods. Alice Springs Telegraph Station, Yeperenye, Arltunga, Kunoth Bore, Simpsons Gap, Yulara, Uluru-Kata Tjuta NP.
Reed-Warbler	**Australian Reed-Warbler** *Acrocephalus australis*	M	Wetlands, reedbeds, long rank grasses. Fogg Dam, Leanyer WTP, Borroloola, Mamukala Wetland,

			Newcastle Waters, Jabiru L, Glen Helen Gorge, Finke Gorge.
	Oriental Reed-Warbler *Acrocephalus orientalis*	V, S	Wetlands, reedbeds. Fogg Dam.
Ringneck	**Australian Ringneck** *Barnardius zonarius* Only *Port Lincoln* ssp. in NT.	M	Arid scrub, open woodland, near people dwellings. Olive Pink BG, Santa Teresa Rd, Yeperenye, Stuart Hwy, West McDonnell Ranges, Newhaven, Watarrka NP.
Robin	**Buff-sided Robin** *Poecilodryas cerviniventris*	U	Dense riparian forest, thickets of pandanus and paperbarks, bamboo. Timber Creek, Judbarra Gregory NP, Berry Springs, Adelaide River, Kakadu, Borroloola, Mt Bundy Station, Elsey NP
	Hooded Robin *Melanodryas cucullata*	M	Grassy woodland, open forest, stony hills. Watarrka NP, Uluru-Kata Tjuta NP, Karlu Karlu, Newhaven, Rainbow Valley, West McDonnell Ranges, Elsey.
	Mangrove Robin *Peneoenanthe pulverulenta*	U	Mangroves, mostly on the seaward side. Charles Darwin NP, Tiger Brennan Dr, Ludmilla Creek, Buffalo Creek, Shady Camp, Channel Is, Tiwi Is.
	Red-capped Robin *Petroica goodenovii*	M	Dry woodland, lightly timbered grassland. Newhaven, Olive Pink BG, Alice Springs Desert Park, Knuckey Lagoons, Stuart Hwy, Uluru-Kata Tjuta NP, Watarrka NP.
Rock-Pigeon	**Chestnut-quilled Rock-Pigeon** *Petrophassa rufipennis*	U, E	Sandstone escarpment, rocky outcrops. Nitmiluk NP, Nourlangie Rock, Ubirr, Bardedjilidji, Jim Jim Falls, Gubarra Wk, Nawurlandja Lookout, Yurmikmik Walk.
	White-quilled Rock-Pigeon *Petrophassa albipennis*	M	Sandstone escarpment, rocky outcrops. Judbarra Gregory NP, Jasper Gorge, Saddle Creek RA, Keep R NP.
Rosella	**Northern Rosella** *Platycercus venustus*	M	Open forest, savannah, riparian vegetation. Tiwi Is, Litchfield NP, Kakadu NP, Pine Creek, Marrakai Rd, Timber Creek, Judbarra Gregory NP.
Ruff	**Ruff** *Calidris pugnax*	V, S	Inland and coastal wetlands, sewage ponds. Leanyer WTP, Holmes Jungle, Knuckey Lagoons, Tennant Creek WTP, Ilparpa Ponds.
Sanderling	**Sanderling** *Calidris alba*	M, S	Beaches. Off Aralia St, Buffalo Creek, Daribah Rd, Galuru.
Sandpiper	**Broad-billed Sandpiper** *Calidris falcinellus*	R, S	Estuaries, mudflats, sewage ponds. Off Aralia St, Buffalo Creek, Leanyer WTP, Palmerston WTP, Katherine WTP, Nhulunbuy, Ilparpa Ponds.
	Common Sandpiper *Actitis hypoleucos*	M, S	Freshwater, rocky coast, mangroves, mudflats, sewage ponds. Bicentennial Park, East Pt, Buffalo Creek, Dundee Beach, Kakadu, Nitmiluk NP, Bing Bong Port, Ilparpa Ponds.

	Curlew Sandpiper *Calidris ferruginea*	U, S	Estuaries, inland wetlands, sewage ponds. Palmerston WTP, Katherine WTP, Groote Eylandt, Nhulunbuy, Newhaven, Ilparpa Ponds, Dundee B.
	Marsh Sandpiper *Tringa stagnatilis*	M, S	Freshwater swamps, lagoons, estuaries. Leanyer WTP, Knuckey Lagoons, McMinns Lagoon, Yellow Waters, Leach Lagoon, Katherine WTP.
	Pectoral Sandpiper *Calidris melanotos*	R, S	Sewage ponds, lagoons, mudflats. Leanyer WTP, Knuckey Lagoons, Anbangbang Billabong, Tennant Creek WTP, Ilparpa Ponds.
	Sharp-tailed Sandpiper *Calidris acuminata*	C, S	Coastal and inland wetlands, mudflats, sewage ponds. Leanyer WTP, Batchelor WTP, Ilparpa Ponds, Bird Billabong, Jabiru L, Tablelands Hwy.
	Terek Sandpiper *Xenus cinereus*	M, S	Mangroves, mudflats, beaches. East Pt, Far End Shore, off Aralia St, Wagait Beach, Dundee Beach, Tiwi Is, Elcho Is.
	Wood Sandpiper *Tringa glareola*	U, S	Freshwater swamps and lagoons, sewage ponds. Leanyer WTP, Knuckey Lagoons, McMinns Lagoon, Leaning Tree Lagoon, Ilparpa Ponds, Yellow Waters, Newcastle Waters, Barkly H.
Scrubfowl	**Orange-footed Scrubfowl** *Megapodius reinwardt*	C	Coastal scrub, monsoon forest, mangroves, gardens, parks.
Sea-Eagle	**White-bellied Sea-Eagle** *Haliaeetus leucogaster*	M	Beaches, estuaries, inland wetlands, islands, large rivers and lakes.
Shearwater	**Streaked Shearwater** *Calonectris leucomelas*	V	Offshore waters. Buffalo Creek, Tiwi Is.
	Tropical Shearwater *Puffinus bailloni*	V	Inshore and offshore waters. Tiwi Is.
Shelduck	**Australian Shelduck** *Tadorna tadornoides*	V	Wetlands, grassland. Leanyer WTP, Ilparpa Ponds, Newcastle Waters.
	Radjah Shelduck *Radjah radjah*	C	Coastal wetlands, mudflats, sewage ponds. Kakadu, Mary R NP, Adelaide R WTP, Knuckey Lagoons, Elsey NP, Tiwi Is, Nhulunbuy, Fogg Dam, Borroloola.
Shoveler	**Australasian Shoveler** *Spatula rhynchotis*	R	Wetlands, sewage ponds. Leanyer WTP, Tablelands Hwy, Ilparpa Ponds, Ilparpa Claypans.
Shrike-thrush	**Grey Shrike-thrush** *Colluricincla harmonica*	M	Woodland, forest, parkland, rocky outcrops.
	Little Shrike-thrush *Colluricincla megarhyncha*	M	Monsoon forest, mangroves, bamboo, coastal scrub. Charles Darwin NP, Howard Springs, Berry Springs, Litchfield NP, Kakadu NP, Tiwi Is.
	Sandstone Shrike-thrush *Colluricincla woodwardi*	U	High rocky country, gorges and escarpment. Ubirr, Nourlangie Rock, Gubarra, Jim Jim Falls, Yurmikmik Wk, Judbarra Gregory NP, Jasper Gorge, Keep R NP, Limmen NP, Caranbirini.
Shrike-tit	**Northern Shrike-tit** *Falcunculus whitei*	R	**Split from Crested Shrike-tit**. Dry eucalypt woodland, open forest. Central Arnhem Rd, Fergusson R, Edith

			Falls Rd, Chinaman Creek, Warloch Ponds, Buntine Hwy, Elsey NP, Caranbirini.
Sittella	**Varied Sittella** *Daphoenositta chrysoptera*	U	Woodland, dry forest. Pine Creek, Edith Falls Rd, Central Arnhem Rd, Warloch Ponds, Buntine Hwy, Stuart Hwy, Keep R NP, Watarrka NP, Redbank Gorge.
Snipe	**Latham's Snipe** *Gallinago hardwickii*	V, S	Sewage ponds. Tennant Creek WTP, Barkly Homestead, Ilparpa Ponds.
	Swinhoe's Snipe *Gallinago megala*	U, S	Freshwater wetlands with short, sparse grasses, sewage ponds. Leanyer WTP, Holmes Jungle, Tiwi Is, Knuckey Lagoons, McMinns Lagoon, Fogg Dam, Jabiru L, Katherine WTP, Borroloola.
Songlark	**Brown Songlark** *Cincloramphus cruralis*	M, W	Grassland, floodplains. Abundant at some sites. Holmes Jungle, Fogg Dam, Timber Creek, Barkly Hwy, Tablelands Hwy, Connells Lagoon, Newhaven, Santa Teresa Rd, Simpsons Gap.
	Rufous Songlark *Cincloramphus mathewsi*	M, W	Grassy woodland, wooded roadsides, floodplains. Knuckey Lagoons, Central Arnhem Rd, Marrakai Rd, Buchanan Hwy, Barkly Hwy, Aileron RH, Trephina Gorge, Stuart Hwy, Yulara.
Sparrow	**Eurasian Tree Sparrow** *Passer montanus*	V, I	Urban areas, arriving on boats. Darwin Harbour.
	House Sparrow *Passer domesticus*	R, I	Urban areas. Small populations, mostly around roadhouses. Barkly Homestead, Renner Springs, Tenant Creek WTP, Rapid Creek estuary.
Sparrowhawk	**Collared Sparrowhawk** *Accipiter cirrocephalus*	M	Woodland, forest, urban areas.
Spinifexbird	**Spinifexbird** *Poodytes carteri*	M	Restricted to spinifex grassland. West McDonnell Ranges, Santa Teresa Rd, Newhaven, Mary Ann Dam, Trephina.
Spoonbill	**Royal Spoonbill** *Platalea regia*	C	Wetlands, estuaries, floodplains.
	Yellow-billed Spoonbill *Platalea flavipes*	R	Inland wetlands, farm dams, sewage ponds. Corroboree Billabong, Leach Lagoon, Renner Springs, Katherine WTP, Newhaven, Finke R Bridge.
Starling	**Common Starling** *Sturnus vulgaris*	V, I	Roadhouses, grassland. Erldunda RH, Kunoth Bore.
Stilt	**Banded Stilt** *Cladorhynchus leucocephalus*	V	Sewage ponds. Ilparpa Ponds.
	Pied Stilt *Himantopus leucocephalus*	C	Freshwater and coastal wetlands, sewage ponds.
Stint	**Little Stint** *Calidris minuta*	V, S	Inland and coastal wetlands, sewage ponds. Buffalo Creek, Leanyer WTP, Palmerston WTP.
	Long-toed Stint *Calidris subminuta*	R, S	Freshwater and coastal wetlands, sewage ponds. Knuckey Lagoons,

			Palmerston WTP, Katherine WTP, Tennant Creek WTP, Ilparpa Ponds.
	Red-necked Stint *Calidris ruficollis*	C, S	Inland and coastal wetlands, mudflats, beaches.
Stone-curlew	**Beach Stone-curlew** *Esacus magnirostris*	U	Beaches, estuaries. East Pt, Buffalo Creek, Channel Is, Tree Pt CR, Wagait Beach, Dundee Beach, Bing Bong Port, Tiwi Is, Groote Eylandt, Elcho Is.
	Bush Stone-curlew *Burhinus grallarius*	M	Islands, woodland, parkland, edges of mangroves, savannah. Kakadu NP, East Pt, Bicentennial Park, Casuarina CR, Adelaide River, Pine Creek.
Stork	**Black-necked Stork** *Ephippiorhynchus asiaticus*	M	Wetlands, flooded grassland. Kakadu NP, Mary R NP.
Storm-Petrel	**Matsudaira's Storm-Petrel** *Hydrobates matsudairae*	V	Offshore waters. Casuarina CR.
	Wilson's Storm-Petrel *Oceanites oceanicus*	V	Offshore waters. Tiwi Is.
Swallow	**Barn Swallow** *Hirundo rustica*	U, S	Regular summer visitor from Northern Hemisphere, Nov-Mar, on powerlines. Leanyer WTP, off Aralia St, Katherine WTP, Lee Pt, Nhulunbuy, Groote Eyl.
	Red-rumped Swallow *Cecropis daurica*	R, S	Over open areas, on powerlines. Casuarina CR, Rapid Creek, Muirhead Bushland, Leanyer WTP, Katherine Showgrounds.
	Welcome Swallow *Hirundo neoxena*	R	Wetlands, woodland, forest, urban areas, sewage ponds. Off Aralia St, Howard Springs, Jabiru, Kulgera RH, Renner Springs, Yulara.
	White-backed Swallow *Cheramoeca leucosterna*	U	Open, lightly timbered habitat. Karlu Karlu, Newhaven, Yeperenye, Santa Teresa Rd, Ormiston Gorge, Yulara, Old Andado, Stuart Hwy, Watarrka NP.
Swamphen	**Purple Swamphen** *Porphyrio porphyrio*	C	Wetlands with reedy margin.
Swan	**Black Swan** *Cygnnus atratus*	R	Wetlands, rivers, sewage ponds. Ellery Creek Big Hole, McMinns Lagoon, Glen Helen Gorge, Leaning Tree Lagoon.
Swift	**Fork-tailed Swift** *Apus pacificus*	U	Aerial over any habitat. Bicentennial Park, Dundee Beach, Newhaven, Pine Creek, Daly R, Ilparpa Ponds.
	House Swift *Apus nipalensis*	V	Aerial over any habitat. East Pt, Casuarina CR, Rapid Creek estuary.
Tattler	**Grey-tailed Tattler** *Tringa brevipes*	C, S	Coastal wetlands, rocky shores. estuaries.
Teal	**Chestnut Teal** *Anas castanea*	V	Sewage ponds. Leanyer WTP, Nhulunbuy, Ilparpa Ponds.
	Grey Teal *Anas gracilis*	A	Wetlands, estuaries, sewage ponds. Nomadic.
Tern	**Australian Gull-billed Tern** *Gelochelidon macrotarsa*	C	**Split from Gull-billed Tern.** Inland and coastal wetlands, flooded grassland. East Pt, Buffalo Creek, Bird Billabong, Dundee Beach, Fogg Dam,

			Newcastle Waters, McMinns Lagoon, Ilparpa Ponds, Groote Eylandt, Tiwi Is.
	Black-naped Tern *Sterna sumatrana*	M	Coastal waters, mostly offshore islands. Darwin Harbour, Sir Edward Pellew Is, Groote Eylandt, Elcho Is, Nhulunbuy, Tiwi Is.
	Bridled Tern *Onychoprion anaethetus*	U	Inshore and offshore waters, islands. Darwin Harbour, East Pt, Dundee Beach, Tiwi Is, Sir Edward Pellew Is, Groote Eylandt, Nhulunbuy.
	Caspian Tern *Hydroprogne caspia*	M	Inland and coastal waters, beaches. East Pt, Buffalo Creek, Dundee Beach, Katherine WTP, Policemans Pt.
	Common Gull-billed Tern *Gelochelidon nilotica*	R, S	**Split from Gull-billed Tern.** Coastal waters, beaches, mudflats. Buffalo Creek, Palmerston WTP, Dundee Beach.
	Common Tern *Sterna hirundo*	U, S	Coastal waters, beaches, estuaries, sewage ponds. Forming large flocks before migration north. Darwin Harbour, Buffalo Creek, Leanyer WTP, Dundee Beach, Katherine WTP, Tiwi Is.
	Greater Crested Tern *Thallaseus bergii*	A	Coastal waters, beaches, islands.
	Lesser Crested Tern *Thalasseus bengalensis*	U	Coastal waters, beaches, islands. East Pt, off Aralia St, Buffalo Creek, Dundee Beach, Bing Bong Port, Elcho Is, Groote Eylandt, Tiwi Is.
	Little Tern *Sternula albifrons*	M, S	Beaches, estuaries, islands. Most are migrants from Northern Hemisphere. East Pt, off Aralia St, Buffalo Creek, Dundee Beach, Nhulunbuy, Tiwi Is, Groote Eylandt, Sir Edward Pellew Is.
	Roseate Tern *Sterna dougallii*	M	Offshore waters, islands. Sir Edward Pellew Is, Groote Eylandt, Nhulunbuy, Elcho Is, Darwin Harbour, Tiwi Is.
	Sooty Tern *Onychoprion fuscata*	V	Inshore and offshore waters. Elcho Is, Tiwi Is.
	Whiskered Tern *Chlidonias hybrida*	C	Freshwater and coastal wetlands. Plenty at Yellow Waters.
	White-winged Black Tern *Chlidonias leucopterus*	M, S	Inshore waters, freshwater wetlands. Buffalo Creek, Leanyer WTP, off Aralia St, Dundee Beach, Katherine WTP, Bird Billabong, Groote Eylandt, Tiwi Is.
Thornbill	**Chestnut-rumped Thornbill** *Acanthiza uropygialis*	M	Open woodland, shrubland with understory of small shrubs. Olive Pink BG, Newhaven, Gemtree RH, Stuart Hwy, Yeperenye, Simpsons Gap.
	Inland Thornbill *Acanthiza apicallis*	M	Dry woodland and shrubland with dense understory. Olive Pink BG, West McDonnell Ranges, Kunoth Bore, Newhaven, Stuart Hwy, Uluru-Kata Tj.
	Slaty-backed Thornbill *Acanthiza robustirostris*	U	Mulga woodland with eremophila understory. Barrow Creek, Gemtree

			RH, Newhaven, Alice Springs Desert Park, Kunoth Bore, Trephina Gorge, West McDonnell Ranges, Stuart Hwy.
	Yellow-rumped Thornbill *Acanthiza chrysorrhoa*	R	Woodland, parkland, roadsides, feeding on the ground. Alice Springs Telegraph Station, Newhaven, Kunoth Bore, Ross R Resort, Ormiston Gorge.
Treecreeper	**Black-tailed Treecreeper** *Climacteris melanurus*	M	Open forest, savannah. Arnhem Hwy, Marrakai Rd, Kakadu NP, Pine Creek, Chainman Creek, Edith Falls Rd, Central Arnhem Rd, Timber Creek.
	White-browed Treecreeper *Climacteris affinis*	R	Arid woodland with tall shrubs. Prowse Gap, Santa Teresa Rd, Stuart Hwy, Serpentine Gorge, Watarrka NP.
Triller	**Varied Triller** *Lalage leucomela*	C	Monsoon forest, mangroves, gardens. Litchfield NP, Casuarina CR, Wagait Beach, McMinns Lagoon, Fogg Dam, Kakadu NP, Nitmiluk NP, Tiwi Is.
	White-winged Triller *Lalage tricolor*	C	Dry forest, savannah, edges of mangroves, roadsides. Fogg Dam, Bird Billabong, Newcastle Waters, Judbarra Gregory NP, Kakadu NP, Watarrka NP.
Turnstone	**Ruddy Turnstone** *Arenaria interpres*	U, S	Beaches, rocky shores. Darwin Harbour, East Pt, Buffalo Creek, Wagait Beach, Dundee Beach, Bing Bong Port, Elcho Is.
Wagtail	**Citrine Wagtail** *Motacilla citreola*	V, S	Sewage ponds, wet grassy areas. Katherine WTP.
	Eastern Yellow Wagtail *Motacilla tschutschensis*	M, S	Wet, grassy areas, sewage ponds, mudflats. Leanyer WTP, Palmerston WTP, Holmes Jungle, McMinns Lagoon, Knuckey Lagoons, Fogg Dam, Katherine WTP, Ilparpa Ponds, Tiwi Is.
	Grey Wagtail *Motacilla cinerea*	R, S	Wet grassy areas, sewage ponds. Darwin BG, Charles Darwin University, Leanyer WTP, Palmerston WTP, Jim Jim Falls, Edith Falls, Ilparpa Ponds.
	White Wagtail *Motacilla alba*	V, S	Wet grassy areas, sewage ponds, wetland edges. Leanyer WTP, Batchelor WTP, Mamukala Wetlands.
	Willie Wagtail *Rhipidura leucophrys*	C	Woodland, parkland, urban and rural areas.
Wedgebill	**Chiming Wedgebill** *Psophodes occidentalis*	U	Dense vegetation near claypans, tall scrub. Connors Well, Alice Springs Desert Park, Corroboree Rock, Santa Teresa Rd, Simpsons Gap, Stuart Hwy, Lasseter Hwy, Yulara.
Weebill	**Weebill** *Smicrornis brevirostris*	M	Woodland, dry open forest, parkland, islands.
Whimbrel	**Whimbrel** *Numenius phaeopus*	M, S	Mudflats, mangroves, coastal wetlands. Darwin Harbour, East Pt, off Aralia St, Wagait Beach, Dundee Beach, Bing Bong Port, Tiwi Is.
Whistler	**Brown Whistler** *Pachycephala simplex*	M, E	**Split from Grey Whistler.** Mangroves, monsoon forest and adjacent mixed forest, islands. Fogg

			Dam, East Pt, Buffalo Creek, Howard Springs, Berry Springs, Adelaide River, Kakadu, Daly R, Groote Eylandt, Tiwi Is
	Mangrove Golden Whistler *Pachycephala melanura*	U	Mangroves, tidal stretches of rivers, bamboo, monsoon forest. Adelaide River Bridge, Shady Camp, Daly R, Bing Bong Port, off Aralia St, Buffalo Creek.
	Rufous Whistler *Pachycephala rufiventris*	M	Woodland, forest, parkland.
	White-breasted Whistler *Pachycephala lanioides*	R	Mangroves, islands. Charles Darwin NP, off Orchard Rd, Palmerston WTP, Borroloola, Bing Bong Port.
Whistling-Duck	**Plumed Whistling-Duck** *Dendrocygna eytoni*	A	Wetlands, flooded grassland. Gregarious.
	Spotted Whistling-Duck *Dendrocygna guttata*	R	Wetlands, sewage ponds. Leanyer WTP, Tiwi Is (regular on the sewage ponds).
	Wandering Whistling-Duck *Dendrocygna arcuata*	A	Wetlands, flooded grassland. Gregarious.
White-eye	**Australian Yellow White-eye** *Zosterops luteus*	M	Mangroves and adjacent vegetation, open forest. Tiger Brennan Dr, East Pt, Buffalo Creek, Leanyer WTP, Dundee Beach, Mary R NP, Borroloola.
Whiteface	**Banded Whiteface** *Aphelocephala nigricincta*	R	Arid shrubland, mulga, grassland with scattered trees and shrubs. Stuart Hwy, Newhaven, Lasseter Hwy, Uluru-Kata Tjuta NP, Old Andado, Santa Teresa Rd, Mac Clark CR.
	Southern Whiteface *Aphelocephala leucopsis*	U	Open woodland, tall shrubland. Gemtree RH, Aileron RH, Ilparpa Ponds, Mac Clark CR, Stuart Hwy, Ormiston Gorge, Luritja Rd.
Woodswallow	**Black-faced Woodswallow** *Artamus cinereus*	A	Woodland, grassland, open plains.
	Little Woodswallow *Artamus minor*	M	Hills and ridges and over the nearby open forest and woodland. Litchfield NP, Kakadu NP, Nitmiluk NP, Central Arnhem Rd, Judbarra Gregory NP, Keep R NP, Limmen NP, Trephina Gorge, West McDonnell Ranges, Watarrka NP, Uluru-Kata Tjuta NP.
	Masked Woodswallow *Artamus personatus*	C	Woodland, shrubland, open plains. Often in huge flocks. Nomadic.
	White-breasted Woodswallow *Artamus leucorynchus*	C	Around freshwater bodies, estuaries and floodplains. Muirhead Bushland, Casuarina CR, Berry Springs, Darwin Harbour, Adelaide R, S Alligator boat ramp, Fogg Dam, Pine Creek, Timber C
	White-browed Woodswallow *Artamus superciliosus*	R	Woodland, shrubland, open eucalypt forest. Marrakai Rd, Umbrawarra Gorge, Timber Creek, Tablelands Hwy, Tenant Creek WTP, Redbank Gorge, Yulara, Simpsons Gap.

Site Index

D

E

F

G

H

I

J

K

L

M

N

O

P

R

S

T

U

V

W

Y

List of Wader Sites

www.ingramcontent.com/pod-product-compliance
Lightning Source LLC
LaVergne TN
LVHW060932110826
845147LV00029B/743

* 9 7 8 0 6 4 8 9 5 6 4 5 7 *